MATHEMATICS
3000

MATHEMATICS 3000

Science OPTION

Québec Education Program

Secondary 5

Chantal Buzaglo

Gérard Buzaglo

Guérin Montreal Toronto

4501 Drolet Street
Montreal (Quebec) Canada H2T 2G2
Telephone: 514-842-3481
Fax: 514-842-4923
Internet: http://www.guerin-editeur.qc.ca
E-mail: francel@guerin-editeur.qc.ca

Translators
Jean Guérin
Doug Neal

Legal deposit

ISBN 978-2-7601-7107-8

Bibliothèque et Archives nationales du Québec, 2009
Bibliothèque et Archives Canada, 2009

PRINTED IN CANADA

We acknowledge the financial support of the Government of Canada through the Book
Publishing Industry Development Program for our publishing activities.

Canadä

PHOTOCOPYING KILLS BOOKS

Introduction

At the beginning of the third millennium, Guérin, éditeur is pleased to make available to Quebec teachers the exercise book, Math 506, **Science option**, of the **Mathematics 3000** collection.

This is an exercise book whose content, in accordance with the Quebec Education Program, is geared towards skill development, especially the three disciplinary skills: "**Solving a situational problem**", "**Using mathematical reasoning**", and "**Communicating by using mathematical language**".

Each book in the collection is divided into chapters that cover the various fields of mathematics such as arithmetic, algebra, geometry, probabilities and statistics.

Each chapter begins with the **Challenge** section where the student is invited, alone or in a team, to **solve situational problems** that have not been presented previously. The solution of each situation requires a combination of rules or principles that the student may have learned or not. In this section, the student is confronted with various situations that will provide him with the motivation to seek inside the chapter the elements allowing him to solve them.

Each of the other sections of a chapter starts with **learning activities** where the student is led step by step to the discovery of the concepts. Activities lead to highlighted **sections** summarizing the essential material of the course, and supported by **examples**. The student will find, in these highlights, complete references that will be useful throughout his learning process. The highlights are followed by a series of graded **exercises and problems** that will allow the student to **develop his skills** by solving situational problems, by using mathematical reasoning and by communicating using mathematical language. Each time the situation allows it, the student will have to explain the steps he used, justify his reasoning and finally communicate his answer in an appropriate manner.

Each chapter ends with an **Evaluation** section that will allow the student to ascertain if the knowledge has been acquired and if the skills have been attained.

A detailed **list of symbols** and an **index** at the end of each book will allow the student to easily find everything he needs during his learning.

This pedagogical tool, focused on skill development, is written in a clear and simple language and aims to be accessible to every student without sacrificing mathematical rigor.

Table of contents

Chapter *1*

Arithmetic and algebraic expressions

CHALLENGE 1

1. Under what conditions does $\sqrt[n]{a}$ not exist in $\mathbb{R}$? _____

2. Write the expression $\dfrac{8^2 \times \sqrt{32}}{4^4 \times \sqrt[5]{16}}$ as a power of 2.

_____

3. Rationalize the denominator of the expression $\dfrac{5}{\sqrt{2}}$.

_____

4. Find an equivalent fraction to $\dfrac{\sqrt{5} + \sqrt{2}}{\sqrt{5} - \sqrt{2}}$ with a rational denominator.

_____

5. For which values of x is the expression $\sqrt{2x^2 + x - 6}$ defined?

_____

6. Under what conditions is the trinomial $ax^2 + bx + c$ factorable in the set of real numbers?

_____

7. Factor the trinomial $x^2 + 2x - 2$. _____

8. For what values of m does the trinomial $mx^2 + (m - 1)x + m$ factor as a product of two distinct first degree factors?

_____

1.1 Powers with integer exponent

ACTIVITY 1 Real numbers

a) Complete the following with the term "rational" or "irrational".

1. Any real number that has an infinite repeating decimal representation is __rational__

2. Any real number that has an infinite non-repeating decimal representation is __irrational__

b) Place the following real numbers in the Venn diagram below.

-2; 5; π; $\frac{2}{3}$; 3.14; $\sqrt{2}$; $1.\overline{6}$

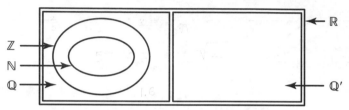

c) We represent the set of rational numbers by $\mathbb{Q}$ and the set of irrational numbers by $\mathbb{Q}'$.

Complete. 1. $\mathbb{Q} \cap \mathbb{Q}' =$ _____ 2. $\mathbb{Q} \cup \mathbb{Q}' =$ _____

d) 1. If a is a natural number, what condition must be set on the number a such that $\sqrt{a}$ is a rational number? _____

2. Complete the following using the appropriate symbol $\mathbb{Q}$ or $\mathbb{Q}'$.

1) $\sqrt{16} \in$ _____ 2) $\sqrt{17} \in$ _____

REAL NUMBERS

- Any real number with an **infinite repeating** decimal representation is **rational**.
  Any real number with an **infinite non-repeating** decimal representation is irrational.

- $\mathbb{Q}$ represents the set of rational numbers, $\mathbb{Q}'$ the set of **irrationals** and $\mathbb{R}$ the set of **real numbers**. We have:

$$\boxed{\mathbb{Q} \cup \mathbb{Q}' = \mathbb{R}} \qquad \boxed{\mathbb{Q} \cap \mathbb{Q}' = \varnothing}$$

$\mathbb{R}_+$ represents the set of **positive real numbers** including zero.
$\mathbb{R}_-$ represents the set of **negative real numbers** including zero.
$\mathbb{R}^*$ represents the set of **non-zero real numbers**.

- Every real number corresponds to a point on the number line, and every point on the number line corresponds to a real number.

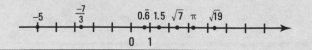

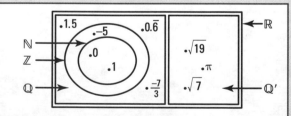

$\mathbb{N}$ represents the set of natural numbers.
$\mathbb{N} = \{0, 1, 2, ...\}$
$\mathbb{Z}$ represents the set of integers.
$\mathbb{Z} = \{..., -2, -1, 0, 1, 2, ...\}$
We have: $\mathbb{N} \subseteq \mathbb{Z} \subseteq \mathbb{Q} \subseteq \mathbb{R}$.

---

a) Consider the power a^n. Complete.

1. a is called: _____ 2. n is called: _____

b) 1. What is the definition of a^n? ($n \in \mathbb{N}$, $n \geqslant 2$) _____
2. Complete. 1) $a^1 =$ _____ 2) $a^0 =$ _____ ($a \neq 0$)

c) Calculate.

1. 2^4 _____ 2. $(-2)^4$ _____ 3. 2^3 _____ 4. $(-2)^3$ _____

d) Under what conditions will the power a^n be negative? _____

e) Complete.

1. $a^m \times a^n =$ _____ 2. $a^m \div a^n =$ _____

3. $(a \times b)^n =$ _____ 4. $\left(\dfrac{a}{b}\right)^n =$ _____

5. $(a^m)^n =$ _____

f) What is the definition of a^{-n} when a is non-zero? _____

g) Calculate.

1. 2^{-2} _____ 2. $(-2)^{-2}$ _____ 3. 2^{-3} _____ 4. $(-2)^{-3}$ _____

POWERS WITH INTEGER EXPONENT

• **Definitions**

$$a^n = \underbrace{a \times a \times \ldots \times a}_{n \text{ factors}} \ (n \in \mathbb{N} \text{ and } n \geqslant 2) \qquad a^1 = a \qquad a^0 = 1 \ (a \neq 0) \qquad a^{-n} = \frac{1}{a^n}(a \neq 0)$$

• **Laws of exponents**
1. Product of two powers with the same base:
2. Quotient of two powers with the same base:
3. Power of a product:
4. Power of a quotient:
5. Power of a power:

$$a^m \times a^n = a^{m+n}$$
$$\frac{a^m}{a^n} = a^{m-n}$$
$$(ab)^n = a^n b^n$$
$$\left(\frac{a}{b}\right)^n = \frac{a^n}{b^n}$$
$$(a^m)^n = a^{mn}$$

---

1. Calculate the following.

a) $(-2)^5$ _____ **b)** 2^5 _____ **c)** $(-3)^4$ _____ **d)** -3^4 _____

e) 3^{-2} _____ **f)** $(-3)^{-2}$ _____ **g)** $(-5)^{-2}$ _____ **h)** -5^{-2} _____

i) $\left(-\dfrac{2}{3}\right)^2$ _____ **j)** $\left(-\dfrac{2}{3}\right)^{-2}$ _____ **k)** $-\left(-\dfrac{3}{4}\right)^{-2}$ _____ **l)** $-\left(-\dfrac{3}{4}\right)^{-1}$ _____

2. Using the laws of exponents, write the following as a single power and then evaluate it.

a) $(-3)^2 \times (-3)^3 = $ _____

b) $2^3 \times 2^{-5} \times 2 = $ _____

c) $\left(\frac{3}{4}\right)^2 \left(\frac{3}{4}\right)^{-2} = $ _____

d) $\frac{(-5)^5}{(-5)^3} = $ _____

e) $\frac{2^3}{2^5} = $ _____

f) $(2^3)^2 = $ _____

g) $[(-2)^2]^4 = $ _____

h) $(-2^3)^2 = $ _____

i) $-(2^3)^2 = $ _____

3. Simplify the following expressions using the laws of exponents.

a) $a^2 \times a^3 = $ _____

b) $(a^3)^2 = $ _____

c) $\frac{a^5}{a^2} = $ _____

d) $\left(\frac{a^3}{b^2}\right)^2 = $ _____

e) $(2a^3b^2)^2 = $ _____

f) $(3a^2b) \cdot (2a^3b^2) = $ _____

4. Simplify the following expressions using the laws of exponents.

a) $(3x^2)^2 = $ _____

b) $(-2x^3y^2)^2 = $ _____

c) $\left(\frac{3x}{2y}\right)^3 = $ _____

d) $\left(\frac{2x^3}{3y^2}\right)^2 = $ _____

e) $\frac{12x^3y^2}{6x^2y^4} = $ _____

f) $\frac{(2x^2y)^3}{4x^4y^2} = $ _____

5. Simplify the following expressions using the laws of exponents.

a) $(2a)^3(3a)^2 = $ _____

b) $(2a^2b)^3 \cdot (3ab^2)^2 = $ _____

c) $\frac{12a^3b^2}{6a^2b^4} = $ _____

d) $\left(\frac{-2a^2}{3b}\right)^2 = $ _____

e) $\left(\frac{2a^2}{3b}\right)^3 \cdot \left(\frac{3a^2}{2b^2}\right)^3 = $ _____

f) $\left(\frac{2a^2}{3b}\right)^3 \div \left(\frac{a^2}{b}\right)^3 = $ _____

6. Simplify the following expressions using the laws of exponents.

a) $2a^{-2} \times 3a = $ _____

b) $(2a^{-2})^{-3} = $ _____

c) $\frac{12a^{-2}}{4a^{-5}} = $ _____

d) $(2a^{-3})^{-1} \times (3^{-1}a^2)^{-2} = $ _____

e) $\left(\frac{2a^{-1}}{3a^2}\right)^{-3} = $ _____

f) $(2a^2b^{-1}) \cdot (-3a^{-1}b^2) = $ _____

g) $(-2a^2b)^{-1} \times (3a^{-2}b)^2 = $ _____

h) $\left(\frac{3a^{-2}b}{4ab^{-2}}\right)^{-2} = $ _____

i) $\left(\frac{-2a^2b^{-1}}{3a}\right)^{-1} \cdot \left(\frac{3a^{-2}b}{2a}\right)^{-2} = $ _____

7. Write the following expressions as a power of 2.

a) $(2^4)^5 \times 16^3$ _____

b) $16^2 \times 8^4 \times 4^0$ _____

c) $\frac{4^4 \times 2^2 \times 16}{2^5 \times 8^2}$ _____

d) $\frac{(2^3)^2 \times (4^2)^3}{(2^2)^3 \times 8^4}$ _____

8. Compare the numbers $A = (25)^4 \times 5^5$ and $B = (25^2 \times 125)^2 \times 5^0$ after expressing each of these numbers as a power of 5.

_____

9. Compare the numbers $A = (2^{-4} \times 4^3)^2 \times \frac{1}{8}$ and $B = \frac{1}{32} \times (2^{-4} \times 8^2)^2$ after expressing each of these numbers as a power of 2.

_____

10. Simplify the following expressions using the laws of exponents. $(a \neq 0)$

a) $a^{2n} \times a^n$ _____

b) $a^{2n-1} \times a^{3-n}$ _____

c) $a^{3n+1} \div a^{2n-1}$ _____

d) $(a^{2n+1})^2$ _____

e) $\dfrac{a^{3n-2}}{a^{n+2}}$ _____

f) $(a^{n+1} \times a^{n-1})^2$ _____

11. Simplify the following expressions using the laws of exponents. $(a \neq 0)$

a) $(a^{n+1})^3 \times (a^{n-1})^2$ _____

b) $\dfrac{(a^{2n+1})^3}{(a^{2n-1})^2}$ _____

c) $\dfrac{(a^{n-1})^3 \times (a^{2n+1})^2}{a^{5n+4}}$ _____

d) $\dfrac{(a^{n-1})^2 \times (a^{n+1})^3}{a^{3n+1} \times a^{2n-1}}$ _____

12. Express $(4^{2n+4} \times 2^{4n-5}) \div 16^{2n}$ as a power of 2.

_____

13. If $x = a^3$ and $y = 3a^2$, write the following expressions in terms of a.

a) $3x^2y$ _____

b) x^2y^3 _____

c) $(2x^3y)^2$ _____

d) $4xy^2 \div 2xy$ _____

e) $3x^2y^4 \div (2xy)^2$ _____

f) $\left(\dfrac{2xy^2}{3xy}\right)^2$ _____

g) $x^{-2}y^2$ _____

h) $9x^2y^{-2}$ _____

14. The population of a city is given by $P = (1.02)^t$, where P is expressed in millions of people and t represents the number of years since 2005.

a) What will the population of this city be in 2010? _____

b) What was the population of this city in 2000? _____

15. In 2005, an employee of a company earned an annual salary of $30 000. This company gives an annual 4 % raise to its employees. The equation $s = 30(1.04)^t$ expresses the employee's salary s (in thousands of dollars) as a function of the number of years t since 2005.

a) What was the employee's salary in

1. 2004? _____ 2. 2000? _____

b) What will the employee's salary be in

1. 2010? _____ 2. 2015? _____

1.2 Binary system

ACTIVITY 1 Decomposition of a number into a sum of powers

a) Raphael must empty 27 litres of water into a minimum number of containers.

1. If Raphael can only use 10 l or 1 l containers, how many containers of each kind will he use? _____

2. If Raphael can only use 16 l, 8 l, 4 l, 2 l, or 1 l containers, how many containers of each kind will he use?

_____

> The numbers 16, 8, 4, 2 and 1 are powers of 2.

b) Any natural number can be decomposed into a **sum of powers** of any natural number greater than 1.

For example, the number 31 can be decomposed into a sum of powers of 2.

$$\begin{aligned}
31 &= 16 + 15 && \text{(The largest power of 2 going into 31 is 16 (2^4))} \\
&= 16 + (8 + 7) && \text{(The largest power of 2 going into 15 is 8 (2^3))} \\
&= 16 + 8 + (4 + 3) && \text{(The largest power of 2 going into 7 is 4 (2^2))} \\
&= 16 + 8 + 4 + (2 + 1) && \text{(The largest power of 2 going into 3 is 2 (2^1))} \\
&= 2^4 + 2^3 + 2^2 + 2^1 + 2^0 && \text{Note that } 1 = 2^0.
\end{aligned}$$

Decompose the number 100 into

1. a sum of powers of 2.

_____

_____

_____

_____

2. a sum of powers of 3.

_____

_____

_____

_____

SYSTEM IN BASE 2

Given a number composed of digits, the **value** of a digit depends on its **position** in the number as well as the numeration system.

– The decimal system, or system in base 10, uses the 10 digits 0, 1, 2, ..., 9.

In the decimal system, the value of a digit a in position n is: $a \times 10^n$.

Ex.: Consider, in the decimal system, the number 7445.

The following table gives the position and the value of each digit.

Digit	7	4	4	5
Position	3	2	1	0
Value	7×10^3	4×10^2	4×10^1	5×10^0

> Note that the positions are numbered from right to left: 0, 1, 2, ...

The decomposition of the number 7445 into a sum of powers of 10 is:

$$7445 = 7 \times 10^3 + 4 \times 10^2 + 4 \times 10^1 + 5 \times 10^0.$$

– The binary system, or system in base 2, uses the digits 0 and 1.

In the binary system, the value of a digit a in position n is: $a \times 2^n$.

Ex.: Consider, in the binary system, the number 1101, written 1101_2.

The following table gives the position and the value of each digit.

Digit	1	1	0	1
Position	3	2	1	0
Value	1×2^3	1×2^2	0×2^1	1×2^0

The decomposition of the number 1101_2 into a sum of powers of 2 is:

$$1101_2 = 1 \times 2^3 + 1 \times 2^2 + 0 \times 2^1 + 1 \times 2^0.$$

By doing the sum of these powers of 2, we get the equivalent to the number 1101_2 in the decimal system.

$$1101_2 = 1 \times 8 + 1 \times 4 + 0 \times 2 + 1 \times 1 = 13$$

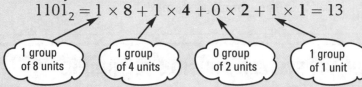

| 1 group of 8 units | 1 group of 4 units | 0 group of 2 units | 1 group of 1 unit |

1. **a)** Expand the following numbers into a sum of powers of 2.

1. 27 = _____

2. 22 = _____

3. 49 = _____

4. 38 = _____

b) Write each of the preceding numbers in the binary system.

1. 27 = _____ 2. 22 = _____

3. 49 = _____ 4. 38 = _____

2. The following numbers are in the binary system. Write each number as a sum of powers of 2 and find the equivalent of each number in the decimal system.

a) 100_2: _____

b) 101_2: _____

c) 1101_2: _____

d) 1010_2: _____

e) $11\ 101_2$: _____

3. We must arrange 14 chocolate bars into a minimum of packages. Each package contains 1, 2, 4 or 8 bars. How many packages of each kind must we make?

_____

4. Find the minimum of quarters, nickels and pennies that are required to get an amount of

    a) 118 ¢. _____

    b) 122 ¢. _____

    c) 134 ¢. _____

    d) 47 ¢. _____

5. Write each of the preceding amounts in the form of a sum of powers of 5.

    a) 118 _____   **b)** 122 _____

    c) 134 _____   **d)** 47 _____

6. Write each of the preceding numbers in a system in base 5.

    a) 118 _____   **b)** 122 _____   **c)** 134 _____   **d)** 47 _____

7. Write the first 10 natural numbers 0, 1, …, 9 in the binary system.

CONVERSION TO THE BINARY SYSTEM: DIVISION TECHNIQUE

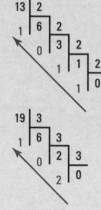

- To convert a number from the decimal system into base 2, we perform many successive divisions by 2 until we get a zero quotient.

  Use the remainders, in the order indicated by the arrow, to write the number.

  Ex.: Converting 13 from the decimal system into base 2.

      We get: $13_{10} = 1101_2$.

      Verification: $13_{10} = 1 \times 2^3 + 1 \times 2^2 + 0 \times 2^1 + 1 \times 2^0$

- To convert a number from the decimal system into base 3, we proceed in the same way by performing many successive divisions by 3.

  Ex.: Converting 19 from the decimal system into base 3.

      We get: $19_{10} = 201_3$.

      Verification: $19_{10} = 2 \times 3^2 + 0 \times 3^1 + 1 \times 3^0$

---

8. Convert the following numbers

       1. into base 2.   2. into base 3.   3. into base 5.

    a) 17 1. _____   2. $3^2 + 3^2 - 3^0$ _____   3. _____

    b) 35 1. _____   2. _____   3. _____

    c) 72 1. _____   2. _____   3. _____

9. Perform the following operations and express each answer in base 2.

    a) $101_2 + 111_2$ _____   **b)** $101_2 - 11_2 =$ _____

    c) $110_2 \times 10_2$ _____   **d)** $1010_2 \div 101_2 =$ _____

    e) $100_2 \times 101_2$ _____   **f)** $1001_2 - 100_2 =$ _____

1.3 Powers with rational or irrational exponent

ACTIVITY 1 n^{th} root of a real number

a) Complete.

1. $\sqrt[2]{64} =$ _____ because _____
2. $\sqrt[2]{-64}$ does not exist in $\mathbb{R}$ because _____
3. $\sqrt[3]{64} =$ _____ because _____
4. $\sqrt[3]{-64} =$ _____ because _____

b) Complete. $\sqrt[n]{a} = b \Leftrightarrow$ _____

c) Under what conditions does $\sqrt[n]{a}$ not exist in $\mathbb{R}$?

_____

---

n^{th} ROOT OF A REAL NUMBER

Given a natural number n and a real number a, the nth root of the real number a, written $\sqrt[n]{a}$, is the unique real number b for which $b^n = a$.

$$\boxed{\sqrt[n]{a} = b \Leftrightarrow b^n = a}$$

> *n is called the index, a is the radicand, and $\sqrt{}$ is the radical.*

Note that $\sqrt[n]{a}$ does not exist in $\mathbb{R}$ when **n is even** and **a is negative**.

By convention, we do not write the index 2. Thus, $\sqrt[2]{a} = \sqrt{a}$.

Ex.: $\sqrt[4]{16} = 2$ because $2^4 = 16$; $\sqrt[3]{8} = 2$ because $2^3 = 8$; $\sqrt[3]{-8} = -2$ because $(-2)^3 = -8$
$\sqrt[4]{-16} \notin \mathbb{R}$ because the index 4 is even and the radicand -16 is negative.

---

1. Determine, if possible.

a) $\sqrt{25}$ _____ **b)** $\sqrt{-25}$ _____ **c)** $\sqrt[3]{27}$ _____ **d)** $\sqrt[3]{-27}$ _____

e) $\sqrt[4]{81}$ _____ **f)** $\sqrt[4]{-81}$ _____ **g)** $\sqrt{(-7)^2}$ _____ **h)** $\sqrt[3]{(-2)^3}$ _____

2. Using a calculator, find the value of the following expressions (round your answer to the nearest thousandth).

a) $\sqrt{2}$ _____ **b)** $\sqrt{3}$ _____ **c)** $\sqrt[3]{2}$ _____ **d)** $\sqrt[3]{3}$ _____

3. True or false?

a) The equation $x^2 = 25$ has 2 real solutions 5 and -5. _____

b) The equation $x^2 = -25$ has no real solutions. _____

c) The equation $x^3 = 8$ has the number 2 as its only solution. _____

d) The equation $x^3 = -8$ has the number -2 as its only solution. _____

4. Simplify $\sqrt{x^2}$ if

a) x is positive. _____ **b)** x is negative. _____

ACTIVITY 2 Powers with rational exponent

a) For any real number a, and any non-zero natural number n, we have: $a^{\frac{1}{n}} = \sqrt[n]{a}$.
Evaluate, if possible.

1. $16^{\frac{1}{4}}$ _____ 2. $(-16)^{\frac{1}{4}}$ _____ 3. $8^{\frac{1}{3}}$ _____ 4. $(-8)^{\frac{1}{3}}$ _____

b) If $a^{\frac{1}{n}}$ exists in $\mathbb{R}$, then for any natural number m, we have: $a^{\frac{m}{n}} = \left(\sqrt[n]{a}\right)^m$.
Evaluate, if possible.

1. $16^{\frac{3}{2}}$ _____ 2. $(-8)^{\frac{2}{3}}$ _____ 3. $(-16)^{\frac{3}{4}}$ _____ 4. $64^{\frac{2}{3}}$ _____

POWERS WITH RATIONAL EXPONENT

- **Definitions**

  - For any real number a, and any non-zero natural number n, we have:

$$a^{\frac{1}{n}} = \sqrt[n]{a}$$

  Ex.: $16^{\frac{1}{4}} = \sqrt[4]{16} = 2$; $(-64)^{\frac{1}{3}} = \sqrt[3]{-64} = -4$; $(-81)^{\frac{1}{4}} = \sqrt[4]{-81} \notin \mathbb{R}$

  The power $a^{\frac{1}{n}}$ does not exist in $\mathbb{R}$ when n is even and a is negative.

  - If $a^{\frac{1}{n}}$ exists in $\mathbb{R}$, then for any natural number m, we have:

$$a^{\frac{m}{n}} = \left(\sqrt[n]{a}\right)^m$$

  Ex.: $16^{\frac{3}{2}} = \left(\sqrt[2]{16}\right)^3 = 4^3 = 64$; $(-8)^{\frac{2}{3}} = \left(\sqrt[3]{-8}\right)^2 = (-2)^2 = 4$

- **Laws of exponents**

  The five laws of exponents also apply when the exponents m and n are **rational** numbers.

  Ex.: 1. $a^{\frac{1}{2}} \times a^{\frac{1}{3}} = a^{\frac{1}{2}+\frac{1}{3}} = a^{\frac{5}{6}}$ 2. $a^{\frac{3}{2}} \div a^{\frac{2}{3}} = a^{\frac{3}{2}-\frac{2}{3}} = a^{\frac{5}{6}}$

  3. $(a \cdot b)^{\frac{1}{2}} = a^{\frac{1}{2}}b^{\frac{1}{2}}$ 4. $\left(\dfrac{a}{b}\right)^{\frac{3}{2}} = \dfrac{a^{\frac{3}{2}}}{b^{\frac{3}{2}}}$ 5. $\left(a^{\frac{2}{3}}\right)^{\frac{3}{4}} = a^{\frac{1}{2}}$

---

5. Calculate the following real numbers.

a) $25^{\frac{3}{2}}$ _____ b) $(-27)^{\frac{2}{3}}$ _____ c) $16^{1.5}$ _____

d) $9^{-\frac{3}{2}}$ _____ e) $8^{-\frac{2}{3}}$ _____ f) $4^{-2.5}$ _____

6. **a)** If $a^{\frac{1}{n}}$ exists, show that $\left(\sqrt[n]{a}\right)^m = \sqrt[n]{a^m}$. _____

  b) Calculate $4^{\frac{3}{2}}$ in two different ways. 1. _____ 2. _____

© Guérin, éditeur ltée

7. Apply the laws of exponents to simplify the following expressions.

a) $x^{\frac{2}{3}} \cdot x^{-\frac{1}{2}} = $ _____

b) $\left(x^{-2}\right)^{-\frac{3}{2}} = $ _____

c) $\dfrac{x^{-\frac{2}{3}}}{x^{-\frac{3}{2}}} = $ _____

d) $\left(x^{-2}y^3\right)^{\frac{1}{6}} = $ _____

e) $\left(\dfrac{x^{-2}}{y^2}\right)^{-\frac{3}{2}} = $ _____

f) $\left(x^3y^{-1}\right)^{\frac{2}{3}} \cdot \left(xy^2\right)^{\frac{1}{2}} = $ _____

g) $\left(\dfrac{x^2}{y^{-1}}\right)^{\frac{1}{2}} \cdot \left(\dfrac{x^3}{y}\right)^{\frac{1}{3}} = $ _____

h) $\left(4x^2y^4\right)^{\frac{1}{2}} = $ _____

i) $\left(\dfrac{8x^3y^6}{27}\right)^{\frac{2}{3}} = $ _____

8. Write the expression $\dfrac{4^3 \times \sqrt{8}}{8^2 \times \sqrt[3]{16}}$ as a power of 2. _____

9. Write the expression $\dfrac{\sqrt{5} \times \sqrt[3]{25}}{\sqrt[6]{625}}$ as a power of 5. _____

10. Given that $a > 0$, simplify the expression $\dfrac{a^2 \cdot \sqrt{a^3}}{\sqrt[3]{a^2} \cdot \sqrt{a^4}}$. _____

ACTIVITY 3 Powers with irrational exponent

a) Calculate the following powers with rational exponents.

1. 2^3 _____
2. 2^{-3} _____
3. $4^{\frac{1}{2}}$ _____
4. $27^{\frac{2}{3}}$ _____
5. 5^0 _____

b) Use a calculator to calculate the following powers with irrational exponent (round to the nearest hundredth).

1. $2^{\sqrt{2}}$ _____
2. 2^{π} _____
3. $2^{-\pi}$ _____

POWERS OF A POSITIVE REAL NUMBER

- Given a positive real number a and a rational or irrational number x, the xth power of the number a, written a^x, exists for any x.

  Ex.: Using a calculator, we get (rounded to the thousandth)
  $$\left(\sqrt{2}\right)^{\pi} = 2.971; \quad \pi^{\sqrt{2}} = 5.047$$

- The five laws of exponents also apply when the exponents are **real** numbers.

  Ex.: 1. $a^x \cdot a^y = a^{x+y} \ (a \geqslant 0)$ 2. $\dfrac{a^x}{a^y} = a^{x-y} \ (a > 0)$

       3. $(a \cdot b)^x = a^x \cdot b^x \ (a \geqslant 0, b \geqslant 0)$ 4. $\left(\dfrac{a}{b}\right)^x = \dfrac{a^x}{b^x} \ (a \geqslant 0, b > 0)$

       5. $(a^x)^y = a^{xy} \ (a \geqslant 0)$

---

11. Given $f(x) = 3 \times 4^x$. Calculate.

a) $f(0)$ _____
b) $f(2)$ _____
c) $f(-2)$ _____
d) $f\left(\frac{1}{2}\right)$ _____
e) $f\left(-\frac{3}{2}\right)$ _____

12. Given $f(x) = -2 \times 9^x$. Calculate.

a) $f(0)$ _____
b) $f(1)$ _____
c) $f(-1)$ _____
d) $f\left(\frac{1}{2}\right)$ _____
e) $f\left(-\frac{1}{2}\right)$ _____

13. Given $f(x) = 3^x$. Use a calculator to determine (round to the nearest hundredth)

a) $f\left(\frac{1}{2}\right)$ _____
b) $f\left(-\frac{1}{2}\right)$ _____
c) $f(\sqrt{2})$ _____
d) $f(\pi)$ _____

1.4 Square root of a real number

Square root of a real number

Activity 1 Properties of radicals

a) Consider two real numbers a and b and the equality $\sqrt{a} = b$.

1. What conditions must we put on the real numbers a and b? _____

2. Complete: $\sqrt{a} = b \Leftrightarrow$ _____

b) True or false?

1. $\sqrt{4 \times 25} = \sqrt{4} \times \sqrt{25}$ _____

2. $\sqrt{\dfrac{100}{25}} = \dfrac{\sqrt{100}}{\sqrt{25}}$ _____

3. $\sqrt{16+9} = \sqrt{16} + \sqrt{9}$ _____

4. $\sqrt{25-9} = \sqrt{25} - \sqrt{9}$ _____

c) Justify the steps showing that $\sqrt{ab} = \sqrt{a} \times \sqrt{b} \left(a \in \mathbb{R}_+, b \in \mathbb{R}_+ \right)$.

$\sqrt{ab} = (ab)^{\frac{1}{2}}$ _____

$\quad = a^{\frac{1}{2}} b^{\frac{1}{2}}$ _____

$\quad = \sqrt{a}\sqrt{b}$ _____

d) Justify the steps showing that $\sqrt{\dfrac{a}{b}} = \dfrac{\sqrt{a}}{\sqrt{b}} \left(a \in \mathbb{R}_+ \text{ and } b \in \mathbb{R}_+^* \right)$.

$\sqrt{\dfrac{a}{b}} = \left(\dfrac{a}{b} \right)^{\frac{1}{2}}$ _____

$\quad = \dfrac{a^{\frac{1}{2}}}{b^{\frac{1}{2}}}$ _____

$\quad = \dfrac{\sqrt{a}}{\sqrt{b}}$ _____

PROPERTIES OF RADICALS

- The square root of a zero or positive real number a, written $\sqrt{a}$, is the zero or positive real number b such that $b^2 = a$.

  If $a \in \mathbb{R}_+$ and $b \in \mathbb{R}_+$, $\boxed{\sqrt{a} = b \Leftrightarrow b^2 = a}$ **Ex.:** $\sqrt{25} = 5$ because $5^2 = 25$

- If $a \in \mathbb{R}^+$ and $b \in \mathbb{R}^+$, we have:

  $\boxed{\sqrt{a \times b} = \sqrt{a} \times \sqrt{b}}$ **Ex.:** $\sqrt{16 \times 9} = \sqrt{16} \times \sqrt{9}$

  $\boxed{\sqrt{\dfrac{a}{b}} = \dfrac{\sqrt{a}}{\sqrt{b}}} \quad (b \neq 0)$ **Ex.:** $\sqrt{\dfrac{16}{100}} = \dfrac{\sqrt{16}}{\sqrt{100}}$

  $\boxed{\sqrt{a+b} \neq \sqrt{a} + \sqrt{b}} \quad (ab \neq 0)$ **Ex.:** $\sqrt{64+36} \neq \sqrt{64} + \sqrt{36}$

  $\boxed{\sqrt{a-b} \neq \sqrt{a} - \sqrt{b}} \quad (ab \neq 0)$ **Ex.:** $\sqrt{100-64} \neq \sqrt{100} - \sqrt{64}$

---

1. **a)** Is the square root of a positive number unique? _____

   b) Does the square root of a negative number exist in the set of real numbers? _____

   c) Can the square root of a number be negative? _____

2. Calculate.

   a) $\sqrt{25} \times \sqrt{64}$ _____

   b) $\sqrt{8} \times \sqrt{2}$ _____

   c) $\left(\sqrt{5}\right)^2$ _____

   d) $\sqrt{\dfrac{100}{64}}$ _____

   e) $\dfrac{\sqrt{75}}{\sqrt{3}}$ _____

   f) $\sqrt{72} \div \sqrt{2}$ _____

   g) $\sqrt{81+144}$ _____

   h) $\sqrt{225-81}$ _____

   i) $\dfrac{\sqrt{8} \times \sqrt{12}}{\sqrt{6}}$ _____

3. The associative property of multiplication in the set $\mathbb{R}$ of real numbers enables you to establish that:

$$a\sqrt{b} \times c\sqrt{d} = ac\sqrt{bd} \qquad (b \geqslant 0, d \geqslant 0)$$
$$a\sqrt{b} \div c\sqrt{d} = \dfrac{a}{c}\sqrt{\dfrac{b}{d}} \qquad (b \geqslant 0, c > 0, d > 0)$$

Perform the following operations using this property.

   a) $3\sqrt{2} \times \sqrt{5}$ _____

   b) $2 \times 5\sqrt{3}$ _____

   c) $-3\sqrt{2} \times 5\sqrt{3}$ _____

   d) $12\sqrt{6} \div 4\sqrt{3}$ _____

   e) $12\sqrt{2} \div 2$ _____

   f) $12\sqrt{20} \div 4\sqrt{5}$ _____

ACTIVITY 2 Reducing the radicand

Justify the steps which enable you to reduce the radicand.

$\sqrt{75} = \sqrt{25 \times 3}$ _____

$\quad = \sqrt{25} \times \sqrt{3}$ _____

$\quad = 5\sqrt{3}$ _____

REDUCING THE RADICAND

- Let us illustrate the procedure in the following example.

   Ex.: $\sqrt{80} = \sqrt{16 \times 5}$ The radicand is written as the product of 2 factors with one factor being a perfect square number.

   $\quad = \sqrt{16} \times \sqrt{5}$ Apply the property $\sqrt{ab} = \sqrt{a} \times \sqrt{b}$.

   $\quad = 4 \times \sqrt{5}$ Evaluate the square root of the square number factor.

   $\quad = 4\sqrt{5}$

- The list of perfect square numbers less than 200 are:

   0, 1, 4, 9, 16, 25, 36, 49, 64, 81, 100, 121, 144, 169, 196.

4. Write each of the following numbers in the form $a\sqrt{b}$, where b is the smallest possible integer.

   a) $\sqrt{32}$ _____

   b) $\sqrt{98}$ _____

   c) $\sqrt{180}$ _____

   d) $\sqrt{720}$ _____

   e) $\sqrt{500}$ _____

   f) $2\sqrt{40}$ _____

   g) $\sqrt{567}$ _____

   h) $\sqrt{1944}$ _____

   i) $\dfrac{3}{5}\sqrt{250}$ _____

5. The distributive property of multiplication over addition in the set $\mathbb{R}$ of real numbers enables you to establish that: $a\sqrt{b} \pm c\sqrt{b} = (a \pm c)\sqrt{b}$ $(b \geqslant 0)$. Perform the following operations using this property.

a) $2\sqrt{5} + 4\sqrt{5}$ _____

b) $7\sqrt{2} - 2\sqrt{2}$ _____

c) $5\sqrt{18} - 6\sqrt{2}$ _____

d) $-3\sqrt{18} + 4\sqrt{8}$ _____

e) $2\sqrt{45} - 2\sqrt{28} + 3\sqrt{20} + 3\sqrt{63}$ _____

f) $2\sqrt{75} - 2\sqrt{108} + 5\sqrt{48} - \sqrt{27} + 3\sqrt{12}$ _____

g) $\sqrt{3} - \dfrac{\sqrt{3}}{3}$ _____

h) $3\sqrt{20} - 2\sqrt{12} + \sqrt{45} + 4\sqrt{27}$ _____

6. Perform the following operations.

a) $\left(-2\sqrt{5}\right)^2$ _____

b) $3\sqrt{5} \times -2\sqrt{3}$ _____

c) $4\sqrt{3} \times 2\sqrt{15}$ _____

d) $5\sqrt{18} - 6\sqrt{2}$ _____

e) $2\sqrt{3}\left(5\sqrt{3} + \sqrt{5}\right)$ _____

f) $\left(4\sqrt{5} + 3\right)\left(4\sqrt{5} - 3\right)$ _____

g) $3\sqrt{2}\left(\sqrt{2} + 1\right)$ _____

h) $2\sqrt{3}\left(2\sqrt{3} - \sqrt{2}\right)$ _____

i) $5\sqrt{18} - 4\sqrt{50}$ _____

j) $5\sqrt{8} - 2\sqrt{27} + 2\sqrt{75} - 3\sqrt{18}$ _____

ACTIVITY 3 Rationalizing the denominator

a) 1. Given a rational number x. Show that $\left(\sqrt{x}\right)^2$ is rational.

_____

2. Consider the expression $\dfrac{a}{\sqrt{b}}$ where $b \in \mathbb{Q}^*$. Justify the steps which enable you to make the denominator a rational number.

$\dfrac{a}{\sqrt{b}} = \dfrac{a \cdot \sqrt{b}}{\sqrt{b} \cdot \sqrt{b}}$ _____

$= \dfrac{a\sqrt{b}}{\left(\sqrt{b}\right)^2}$ _____

$= \dfrac{a\sqrt{b}}{b}$ _____

b) Use the identity $(a + b)(a - b) = a^2 - b^2$ to expand the following products.

1. $\left(\sqrt{5} + 2\right)\left(\sqrt{5} - 2\right)$ _____

2. $\left(\sqrt{7} + \sqrt{3}\right)\left(\sqrt{7} - \sqrt{3}\right)$ _____

3. $\left(2 - \sqrt{3}\right)\left(2 + \sqrt{3}\right)$ _____

4. $\left(2\sqrt{3} + 1\right)\left(2\sqrt{3} - 1\right)$ _____

c) The expression $(a - b)$ is called the **conjugate** of the expression $(a + b)$.

1. What is the conjugate of $\left(3 + \sqrt{2}\right)$? _____

2. Verify that the product of $\left(3 + \sqrt{2}\right)$ by its conjugate is a rational number.

_____

d) Consider the expression $\dfrac{7}{\sqrt{5} + \sqrt{2}}$. Justify the steps which enable you to make the denominator a rational number.

$\dfrac{7}{\sqrt{5} + \sqrt{2}} = \dfrac{7\left(\sqrt{5} - \sqrt{2}\right)}{\left(\sqrt{5} + \sqrt{2}\right)\left(\sqrt{5} - \sqrt{2}\right)}$ _____

$= \dfrac{7\left(\sqrt{5} - \sqrt{2}\right)}{\left(\sqrt{5}\right)^2 - \left(\sqrt{2}\right)^2}$ _____

$= \dfrac{7\left(\sqrt{5} - \sqrt{2}\right)}{3}$ _____

RATIONALIZING THE DENOMINATOR

Rationalizing the denominator of an irrational expression consists of determining an equivalent expression with a rational denominator.

There are 2 cases:

1. To rationalize the expression $\dfrac{a}{\sqrt{b}}$, we multiply the numerator and denominator by the denominator.

$$\frac{a}{\sqrt{b}} = \frac{a \cdot \sqrt{b}}{\sqrt{b} \cdot \sqrt{b}} = \frac{a\sqrt{b}}{\left(\sqrt{b}\right)^2} = \frac{a\sqrt{b}}{b}$$

Ex.: $\dfrac{2}{\sqrt{3}} = \dfrac{2 \cdot \sqrt{3}}{\sqrt{3} \cdot \sqrt{3}} = \dfrac{2\sqrt{3}}{\left(\sqrt{3}\right)^2} = \dfrac{2\sqrt{3}}{3}$

2. To rationalize the expression $\dfrac{a}{\sqrt{b}+\sqrt{c}}$, we multiply the numerator and denominator by the conjugate of the denominator.

$$\frac{a}{\sqrt{b}+\sqrt{c}} = \frac{a\left(\sqrt{b}-\sqrt{c}\right)}{\left(\sqrt{b}+\sqrt{c}\right)\left(\sqrt{b}-\sqrt{c}\right)} = \frac{a\left(\sqrt{b}-\sqrt{c}\right)}{\left(\sqrt{b}\right)^2 - \left(\sqrt{c}\right)^2} = \frac{a\left(\sqrt{b}-\sqrt{c}\right)}{b-c}$$

Ex.: $\dfrac{1}{\sqrt{5}+\sqrt{3}} = \dfrac{\left(\sqrt{5}-\sqrt{3}\right)}{\left(\sqrt{5}+\sqrt{3}\right)\left(\sqrt{5}-\sqrt{3}\right)} = \dfrac{\left(\sqrt{5}-\sqrt{3}\right)}{\left(\sqrt{5}\right)^2 - \left(\sqrt{3}\right)^2} = \dfrac{\sqrt{5}-\sqrt{3}}{5-3} = \dfrac{\sqrt{5}-\sqrt{3}}{2}$

Note that the **conjugate** of $(a+b)$ is $(a-b)$ and that $(a+b)(a-b) = a^2 - b^2$.

---

7. Rationalize the denominator of the following expressions.

a) $\dfrac{3}{\sqrt{5}}$ _____

b) $\dfrac{5}{\sqrt{10}}$ _____

c) $\dfrac{1}{\sqrt{2}}$ _____

d) $\dfrac{2}{3\sqrt{5}}$ _____

e) $\dfrac{\sqrt{2}}{\sqrt{3}}$ _____

f) $\sqrt{\dfrac{2}{5}}$ _____

g) $\dfrac{1+\sqrt{2}}{\sqrt{5}}$ _____

h) $\dfrac{1-\sqrt{3}}{\sqrt{3}}$ _____

8. For each of the following expressions,
   1. find the conjugate expression.   2. multiply the expression by its conjugate.

a) $\sqrt{3}+1$ 1. _____   2. _____

b) $\sqrt{5}-2$ 1. _____   2. _____

c) $\sqrt{3}+\sqrt{2}$ 1. _____   2. _____

d) $2\sqrt{3}-3$ 1. _____   2. _____

9. Rationalize the denominator of the following expressions.

a) $\dfrac{1}{\sqrt{6}+2}$ _____

b) $\dfrac{\sqrt{3}}{\sqrt{5}-1}$ _____

c) $\dfrac{3}{\sqrt{5}-\sqrt{3}}$ _____

d) $\dfrac{\sqrt{3}+\sqrt{2}}{\sqrt{3}-\sqrt{2}}$ _____

e) $\dfrac{3\sqrt{2}-2\sqrt{3}}{3\sqrt{2}+2\sqrt{3}}$ _____

f) $\dfrac{\sqrt{2}}{5\sqrt{2}-2\sqrt{5}}$ _____

10. Rationalize the numerator of the following expressions.

a) $\dfrac{\sqrt{3}+1}{2}$ _____

b) $\dfrac{\sqrt{5}+\sqrt{2}}{6}$ _____

c) $\dfrac{3\sqrt{2}-\sqrt{3}}{3\sqrt{2}+\sqrt{3}}$ _____

11. Rationalize the numerator of the expression $\dfrac{\sqrt{x+h}-\sqrt{x}}{h}$. $(h \neq 0)$

_____

12. Rationalize the denominator of the following expressions.

a) $\dfrac{1}{\sqrt{x+1}+\sqrt{x}}$ _____

b) $\dfrac{x-4}{x-1-\sqrt{2x+1}}$ $(x \neq 4)$_____

c) $\dfrac{x^2-3x}{x-1-\sqrt{x+1}}$ $(x \neq 0 \text{ and } x \neq 3)$ _____

13. Consider the second degree equation $x^2 - 2x - 1 = 0$ in the form $ax^2 + bx + c = 0$.

a) Determine the solutions x_1 and x_2 of this equation._____

b) Verify the following properties.

    1. $x_1 + x_2 = \dfrac{-b}{a}$._____

    2. $x_1 \cdot x_2 = \dfrac{c}{a}$._____

14. The quadratic function f on the right has two zeros x_1 and x_2.
If $x_1 = 2 - \sqrt{3}, x_2 = 2 + \sqrt{3}$ and $f(1) = 2$, determine

a) the rule of function f.

_____

_____

_____

_____

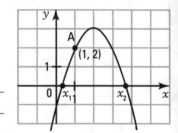

b) max f. _____

15. For what values of x are the following expressions defined?

a) $\sqrt{x-2}$ _____   **b)** $\sqrt[3]{x-2}$ _____

c) $\sqrt{2x-6}$ _____   **d)** $\sqrt{-3x+6}$ _____

e) $\dfrac{1}{\sqrt{x-2}}$ _____   **f)** $\dfrac{x-1}{\sqrt{x-1}}$ _____

16. For what values of x are the following expressions defined?

a) $\sqrt{x^2-9}$ _____   **b)** $\sqrt{x^2+1}$_____

c) $\sqrt{1-x^2}$ _____   **d)** $\sqrt{x^2-5x+6}$ _____

17. For what values of x are the following expressions defined?

a) $\sqrt{\dfrac{x-1}{x+2}}$ _____

b) $\sqrt{\dfrac{x^2-1}{x^2-9}}$ _____

1.5 Factoring a polynomial

Factor the following polynomials.

a) $15x^4 + 20x^3 - 10x^2$ _____

b) $6x^2 - 2xy + 9x - 3y$ _____

c) $16x^2 - 9$ _____

d) $9x^2 + 12x + 4$ _____

e) $x^2 - 8x + 15$ _____

f) $2x^2 + 7x + 3$ _____

FACTORING A POLYNOMIAL

- **Factoring** a polynomial means writing the polynomial as a product of factors.
- **Removing a common factor** is a method which can be used to factor a polynomial composed of monomials which all have a common factor. To factor, you need to apply the distributive property of multiplication over addition.

$$ab + ac = a(b + c)$$

factor / expand

Ex.: $P(x) = 6x^4 + 15x^3 - 18x^2$
$= 3x^2(2x^2 + 5x - 6)$

- **Factoring by grouping** is a method which enables you to factor polynomials by grouping the terms which contain a common factor. You then remove the common factor in each of the groupings.

Ex.: Factor the following expression using factoring by grouping.

$\underline{9x^2 - 12xy^2} + \underline{6xy - 8y^3}$ ← Group the terms containing a common factor.

$= 3x(3x - 4y^2) + 2y(3x - 4y^2)$ ← Remove the common factor in each grouping.

$= (3x - 4y^2)(3x + 2y)$ ← Remove the common factor a 2nd time.

- A **difference of two squares** is factorable.

$$a^2 - b^2 = (a + b)(a - b)$$

Ex.: $9x^2 - 4y^2 = (3x + 2y)(3x - 2y)$

- **Perfect square trinomials** are factorable.

$$a^2 + 2ab + b^2 = (a + b)^2$$
$$a^2 - 2ab + b^2 = (a - b)^2$$

Ex.: $4x^2 + 12x + 9 = (2x + 3)^2$
$9x^2 - 30xy + 25y^2 = (3x - 5y)^2$

- The **"product and sum"** method enables you to factor a second degree trinomial. Let us illustrate this method by factoring $P(x) = 2x^2 + 7x + 6$.

1. **Identify** the coefficients a, b and c.	1. $a = 2; b = 7; c = 6$
2. **Find** two integers m and n such that $\begin{cases} m \cdot n = ac \leftarrow \text{product of the end coefficients} \\ m + n = b \leftarrow \text{middle coefficient.} \end{cases}$	2. $\begin{cases} mn = 12 \\ m + n = 7 \end{cases}$ $m = 4, n = 3$
3. **Write:** $ax^2 + bx + c = ax^2 + mx + nx + c$ and **factor** by grouping.	3. $2x^2 + 7x + 6 = 2x^2 + 4x + 3x + 6$ $= 2x(x + 2) + 3(x + 2)$ $= (x + 2)(2x + 3)$

1. Factor the following polynomials.

a) $6x^3y^3 - 9x^3y + 6x^2y^2$ _____

b) $25x^2 - 9y^2$ _____

c) $2x^2 + 3xy - 10x - 15y$ _____

d) $x^3 + x^2 + x - 3$ _____

e) $16x^2 - (x + 2)^2$ _____

f) $(x + 1)^2 - (2x + 3)^2$ _____

g) $4x^2 - 4x + 1$ _____

h) $9x^2 + 12xy + 4y^2$ _____

i) $x^2 - 8x + 15$ _____

j) $2x^2 - 7x + 3$ _____

k) $2x^2 - 9x + 4$ _____

l) $3x^2 - 4x - 4$ _____

2. Factor the following polynomials completely.

a) $2x^2 - 50x$ _____

b) $12x^3 - 12x^2 + 3x$ _____

c) $4x^3 - 4x^2 - 8x$ _____

d) $x^4 - 81$ _____

e) $(x^2 - 4) + (x - 2)^2$ _____

f) $x^4 - 8x^2 + 16$ _____

ACTIVITY 2 Factoring a second degree trinomial: Method of completing the square.

a) Fill in the missing term to obtain a perfect square trinomial and then factor.

1. $x^2 + 6x +$ _____ $=$ _____

2. $x^2 - 5x +$ _____ $=$ _____

3. $x^2 + \frac{5}{2}x +$ _____ $=$ _____

4. $x^2 - \frac{7}{3}x +$ _____ $=$ _____

b) Justify the steps which enable you to factor a trinomial of the form $ax^2 + bx + c$.

Steps	Justifications
$P(x) = 2x^2 + 5x + 2$	$a = 2, b = 5, c = 2$
$= 2\left(x^2 + \frac{5}{2}x + 1\right)$	
$= 2\left(x^2 + \frac{5}{2}x + \ldots + 1 - \ldots\right)$	
$= 2\left[x^2 + \frac{5}{2}x + \frac{25}{16} + 1 - \frac{25}{16}\right]$	
$= 2\left[\left(x + \frac{5}{4}\right)^2 - \frac{9}{16}\right]$	
$= 2\left(x + \frac{5}{4} + \frac{3}{4}\right)\left(x + \frac{5}{4} - \frac{3}{4}\right)$	
$= 2(x + 2)\left(x + \frac{1}{2}\right)$	
$= (x + 2)(2x + 1)$	

FACTORING A SECOND DEGREE TRINOMIAL: METHOD OF COMPLETING THE SQUARE

The method of completing the square is illustrated below by factoring $P(x) = 2x^2 + 7x + 6$.

$P(x) = 2x^2 + 7x + 6$

$= 2\left(x^2 + \frac{7}{2}x + 3\right)$ ← Factor out the coefficient $a = 2$.

$= 2\left[\left(x^2 + \frac{7}{2}x + \frac{49}{16}\right) + 3 - \frac{49}{16}\right]$ ← Complete the perfect square trinomial.

> $\frac{49}{16}$ is the square of half of the coefficient $\frac{7}{2}$ of the middle term.

$= 2\left[\left(x + \frac{7}{4}\right)^2 - \frac{1}{16}\right]$ ← Factor the perfect square trinomial.

$= 2\left[\left(x + \frac{7}{4} + \frac{1}{4}\right)\left(x + \frac{7}{4} - \frac{1}{4}\right)\right]$ ← Factor the difference of two squares.

$= 2(x + 2)\left(x + \frac{3}{2}\right)$ ← Simplify.

$= (x + 2)(2x + 3)$ ← Write as a product of two binomials.

3. Factor the following second degree trinomials by completing the square.

a) $x^2 - 10x + 21$ _____

b) $x^2 - 5x - 14$ _____

c) $x^2 - 7x + 12$ _____

d) $x^2 - 9x + 20$ _____

e) $2x^2 + 7x + 3$ _____

f) $3x^2 + 5x - 2$ _____

g) $6x^2 + x - 2$ _____

h) $10x^2 - 19x + 6$ _____

ACTIVITY 3 Factoring a second degree trinomial: The roots method.

a) Justify the steps which enable you to write a second degree trinomial in standard form.

$ax^2 + bx + c = a\left(x^2 + \frac{b}{a}x + \frac{c}{a}\right)$ _____

$= a\left(x^2 + \frac{b}{a}x + \frac{b^2}{4a^2} + \frac{c}{a} - \frac{b^2}{4a^2}\right)$ _____

$= a\left[\left(x + \frac{b}{2a}\right)^2 + \frac{4ac - b^2}{4a^2}\right]$ _____

$= a\left[\left(x + \frac{b}{2a}\right)^2 - \frac{\Delta}{4a^2}\right]$ _____

b) From the standard form $a\left[\left(x + \frac{b}{2a}\right)^2 - \frac{\Delta}{4a^2}\right]$,

1. show that when Δ is positive, the trinomial $ax^2 + bx + c$ is factorable into a product of two 1st degree factors, that is to say $ax^2 + bx + c = a(x - x_1)(x - x_2)$ where x_1 and x_2 are the roots of the trinomial.

2. Explain why the trinomial $ax^2 + bx + c$ is not factorable in $\mathbb{R}$ when Δ is negative.

_____

_____

3. Factor the trinomial $ax^2 + bx + c$ when Δ is zero.

_____

FACTORING A SECOND DEGREE TRINOMIAL: THE ROOTS METHOD

The second degree trinomial $ax^2 + bx + c$ is factorable in $\mathbb{R}$ if and only if the discriminant Δ is positive or zero.

$$\boxed{\Delta \geqslant 0: ax^2 + bx + c = a(x - x_1)(x - x_2)}, \Delta = b^2 - 4ac$$

where $x_1 = \dfrac{-b - \sqrt{\Delta}}{2a}$ and $x_2 = \dfrac{-b + \sqrt{\Delta}}{2a}$ are the roots of the trinomial.

$$\boxed{\Delta < 0: ax^2 + bx + c \text{ cannot be factored in } \mathbb{R}.}$$

Ex.: Factor $2x^2 + 7x + 6$.

$a = 2, b = 7, c = 6; \Delta = 1; x_1 = -2, x_2 = -\dfrac{3}{2}$.

$2x^2 + 7x + 6 = 2(x + 2)\left(x + \dfrac{3}{2}\right)$

$\qquad\qquad\quad = (x + 2)(2x + 3)$

Ex.: Factor $4x^2 - 12x + 9$.

$a = 4, b = -12, c = 9; \Delta = 0; x_1 = x_2 = \dfrac{3}{2}$.

$4x^2 - 12x + 9 = 4\left(x - \dfrac{3}{2}\right)^2$

Ex.: $x^2 + x + 1$ is not factorable in $\mathbb{R}$ since $\Delta < 0$.
Indeed, $a = 1, b = 1, c = 1$ and $\Delta = -3$.

4. For each of the following trinomials, indicate if the trinomial is factorable.

a) $2x^2 + 3x + 1$ _____

b) $2x^2 - x - 6$ _____

c) $x^2 - x + 1$ _____

d) $4x^2 - 28x + 49$ _____

e) $x^2 + 2x - 1$ _____

f) $4x^2 - 12x + 10$ _____

5. Factor the following trinomials using the roots method.

a) $2x^2 + 13x + 15$ _____

b) $4x^2 + 12x + 9$ _____

c) $-4x^2 + 4x - 1$ _____

d) $4x^2 + 4x - 3$ _____

e) $x^2 + 2x - 1$ _____

f) $2x^2 + 4x - 4$ _____

g) $6x^2 - 7x + 2$ _____

h) $8x^2 + 2x - 1$ _____

6. Simplify the following rational expressions after indicating the restrictions.

a) $\dfrac{x^2 - 3x + 2}{(x-1)^2} =$ _____

b) $\dfrac{x^2 - 9}{x^2 - 8x + 15} =$ _____

c) $\dfrac{2x^2 - 3x - 2}{2x^2 - 5x - 3} =$ _____

d) $\dfrac{2x^2 - 12x^2 + 18x}{2x^3 - 18x} =$ _____

7. Solve the following equations.

a) $2x^2 - 9x - 5 = 0$

b) $9x^2 - 12x + 4 = 0$

c) $x^2 + 2x + 3 = 0$

d) $x^3 - x = 0$

e) $x^2 + 4x + 1 = 0$

f) $-4x^2 + 4x - 1 = 0$

8. Determine the sign of the following polynomials.

a) $P(x) = 2x - 6$

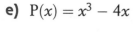

b) $P(x) = -2x^2 + 10$

c) $P(x) = x^2 - 8x + 15$

d) $P(x) = -2x^2 - 5x + 3$

e) $P(x) = x^3 - 4x$

f) $P(x) = x^3 - 4x^2 + 4x$

9. The polynomial $R = -t^2 + 12t - 32$ gives the net revenue R, in thousands of dollars, of a bakery t months after opening ($0 \leqslant t \leqslant 12$). Determine and interpret the sign of this polynomial.

Evaluation 1

1. Write, as a power of 2, the expression: $\dfrac{16^3 \times 2^{-4} \times \sqrt{24}}{\sqrt{6} \times 8^{\frac{3}{2}}}$. _____

2. Simplify the following expressions.

   a) $x^{-3} \cdot x^5$ _____ **b)** $\left(x^{-\frac{2}{3}}\right)^{-6}$ _____ **c)** $(x^2y^{-3})^2 \cdot (3x^2y)^{-1}$ _____

   d) $\left(\dfrac{3x^{-2}}{2x^{-1}}\right)^2$ _____ **e)** $\sqrt{4x^8y^4}$ _____ **f)** $\sqrt[3]{8x^6y^9}$ _____

3. Reduce the radicand.

   a) $\sqrt{72}$ _____ **b)** $\sqrt{288}$ _____

4. Perform the following operations.

   a) $\sqrt{18} - \sqrt{12} - \sqrt{8} + 2\sqrt{3}$ _____ **b)** $\left(2\sqrt{3} + 3\sqrt{2}\right)\left(2\sqrt{3} - 3\sqrt{2}\right)$ _____

5. Rationalize the denominator.

   a) $\dfrac{2\sqrt{3}}{\sqrt{5}}$ _____ **b)** $\dfrac{\sqrt{2}}{\sqrt{5} - \sqrt{3}}$ _____ **c)** $\dfrac{\sqrt{5} - \sqrt{2}}{\sqrt{5} + \sqrt{2}}$ _____

6. For what values of x are the following expressions defined?

   a) $\sqrt{-2x + 6}$ _____

   b) $\sqrt{9 - x^2}$ _____

   c) $\sqrt{x^2 - 6x + 8}$ _____

   d) $\sqrt{\dfrac{x^2 - 1}{16 - x^2}}$ _____

7. Write the number 28 of the decimal system

   a) in base 2. _____ **b)** in base 3. _____ **c)** in base 5. _____

8. Convert the following numbers into the decimal system.

   a) 1010_2 _____ **b)** 211_3 _____ **c)** 342_5 _____

9. Factor the trinomial $2x^2 + 7x + 6$ by completing the square.

10. Factor the trinomial $x^2 + 2x - 1$.

_____

_____

11. Factor the following polynomials completely.

   a) $x^4 - 16$ _____

   b) $x^4 - 18x^2 + 81$ _____

   c) $(x^2 + 1)^2 - 4x^2$ _____

   d) $2x^5 - 4x^3 + 2x$ _____

12. Simplify the following rational expressions after indicating the restrictions.

   a) $\dfrac{x^2 - 9}{x^2 + 8x + 15}$ _____
      b) $\dfrac{2x^2 - 3x - 2}{x^2 - 7x + 10}$ _____

13. Explain why the trinomial $x^2 + x + 1$ is not factorable in the set $\mathbb{R}$.

_____

14. For what values of m is the trinomial $mx^2 + (m + 1)x + m$ factorable in $\mathbb{R}$?

_____

15. For what values of m does the equation $mx^2 + mx + 1 = 0$ yield

   a) two distinct solutions? _____

   b) only one solution? _____

   c) no solution? _____

16. The polynomial R $= 2t^2 - 18t + 36$ gives the net revenue R in thousands of dollars of a restaurant t months after the opening of a competing restaurant. $(0 \leqslant t \leqslant 12)$
Determine and interpret the sign of this polynomial.

_____

_____

_____

_____

Chapter 2

Optimization

CHALLENGE 2

1. During the summer, Adel grows strawberries on his farm in the St-Laurent Lowlands. His wife Denise makes jam that she sells in her general store. She fills 400 ml jars and 500 ml jars.

- Every week she uses a maximum of 30 litres of jam.
- She wants to produce at least 50 jars per week.
- She also wants to produce, weekly, at least 20 jars but at most forty 500 ml jars.
- Moreover, she wants to produce, weekly, at least twenty 400 ml jars.

How many jars of each size must she produce weekly in order to maximize her profit if she sells each 400 ml jar for $7 and each 500 ml jar for $9?

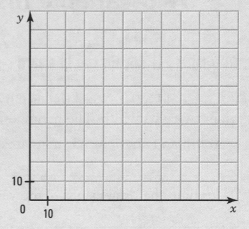

2.1 Two-variable first degree equations

ACTIVITY 1 Laying sod in a yard

Mr. Quinn would like to have sod installed in his rectangular yard. The length of the yard is 50 m more than twice its width. The perimeter of the yard is equal to 340 m.

a) Establish an equation that translates this situation.

_____

b) Determine the dimensions of the yard.

_____

c) Find the cost of the sod, knowing that it costs \$0.80/m². _____

ONE-VARIABLE FIRST DEGREE EQUATION

- A **one-variable first degree equation** is an equation that can be written as:

$$\boxed{ax + b = 0} \qquad a \neq 0$$

Ex.: $2x + 6 = 0$ is a one-variable first degree equation.

- Solving a first degree equation in one variable x consists in finding the value of x which transforms the equation into a true equality. The value of x we obtain is called **solution** of the equation.

Ex.: $3x - 5 = 13$
$$\begin{array}{ll} \downarrow + 5 \quad \downarrow + 5 & \text{We add 5 to both sides of the equation.} \\ 3x = 18 & \\ \downarrow \div 3 \quad \downarrow \div 3 & \text{We divide each side of the equation by 3.} \\ x = 6 & \end{array}$$

The solution of the equation is 6.

ACTIVITY 2 Two-variable first degree equation

Consider the two-variable first degree equation $2x - 5y = -10$.

a) Do the coordinates of the point A(5,4) verify this equation?

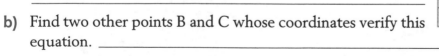

b) Find two other points B and C whose coordinates verify this equation. _____

c) Place points A, B and C in the Cartesian plane on the right. What is the position of these three points? _____

d) What is the solution set of the equation $2x - 5y = -10$? Represent it in the Cartesian plane.

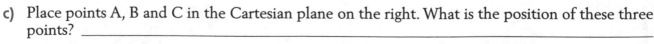

ACTIVITY 3 Manufacturing furniture

A furniture manufacture makes chairs and armchairs. The number of hours spent on finishing a chair is 3 hours and the number of hours spent finishing an armchair is 5 hours. In one week, the time spent on finishing these two pieces of furniture is equal to 45 hours.

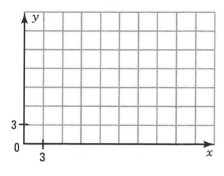

a) If x and y represent respectively the number of chairs and the number of armchairs produced in one week, translate into a two-variable equation the constraint stating that the total time spent during one week to make these two items is 45 hours.

_____

b) Construct a table of values satisfying the constraint established in a).

x			
y			

c) In this situation, the variables x and y take only positive values. Represent the solution set of the equation established in a) in the 1st quadrant above.

TWO-VARIABLE FIRST DEGREE EQUATION

- A two-variable first degree equation is an equation that can be written as:

$$ax + by + c = 0 \qquad a \neq 0, b \neq 0$$

- The solution set of such an equation is represented graphically by a line.

  Ex.: Consider the equation $3x - 4y + 12 = 0$.

  Table of values

x	−4	0	4
y	0	3	6

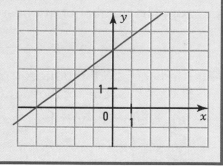

  The solution set of the equation $3x - 4y + 12 = 0$ is represented by the set of points on the line on the right.

---

1. Determine if the coordinates of the point P(−2, 3) verify each of the following equations.

a) $3x + 4y = 6$ b) $-2x + y = 5$ c) $y = 5x + 7$ d) $\dfrac{x}{2} + \dfrac{y}{1.5} = 1$

_____   _____   _____   _____

2. Represent graphically the solution set of each of the following equations.

a) $3x + 4 = 10$

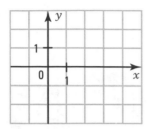

b) $x + y = 2$

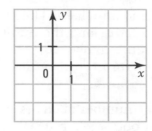

c) $x + 2y = 3$

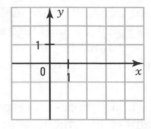

d) $3x - 2y = 3$

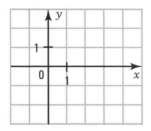

e) $y = -2x + 4$

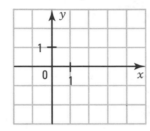

f) $4y = -4$

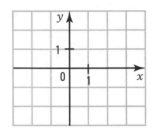

3. The management of a tennis club wishes to hire personnel for its summer season. It wants to hire instructors and attendants. If x represents the number of instructors and y the number of attendants, translate each of the following constraints into a two-variable first degree equation.

a) The total number of people hired is equal to 8. _____

b) The number of instructors exceeds the number of attendants by 4. _____

c) There are three times as many instructors as attendants. _____

d) The number of instructors increased by twice the number of attendants is equal to 10.

_____

e) The number of attendants is equal to one third the number of instructors decreased by 1.

_____

4. A grocery store produces strawberry jam. It produces 250 ml jars and 500 ml jars. The total quantity of jam it wants to package is 6000 ml.

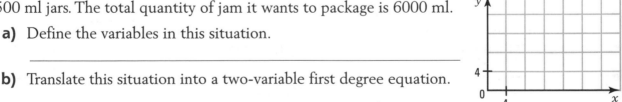

a) Define the variables in this situation.

_____

b) Translate this situation into a two-variable first degree equation.

_____

c) Represent the solution set of the equation established in b) in the Cartesian plane on the right.

d) Give a solution couple for this equation. What does it represent?

_____

2.2 Two-variable first degree inequalities

ACTIVITY 1 Fence around a field

M. Addison would like to put a fence around a rectangular field whose length measures 6 m more that three times its width. He has a maximum of 84 m of fencing.

a) Write an inequality that translates this situation.

_____

b) In which interval is the width of this field contained?

_____

ACTIVITY 2 Properties of the inequality relation

Let a, b and c be any three real numbers. Complete the following equivalences using the appropriate symbol $\geqslant$ or $\leqslant$.

a) $a \leqslant b \Leftrightarrow a + c \underline{\hspace{1cm}} b + c$.

b) $a \leqslant b \Leftrightarrow a - c \underline{\hspace{1cm}} b - c$.

c) 1. $a \leqslant b$ and $c > 0 \Leftrightarrow ac \underline{\hspace{1cm}} bc$.
   2. $a \leqslant b$ and $c < 0 \Leftrightarrow ac \underline{\hspace{1cm}} bc$.

d) 1. $a \leqslant b$ and $c > 0 \Leftrightarrow \dfrac{a}{c} \underline{\hspace{1cm}} \dfrac{b}{c}$.

   2. $a \leqslant b$ and $c < 0 \Leftrightarrow \dfrac{a}{c} \underline{\hspace{1cm}} \dfrac{b}{c}$.

ONE-VARIABLE FIRST DEGREE INEQUALITY

- A **one-variable first degree inequality** is an inequality that can be written as:

$$\boxed{ax + b \geqslant 0} \qquad a \neq 0 \qquad (\leqslant, >, <)$$

  Ex.: $3x + 9 \geqslant 0$ is a one-variable first degree inequality.

- Solving a first degree inequality in one variable x consists in finding the set of solutions that transforms the inequality into a true inequality.

  Ex.: $-2x + 3 \geqslant 15$
     $\downarrow -3 \quad \downarrow -3$ We subtract 3 from both sides of the inequality.

   $-2x \geqslant 12$
     $\downarrow \div (-2) \ \downarrow \div (-2)$ We divide each side of the inequality by -2.
     $x \leqslant -6$ We **change** the direction of the inequality because we divide each side by the negative number -2.

   $S = {]-\infty, -6]}$

ACTIVITY 3 Two-variable first degree inequality

Consider the line l with equation: $2x + 5y - 10 = 0$. Line l divides the plane into 2 half-planes: the colored half-plane containing the origin 0 and the grey half-plane that doesn't contain it. This line l is called **boundary** for each of the half-planes. In which half-plane is the set of points verifying the following inequality located?

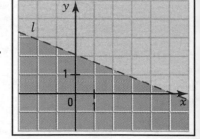

a) $2x + 5y - 10 > 0$? _____

b) $2x + 5y - 10 < 0$? _____

ACTIVITY 4 At a financial centre

A financial centre employs regular staff and contract staff. Each regular employee receives a \$20/hour salary and each contract employee receives a \$25/hour salary. The centre has a maximal budget of \$2000 per week.

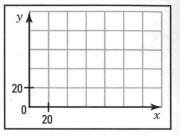

a) If x represents the number of working hours of a regular employee and y represents the number of working hours of a contract employee, translate this situation into two-variable first degree inequality. _____

b) Explain why the possible solutions for x and y must be in the 1st quadrant.

_____

c) Draw the boundary line that divides the plane into two half-planes.

d) Color, in the 1st quadrant, the region of the plane that represents the solution set of the inequality given in a).

e) Give two solution couples for this inequality. _____

TWO-VARIABLE INEQUALITY – REPRESENTATION OF THE SOLUTION SET

The solution set of the two-variable first degree inequality $ax + by + c > 0$ is represented by a **half-plane** whose **boundary** is the line $l: ax + by + c = 0$.

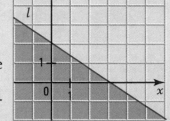

Ex.: To determine the solution set of the inequality $2x + 3y - 6 \leqslant 0$,
1. we draw the line $l: 2x + 3y - 6 = 0$, boundary of the half-plane we seek.
2. if the origin 0(0, 0) verifies the inequality, the solution half-plane is the one that contains the origin.

The boundary is drawn as a **solid line** to show that the points on the boundary are solutions, as a **dotted line** otherwise.
3. we color the solution half-plane.

$2x + 3y - 6 < 0$

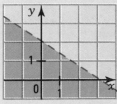

$2x + 3y - 6 > 0$

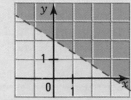

$2x + 3y - 6 \geqslant 0$

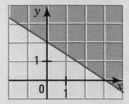

---

1. Represent graphically the solution set of the following inequalities.

a) $-4x + 5y - 10 \leqslant 0$

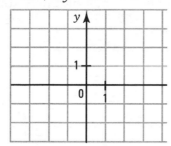

b) $x - 3y < 0$

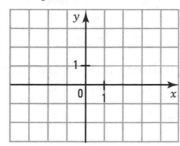

c) $y > x - 2$

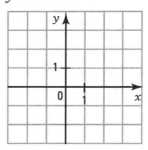

d) $y \geqslant -1$

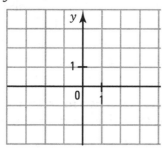

e) $x \leqslant 3$

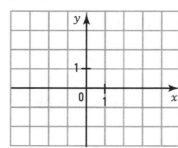

f) $x + y \leqslant 3$

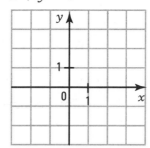

2. Determine if the coordinates of the point P(3, –2) verify each of the following inequalities.

a) $5x - 4y > 10$

b) $x \leqslant 4y$

c) $x < 2y + 4$

d) $-3x + 2y + 5 \leqslant 0$

e) $x \leqslant 8$

f) $\frac{x}{3} + \frac{y}{2} < 1$

3. For each of the following situations,
1. identify the variables.
2. translate the situation into a two-variable first degree inequality.

a) The total number of boys and girls on a field trip is less than or equal to 150.

b) The perimeter of a rectangle is greater than 250 cm.

c) At a summer camp, counsellors are paid $9.50 an hour and sports instructors are paid $15 an hour. The budget for these employees' salary is less than $9000.

d) At a food products company, salad dressing is packaged in 100 ml bottles and 250 ml bottles. The total amount of dressing packaged in bottles is at least equal to 50 litres.

e) In a group of tourists, there are at most three times as many Francophones as there are Anglophones.

4. To raise money for their graduation party, secondary 5 students sell shirts and caps. Each shirt sells for $15 and each cap sells for $8. Translate each of the following constraints into a two-variable first degree inequality, knowing that x represents the number of shirts sold and y represents the number of caps sold.

a) The students want to raise at least $850. _____

b) They want to sell at most three times as many shirts as caps. _____

c) They sold more than 70 items. _____

d) They sold a maximum of 40 shirts. _____

e) They sold at least as many shirts as caps. _____

5. At a fundraising concert to help homeless people, organizers sell adult tickets for $25 and student tickets for $10. If x represents the number of adult tickets sold and y represents the number of student tickets sold, use a two-variable first degree inequality to translate each of the following statements and represent the solution set of the inequality in the Cartesian plane with an appropriate choice of scale.

a) The organizers raised more than $4000.   b) There were at least four times as many adult tickets sold as student tickets.

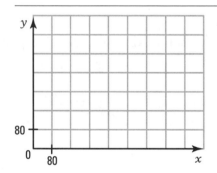   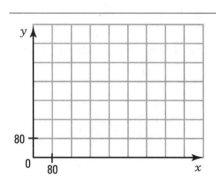

c) The number of tickets sold is less than 400. d) The number of adult tickets sold is greater than or equal to 240.

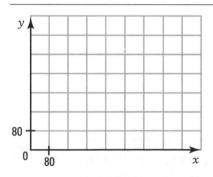   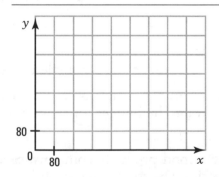

6. For each of the following situations,
1. define the variables involved in the situation;
2. translate the situation into an inequality;
3. represent the situation in the Cartesian plane.

a) A garden has an area of 75 m². Each fruit patch occupies 3 m² and each vegetable patch occupies 5 m².

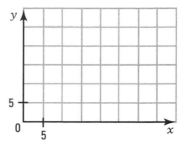

_____

_____

_____

b) In Quebec's logging industry, timber production exceeds pulp and paper production by at least 2%.

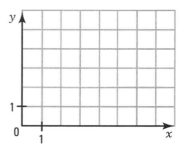

_____

_____

_____

c) Quebec's tourist industry announces that there are at least 6 times as many tourists from Quebec as there are tourists from other parts of Canada.

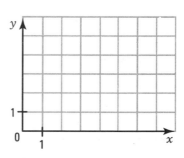

_____

_____

_____

7. The manager of employees for a pharmaceutical company wishes to hire employees for the research department and employees for management. Research employees are paid $40 an hour and management employees are paid $16 an hour. If x represents the number of research employees and y the number of management employees, translate each of the following graphs into an inequality.

a)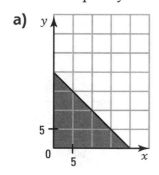

b)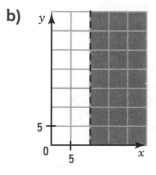

c)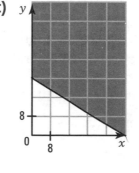

d)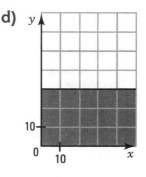

_____   _____   _____   _____

2.2 Two-variable first degree inequalities

2.3 System of two-variable first degree equations

a) Represent, in the Cartesian plane on the right, the following system of equations and determine the solution set of the system.

$$\begin{cases} 2x + 5y = 1 \\ x = 2y + 5 \end{cases}$$ _____

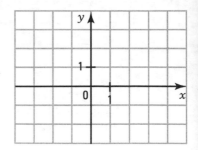

b) Solve the following system using the addition method.

$$\begin{cases} 2x + 3y = 6 \\ 5x + 4y = 1 \end{cases}$$ _____

c) Solve the following system using the substitution method.

$$\begin{cases} 3x + 8y = 1 \\ x = 4y - 3 \end{cases}$$ _____

d) Solve the following system using the comparison method.

$$\begin{cases} y = 4x + 8 \\ y = 3x + 5 \end{cases}$$ _____

SYSTEM OF TWO-VARIABLE FIRST DEGREE EQUATIONS

- A **system of two-variable first degree equations** is a system that can be written as:

$$\begin{cases} a_1x + b_1y = c_1 \\ a_2x + b_2y = c_2 \end{cases}$$

where x and y are the variables and a_1, b_1, c_1, a_2, b_2, c_2 are real numbers.

- Solving a system: **Graphical method**
  Solving graphically a system of two first degree equations consists in representing graphically each of the equations and determining the set of couples that verify both equations simultaneously.

  Ex.: The solution set of the system $\begin{cases} 3x + y = -5 \\ x + 2y = 0 \end{cases}$ is: $S = \{(-2, 1)\}$

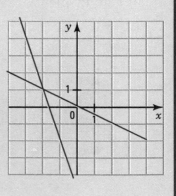

- Solving a system: Addition method

The addition method (also called reduction method) is illustrated in the following example.

Consider the system: $\begin{cases} 2x + 5y = -4 \\ 3x - 2y = 13 \end{cases}$

- We multiply both members of each equation by a nonzero real number in order to have opposite coefficients for the variable x (or the variable y).
- We add the corresponding sides of the equations in order to obtain an equation in only one variable.
- We determine the value of this variable.
- We, then, substitute the value obtained into one of the equations of the system and we deduce the value of the other variable.
- We establish the solution set S of the system.

$\begin{array}{c} \times 3 \\ \times -2 \end{array} \begin{cases} 2x + 5y = -4 \\ 3x - 2y = 13 \end{cases}$

$\begin{cases} 6x + 15y = -12 \\ -6x + 4y = -26 \end{cases}$

$19y = -38$
$y = -2$
$2x + 5(-2) = -4$
$x = 3$

$S = \{(3, -2)\}$

- Solving a system: Substitution method

The substitution method is illustrated in the following example.

Consider the system: $\begin{cases} 3x + 4y = -6 \\ 2x + y = 1 \end{cases}$

- We isolate one of the variables using one of the equations of the system.
- In the other equation, we substitute the isolated variable with the expression obtained.
- We solve the equation.
- We, then, substitute the value obtained into one of the equations of the system and we deduce the value of the other variable.
- We establish the solution set S of the system.

$y = -2x + 1$
$3x + 4(-2x + 1) = -6$

$3x - 8x + 4 = -6$
$x = 2$
$3(2) + 4y = -6$
$y = -3$
$S = \{(2, -3)\}$

- Solving a system: Comparison method

The comparison method is illustrated in the following example.

Consider the system: $\begin{cases} -2x + y = 1 \\ 3x + 2y = 9 \end{cases}$

- We isolate the same variable in each equation.

- We deduce by transitivity an equation in only one variable.

- We solve the equation that we obtained.

- We substitute the value obtained into one of the equations of the system and we deduce the value of the other variable.
- We establish the solution set S of the system.

$\begin{cases} y = 2x + 1 \\ y = -\dfrac{3}{2}x + \dfrac{9}{2} \end{cases}$

$2x + 1 = -\dfrac{3}{2}x + \dfrac{9}{2}$

$4x + 2 = -3x + 9$
$x = 1$
$y = 2 \times 1 + 1$
$y = 3$
$S = \{(1, 3)\}$

2.3 System of two-variable first degree equations

1. Solve the following systems using the appropriate method.

a) $\begin{cases} 3x + 2y = -5 \\ 5x + 3y = -7 \end{cases}$

b) $\begin{cases} x = 3y - 8 \\ x = \frac{1}{2}y - 3 \end{cases}$

c) $\begin{cases} 3x + y = -4 \\ x = 2y - 13 \end{cases}$

d) $\begin{cases} y = -2x - 3 \\ 5x + y = -3 \end{cases}$

e) $\begin{cases} y = 4x + \frac{1}{2} \\ y = 2x + 1 \end{cases}$

f) $\begin{cases} 4x + 3y = -28 \\ 3x - 2y = 13 \end{cases}$

2. In each of the following situations,
1. identify the variables;
2. write a system of two-variable first degree equations;
3. determine the solution of the system.

a) In a real estate project, there are three times as many condominiums as single-family houses. There is a total of 240 homes. How many condominiums are there?

b) In a warehouse, there are 1250 boxes. Each small box occupies a volume of 7 dm³ and each large box occupies a volume of 45 dm³. The total volume occupied by the boxes is 42 950 dm³. How many boxes of each size are there?

c) Determine the area of a rectangle if its length is 5 m more than twice its width and the perimeter of the rectangle is equal to 37 m.

d) A car rental agency offers two options. The 1st one consists in paying a $30 fixed amount and a $0.08 amount per kilometre. The 2nd consists in paying a $20 fixed amount and a $0.10 amount per kilometre. Determine the number of kilometres that we must travel so that both options carry the same cost.

2.4 System of two-variable first degree inequalities

Consider the following system of inequalities.

$$\begin{cases} 3x + y \geqslant 5 & (1) \\ 2x - 3y < 7 & (2) \end{cases}$$

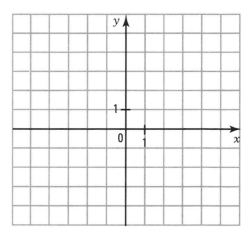

a) Represent the solution set of inequality (1) in the Cartesian plane on the right.

b) Represent the solution set of inequality (2) in the Cartesian plane on the right.

c) Color the region corresponding to the set of points that verify both inequalities simultaneously.

This set of points is the **solution set** *of the system.*

ACTIVITY 2 At the restaurant

Ava and Richard are at a restaurant with their children. They order dishes from the daily menu at $15 each and beverages at $3 each. Their budget allows them to spend a maximum of $90. They wish to order at least 4 dishes.

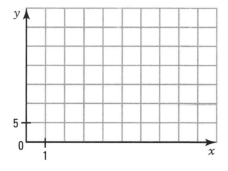

a) Identify the variables in this situation.

_____

b) Write a system of two-variable first degree inequalities that represents the constraints of this situation.

_____

c) Represent this system in the Cartesian plane on the right and color the solution set of the system.

d) Give all solutions couples of the system. _____

SYSTEM OF TWO-VARIABLE FIRST DEGREE INEQUALITIES

- A **system of two-variable first degree inequalities** is a system that can be written in the form:

$$\begin{cases} a_1x + b_1y \geqslant c_1 \\ a_2x + b_2y \geqslant c_2 \end{cases} \quad (\leqslant, >, <)$$

- The **solution set** of a of two-variable first degree inequalities is obtained by determining the intersection of the solution sets of each of the inequalities of the system.

Ex.: To solve the system $\begin{cases} 3x + 5y \leqslant 13 \\ x > 2y - 3 \end{cases}$, we proceed in the following way:

$\boxed{1}$ We represent the solution set of the inequality:	$\boxed{2}$ We represent the solution set of the inequality:	$\boxed{3}$ We deduce the solution set of the system.
$3x + 5y \leqslant 13$	$x > 2y - 3$	

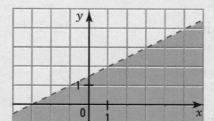 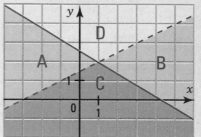 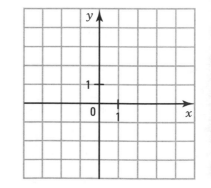

Any point belonging to region A verifies inequality (1) only.

Any point belonging to region B verifies inequality (2) only.

Any point belonging to region D verifies neither inequality.

Any point belonging to region C verifies both inequalities simultaneously and represents the solution set of the system.

1. Determine graphically the solution set of the following systems.

a) $\begin{cases} -4x + y \leqslant -8 \\ x + y \leqslant 2 \end{cases}$

b) $\begin{cases} y > -2x + 3 \\ x \leqslant 2 \end{cases}$

c) $\begin{cases} x \geqslant -2 \\ y < 2 \end{cases}$

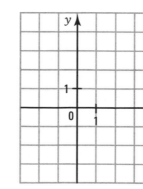

d) $\begin{cases} x + 3y \geqslant 0 \\ 3x + 2y \leqslant 7 \end{cases}$

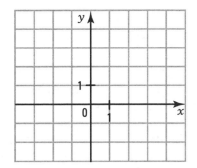

e) $\begin{cases} x + y \leqslant 3 \\ x > 2y \end{cases}$

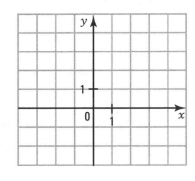

f) $\begin{cases} 5x + 6y \leqslant -1 \\ x + 5y > 4 \end{cases}$

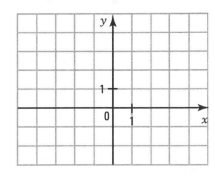

2. In each of the following situations
   1. identify the variables involved;
   2. write a system that translates the constraints of the situation;
   3. represent this system in the Cartesian plane and determine the solution set.

   a) A rectangle has a height equal to at least three times its width. Its perimeter is less than 12 cm.

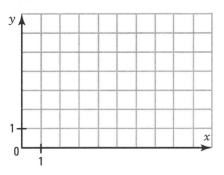

   _____

   b) In an aquarium, there are at least five more fishes as there are plants. The total number of species is at most equal to 30.

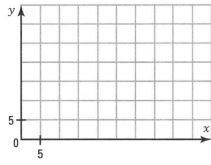

   _____

   c) In a 720 m² parking lot, each car occupies an area of 6 m² and each bus an area of 18 m². There are less than 50 vehicles.

   _____

2.5 Polygon of constraints

ACTIVITY 1 Constraints of a situation

To raise funds for learning disabilities, members of an association organize a concert in a theater. They want to allocate seats for donors and the rest of the seats are reserved for general admission. The theater contains a maximum of 500 seats. In order to satisfy the fundraising campaign requirements, there must be three times as many seats for general admission than seats reserved for donors. Organizers wish to have at least 50 seats reserved for donors and a maximum of 300 seats for general admission.

a) Identify the variables in this situation.

_____

_____

b) What are the two inequalities that translate the fact that, in a situation, the variables usually take positive or zero values? _____

c) Translate each of the constraints of this situation into an inequality. _____

_____

_____

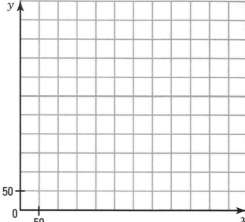

d) Represent each of the constraints in the Cartesian plane on the right and color the region that satisfies all the constraints. The region obtained is a closed polygon called **polygon of constraints**.

e) Determine the vertices of the polygon of constraints.

POLYGON OF CONSTRAINTS

- A **polygon of constraints** is a convex polygon (open or closed) representing the solution set of a system of inequalities translating, in a situation, the constraints on the variables.

- In a situation, since the variables usually take non negative values, the polygon of constraints is represented in the 1st quadrant.

  Ex.: The polygon of constraints corresponding to the solution set of the following system is represented on the right.
  $$\begin{cases} x \geq 0 \\ y \geq 0 \\ x + y \leq 7 \\ x \geq 2 \\ y \geq 2 \\ x \leq 2y \end{cases}$$

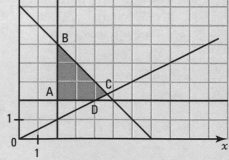

The vertices of this polygon of constraints are: A(2, 2), B(2, 5), C$\left(\frac{14}{3}, \frac{7}{3}\right)$ and D (4, 2).

© Guérin, éditeur ltée

ACTIVITY 2 Vertices of the polygon of constraints

Consider the following system of inequalities and polygon of constraints.

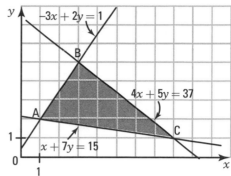

$$\begin{cases} x \geqslant 0 \\ y \geqslant 0 \\ -3x + 2y \leqslant 1 \\ x + 7y \geqslant 15 \\ 4x + 5y \leqslant 37 \end{cases}$$

a) What system of equations allows you to find vertex A of the polygon of constraints?

_____

b) Solve this system using an appropriate method. _____

c) Determine the polygon's other 2 vertices. _____

VERTICES OF THE POLYGON OF CONSTRAINTS

To determine the coordinates of the vertices of a polygon of constraints, we solve, for each vertex, the appropriate system of equations.

Ex.: See activity 2

---

1. Determine the polygon of constraints corresponding to the solution set of each of the following systems of inequalities and find the coordinates of the polygon's vertices.

a) $y \leqslant x + 2$
$x + y \leqslant 3$
$x - 6y \leqslant 3$

b) $3x + 2y \leqslant 6$
$x \geqslant -1$
$x - y \leqslant 0$

c) $y \leqslant -x + 4$
$x - 2y \leqslant 4$
$x \geqslant 0$
$y \leqslant 2$

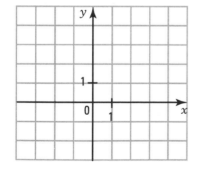

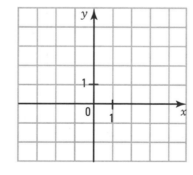

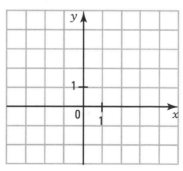

_____   _____   _____

2. Determine the polygon of constraints corresponding to the solution set of each of the following systems of inequalities and find the coordinates of the polygon's vertices.

a) $x \geqslant 0$
$y \geqslant 0$
$x + y \leqslant 5$
$x \geqslant 2y$
$y \leqslant 1$

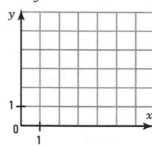

b) $x \geqslant 0$
$y \geqslant 0$
$x - y > 3$
$y \leqslant 2x$
$x + y < 4$

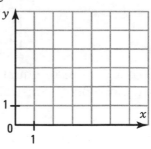

c) $x \geqslant 0$
$y \geqslant 0$
$x - y \leqslant 4$
$y < x + 2$
$y < 3$

_____   _____   _____

3. In each of the following cases, construct the polygon of constraints corresponding to the system of inequalities and determine, algebraically, the polygon of constraints' vertices.

a) $2x - 3y \geqslant -8$
$5x + y \leqslant 14$
$3x + 4y \geqslant 5$

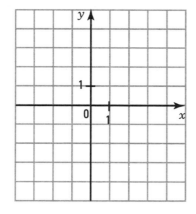

b) $y \geqslant x + 2$
$-x \leqslant 2y$
$x - 3y \geqslant -10$

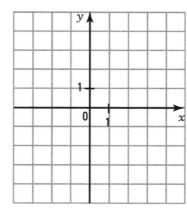

c) $y \leqslant -\frac{1}{2}x + 5$
$x \leqslant 4$
$4x + 5y \geqslant 1$
$y \leqslant 4x + 5$

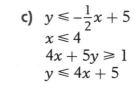
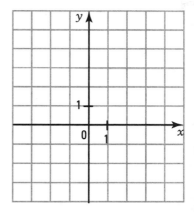

_____   _____   _____

4. For each of the following situations,
  1. identify the variables;
  2. determine the system of inequalities that translates the constraints of the situation;
  3. construct the polygon of constraints;
  4. determine the vertices of the polygon of constraints.

a) A farmer grows tomatoes and potatoes on an area of at most 40 hectares. The area allotted to tomatoes is at most equal to 20 hectares. The area allotted to potatoes is at most equal to twice the area allotted to tomatoes.

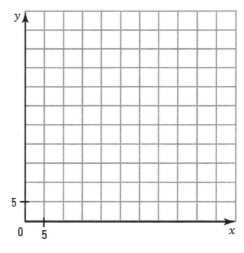

b) A sports centre wishes to hire students for its summer camp. To meet the needs of its members, the centre must hire at most 20 students, a minimum of 6 girls, at most as many boys as girls and a maximum of 8 boys.

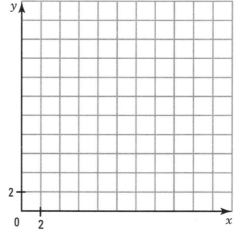

2.6 Optimization of a situation

a) At a theater, floor seats cost $12 and balcony seats cost $16. Let x represent the number of floor seats sold and y the number of balcony seats sold.

Express the proceeds R of the theater as a function of the variables x and y. _____

b) A company produces tables and chairs. The production costs are $150 per table and $50 per chair. Let x and y represent respectively the number of tables and the number of chairs produced.

Express the production cost C as a function of the variables x and y. _____

OPTIMIZATION OF A FUNCTION

Optimizing a function of two variables x and y consists in finding the couple (x, y) which, depending on context, **maximizes** or **minimizes** the function.

In general, we seek the couple (x, y) which maximizes a revenue function or minimizes a cost function.

Activity 2 Maximization of a revenue function

At the end of the season, the manager of a nursery garden wants to clear his inventory which contains 1500 flower boxes and 2000 shrubs.

Let x and y represent respectively the number of flower boxes and the number of shrubs sold.

The constraints associated with the sale of the flower boxes and shrubs are represented by the polygon of constraints on the right. The revenue R (in $) generated by selling x flower boxes and y shrubs is given by $R = 3x + 8y$.

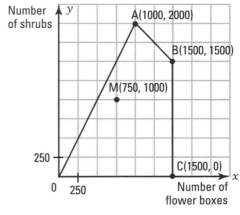

a) The interior point M(750, 1000) of the polygon satisfies the constraints and corresponds to the sale of 750 flower boxes and 1000 shrubs. What is the revenue R generated by this sale?

_____

b) Evaluate, for each vertex of the polygon of constraints, the revenue associated with the sale.

Vertices	Revenue: $R = 3x + 8y$
0 (0, 0)	
A (1000, 2000)	
B (1500, 1500)	
C (1500, 0)	

c) 1. Among the vertices 0, A, B and C, which one corresponds to the maximal revenue? _____

   What is this maximal revenue? _____

2. Among the vertices 0, A, B and C, which one corresponds to the minimal revenue? _____

   What is this minimal revenue? _____

d) 1. Choose a random point in the interior of the polygon of constraints. Evaluate the revenue associated with the chosen point and verify that the revenue obtained is contained between the minimal revenue and the maximal revenue computed in c).

   _____

2. What is the couple (x, y) verifying the constraints and which maximizes the revenue function? _____

   Interpret your result. _____

   _____

ACTIVITY 3 Minimization of a cost function

A company produces square tables and round tables. Let x and y represent respectively the number of square tables and the number of round tables. The constraints associated with the production of the tables are represented by the polygon of constraints on the right.

The cost C (in $) associated with the production of x square tables and y round tables is given by $C = 120x + 140y$.

a) Evaluate, for each vertex of the polygon of constraints, the cost associated to the production.

b) 1. Among the vertices A, B, C and D, which one corresponds to the minimal cost? ___ What is this minimal cost? _____

2. Among the vertices A, B, C and D, which one corresponds to the maximal cost? _____

   What is this maximal cost? _____

c) 1. Choose a random point in the interior of the polygon of constraints and verify that the cost obtained is contained between the minimal cost and the maximal cost established in b).

Vertices	Cost: $C = 120x + 140y$
A (100, 100)	
B (150, 250)	
C (250, 150)	
D (150, 50)	

_____

2. What is the couple (x, y), verifying the constraints, which minimizes the cost function?

_____

Interpret your result. _____

_____

At lunchtime, a cafeteria sells sandwiches and beverages. Let x and y represent respectively the number of sandwiches sold and the number of beverages sold.

The constraints associated with the sale of these items are represented by the polygon of constraints on the right.

The revenue R (in $) generated by selling x sandwiches and y beverages is given by $R = 2x + y$.

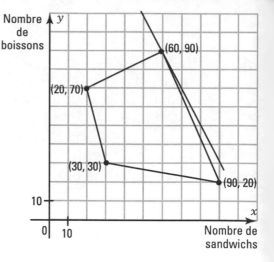

a) On Monday, the cafeteria's revenue was $150.

1. Name three possible couples (x, y) which result in this $150 revenue and which satisfy the constraints. _____

_____

_____

2. The three couples obtained verify the equation of the line m: $2x + y = 150$. Draw line m and verify that it passes through the three points obtained in 1.

b) On Tuesday, the cafeteria's revenue was $180.

The couples which result in a revenue of $180 verify the equation of the line t: $2x + y = 180$.

1. Draw line t.

2. Give a point on line t which satisfies the constraints and one point which does not satisfy the constraints. _____

3. Explain why lines m and t are parallel. _____

c) When we vary the revenue R in the equation $2x + y = R$, the line $2x + y = R$ moves in the same direction.

The line $2x + y = R$ is called scanning line.

The lines m: $2x + y = 150$ and t: $2x + y = 180$ are thus two positions for the scanning line.

On Wednesday, the cafeteria's revenue was $200. Give the equation of the line w corresponding to Wednesday's revenue and draw the scanning line corresponding to Wednesday.

_____

d) 1. Draw the line l: $2x + y = 220$ corresponding to a position of the scanning line. Can we find, on this line l, a point (x, y) satisfying the constraints? Justify your answer.

_____

2. Then, is a revenue of $220 possible? _____

e) 1. What is the point of the polygon of constraints through which the scanning line giving the maximal revenue must pass? _____

2. What is the maximal revenue? _____

3. Draw in red the scanning line passing through the point found and then give the equation of the line passing through the point found.

_____

OPTIMIZATION OF A FUNCTION UNDER CONSTRAINTS

- Given a polygon of constraints and the function to be optimized $F = ax + by + c$, optimizing the function F consists in determining the points, if they exist, of the polygon of constraints whose coordinates maximize or minimize, depending on context, the function F.

- If the function to be optimized possesses a maximal or minimal value, then this value is attained at, at least, one of the vertices of the polygon of constraints.

- In practice, it is sufficient to evaluate the function to be optimized at each of the vertices of the polygon of constraints to establish the maximal (or minimal) value of the function to be optimized and thus deduce the couple which maximizes (or minimizes) the function.

1. The board of directors of a music competition hires paid staff and volunteers for its fundraising campaign. The constraints associated with the hiring process are represented by the polygon of constraints below.

The function F giving the costs (in \$) associated with the hiring process is defined by $F = 120p + 50v$ where p and v represent respectively the number of paid staff and the number of volunteers.

a) Evaluate the function to be optimized for each vertex of the polygon of constraints.

Vertex	F = 120p + 50v

b) 1. Taking the constraints into account, what is the minimal cost associated with the hiring process for this fundraising campaign? _____

2. How many paid staffs and how many volunteers must the board hire in order to minimize costs? _____

2. The vertices of a polygon of constraints are represented on the graph on the right.

The function to be optimized is defined by $R = 2x + 4y - 12$.

a) What is the couple which maximizes this function? _____

b) Verify your result using the scanning line.

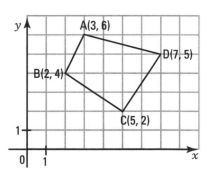

2.6 Optimization of a situation   **51**

3. To raise money for their graduation party, secondary 5 students organize a car wash for cars and minivans.
The students charge $5 per car and $10 per minivan.
This event is organized with the following constraints.
- They can wash at most 100 vehicles.
- They must wash at least 50 vehicles in order to raise enough money.
- They expect to wash at least four times as many cars as minivans.

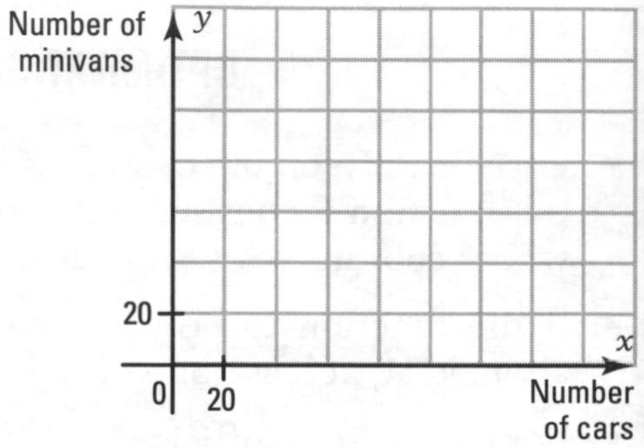

a) Identify the variables in this situation.

_____

b) Translate the constraints into a system of inequalities.

c) Draw the polygon of constraints.

d) Establish the rule of the function to be optimized.

_____

Vertices	R = 5x + 10y

e) Evaluate the function to be optimized at each vertex of the polygon of constraints.

f) How many cars and minivans must the students wash in order to maximize the profit? _____

g) Verify your result by drawing the scanning line and by making it vary.

_____

_____

4. A cell phone company makes Nat model phones and Val model phones.

The company expects a revenue of $40 per Nat phone and $60 per Val phone.

To satisfy production constraints, the company must produce monthly,

– at most 400 cell phones;
– at least 150 Nat phones;
– at most 200 Val phones.

a) Identify the variables in this situation.

_____

b) Translate the constraints into a system of inequalities.

c) Draw the polygon of constraints.

d) Establish the rule of the function to be optimized.

_____

Vertices	R = 40x + 60y

e) Evaluate the function to be optimized at each vertex of the polygon of constraints.

f) How many cell phones of each model must the company make in order to maximize its revenue?

_____

g) After one week of production, the company decides to make at least 100 more Nat phones than Val phones.

Translate this additional constraint into an inequality. _____

h) Evaluate the function to be optimized at each vertex of the new polygon of constraints then determine the number of cell phones of each model the company must make in order to maximize its revenue.

Vertices	R = 40x + 60y

_____

i) Did the maximal revenue increase or decrease as a result of this additional constraint?

_____

SOLVING AN OPTIMIZATION PROBLEM

The following steps allow us to solve an optimization problem.
1. Identify the variables.
2. Translate the constraints of the situation into a system of inequalities.
3. Draw the polygon of constraints.
4. Determine the coordinates of the vertices of the polygon of constraints.
5. Establish the rule of the function to be optimized.
6. Evaluate the function to be optimized at each vertex of the polygon of constraints.
7. Deduce the vertex whose coordinates maximize (or minimize) the function to be optimized.

5. A landscape architect was hired by a cultural centre to design the exterior of the centre. The architect must observe the following constraints.

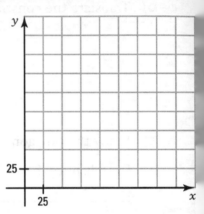

- The total area to be landscaped is at most 150 m².
- She must allot, at most, 75 m² for a flower bed and at most 100 m² for shrubs.
- She must allot, at most, an area twice as large for flowers as for shrubs.

Knowing that she charges $200 per m² for flowers and $125 per m² for shrubs, what area should she allot for each type of plant in order to maximize her revenue?

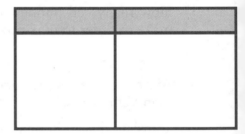

The function $R = 1.25x + 2.50y$ gives the revenue of a baker who sells x regular croissants and y chocolate croissants.

The polygon of constraints is represented on the right.

a) Evaluate the revenue at each vertex of the polygon of constraints.

A: _____ B: _____ C: _____ D: _____ E: _____

b) Verify that the revenue is maximal at the two consecutive vertices B and C of the polygon of constraints.

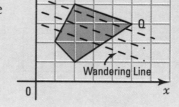

Number of chocolate croissants

B(4, 8)

C(10, 5)

D(10, 3)

A(2, 2)

E(9, 2)

Number of regular croissants

c) Draw a few positions for the scanning line and verify that the extreme position of the wandering line that verifies the constraints is the line BC.

d) What is the equation of line BC? _____

e) Is it true that any point on edge BC of the polygon of constraints whose coordinates are integers corresponds to a sale that maximizes the revenue? _____

f) Give the 4 solution couples that maximize the revenue. _____

NON UNIQUE OPTIMAL SOLUTION

If a function to be optimized attains its maximal (or minimal) value at two consecutive vertices P and Q of a polygon of constraints, then this function attains this same maximal (or minimal) value at each point of the edge PQ of the polygon.

This situation occurs when the scanning line is parallel to one of the edges of the polygon of constraints.

Ex.: See activity 3.

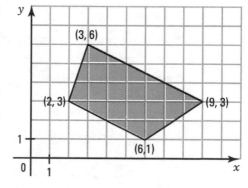

P

Q

Wandering Line

6. The polygon of constraints of an optimization problem is represented on the graph on the right.

The rule of the function to be optimized is: $R = 3x + 6y$ where x and y are integers.

How many couples maximize function R? _____

Name them: _____

(3, 6)

(2, 3)

(9, 3)

(6, 1)

Evaluation 2

1. Represent graphically the solution set of the following inequalities.

   a) $2x + 5y \geqslant 10$

   b) $y \geqslant 2x - 3$

   c) $x + y < 3$

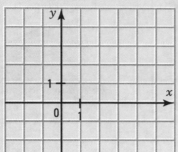 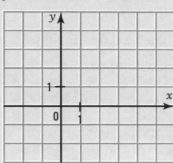 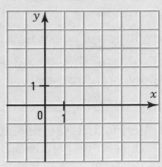

2. A bakery sells each day fresh bread and baguettes.

   The price of a loaf of bread is \$3 and that of a baguette is \$1.50. In a day, the amount sold is at most equal to \$1200.

   Represent this situation in the Cartesian plane.

   _____

   _____

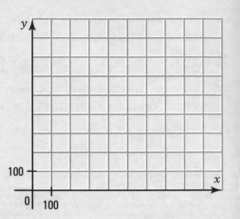

3. Represent graphically the solution set of the following systems of inequalities.

   a) $\begin{cases} 3x + 2y \leqslant 7 \\ x - 3y > -5 \end{cases}$

   b) $\begin{cases} y > -2x + 7 \\ x - y < 2 \end{cases}$

   c) $\begin{cases} x \geqslant -1 \\ x > 3y \end{cases}$

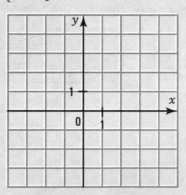 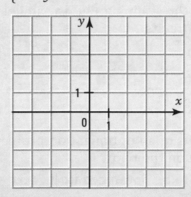 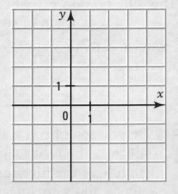

4. At a music camp, the main instruments taught are piano and violin. The camp managers expect that there will be at least twice as many campers playing piano as campers playing the violin. In addition, they expect a maximum of 300 campers playing one of these two instruments.

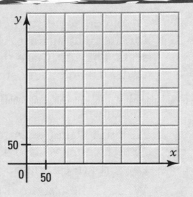

   a) Represent this situation in the Cartesian plane.

   _____

   _____

   _____

   _____

   b) Give a solution couple of the system which satisfies these constraints.

   _____

5. Represent, for each of the following systems of inequalities, the polygon of constraints corresponding to the solution set of the system and then determine the polygon's vertices.

   a) $-4x + 5y \leqslant 7$

   $x \leqslant 3y$
   $x \leqslant 2$

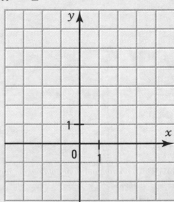

   _____

   b) $2x + 3y \geqslant 6$

   $x \leqslant y + 2$
   $y \leqslant 3$

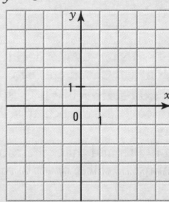

   _____

   c) $y \leqslant \dfrac{5}{2}x + 4$

   $x + y \leqslant 4$
   $x \leqslant 2y$

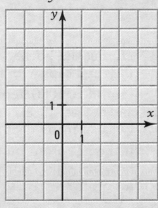

   _____

6. A concert is performed at the Athletes Park to raise funds for the fight against AIDS. Organizers have installed 8000 seats. They estimate that there will be at least 3000 youths under 18 and at most 4000 adults.

They want to organize this concert for at least 4000 spectators.

A youth ticket sells for $15 and an adult ticket sells for $25. Expenses associated with the organization of this concert are estimated at $20 000.

What is the maximal net revenue that the organizers can obtain?

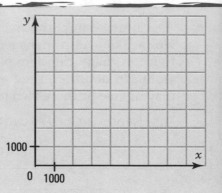

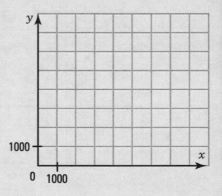

7. During the hockey playoffs, a shop owner decides to sell flags and caps with the Montreal Canadiens logo.

He orders 6000 items and expects to sell at least 3000 flags and at least 1000 caps. Moreover, he expects to sell at least twice as many flags as caps.

If the net profit on a flag is $15 and that on a cap is $12, how many flags and caps must he sell in order to maximize his profit?

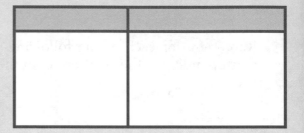

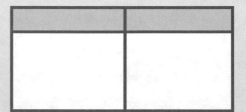

8. The graduation committee at a school organizes a cookie and muffin sale to raise money for the graduation party. The two coordinators of the committee, Laura and Russ, offer the following propositions to their members.

Laura's proposition	Russ' proposition
• Price of a cookie: $2 • Price of muffin: $3 **Polygon of constraints** 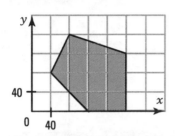	• Price of a cookie: $2.50 • Price of a muffin: $2.50 **Constraints** The committee must sell – a maximum of 320 items; – at least 120 cookies; – at most 160 muffins; – at most 4 times as many cookies as muffins.

Let x represent the number of cookies and y the number of muffins.

Which proposition should the committee accept in order to maximize profits?

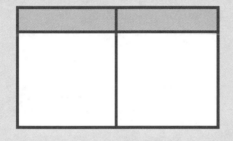

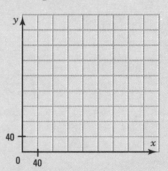

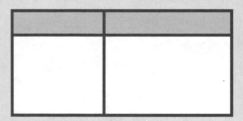

Chapter 3

Real functions

CHALLENGE 3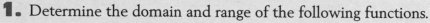

1. Determine the domain and range of the following functions.

    a) $f(x) = -2|x - 3| + 1$ **b)** $f(x) = -\sqrt{-x + 1} + 1$ **c)** $f(x) = \frac{2}{3(x - 1)} - 1$

    _____   _____   _____

    _____   _____   _____

2. Consider the functions $f(x) = 2x - 1$ and $g(x) = 3x^2 - 2x + 1$. Find the rule of

    a) $g \circ f$ **b)** $f \circ g$

3. Determine the zeros of the following functions.

    a) $f(x) = -2|x - 1| + 6$ **b)** $f(x) = -2\sqrt{x - 3} + 6$ **c)** $f(x) = \frac{-3}{2(x + 1)} + 1$

4. What are the equations of the asymptotes of the function $f(x) = \frac{2}{5(x - 1)} - 4$?

5. Study the sign of the following functions.

    a) $f(x) = 4\left|-\frac{1}{2}(x - 1)\right| - 4$

    b) $f(x) = -2\sqrt{x + 3} + 4$

    c) $f(x) = \frac{4}{x - 3} + 2$

6. Describe the variation of the following functions.

    a) $f(x) = -\frac{2}{3}|x - 2| + 4$

    b) $f(x) = -\frac{1}{2}\sqrt{-2(x - 1)} + 1$

    c) $f(x) = \frac{2}{x - 1} + 1$

7. Find the rule of

    a) an absolute value function whose graph has a vertex at V(−2, 6) and passes through the point A(1, −3).

    b) a rational function passing through the point A(3, 4) with asymptotes defined by the lines $x = 1$ and $y = 2$.

    c) a square root function whose graph has a vertex at V(−4, −2) and passes through the point A(5, 4).

3.1 Function

a) Consider the mapping diagram of the relation R represented on the right.

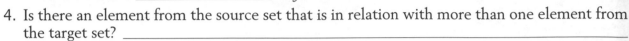

1. What is the source set? _____
2. What is the target set? _____
3. Complete: An element x from set A is in relation with an element y from set B if x is _____ of y.
4. Is there an element from the source set that is in relation with more than one element from the target set? _____
5. Is this relation a function? Justify your answer.

   _____

b) Consider the Cartesian graph of the relation S represented on the right. The point $(1, 3)$ means that the element 1 from the source set is in relation with the element 3 from the target set.

1. What is the image of 4? _____
2. What is the antecedent of 2? _____
3. Is there an element from the source set that is in relation with more than one element from the target set? _____
4. Is this relation a function? Justify your answer.

   _____

   _____

DEFINITION OF A FUNCTION

- A relation given by a source set A to a target set B is a function if each element from A is associated with at most one element from B.

- **Mapping diagram**

   Given the mapping diagram of a relation, this relation is a function if, from each element of the source set, at most one arrow is drawn.

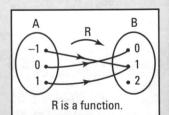

R is a function.

- **Cartesian graph**

   Given the Cartesian graph of a relation, this relation is a function if any vertical line intersects the graph of this relation in at most one point.

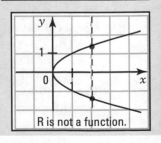

R is not a function.

- Set of ordered pairs

  Given a relation's set of ordered pairs, this relation is a function if the first coordinate of each pair verifying the relation appears only once.

1. In each of the following cases, indicate if the relation is a function.

a)
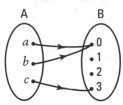

b)
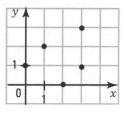

c) $G = \{(0, 0), (1, -1), (1, 1)\}$

d)
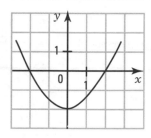

e)
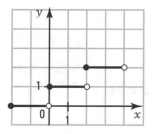

f)
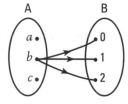

g) $G = \{(4, 3), (5, 3), (6, 3)\}$

h)
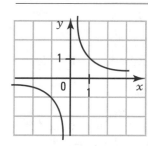

i)
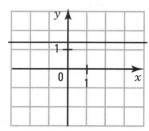

j)
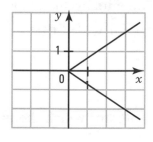

k)
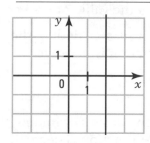

l)
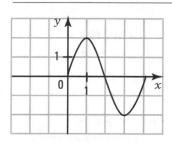

Activity 2 Properties of functions

Consider the function *f* represented on the right.

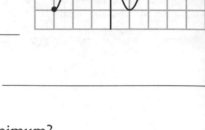

a) What is the domain of *f*? _____

b) What is the range of *f*? _____

c) What are the zeros of *f*? _____

d) What is the initial value of *f*? _____

e) Over what interval is the function *f*

    1. positive? _____ 2. negative? _____

f) Over what interval is the function *f*

    1. increasing? _____ 2. decreasing? _____

g) What is, for function *f*, its

    1. absolute maximum? _____ 2. absolute minimum? _____

PROPERTIES OF FUNCTIONS

Consider the function *f* represented on the right.

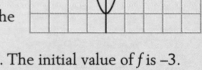

- The **domain** of a function *f* is the subset of the elements of the source set which have an image in *f*.

  dom $f = [-2, 4]$

- The **range** of a function *f* is the subset of the elements of the target set which are images by *f*.

  ran $f = [-3, 4]$

- The **zeros** of the function *f* are the values of *x* for which the function is equal to zero. The zeros of *f* are: -1, 1 and 3.

- The **initial value** of the function *f* is the value of *y* when $x = 0$. The initial value of *f* is -3.

- Studying the **sign** of a function consists of finding the values of *x* for which the function is positive or those for which the function is negative.

  $f(x) \geqslant 0$ if $x \in [-2, -1] \cup [1, 3]$.
  $f(x) \leqslant 0$ if $x \in [-1, 1] \cup [3, 4]$.

- Studying the **variation** of a function consists of finding the values of *x* for which the function is increasing or those for which the function is decreasing..

  f is increasing if $x \in [0, 2]$.
  f is decreasing if $x \in [-2, 0] \cup [2, 4]$.

- The **absolute maximum** (or **minimum**) of a function is the highest image (or the lowest image) when it exists.

  max $f = 4$, min $f = -3$

2. Consider the function f represented on the right. Determine

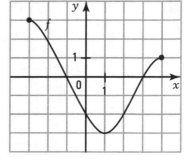

   a) 1. dom $f =$ _____ 2. ran $f =$ _____

   b) 1. the zeros of f: _____

        2. the initial value: _____

   c) the values of x for which the function f is

        1. positive: _____ 2. negative: _____

   d) the values of x for which the function f is

        1. increasing: _____   2. decreasing: _____

   e) 1. the maximum of f: _____   2. the minimum of f: _____

3. Draw the graph of a function satisfying the following conditions.

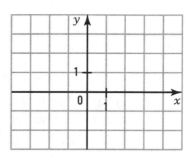

   1. dom $f = [-1, 4]$.

   2. ran $f = [-2, 3]$.

   3. The zeros of f are: 1 and 3.

   4. The initial value is -1.

   5. The function is negative when $x \in [-1, 1] \cup [3, 4]$.

   6. The function is increasing when $x \in [-1, 2]$ and decreasing when $x \in [2, 4]$.

   7. max $f = 3$ and min $f = -2$.

4. Study the following functions by completing the table below.

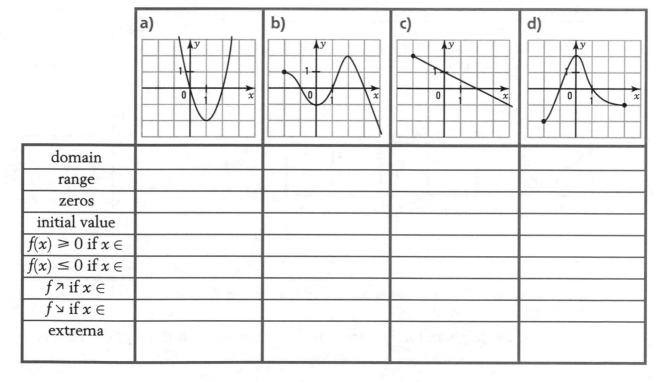

	a)	b)	c)	d)
domain				
range				
zeros				
initial value				
$f(x) \geqslant 0$ if $x \in$				
$f(x) \leqslant 0$ if $x \in$				
$f \nearrow$ if $x \in$				
$f \searrow$ if $x \in$				
extrema				

5. Determine the domain and range of the following functions.

a)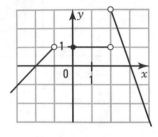

_____

_____

b)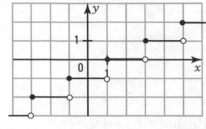

_____

_____

c)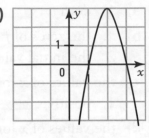

_____

_____

Activity 3 Inverse of a function

Let *s* represent the side of a square and A represent its area.

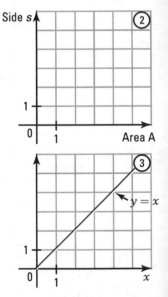

a) 1. What is the rule of the function *f* that associates, to the square's side *s*, its area? _____

2. Complete the table of values below and represent the function *f* in the Cartesian plane ①.

Side *s*	0	0.5	1	1.5	2
Area A					

b) 1. What is the rule of the inverse f^{-1} that associates, to the square's area A, its side length *s*?

_____

2. Complete the table of values below and represent the function f^{-1} in the Cartesian plane ②.

Area A	0	0.25	1	2.25	4
Side *s*					

3. Explain why the inverse f^{-1} is a function.

_____

_____

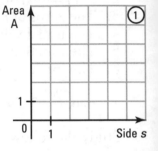

c) 1. Reproduce the two graphs in the same Cartesian plane ③ where the axes are not labeled.

2. Verify that the graphs of *f* and f^{-1} are symmetrical about the bisector of the 1st quadrant.

ACTIVITY 4 Functions whose inverse is not a function

a) Consider the sets A and B on the right, and the function f of A toward B with the rule $f(x) = x^2$.

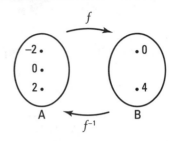

1. Use a mapping diagram to represent function f.
2. Deduce the mapping diagram of the inverse f^{-1}.
3. Explain why f^{-1} is not a function.

_____

_____

b) Consider the table of values on the right of a function f.

x	–2	–1	0	1	2
f(x)	2	1	0	1	2

x					
f⁻¹(x)					

1. Deduce a table of values for f^{-1}.
2. Explain why f^{-1} is not a function.

_____

c) The function f on the right has the rule $f(x) = x^2$.

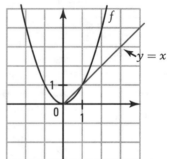

1. Deduce, by symmetry about the bisector of the 1st quadrant, the graph of the inverse f^{-1}.

2. Explain why the inverse f^{-1} is not a function.

_____

3. True or false?

The inverse of f is not a function when a horizontal line can be drawn to intersect the graph of f at more than one point. _____

INVERSE OF A FUNCTION

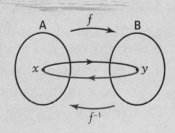

- If f is the function of a source set A toward a target set B, the **inverse** of f, written f^{-1}, has the source set B and the target set A.

- The inverse of a function is not necessarily a function.

Ex.: $f: A \to B$
$$x \mapsto y = 2x$$

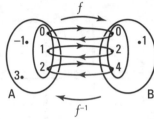

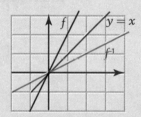

f^{-1} is a function.
$$\mathrm{dom}f = \mathrm{ran}f^{-1} = \{0, 1, 2\}$$
$$\mathrm{ran}f = \mathrm{dom}f^{-1} = \{0, 2, 4\}$$

Ex.: $f: A \to B$
$$x \mapsto y = x^2$$

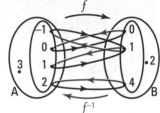

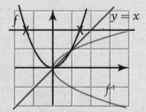

f^{-1} is not a function.
$$\mathrm{dom}f = \mathrm{ran}f^{-1} = \{-1, 0, 1, 2\}$$
$$\mathrm{ran}f = \mathrm{dom}f^{-1} = \{0, 1, 4\}$$

- For any function f, we have: $\boxed{\mathrm{dom}f = \mathrm{ran}f^{-1}}$ and $\boxed{\mathrm{ran}f = \mathrm{dom}f^{-1}}$

- The Cartesian graphs of a function and its inverse are **symmetrical about the line** with the equation $y = x$.

f^{-1} is a function.

f^{-1} is not a function.

- The inverse of a function f is not a function when a **horizontal line** can be drawn to intersect the graph of f at more than one point.

6. Consider the mapping diagram of a function f.

  a) Deduce the mapping diagram of f^{-1}.

  b) Explain why f^{-1} is a function.

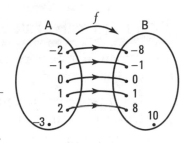

  _____

  c) Determine

  1. dom$f$. _____ 2. ran f. _____
  3. domf^{-1}. _____ 4. ran f^{-1}. _____

  d) Verify that

  1. dom$f$ = ranf^{-1}. 2. ran$f$ = domf^{-1}.

7. Indicate which of the following functions have an inverse that is also a function.

  a)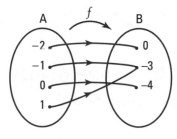

  b)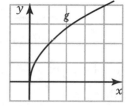

  _____

  c) $h = \{(-2, -4), (-1, -2), (0, 0), (1, 2), (2, 4)\}$ **d)**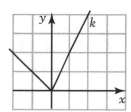

  _____

8. For each of the following functions,

  1. deduce the graph of the inverse.
  2. indicate if the inverse is a function.

  a)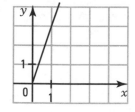

  _____

  b)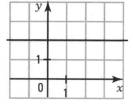

  _____

  c)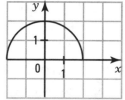

  _____

  d)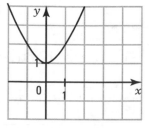

  _____

  e)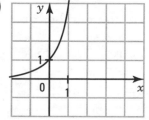

  _____

  f)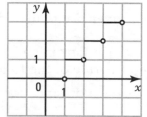

  _____

ACTIVITY 5 Rule of the inverse

A salesman in a store receives a weekly base salary of $250 and a sales commission of $10 per item sold for the week.

a) Let a represent the number of items sold for the week, and s represent the total weekly salary. Determine the rule of

    1. the function f which gives the total salary s as a function of the number of items sold a. _____

    2. the function f^{-1} which associates, to a given salary s, the number of items sold a. _____

b) Complete the table of values on the right for the functions f and f^{-1}.

$f\Big($

a	0	5	10	15	20
s					

$\Big)f^{-1}$

RULE OF THE INVERSE

Given the function f with the rule: $y = 2x + 6$. To determine the rule of the inverse f^{-1},

1. we isolate x in the rule of f.

$$y = 2x + 6$$
$$2x = y - 6$$
$$x = \tfrac{1}{2}y - 3$$

2. we switch the letters x and y.

$$y = \tfrac{1}{2}x - 3$$

f^{-1} therefore has the rule: $y = \tfrac{1}{2}x - 3$.

> We interchange the letters x and y to respect the convention of function notation which assigns x as elements of the source set and y as elements of the target set.

9. For each of the following rules of functions, find the rule of its inverse.

a) $y = 5x$

b) $y = 3x - 6$

c) $y = -2x + 10$

d) $y = 0.1x + 100$

e) $y = \tfrac{2}{3}x - 6$

f) $y = -\tfrac{3}{4}x + 12$

10. A capital of $1000 is invested on January 1st, 2009 at an annual interest rate of 10%. Find the rule which associates

a) a given number of elapsed years t since the beginning, to the accumulated capital C. _____

b) a given accumulated capital C, to the number of elapsed years t. _____

11. A car's gas tank initially contains 60 litres of gas. This car consumes on average 12 litres/100 km. Find the rule of the function which associates,

a) a given distance traveled d (in km) to the quantity q of gas remaining in the tank. _____

b) a given quantity q of gas remaining in the tank, to the distance traveled d (in km). _____

ACTIVITY 6 Composition of functions

Consider the function f defined by $f(x) = x + 5$ and the function g defined by the rule $g(x) = 2x$.

a) Determine
   1. $f(1)$ _____
   2. $g(f(1))$ _____

b) The composition of f by g, written $g \circ f$ is defined by $g \circ f(x) = g(f(x))$.
   1. Calculate $g \circ f(1)$ _____
   2. Determine the rule of $g \circ f$. _____

c) Determine
   1. $g(1)$ _____
   2. $f(g(1))$ _____

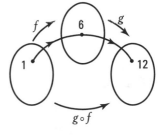

d) The composition of g by f, written $f \circ g$, is defined by $f \circ g(x) = f(g(x))$.
   1. Calculate $f \circ g(1)$ _____
   2. Determine the rule of $f \circ g$. _____

e) Compare the rules of $g \circ f$ and $f \circ g$.
_____

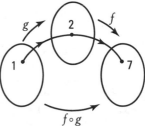

COMPOSITION OF FUNCTIONS

- Given two functions f and g,
  - the composition of f by g, written $g \circ f$, is defined by the rule:

$$g \circ f(x) = g(f(x))$$

  - the composition of g by f, written $f \circ g$, is defined by the rule:

$$f \circ g(x) = f(g(x))$$

Ex.: Given $f(x) = x + 3$ and $g(x) = x^2$, we have:

$g \circ f(1) = g(f(1)) = g(4) = 16$; $f \circ g(1) = f(g(1)) = f(1) = 4$
$g \circ f(x) = g(x + 3) = (x + 3)^2$; $f \circ g(x) = f(x^2) = x^2 + 3$

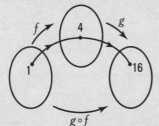

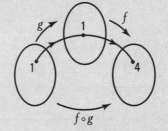

Note that, in general, $g \circ f(x) \neq f \circ g(x)$.

---

12. Consider the functions $f(x) = 3x - 5$ and $g(x) = -2x + 8$. Determine

   a) $g \circ f(2) =$ _____
   b) $f \circ g(-1) =$ _____
   c) $f \circ g(4) =$ _____

   d) $g \circ f(0) =$ _____
   e) $g \circ g(7) =$ _____
   f) $f \circ g(-5) =$ _____

13. Consider the functions $f(x) = -2x + 5$ and $g(x) = 4x - 3$.
Determine the rules of the following functions.

a) $f \circ g(x) =$ _____

b) $g \circ f(x) =$ _____

c) $f \circ f(x) =$ _____

d) $g \circ g(x) =$ _____

14. Consider the functions $f(x) = 2x + 3$ and $g(x) = 3x - 2$.

a) Determine the rule of

1. $g \circ f$. _____   2. $f \circ g$. _____

b) Verify that $g \circ f(x) \neq f \circ g(x)$.

15. Consider $f(x) = x + 5$ and $g(x) = x - 2$. Verify that, $g \circ f(x) = f \circ g(x)$.

_____

16. Consider the function $f(x) = 2x + 8$.

a) Determine the rule of the inverse f^{-1}. _____

b) 1. Determine the rule of the composite $f^{-1} \circ f$.

_____

2. Determine the rule of the composite $f \circ f^{-1}$.

_____

3. Verify that $f^{-1} \circ f(x) = f \circ f^{-1}(x) = x$.

c) Repeat this exercise with the function $f(x) = -5x + 10$.

_____

17. Consider the functions $f(x) = x + 5$ and $f(x) = 3x + 4$.

a) Determine the rule of the functions f^{-1} and g^{-1}.

_____

b) Determine

1. $f \circ f^{-1}(x) =$ _____

2. $g \circ g^{-1}(x) =$ _____

3. $f \circ g(x) =$ _____

4. $g \circ f(x) =$ _____

c) Determine

1. $(f \circ g)^{-1}(x) =$ _____   2. $(g \circ f)^{-1}(x) =$ _____

3. $g^{-1} \circ f^{-1}(x) =$ _____   4. $f^{-1} \circ g^{-1}(x) =$ _____

d) What can you deduce? _____

18. Consider the functions $f(x) = x^2 + 4x - 5$ and $g(x) = 2x - 1$.

a) Determine the rule of the composite $f \circ g$.

_____

b) Determine $f \circ g(2)$ in two different ways:
1. by finding $f(g(2)) = $ _____
2. by using the rule found in a). _____

19. In Quebec, every purchase is taxable. The goods and services tax (GST) is 5 %.
The Quebec sales tax (QST) is 7.5 %.
Let f be the function which associates a given purchase amount x to the amount y including GST.
Let g be the function which associates a given purchase amount x to the amount y including QST.

a) Determine the rule of the function
1. f: _____ 2. g: _____

b) 1. Determine the rule of the function $g \circ f$. _____
2. Determine the rule of the function $f \circ g$. _____

c) Compare the rules of the functions $g \circ f$ and $f \circ g$. What can you conclude?

_____

_____

d) 1. What is the final price of a product with a $39.80 price tag? _____
2. What is the initial price tag of a product if the final cost paid is $56.44? _____

20. The weekly salary of a sporting goods store salesman includes a base salary of $300 per week and a $40 bonus for every item sold.

During the holidays, the owner of the store decides to give each employee a 4% bonus on their weekly salary.

Let f be the function which gives the regular weekly salary y as a function of the number of items sold x.

Let g be the function which gives the bonus holiday weekly salary y as a function of the regular weekly salary x.

a) Determine the rule of the function
1. f: _____ 2. g: _____ 3. $g \circ f$: _____

b) What will an employee's salary be, during the holidays, if he sells 4 items during the week? _____

c) How many items did an employee sell if he receives a weekly salary of $561.60 during the holidays? _____

ACTIVITY 7 Operations between functions

Consider the functions $f(x) = x^2 - 9$ and $g(x) = x + 3$. Determine

a) $f(x) + g(x) =$ _____

b) $f(x) - g(x) =$ _____

c) $f(x) \times g(x) =$ _____

d) $\dfrac{f(x)}{g(x)} =$ _____

OPERATIONS BETWEEN FUNCTIONS

Given two real functions f and g, we have:

$(f + g)(x) = f(x) + g(x)$ $(f - g)(x) = f(x) - g(x)$

$(f \cdot g)(x) = f(x) \times g(x)$ $\dfrac{f}{g}(x) = \dfrac{f(x)}{g(x)}$

Ex.: Given $f(x) = x^2 + 2x - 15$ and $g(x) = 2x - 6$, we have:

$(f + g)(x) = f(x) + g(x) = (x^2 + 2x - 15) + (2x - 6) = x^2 + 4x - 21.$

$(f - g)(x) = f(x) - g(x) = (x^2 + 2x - 15) - (2x - 6) = x^2 - 9.$

$(f \cdot g)(x) = f(x) \times g(x) = (x^2 + 2x - 15)(2x - 6) = 2x^3 - 2x^2 - 42x + 90.$

$\dfrac{f}{g}(x) = \dfrac{f(x)}{g(x)} = \dfrac{x^2 + 2x - 15}{2x - 6} = \dfrac{(x-3)(x+5)}{2(x-3)} = \dfrac{x+5}{2}.$

21. Consider the four functions f, g, h, and i. Let $f(x) = x^2 + x - 6$, $g(x) = 2x - 4$, $h(x) = x^2 - 9$ and $i(x) = 3x^2 - 12$.

a) $(f + g + h)(x) =$ _____

b) $(f - g + h)(x) =$ _____

c) $(f \cdot g)(x) =$ _____

d) $(g \cdot h)(x) =$ _____

e) $(f - h - i)(x) =$ _____

f) $\left(\dfrac{f}{g}\right)(x) =$ _____

g) $\left(\dfrac{f \cdot g}{i}\right)(x) =$ _____

h) $\left(\dfrac{g \cdot h}{f}\right)(x) =$ _____

22. The condominium association of a building establishes the following fees to be charged to each of its condo owners.

– Monthly condo fees: $225

– Monthly fees for renovations: $80

– Municipal taxes paid at the beginning of the year: $1500

a) Determine the rule of the function f which gives the cost y of condo fees as a function of the number x of months. _____

b) Determine the rule of the function g which gives the total cost y of renovation fees and municipal taxes as a function of the number x of months. _____

c) Determine the rule of the function $f + g$ and interpret this rule. _____

_____

_____

d) What is the total amount of fees paid by a condo owner after 8 months of occupancy?

_____

3.2 Polynomial functions

ACTIVITY 1 Polynomial functions

a) Among the following functions, indicate which ones are polynomial functions.
If it is a polynomial function, indicate its degree.

1. $P(x) = -5x + 8$ _____

2. $P(x) = -4x^2 - 5x$ _____

3. $P(x) = \dfrac{5}{x} + 3$ _____

4. $P(x) = -3$ _____

5. $P(x) = \sqrt{x} - 7$ _____

6. $P(x) = x^3 + 4x^2 - 5x + 3$ _____

b) Represent the following polynomial functions in the Cartesian plane on the right.

1. $f(x) = 2$
2. $g(x) = 3x - 2$
3. $h(x) = x^2 + 2x - 1$

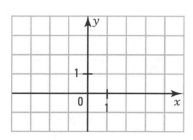

POLYNOMIAL FUNCTIONS

- A polynomial function is any function with a polynomial for a rule.

  Ex.: $f(x) = 2$ is a zero degree polynomial function.

  $g(x) = 2x + 3$ is a 1st degree polynomial function.

  $h(x) = x^2 - 4x + 3$ is a 2nd degree polynomial function.

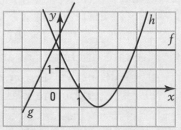

- The following table classifies polynomial functions according to their **degree**.

Degree	Basic polynomial function	Transformed polynomial function	Name
0	$f(x) = 1$	$f(x) = b$ where $b \in \mathbb{R}$	constant function
1	$f(x) = x$	$f(x) = ax$ where $a \in \mathbb{R}^*$	direct variation linear function
		$f(x) = ax + b$ where $a, b \in \mathbb{R}^*$	partial variation linear function
2	$f(x) = x^2$	$f(x) = ax^2 + bx + c$ where $a \in \mathbb{R}^*$	quadratic function
3	$f(x) = x^3$	$f(x) = ax^3 + bx^2 + cx + d$ where $a \in \mathbb{R}^*$	cubic function

ACTIVITY 2 Study of a constant function

Consider the function f given by the rule $y = 3$.

a) Represent this function in the Cartesian plane.

b) Determine

1. dom $f = $ _____   2. ran $f = $ _____

3. the zeros of f if they exist. _____

4. the y-intercept. _____

5. the sign of f _____

6. the variation of f _____   7. the extrema of f _____

c) What is the rate of change between two random points on the graph of f? _____

CONSTANT FUNCTIONS

- A constant function is a zero degree polynomial function. It is described by a rule of the form:
$$\boxed{f(x) = b}, b \in \mathbb{R}$$

- The Cartesian graph of a constant function is a horizontal line with the equation $y = b$.

Study of a constant function
- dom $f = \mathbb{R}$
- ran $f = \{b\}$
- The constant function has no zero unless $b = 0$.
- $f(x) > 0$ over $\mathbb{R}$ if $b > 0$
  $f(x) < 0$ over $\mathbb{R}$ if $b < 0$
- max $f = $ min $f = b$

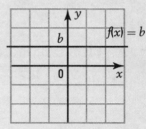

- The rate of change of any constant function is zero.
- A zero function is a constant function described by the rule $f(x) = 0$. Its Cartesian graph is represented by the x-axis.

---

1. A ski resort is open 120 days during the ski season. The cost of a season pass is $450. Consider the function f which gives the total cost y as a function of the number x of days of skiing.

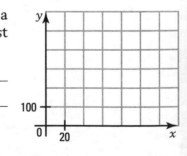

a) How much does it cost to ski for 12 days? _____

b) What is the rule of function f? _____

c) Represent function f in the Cartesian plane.

d) Determine

1. dom $f = $ _____   2. ran $f = $ _____

ACTIVITY 3 Study of a linear function

Consider the functions $f(x) = 3x - 2$ and $g(x) = -\frac{1}{2}x + 2$.

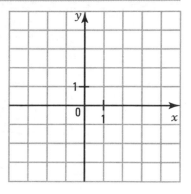

a) Represent the functions f and g in the Cartesian plane on the right.

b) Study the functions f and g and complete the following table.

	Function f	Function g
Domain		
Range		
Zero		
Initial value		
Sign		
Variation		

ACTIVITY 4 Transformations of the basic linear function

The basic 1st degree linear function $f(x) = x$ is represented on the right.

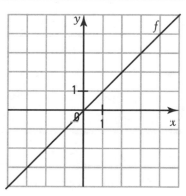

a) 1. Draw the image of function f by the vertical scale change $(x, y) \rightarrow (x, 3y)$ to obtain the graph of function g.

   2. What is the rule of the function g? _____

b) 1. Draw the image of function g by the vertical translation $(x, y) \rightarrow (x, y - 2)$ to obtain the graph of function h.

   2. What is the rule of the function h? _____

LINEAR FUNCTION

- A **linear function** is a 1st degree polynomial function. It is described by a rule of the form:

$$f(x) = ax + b \quad a \in \mathbb{R}^*$$

A linear function represents a situation where the rate of change is **constant**. a represents the rate of change and b represents the initial value (y-intercept).

Ex.: $f(x) = \frac{1}{2}x - 1$ 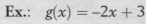 **Ex.:** $g(x) = -2x + 3$

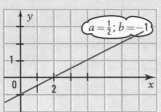 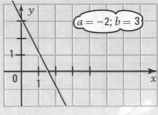

	Function f	Function g
Domain	$\mathbb{R}$	$\mathbb{R}$
Range	$\mathbb{R}$	$\mathbb{R}$
Zero	2	1.5
Initial value	−1	3
Sign	$f(x) \leq 0$ if $x \leq 2$ $f(x) \geq 0$ if $x \geq 2$	$f(x) \geq 0$ if $x \leq 1.5$ $f(x) \leq 0$ if $x \geq 1.5$
Rate of change	$\frac{1}{2}$	−2
Variation	increasing function	decreasing function

- – The function is **increasing** when the rate of change is **positive**.
  – The function is **decreasing** when the rate of change is **negative**.

2. A video game software company establishes that its monthly revenue corresponds to 30% of the amount of sales. The company's fixed monthly operating costs are $12 000 and the company cannot sell for more than $80 000 in one month.

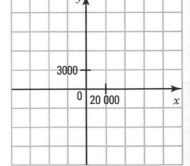

a) What is the rule which gives the net revenue y as a function of the amount x of sales? _____

b) Represent the function in the Cartesian plane.

c) Determine for this function
  1. the domain. _____ 2. the range. _____

d) Determine and interpret
  1. the zero of the function. _____
  2. the initial value of the function. _____

e) Study the sign of this function. _____

f) Study the variation of this function. _____

3. The graph of a linear function passes through the points A(3, 3) and B(5, –3). Determine the interval over which this function is positive. _____

Activity 5 Transformation of the basic quadratic function

The basic quadratic function $f(x) = x^2$ can be transformed into a quadratic function with a rule of the form $g(x) = a(x - h)^2 + k$.

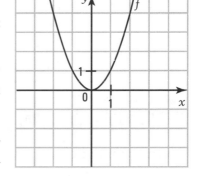

a) Consider the basic quadratic function $f(x) = x^2$ and the quadratic function $g(x) = ax^2$.

Represent, in the same Cartesian plane, the functions $g_1(x) = 2x^2$, $g_2(x) = \frac{1}{2}x^2$ and $g_3(x) = -x^2$ and explain how to deduce the graph of g from the graph of f when

1. $a > 1$: _____
2. $0 < a < 1$: _____
3. $a = -1$: _____

b) Consider the basic quadratic function $f(x) = x^2$ and the function $g(x) = (x - h)^2$.

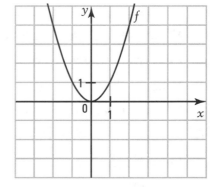

Represent, in the same Cartesian plane, the functions $g_1(x) = (x - 4)^2$ and $g_2(x) = (x + 2)^2$ and explain how to deduce the graph of g from the graph of f when

1. $h > 0$: _____
2. $h < 0$: _____

c) Consider the basic quadratic function $f(x) = x^2$ and the quadratic function $g(x) = x^2 + k$.

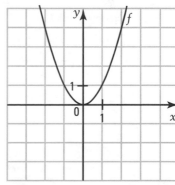

Represent, in the same Cartesian plane, the functions $g_1(x) = x^2 + 2$ and $g_2(x) = x^2 - 3$ and explain how to deduce the graph of g from the graph of f when

1. $k > 0$: _____
2. $k < 0$: _____

ACTIVITY 6   Study of a quadratic function (standard form)

Consider the function f given by the rule $y = -1.5(x - 1)^2 + 6$.

a) Represent this function in the Cartesian plane.

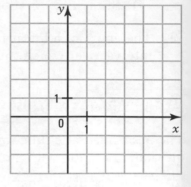

b) Determine

   1. dom $f =$ _____

   2. ran $f =$ _____

   3. the zeros of f. _____

   4. the initial value of f. _____

   5. the sign of f. _____

      _____

   6. the variation of f. _____

      _____

   7. the extrema of f. _____

ACTIVITY 7   Study of a quadratic function (general form)

Consider the function f given by the rule $y = x^2 - 2x - 3$.

a) Is the parabola representing f open upward or downward?

_____

b) What are the coordinates of the vertex? _____

c) Determine the zeros of the function f. _____

d) What is the initial value of f? _____

e) What is the equation of the axis of symmetry? _____

f) Represent this function in the Cartesian plane.

g) Determine:

   1. dom $f =$ _____

   2. ran $f =$ _____

   3. the sign of f. _____

   4. the variation of f. _____

   5. the extrema of f. _____

QUADRATIC FUNCTION

Standard form

$$f(x) = a(x - h)^2 + k$$

$a > 0$ $a < 0$

General form

$$f(x) = ax^2 + bx + c$$

- Vertex: V(h, k)

- Axis of symmetry: $x = h$

- Zeros: $h \pm \sqrt{-\dfrac{k}{a}}$

- Vertex: $\left(-\dfrac{b}{2a}, \dfrac{4ac - b^2}{4a}\right)$

- Axis of symmetry: $x = -\dfrac{b}{2a}$

- Zeros: $\dfrac{-b \pm \sqrt{b^2 - 4ac}}{2a}$

- y-intercept: c

Factored form

$$f(x) = a(x - x_1)(x - x_2)$$

- Zeros: x_1 and x_2

- Axis of symmetry: $x = \dfrac{x_1 + x_2}{2}$

4. Determine the domain and range of the following functions.

     a) $f(x) = -3(x - 2)^2 + 5$ **b)** $f(x) = 2x^2 + 4x - 9$

     _____   _____

     _____   _____

5. Determine the zeros of the function $f(x) = -3(x + 1)^2 + 12.$ _____

6. Determine the y-intercept of $f(x) = -\dfrac{1}{2}(x + 4)^2 + 9.$ _____

7. Determine over what interval the function $f(x) = 2x^2 - 5x - 3$ is positive.

_____

8. Determine over what interval the function $f(x) = 3x^2 + 6x - 5$ is increasing. _____

9. Determine the extrema of the function $f(x) = -2x^2 + 12x - 7.$ _____

10. What is the axis of symmetry of the function $f(x) = -\dfrac{1}{4}x^2 + 3x + 1$? _____

11. Determine the values of x for which the function $f(x) = -3(x + 4)^2 + 5$ is equal to -7.

_____

12. Find the rule of the quadratic function represented by a parabola with a vertex at V$(-1, 5)$ and passing through the point P$(1, 3)$.

_____

13. Consider the functions $f(x) = x + 3$ and $g(x) = -x + 1$ represented on the right.

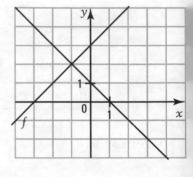

  a) Represent the function s given that $s(x) = f(x) + g(x)$.

  _____

  b) Represent the function p given that $p(x) = f(x) \cdot g(x)$.

  _____

14. A stone is thrown upward from the top of a seaside cliff. The function which gives the stone's height h (in m) above sea level as a function of time t (in sec) since it was thrown has the rule:
$h = -t^2 + 12t + 160$.
Find the interval of time over which the height of the stone is at least 180 m above sea level.

_____

15. The height h, in metres, of a diver relative to the water level is described by the rule $h = \frac{1}{2}t^2 - 6t + 10$ where t represents the elapsed time, in seconds, since the start of the dive. How long did the diver remain underwater?

_____

16. A projectile is thrown upward from a height of 12 m. After 10 seconds, it reaches its maximum height and after 24 seconds, it hits the ground.

Knowing that its trajectory follows the rule of a quadratic function, find the elapsed time between the moment it reaches a height of 6.5 m, on its descent, and the time when it hits the ground.

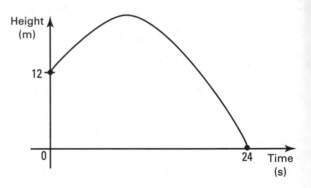

_____

_____

_____

3.3 Absolute value function

ACTIVITY 1 Absolute value of a real number

On a winter day, the temperature (in °C), recorded at noon, has an absolute value of 5.

a) What is the recorded temperature that day if the temperature is:

1. above 0 °C? _____ 2. below 0 °C? _____

b) We represent the absolute value of a number x by $|x|$. Determine:

1. $|+10| =$ _____ 2. $|-10| =$ _____ 3. $|0| =$ _____

c) Is it true to say that two opposite numbers have the same absolute value? _____

ABSOLUTE VALUE OF A REAL NUMBER

The **absolute value** of a real number a, written $|a|$, is defined by:

$$|a| = \begin{cases} a & \text{if } a \geqslant 0 \\ -a & \text{if } a < 0 \end{cases}$$

Ex.: $|+4| = 4$; $|-3| = 3$; $|0| = 0$.

Note that the absolute value of a real number is never negative.

---

1. Determine the following absolute values.

a) $|+8| =$ _____ b) $|-4.7| =$ _____ c) $|0| =$ _____ d) $|\pi| =$ _____

e) $|-6.53| =$ _____ f) $\left|+\dfrac{3}{4}\right| =$ _____ g) $\left|-\dfrac{2}{3}\right| =$ _____ h) $\left|-\dfrac{5}{18}\right| =$ _____

ACTIVITY 2 Properties

Consider a real number a and a non-zero real number b. Answer true or false.

a) $|a| \geqslant 0$ _____ b) $|a| = |-a|$ _____

c) $|a + b| = |a| + |b|$ _____ d) $|a - b| = |a| - |b|$ _____

e) $|a \cdot b| = |a| \cdot |b|$ _____ f) $\left|\dfrac{a}{b}\right| = \dfrac{|a|}{|b|}$ _____

PROPERTIES

For any real number a and any real number b, we have the following properties.

- $|a| \geq 0$ Ex.: $|+5| \geq 0;$ $|-4| \geq 0$
- $|a| = |-a|$ $|4| = |-4|$
- $|a + b| \leq |a| + |b|$ $|7 + (-2)| \leq |7| + |-2|$
- $|a - b| \geq |a| - |b|$ $|5 - (-3)| \geq |5| - |-3|$
- $|ab| = |a| \cdot |b|$ $|8 \times (-3)| = |8| \times |-3|$
- $\left|\dfrac{a}{b}\right| = \dfrac{|a|}{|b|}$ $(b \neq 0)$ $\left|\dfrac{-8}{2}\right| = \dfrac{|-8|}{|2|}$

2. Complete the following using the appropriate symbol $=, >, <$.

a) $|x + 5| \underline{\ >\ } 0$

b) $|x - 3| \underline{\ =\ } |3 - x|$

c) $|2(x - 1)| \underline{\ =\ } 2|x - 1|$

d) $|7 - 12| \underline{\ >\ } |7| - |12|$

e) $\left|\dfrac{x + 2}{x - 1}\right| \underline{\ =\ } \dfrac{|x + 2|}{|x - 1|}$

f) $|-6 + 9| \underline{\ <\ } |-6| + |9|$

ACTIVITY 3 Absolute value equations

a) Today's temperature x, in degrees Celsius, recorded at noon has an absolute value of 20. Determine this temperature if

1. it is warm. _____   2. it is cold. _____

b) What are the solutions to the equation $|x| = 20$? _____

c) Consider the equation $|x| = 0$. What is the unique real number that verifies this equation? ___

d) Consider the equation $|x| = -4$. Is there a real number that verifies this equation? Justify your answer.

_____

ABSOLUTE VALUE EQUATIONS

The number of solutions to the equation:

$$|x| = k$$

depends on the sign of k.

If $k > 0$	If $k = 0$	If $k < 0$
The equation has 2 solutions.	The equation has 1 solution.	The equation has no solution.
$x = -k$ or $x = k$	$x = 0$	
Ex.: $|x| = 3$	Ex.: $|x| = 0$	Ex.: $|x| = -5$
S $= \{-3, 3\}$	S $= \{0\}$	S $= \varnothing$

3. Solve the following equations.

   a) $|x| = 12$

   b) $|x| = -8$

   c) $|x + 5| = 0$

   _____

   _____

   _____

   d) $|2x + 1| = 7$

   e) $\left|\frac{1}{2}x - 5\right| = 4$

   f) $|6 - x| = -3$

   _____

   _____

   _____

4. Solve the following equations.

   a) $2|x - 5| - 4 = 0$

   b) $-2|3x - 1| + 4 = -6$

   c) $12 - |6 - 2x| = 3$

   _____

   _____

   _____

   d) $|x - 5| + 8 = 2$

   e) $-3|2x + 5| + 6 = 6$

   f) $|4x - 5| + 6 = 9$

   _____

   _____

   _____

ACTIVITY 4 Absolute value inequalities

a) Consider the inequality $|x| \leqslant 3$.

On the real number line below, represent the set of all real numbers verifying this inequality and find the solution set.

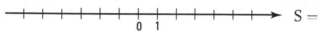 S = _____

b) Consider the inequality $|x| > 4$.

On the real number line below, represent the set of all real numbers verifying this inequality and find the solution set.

 S = _____

ABSOLUTE VALUE INEQUALITIES

Given a **positive** real number k, we have:

$|x| \leqslant k$	$|x| \geqslant k$
$\Leftrightarrow x \geqslant -k$ **and** $x \leqslant k$	$\Leftrightarrow x \leqslant -k$ **or** $x \geqslant k$
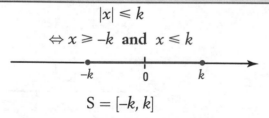	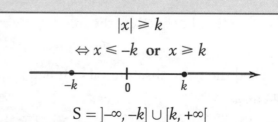
$S = [-k, k]$	$S = \,]-\infty, -k] \cup [k, +\infty[$
Ex.: The inequality $|x| \leqslant 5$ has the solution set: $S = [-5, 5]$.	**Ex.:** The inequality $|x| \geqslant 5$ has the solution set: $S = \,]-\infty, -5] \cup [5, +\infty[$.

---

5. For each of the following inequalities, determine the solution set and represent it on the real number line.

 a) $|x| > 10$ **b)** $|x| \leqslant 4$ **c)** $|x| > -3$

 d) $|x| \leqslant -2$ **e)** $|x| \geqslant 0$ **f)** $|x| \leqslant 0$

ACTIVITY 5   Basic absolute value function

Consider the function f defined by the rule $y = |x|$.

 a) Complete the following table of values.

x	–3	–2	–1	0	1	2	3
y							

 b) Represent the function f in the Cartesian plane.

 c) Determine

  1. dom f. _____   2. ran f. _____

  3. the zero of f. _____   4. the initial value of f. _____

  5. the sign of f. _____

  6. the variation of f. _____

  7. the extrema of f. _____

BASIC ABSOLUTE VALUE FUNCTION

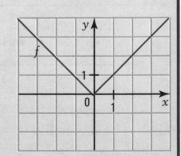

- The function f defined by the rule:
$$f(x) = |x|$$
 is called the basic absolute value function.

- We have:

 dom $f = \mathbb{R}$ ran $f = \mathbb{R}_+$

 The zero of f is 0.   The initial value of f is 0.

 Sign of f: $f(x) \geqslant 0$ over $\mathbb{R}$.

 Variation of f: f is increasing over $\mathbb{R}_+$; f is decreasing over $\mathbb{R}_-$.

 The function f has a minimum of 0.

6. Consider the basic absolute value function $f(x) = |x|$ represented on the right.

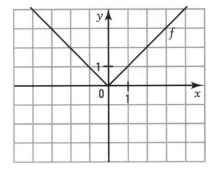

a) Using the graph, find the values of x for which the function $f(x)$ is:

1. equal to 2. _____

2. less than 2. _____

3. less than or equal to 2. _____

4. greater than 2. _____

5. greater than or equal to 2. _____

b) Using the graph, solve the following equations or inequalities:

1. $|x| = 1$ _____   2. $|x| = 0$ _____   3. $|x| = -1$ _____

4. $|x| \leqslant 1$ _____   5. $|x| > 3$ _____   6. $|x| > -1$ _____

Activity 6   Absolute value function $f(x) = a|b(x-h)| + k$

The basic absolute value function $f(x) = |x|$ can be transformed into an absolute value function defined by the rule

$$g(x) = a|b(x - h)| + k$$

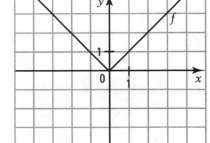

a) Consider the basic absolute value function $f(x) = |x|$ and the absolute value function $g(x) = a|x|$.

Represent, in the same Cartesian plane, the functions $g_1(x) = 2|x|$, $g_2(x) = \frac{1}{2}|x|$ and $g_3(x) = -|x|$ and explain how to deduce the graph of g from the graph of f when

1. $a > 1$: _____

2. $0 < a < 1$: _____

3. $a = -1$: _____

4. Complete: From the graph of $f(x) = |x|$, we obtain the graph of $g(x) = a|x|$ by the transformation $(x, y) \rightarrow$ _____.

5. Is the graph of $g(x) = a|x|$ open upward or downward when

    1) $a > 0$? _____   2) $a < 0$? _____

b) Consider the basic absolute value function $f(x) = |x|$ and the absolute value function $g(x) = |bx|$.

Represent, in the same Cartesian plane, the functions $g_1(x) = |2x|$, $g_2(x) = \left|\frac{1}{2}x\right|$ and $g_3(x) = |-x|$ and explain how to deduce the graph of g from the graph of f when

1. $b > 1$: _____

2. $0 < b < 1$: _____

3. $b = -1$: _____

4. Complete: From the graph of $f(x) = |x|$, we obtain the graph of $g(x) = |bx|$ by the transformation $(x, y) \rightarrow$ _____

5. Compare the graphs of the functions $y = 2|x|$ and $y = |2x|$ obtained in a) and b). Justify your answer. _____

6. Compare the graphs $f(x) = |x|$ and $f(x) = |-x|$. Justify your answer.

_____

c) Consider the basic absolute value function $f(x) = |x|$ and the absolute value function $g(x) = |x - h|$.

Represent, in the same Cartesian plane, the functions $g_1(x) = |x - 3|$ and $g_2(x) = |x + 2|$ and explain how to deduce the graph of g from the graph of f when

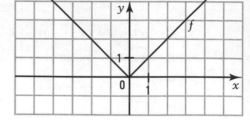

1. $h > 0$: _____

2. $h < 0$: _____

3. Complete: From the graph of $f(x) = |x|$, we obtain the graph of $g(x) = |x - h|$ by the transformation $(x, y) \rightarrow$ _____

d) Consider the basic absolute value function $f(x) = |x|$ and the absolute value function $g(x) = |x| + k$.

Represent, in the same Cartesian plane, the functions $g_1(x) = |x| + 2$ and $g_2(x) = |x| - 3$ and explain how to deduce the graph of g from the graph of f when

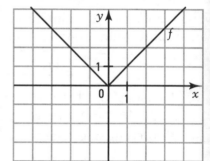

1. $k > 0$: _____

2. $k < 0$: _____

3. Complete: From the graph of $f(x) = |x|$, we obtain the graph of $g(x) = |x| + k$ by the transformation

$(x, y) \rightarrow$ _____

ABSOLUTE VALUE FUNCTION $f(x) = a|b(x - h)| + k$

The graph of the function $f(x) = a|b(x - h)| + k$ is deduced from the graph of the basic absolute value function $y = |x|$ by the transformation:

$$(x, y) \rightarrow \left(\frac{x}{b} + h, ay + k\right)$$

Ex.: The graph of the function $f(x) = -3|\frac{1}{2}(x - 1)| + 4$ is deduced from the graph of the basic absolute value function $g(x) = |x|$ by the transformation: $(x, y) \rightarrow (2x + 1, -3y + 4)$

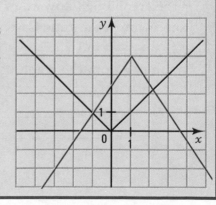

Chapter 3 Real functions

7. The following functions have a rule of the form $f(x) = a|b(x - h)| + k$.
$f_1(x) = 3|x|$, $f_2(x) = |2x|$, $f_3(x) = |x + 4|$, $f_4(x) = |x| + 1$ and $f_5(x) = 2|3(x - 1)| - 4$.
Complete the table on the right by determining, for each function, the parameters a, b, h and k and by giving the rule of the transformation which enables you to obtain the function from the basic absolute value function $g(x) = |x|$.

	a	b	h	k	Rule
$f_1(x) = 3|x|$					
$f_2(x) = |2x|$					
$f_3(x) = |x + 4|$					
$f_4(x) = |x| + 1$					
$f_5(x) = 2|3(x - 1)| - 4$					

8. In each of the following cases, we apply a transformation to the basic absolute value function $y = |x|$. Find the rule of the function obtained by applying the given transformation.

a) $(x, y) \rightarrow (x, -y)$ _____

b) $(x, y) \rightarrow (x - 2, y + 4)$ _____

c) $(x, y) \rightarrow \left(\frac{x}{2}, y\right)$ _____

d) $(x, y) \rightarrow (5x, y)$ _____

e) $(x, y) \rightarrow (3x, -7y)$ _____

f) $(x, y) \rightarrow \left(\frac{x}{3} + 1, 2y - 4\right)$ _____

9. From the basic absolute value function and using the transformation $(x, y) \rightarrow \left(\frac{x}{b} + h, ay + k\right)$, represent the function

$y = -2\left|\frac{1}{3}(x - 1)\right| + 4$ in the Cartesian plane.

_____

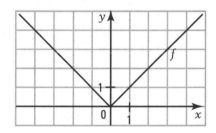

ACTIVITY 7 **Graphing the function $f(x) = a|b(x - h)| + k$**

Consider the function $f(x) = 4\left|-\frac{1}{2}(x - 1)\right| - 4$.

a) Identify the parameters a, b, h and k.

_____

b) Is the graph open upward or downward? Justify your answer.

_____

c) What are the coordinates of the vertex? _____

d) Find the zeros of the function. _____

e) Represent the function f in the Cartesian plane after completing the following table of values.

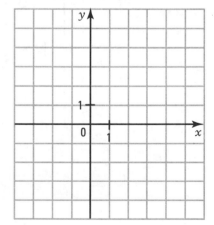

x	-2	1	4
y			

GRAPH OF AN ABSOLUTE VALUE FUNCTION

Consider the **absolute value function** defined by the rule:

$$f(x) = a|b(x - h)| + k$$

- The graph is open:
  - upward if $a > 0$.
  - downward if $a < 0$.
- The graph has the vertex: $V(h, k)$

- The graph has the following line as an axis of symmetry:

$$x = h$$

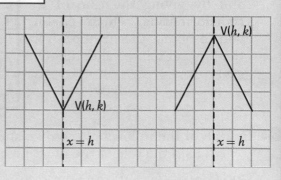

10. Write the rules of the following functions in the form $y = a|x - h| + k$ and identify the parameters a, h and k.

a) $y = -2|3x + 3| + 5$

b) $y = 4|6 - 3x| + 5$

c) $y = -\frac{1}{2}|8x - 4| + 3$

d) $y = -\frac{5}{6}\left|4 - \frac{1}{5}x\right| + 3$

11. Graph the following functions.

a) $y = -2|x - 2| + 3$

b) $y = \frac{1}{8}|4 - 4x| - 2$

c) $y = -\frac{1}{2}|3x - 6| + 4$

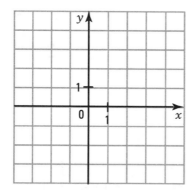

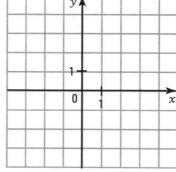

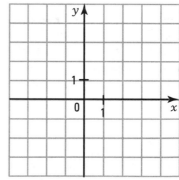

ACTIVITY 8 Determining the sign of an absolute value function

Consider the absolute value function $f(x) = -2|x + 5| + 8$.

a) What are the zeros of this function? _____

b) Determine the sign of this function using a sketch.

⟶

ACTIVITY 9 Study of an absolute value function

Consider the functions $f(x) = \frac{1}{2}|8 - 4x| - 3$ and $g(x) = -\frac{1}{3}|2x - 4| + 4$.

a) Write each of the rules in the form $y = a|x - h| + k$ and represent the functions in the Cartesian plane.

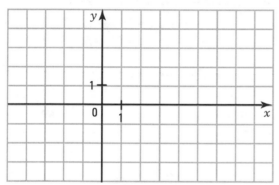 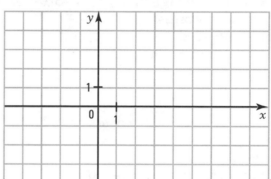

b) Do a study of each of the preceding functions and complete the table below.

Properties	f	g
Domain		
Range		
Zeros		
Initial value		
Sign		
Variation		
Extrema		

STUDY OF AN ABSOLUTE VALUE FUNCTION

Given the absolute value function: $f(x) = a|b(x - h)| + k$, we have:
- $\text{dom} f = \mathbb{R}$.
- $\text{ran} f = [k, +\infty[$ if $a > 0$; $]-\infty, k[$ if $a < 0$.
- The zero(s) of f exist if a and k are opposite signs or if $k = 0$.
- To study the sign of f,
  - we find the zero(s) if they exist;
  - we establish the sign of f from a sketch of the graph.
- Variation
  If $a > 0$, f is decreasing over $]-\infty, h]$.   If $a < 0$, f is increasing over $]-\infty, h]$.
  $\qquad$ f is increasing over $[h, +\infty[$. $\qquad\qquad$ f is decreasing over $[h, +\infty[$.

- Extrema
  If $a > 0$, f has a minimum. $\min f = k$.
  If $a < 0$, f has a minimum. $\max f = k$.

  Ex.: Consider the function $f(x) = -3|x + 2| + 6$. ($a = -3, b = 1, h = -2, k = 6$)
  - Open downward, $a < 0$.
  - Vertex: V(−2, 6).
  - Axis of symmetry: $x = -2$.
  - Zeros: $-3|x + 2| + 6 = 0$
    $\qquad\qquad |x + 2| = 2$

    $\Leftrightarrow$ $\quad x + 2 = -2$ $\quad$ or $x + 2 = 2$
    $\qquad\qquad x = -4$ $\quad$ or $\qquad x = 0$
  - Initial value: $y = 0$.
  - $\text{dom} f = \mathbb{R}$; $\quad$ $\text{ran} f =]-\infty, 6]$
  - Sign of f: $f(x) \geq 0$ over $[-4, 0]$; $f(x) \leq 0$ over $]-\infty, -4] \cup [0, +\infty[$.
  - Variation of f: f is increasing over $]-\infty, -2]$; f is decreasing over $[-2, +\infty[$.
  - $\max f = 6$.

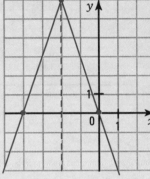

12. Represent the graph and do a study of the function
$f(x) = -\frac{1}{4}|2(x - 1)| + 2$.

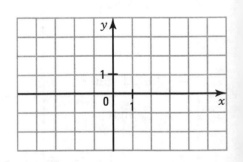

13. Determine the domain and range of each of the following functions.

a) $y = -2|x + 5| - 1$

b) $y = \frac{1}{4}|-2(x - 1)| + 5$

_____ _____

14. Determine the zeros of the following functions.

a) $y = 3|x - 5| - 6$ _____

b) $y = -\frac{1}{2}|6 - 3x| + 4$ _____

c) $y = 4|2x + 1| + 8$ _____

d) $y = -5|6 - x|$ _____

15. Consider the linear function $f(x) = 2x - 3$ and the absolute value function $g(x) = 3|3x + 5| - 4$. Determine the initial value of the composite

a) $g \circ f$: _____

b) $f \circ g$: _____

16. Determine the interval over which each of the following functions is positive.

a) $y = -\frac{1}{3}|x - 5| + 2$

b) $y = 2|3 - 2x| - 4$

_____ _____

c) $y = \frac{3}{4}|-2x + 4| - 3$

d) $y = 3|x - 5| + 6$

_____ _____

17. Determine the interval over which each of the following functions is increasing.

a) $y = 5|6 - 4x| + 2$

b) $y = -3|2x + 4| + 5$

_____ _____

18. Determine the solution set to each of the following inequalities.

a) $|x - 5| > 3$

b) $|6 - x| \leq 1$

c) $|3x - 2| \geq 4$

_____ _____ _____

d) $|2x + 5| \leq 0$

e) $-2|x + 1| + 5 > -5$

f) $3|2 - x| + 4 > 1$

_____ _____ _____

g) $6 - 3|x - 1| \leq 0$

h) $-|2x - 1| + 5 > 0$

i) $\left|\frac{x}{2} - 1\right| > 0$

_____ _____ _____

3.3 Absolute value function

19. Study each of the following functions and complete the following table.

	$f(x) = -2\|x - 1\| + 4$	$f(x) = 3\|x + 2\| - 6$	$f(x) = \frac{1}{2}\|x - 4\| + 3$	$f(x) = -3\|5 - x\|$
Dom f				
Ran f				
Zero(s) if they exist				
Initial value				
Sign				
Variation				
Extrema				

ACTIVITY 10 Finding the rule of an absolute value function

The rule of any absolute value function can be written in the form $f(x) = a\|x - h\| + k$.

a) Consider the function $f(x) = 3\|-2(x - 5)\| + 7$.
Write the rule of this function in the form $f(x) = a\|x - h\| + k$. _____

b) Consider the absolute value function with the vertex V(–2, 4) and passing through the point P(1, –2).

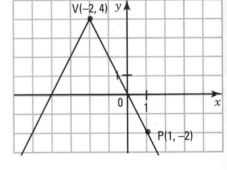

1. Identify h and k. _____

2. Determine a knowing that the coordinates of the point P(1, –2) verify the rule of the function.

_____

_____

_____

_____

3. What is the rule of the function? _____

FINDING THE RULE OF AN ABSOLUTE VALUE FUNCTION

The rule of any absolute value function can be written in the form:

$$f(x) = a|x - h| + k$$

1st case: The vertex V and a point P are given.

1. Identify the parameters h and k.

2. Find a after replacing x and y in the rule by the coordinates of the given point P.

3. Deduce the rule.

1. $h = -1$ and $k = 2$
   $y = a|x + 1| + 2$
2. $-1 = a|2 + 1| + 2$
   $-1 = 3a + 2$
   $a = -1$
3. $y = -|x + 1| + 2$

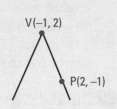

2nd case: Three points, of which two have the same y-coordinate, are given.

1. Identify h as half the sum of the x-coordinates of the points with the same y-coordinates.

2. Find the slope of the ray passing through two given points, and establish parameter a according to the opening of the graph.

3. Find k after replacing x and y in the rule by the coordinates of one of the given points.

4. Deduce the rule.

1. $h = \dfrac{(-6) + (-2)}{2} = -4$

2. Slope $= \dfrac{y_2 - y_1}{x_2 - x_1} = \dfrac{1}{2}$

   $a = -\dfrac{1}{2}$ (open downward)

3. $y = -\dfrac{1}{2}|x + 4| + k$
   $2 = -\dfrac{1}{2}|-2 + 4| + k$
   $k = 3$

4. $y = -\dfrac{1}{2}|x + 4| + 3$

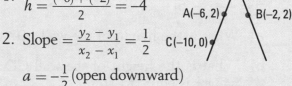

3rd case: Any three points are given.

1. Find the slope of the ray passing through two given points, and establish parameter a according to the opening of the graph.

2. Find the equation of each ray knowing that their slopes are opposite.

3. Find the coordinates (h, k) of the vertex V, which is the intersection of the two rays.

4. Deduce the rule.

1. Slope $= \dfrac{y_2 - y_1}{x_2 - x_1} = \dfrac{3}{4}$

   $a = \dfrac{-3}{4}$ (open downward)

2. $y_1 = \dfrac{3}{4}x + \dfrac{5}{4}$

   $y_2 = -\dfrac{3}{4}x + \dfrac{11}{4}$

3. $\dfrac{3}{4}x + \dfrac{5}{4} = -\dfrac{3}{4}x + \dfrac{11}{4}$

   $6x = 6$
   $x = 1 \Rightarrow y = 2$

   Thus, V(1, 2)

4. $y = -\dfrac{3}{4}|x - 1| + 2$

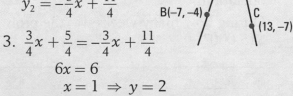
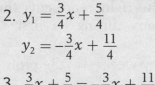

20. Find the rule of an absolute value function whose graph

    a) has the vertex V(3, 4) and passes through the point P(7, 6). _____

    b) passes through the points A(2, –6), B(5, –8) and C(–4, –6). _____

    c) passes through the points A(1, –1), B(3, –5) and C(–4, –3). _____

21. In order to draw the simulated trajectory of a toy airplane, Ethan uses the rule of an absolute value function that gives the airplane's height y, in metres, as a function of elapsed time x, in seconds. The rule of the function is $y = -\frac{5}{4}|x - 8| + 10$.

For how many seconds is the height of the airplane above 7 m? _____

22. In the Cartesian plane on the right, a view of an airplane hangar is represented with the roof of the hangar corresponding to an absolute value function given by the rule $y = -\frac{1}{2}|x - 6| + 8$.

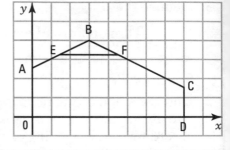

    a) What is the height of the wall A0? _____

    b) What is the height of the wall CD if the width of the hangar is equal to 16 m? _____

    c) The ceiling EF is built at a height of 6.5 m. What is the width of the ceiling? _____

23. The graph on the right represents the evolution of a share's value on the stock market. Eight weeks after its purchase, the share reaches its maximum value of $9. If it initially was worth $7, what will it be worth after 13 weeks?

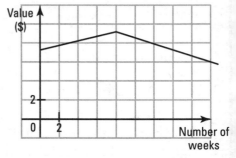

_____

_____

_____

24. The graph on the right represents the profit of a recycling company during its first 40 weeks of operation.

During how many weeks was the profit greater than $15 000?

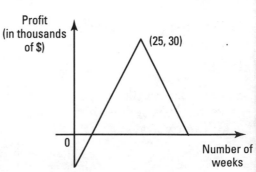

_____

_____

_____

25. The air conditioning system in an office building has been programmed so that it turns on when the outside temperature reaches 23 °C and turns off when it reaches 20 °C.

The outside temperature varies according to the rule of the absolute value function given by $y = -3|x - 6| + 35$ where x represents the elapsed number of hours since 6 a.m. and y represents the outside temperature in °C.

How many hours was the system on?

_____

_____

26. The lateral view of a channelling system is represented in the Cartesian plane on the right, scaled in metres.

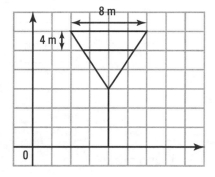

The walls of this system are represented by an absolute value function with the rule: $y = 3|x - 8| + 12$.

A filtering net is placed 4 m below the ceiling of the canal. If the width of the canal is 8 m, what is the width of the filtering net?

_____

_____

27. The graph on the right represents the front of a house. The base of the roof corresponds to the line $y = 5$.

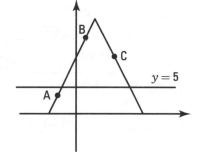

The sides of the roof form the graph of an absolute value function passing through the points A(–2, 3), B(2, 13) and C(8, 8).

What is the area of the triangle limited by the roof and the line?

_____

_____

28. A projectile is thrown from a height of 6 m and follows the trajectory of an absolute value function. It reaches a maximum height of 14 m after 4 seconds. Five seconds after reaching its maximum height, it bounces off a cement block and follows the trajectory of a quadratic function. If the maximum height of the second bounce is 8 m and occurs three seconds after bouncing off the cement block, when will the projectile hit the ground? (Round your answer to the nearest second).

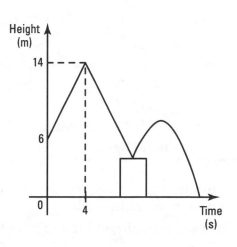

_____

_____

3.3 Absolute value function

3.4 Square root function

ACTIVITY 1 Square root function

Consider the function f defined by the rule $f(x) = \sqrt{x}$.

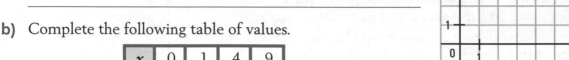

a) What condition must be placed on x for $\sqrt{x}$ to exist in $\mathbb{R}$?

_____

b) Complete the following table of values.

x	0	1	4	9
y				

c) Represent the function f in the Cartesian plane.

d) Determine

1. dom $f =$ _____   2. ran $f =$ _____
3. the zero of f. _____   4. the initial value of f. _____
5. the sign of f. _____
6. the variation of f. _____
7. the extrema of f. _____

BASIC SQUARE ROOT FUNCTION

- The function f defined by the rule:

$$f(x) = \sqrt{x}$$

is called the basic square root function.

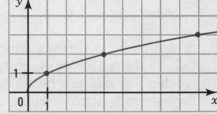

- We have:

dom $f = \mathbb{R}_+$.   ran $f = \mathbb{R}_+$.
The zero of f is 0.   The initial value is 0.
Sign of f: $f(x) \geqslant 0, \forall x \in$ dom f.
Variation of f: f is increasing, $\forall x \in$ dom f.
The function f has a minimum equal to 0.

The point 0 (0, 0) is the vertex of the function.

---

1. Consider the basic square root function $f(x) = \sqrt{x}$ represented on the right.

Using the graph, find the values of x for which

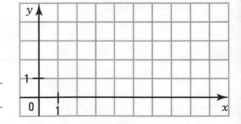

a) $f(x) = 3$ _____

b) $f(x) \geqslant 1$ _____

c) $0 \leqslant f(x) < 2$ _____

d) $f(x) < 0$ _____

e) $1 < f(x) < 3$ _____

ACTIVITY 2 Square root function $f(x) = a\sqrt{b(x - h)} + k$

The basic square root function $f(x) = \sqrt{x}$ can be transformed into a square root function defined by the rule

$$g(x) = a\sqrt{b(x - h)} + k.$$

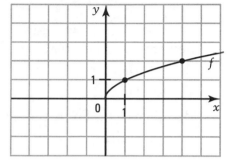

a) Consider the basic square root function $f(x) = \sqrt{x}$ and the square root function $g(x) = a\sqrt{x}$.

Represent, in the same Cartesian plane, the functions $g_1(x) = 2\sqrt{x}$, $g_2(x) = \frac{1}{2}\sqrt{x}$ and $g_3(x) = -\sqrt{x}$ and explain how to deduce the graph of g from the graph of f when

1. $a > 1$: _____
2. $0 < a < 1$: _____
3. $a = -1$: _____
4. Complete: From the graph of $f(x) = \sqrt{x}$, we obtain the graph of $g(x) = a\sqrt{x}$ by the transformation $(x, y) \rightarrow$ _____.
5. Is the graph of $g(x) = a\sqrt{x}$ located in the 1st or 4th quadrant when
   1) $a > 0$? _____   2) $a < 0$? _____

b) Consider the basic square root function $f(x) = \sqrt{x}$ and the square root function $g(x) = \sqrt{bx}$.

Represent, in the same Cartesian plane, the functions $g_1(x) = \sqrt{2x}$, $g_2(x) = \sqrt{\frac{1}{2}x}$ and $g_3(x) = \sqrt{-x}$ and explain how to deduce the graph of g from the graph of f when

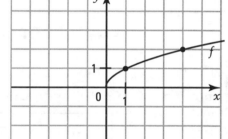

1. $b > 1$: _____
2. $0 < b < 1$: _____
3. $b = -1$: _____
4. Complete: From the graph of $f(x) = \sqrt{x}$, we obtain the graph of $g(x) = \sqrt{bx}$ by the transformation $(x, y) \rightarrow$ _____
5. In which quadrant is the graph of $g(x) = \sqrt{bx}$ when
   1) $b > 0$? _____   2) $b < 0$? _____
6. What can you say about the graph of the function $y = 2\sqrt{x}$ and that of the function $y = \sqrt{4x}$? Justify your answer.

   _____
   _____

c) Consider the basic square root function $f(x) = \sqrt{x}$ and the square root function $g(x) = \sqrt{x-h}$.

Represent, in the same Cartesian plane, the functions $g_1(x) = \sqrt{x-2}$ and $g_2(x) = \sqrt{x+3}$ and explain how to deduce the graph of g from the graph of f when

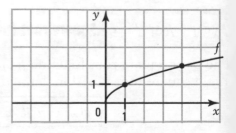

1. $h > 0$: _____

2. $h < 0$: _____

3. Complete: From the graph of $f(x) = \sqrt{x}$, we obtain the graph of $g(x) = \sqrt{x-h}$ by the transformation $(x, y) \rightarrow$ _____

d) Consider the basic square root function $f(x) = \sqrt{x}$ and the square root function $g(x) = \sqrt{x} + k$.

Represent, in the same Cartesian plane, the functions $g_1(x) = \sqrt{x} + 3$ and $g_2(x) = \sqrt{x} - 2$ and explain how to deduce the graph of g from the graph of f when

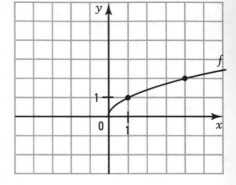

1. $k > 0$: _____

2. $k < 0$: _____

3. Complete: From the graph of $f(x) = \sqrt{x}$, we obtain the graph of $g(x) = \sqrt{x} + k$ by the transformation $(x, y) \rightarrow$ _____

SQUARE ROOT FUNCTION $f(x) = a\sqrt{b(x-h)} + k$

The graph of the function $f(x) = a\sqrt{b(x-h)} + k$ is deduced from the graph of the basic square root function $y = \sqrt{x}$ by the transformation

$$(x, y) \rightarrow \left(\frac{x}{b} + h, \, ay + k \right)$$

Ex.: The basic square root function $y = \sqrt{x}$ and the square root function

$y = -2\sqrt{\frac{1}{2}(x-1)} + 4$ are represented on the right.

The rule of the transformation applied to the graph of the basic square root function is:

$(x, y) \rightarrow (2x + 1, -2y + 4)$.

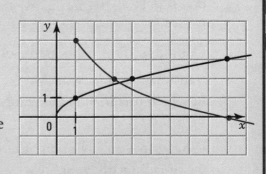

2. The following functions have a rule of the form $f(x) = a\sqrt{b(x-h)} + k$.

$f_1(x) = 3\sqrt{x}, f_2(x) = \sqrt{2x}, f_3(x) = \sqrt{x+4}, f_4(x) = \sqrt{x}+1$ and $f_5(x) = 2\sqrt{3(x-1)}-4$.

Complete the table on the right by determining, for each function, the parameters a, b, h and k and by giving the rule of the transformation which enables you to obtain the function from the basic function $g(x) = \sqrt{x}$.

	a	b	h	k	Rule
$f_1(x) = 3\sqrt{x}$					
$f_2(x) = \sqrt{2x}$					
$f_3(x) = \sqrt{x+4}$					
$f_4(x) = \sqrt{x}+1$					
$f_5(x) = 2\sqrt{3(x-1)}-4$					

3. In each of the following cases, we apply a transformation to the basic square root function $f(x) = \sqrt{x}$. Find the rule of the function obtained by applying the given transformation.

a) $(x, y) \rightarrow (-x, y)$ _____

b) $(x, y) \rightarrow (x - 5, y + 2)$ _____

c) $(x, y) \rightarrow \left(\frac{x}{5}, y\right)$ _____

d) $(x, y) \rightarrow (x, -4y)$ _____

e) $(x, y) \rightarrow (2x, -6y)$ _____

f) $(x, y) \rightarrow \left(\frac{x}{4} + 3, 3y - 5\right)$ _____

4. Consider the functions $f(x) = \sqrt{x}$ and $g(x) = -2\sqrt{\frac{1}{2}(x+1)} + 3$.

a) Give the rule of the transformation which enables you to obtain the graph of g from the graph of f.

_____

b) Draw the graph of g from the graph of f.

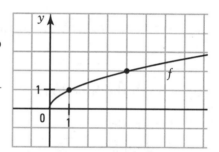

ACTIVITY 3 Graph of a square root function

Consider the function $f(x) = 6\sqrt{-\frac{1}{4}(x-1)} - 3$.

a) Identify the parameters a, b, h and k.

_____

b) Write the rule of the function in the form $f(x) = a\sqrt{-(x-h)} + k$.

_____

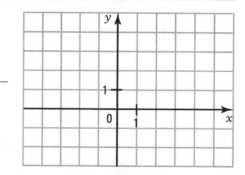

c) What are the coordinates of the vertex? _____

d) Represent the function f in the Cartesian plane after completing the following table of values.

x	-3	0	1
y			

e) What is the zero of f? _____

Activity 4 Finding the zero of a square root function

a) Consider the function with the rule: $y = -2\sqrt{3(x+1)} + 6$.

Justify the steps in finding the zero of this function.

$-2\sqrt{3(x+1)} + 6 = 0$ _____

$\sqrt{3(x+1)} = 3$ _____

$3(x+1) = 9$ _____

$x + 1 = 3$ _____

$x = 2$ _____

b) Under what conditions does the zero of a function $y = a\sqrt{b(x-h)} + k$ exist?

_____

Activity 5 Study of a square root function

Consider the function f with rule $y = -\frac{1}{2}\sqrt{4x+12} + 1$.

a) Write the rule in the form $y = a\sqrt{x-h} + k$.

_____

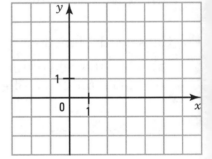

b) Graph the function f.

c) Determine

  1. dom $f =$ _____

  3. the zero of f (if it exists). _____

  5. the sign of f. _____

  6. the variation of f. _____

  7. the extrema of f. _____

  2. ran $f =$ _____

  4. the initial value of f. _____

STUDY OF A SQUARE ROOT FUNCTION

Consider the square root f with the rule:

$$f(x) = a\sqrt{b(x - h)} + k$$

We have the following four cases:

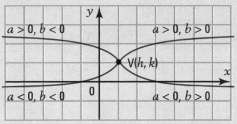

- $\text{dom}\, f = [h, +\infty[$ if $b > 0$; $\text{ran}\, f = [k, +\infty[$ if $a > 0$;
  $\text{dom}\, f =]-\infty, h]$ if $b < 0$. $\text{ran}\, f =]-\infty, k]$ if $a < 0$.
- The zero of f exists if a and k are opposite signs or if $k = 0$.
- To study the sign of f,
  - we find the zero (if it exists);
  - we establish the sign of f from a sketch of the graph.

- **Variation**
  If $ab > 0$, f is increasing over the domain.
  If $ab < 0$, f is decreasing over the domain.

- **Extrema**
  If $a > 0$, f has a minimum. $\min f = k$.
  If $a < 0$, f has a maximum. $\max f = k$.

  Ex.: Consider the function $f(x) = -2\sqrt{x + 4} + 3$ $(a = -2, b = 1, h = -4, k = 3)$.

- Vertex: $V(-4, 3)$
- $\text{dom}\, f = [-4, +\infty[;$ $\text{ran}\, f =]-\infty, 3]$.
- Zero: $-2\sqrt{x + 4} + 3 = 0$
  $$\sqrt{x + 4} = \frac{3}{2}$$
  $$x + 4 = \frac{9}{4}$$
  $$x = -\frac{7}{4}$$

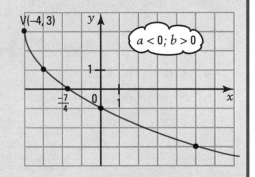

- Initial value: $y = -1$
- Sign of f: $f(x) \geq 0$ over $\left[-4, -\frac{7}{4}\right]$; $f(x) \leq 0$ over $\left[-\frac{7}{4}, +\infty\right[$.
- Variation of f: f is decreasing, $\forall\, x \in \text{dom}\, f$.
- $\max f = 3$.

5. Write the rules of the square root functions in the form $y = a\sqrt{x-h} + k$ or $y = a\sqrt{-(x-h)} + k$.

a) $y = -2\sqrt{4x+8} + 3$

b) $y = 2\sqrt{9x-36} + 4$

_____

_____

c) $y = -\frac{1}{2}\sqrt{18-9x} + 1$

d) $y = -\frac{3}{4}\sqrt{2-4x} + 7$

_____

_____

6. Represent the following square root functions in the Cartesian plane.

a) $y = -2\sqrt{x+5} + 2$

b) $y = \frac{1}{2}\sqrt{4x+8} - 3$

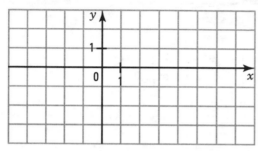

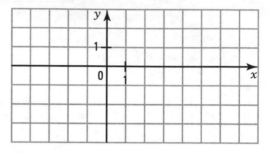

c) $y = -2\sqrt{-2(x-4)} + 3$

d) $y = \sqrt{-2(x-4)} - 2$

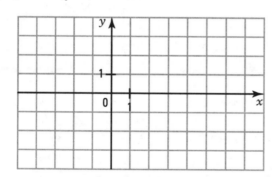

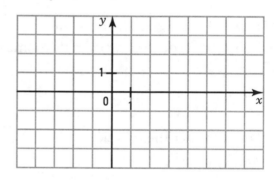

7. Consider the function $f(x) = 2\sqrt{x+4} - 2$.

a) Graph the function f.

b) Study the function f.

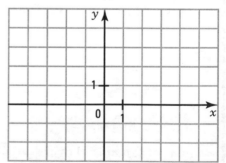

_____

_____

_____

_____

_____

c) Using the graph of f, solve the inequality

1. $f(x) \geqslant 2$ _____

2. $f(x) \leqslant 4$ _____

8. Determine the domain and range of the following functions.

a) $y = -2\sqrt{6 - 3x} + 4$

b) $y = 3\sqrt{4x + 2} - 1$

_____

_____

9. Determine the zero and initial value of the following functions.

a) $y = -3\sqrt{6 - 4x} + 9$

b) $y = 2\sqrt{4x - 1} - 1$

_____

_____

c) $y = 2\sqrt{x - 5} + 4$

d) $y = -2\sqrt{3x + 1}$

_____

_____

10. Consider the absolute value function $f(x) = -2|6 - 2x| + 8$ and the square root function $g(x) = 3\sqrt{\frac{1}{2}(x + 4)} - 5$. Determine

a) $g \circ f(4) =$ _____

b) $f \circ g(-2) =$ _____

11. Determine the interval over which each of these functions is positive.

a) $f(x) = 3\sqrt{x + 5} - 6$

b) $f(x) = -2\sqrt{6 + 4x} + 4$

_____

_____

c) $f(x) = \frac{1}{2}\sqrt{4 - x} + 5$

d) $f(x) = -3\sqrt{-2x + 8} - 1$

_____

_____

12. Solve the following inequalities.

a) $-2\sqrt{x + 3} + 2 \geqslant 0$

b) $\sqrt{3x + 4} < -1$

_____

_____

c) $5\sqrt{2 - x} > 4$

d) $\sqrt{\frac{1}{2}x + 8} > 0$

_____

_____

13. Determine the interval over which each of these functions is increasing.

a) $f(x) = 3\sqrt{-2(x - 1)} + 5$

b) $f(x) = -2\sqrt{-3(x + 4)}$

_____

_____

3.4 Square root function

14. Study each of the following functions and complete the following table.

	$f_1(x) = 3\sqrt{x-2} - 1$	$f_2(x) = -2\sqrt{\frac{1}{2}(x+4)} + 6$	$f_3(x) = \sqrt{2-x} + 1$	$f_4(x) = -2\sqrt{-x} + 4$
Domain				
Range				
Zero				
Initial value				
Sign				
Variation				
Extrema				

Activity 6 Finding the rule of a square root function

Any square root function can be written in the form $f(x) = a\sqrt{x-h} + k$ *or* $f(x) = a\sqrt{-(x-h)} + k$.

a) Consider the functions $f(x) = 3\sqrt{2x+4} - 5$ and $g(x) = 5\sqrt{-4x+8} - 1$.

Write the rule of each function in the form $y = a\sqrt{x-h} + k$ or $y = a\sqrt{-(x-h)} + k$.

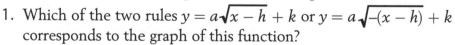

b) We consider the function represented on the right.

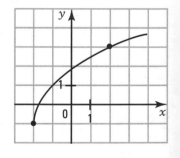

1. Which of the two rules $y = a\sqrt{x-h} + k$ or $y = a\sqrt{-(x-h)} + k$ corresponds to the graph of this function?

_____

2. Identify h and k. _____

3. Determine a knowing that the coordinates of the point P(2, 3) verify the rule of the function.

_____

_____

_____

4. What is the rule of the function? _____

c) Consider the square root function whose graph has a vertex at V(2, –1) and passes through the point P(–2, 5).

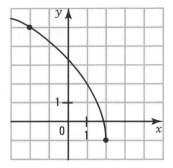

1. Which of the two rules $y = a\sqrt{x - h} + k$ or $y = a\sqrt{-(x - h)} + k$ corresponds to the graph of this function?

_____

2. Identify h and k. _____

3. Determine a knowing that the coordinates of the point P(–2, 5) verify the rule of the function.

_____

4. What is the rule of the function? _____

d) What is the domain of a square root function if its rule is of the form

1. $f(x) = a\sqrt{x - h} + k$. _____ 2. $f(x) = a\sqrt{-(x - h)} + k$. _____

FINDING THE RULE OF A SQUARE ROOT FUNCTION

Any square root function can be written, depending on its domain, in the form:

$$f(x) = a\sqrt{x - h} + k \qquad \text{or} \qquad f(x) = a\sqrt{-(x - h)} + k$$

The vertex V and a point P are given.

1. Determine the form of the rule, $y = a\sqrt{x - h} + k$ or $y = a\sqrt{-(x - h)} + k$.
2. Identify parameters h and k.
3. Determine a after replacing, in the rule, x and y by the coordinates of the point P.
4. Deduce the rule.

Ex.: **a)**

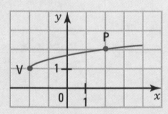

1. $y = a\sqrt{x - h} + k$

2. $y = a\sqrt{x + 2} + 1$

3. $2 = a\sqrt{2 + 2} + 1$

   $1 = 2a$

   $a = \dfrac{1}{2}$

4. rule: $y = \dfrac{1}{2}\sqrt{x + 2} + 1$

b)

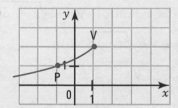

1. $y = a\sqrt{-(x - h)} + k$

2. $y = a\sqrt{-(x - 1)} + 2$

3. $1 = a\sqrt{-(-1 - 1)} + 2$

   $-1 = a\sqrt{2}$

   $a = \dfrac{-1}{\sqrt{2}} = -\dfrac{\sqrt{2}}{2}$

4. rule: $y = -\dfrac{\sqrt{2}}{2}\sqrt{-(x - 1)} + 2$

   or $y = -\dfrac{1}{2}\sqrt{-2(x - 1)} + 2$

---

15. Find the rule of each of the square root functions given its vertex V and a point P on its graph.

a) V(5, 3) and P(9, 3.5)

b) V(–2, –1) and P(–6, –4)

_____

c) V(–2, 4) and P(23, 2)

d) V(5, 3) and P(–13, 5)

_____

ACTIVITY 7 Inverse of a square root function

Consider the function $f(x) = 2\sqrt{x + 3} - 1$.

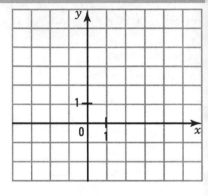

a) In the same Cartesian plane,

  1. graph the function f.
  2. deduce the graph of f^{-1}.

b) Complete: The graphs of the function f and its inverse f^{-1} are symmetrical about the _____

c) Is the inverse f^{-1} a function? Justify your answer.

_____

d) 1. Determine

  1) dom f _____ 2) ran f _____ 3) dom f^{-1} _____ 4) ran f^{-1} _____

  2. Verify that

  1) dom f^{-1} = ran f _____ 2) ran f^{-1} = dom f _____

e) Justify the steps in finding the rule of the inverse function f^{-1}.

  1. Isolate x in the equation $y = 2\sqrt{x + 3} - 1$.

$$y + 1 = 2\sqrt{x + 3}$$ _____

$$\tfrac{1}{2}(y + 1) = \sqrt{x + 3}$$ _____

$$\tfrac{1}{4}(y + 1)^2 = x + 3$$ _____

$$\tfrac{1}{4}(y + 1)^2 - 3 = x$$ _____

  2. Interchange the letters x and y to obtain the rule of the inverse.

  You get: $y = \tfrac{1}{4}(x + 1)^2 - 3$.

  3. What restriction must be set on the variable x? Justify your answer.

_____

_____

_____

_____

INVERSE OF A SQUARE ROOT FUNCTION

The inverse of a square root function is a function whose graph is a semi-parabola.

Ex.: $f(x) = 2\sqrt{x+2} - 1$ has the inverse:

$$f^{-1}(x) = \tfrac{1}{4}(x+1)^2 - 2 \qquad (x \geqslant -1)$$

Note that $\operatorname{dom} f^{-1} = \operatorname{ran} f = [-1, +\infty[$.

The graphs of f and f^{-1} are symmetrical about the bisector of the 1st quadrant.

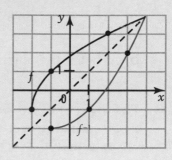

16. Determine the rule of the inverse of the following functions and indicate the domain of the inverse.

a) $y = 2\sqrt{x-1} + 7$

b) $y = -3\sqrt{x+4} - 1$

c) $y = 4\sqrt{-(x+3)} - 2$

d) $y = -2\sqrt{-(x-5)} + 4$

17. At a water park, Raphael is getting ready to go down a slide.

The function f represented on the right gives Raphael's height h (in m) as a function of elapsed time t (in s) since his departure.

At what instant will he be at a height of 4 m?

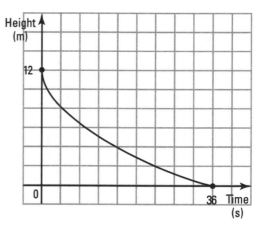

18. The lateral view of a solarium is represented by the graph on the right where the glass ceiling follows the curve of a square root function. A light is located at the centre of the room as indicated in the figure. Determine at what height the base of the light is located. (Round your answer to the nearest tenth.)

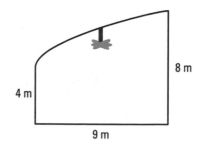

19. A company's logo is drawn using the graphs of two square root functions as illustrated in the figure on the right. The company's name is limited by two line segments.

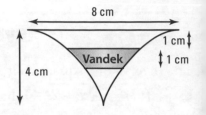

a) What is the length of the upper segment?

_____

b) What is the length of the lower segment? _____

20. The flight of a bird is observed from its takeoff at $t = 0$ from a 150 m high tower until it reaches the ground at $t = 625$ seconds.

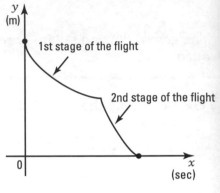

The bird's flight is described by two square root functions represented in the figure on the right.

The 1st stage of its flight lasts 400 s and is described by the rule $y = -3\sqrt{t} + 120$ where t represents the time, in seconds, and y the height of the bird, in metres.

At the instant $t = 400$ s, the bird begins the second stage of its flight.

At what height will the bird be 500 s after the beginning of its flight?

_____

3.5 Greatest integer function

a) The greatest integer of a real number x is represented by $[x]$.

   1. What is the definition of the greatest integer of a real number x?

_____

   2. Calculate

     1) $[3.76]$ _____

     2) $[-1.25]$ _____

   3. In what interval is x located if

     1) $[x] = 2$ _____

     2) $[x] = -2$ _____

b) 1. Graph the basic greatest integer function $f(x) = [x]$ in the Cartesian plane on the right.

   2. Determine

     1) dom f _____

     2) ran f _____

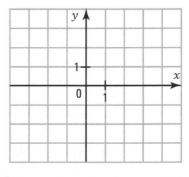

ACTIVITY 2 General greatest integer function $f(x) = a[b(x - h)] + k$

The function $f(x) = -3\left[\frac{1}{2}(x + 4)\right] + 6$ is represented on the right.

a) Identify the parameters a, b, h and k.

_____

b) Verify that

   1. each step has a length of $\dfrac{1}{|b|}$. _____

   2. The height of the counterstep is $|a|$. _____

c) Determine

   1. dom f _____

   2. ran f _____

   3. the zeros of f. _____

   4. the initial value of f. _____

   5. the sign of f. _____

   6. the variation of f. _____

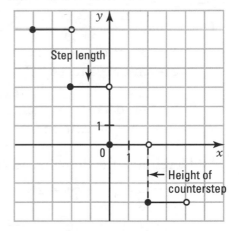

GREATEST INTEGER FUNCTION

We consider the greatest integer function $f(x) = a[b(x - h)] + k$.
- The Cartesian graph is a step function.
- Each step has a length of $\frac{1}{|b|}$.

  – If $b > 0$, the steps are closed on the left and open on the right ($\bullet\!\!-\!\!\circ$).
  – If $b < 0$, the steps are open on the left and closed on the right ($\circ\!\!-\!\!\bullet$).
- The height of the counterstep is $|a|$.
- dom $f = \mathbb{R}$, ran $f = \{y \mid y = am + k, m \in \mathbb{Z}\}$
- – If $ab > 0$, the function is increasing.
  – If $ab < 0$, the function is decreasing.
- The function f has zeros if and only if k is a multiple of a.
- The signs of a and b help us distinguish 4 cases:

$a > 0$ and $b > 0$	$a > 0$ and $b < 0$	$a < 0$ and $b > 0$	$a < 0$ and $b < 0$
	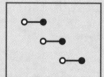	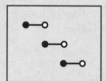	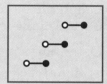

Ex.: Given the function $f(x) = 3\left[-\frac{1}{2}(x - 1)\right] + 2$.

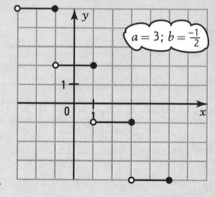

$a = 3; b = \frac{-1}{2}$

We have: $a = 3$; $b = \frac{-1}{2}$; $h = 1$ and $k = 2$.

– The length of a step is $\frac{1}{|b|} = 2$.

– The height of a counterstep is $|a| = 3$.
– dom $f = \mathbb{R}$
– ran $f = \{y \mid y = 3m + 2, m \in \mathbb{Z}\}$
– zeros of f: f has no zeros, since k is not a multiple of a.
– initial value of f: 2.
– $f(x) > 0$ if $x \leqslant 1$; $f(x) < 0$ if $x > 1$
– f is decreasing over $\mathbb{R}$ since $ab < 0$.
– f has no extrema.

1. Determine the domain and range of the following functions.

a) $y = 4\left[\frac{1}{3}(x - 5)\right] - 2$

b) $y = -2[4(x + 1)] + 4$

2. Determine the zeros of the following functions.

a) $y = 2\left[\frac{1}{4}(x + 1)\right] - 6$

b) $y = -3[2(x - 4)] - 12$

c) $y = 4[2x] + 2$

d) $y = -5[x - 8]$

3. Determine the initial value of the function $f(x) = -3\left[\frac{1}{5}(x - 9)\right] + 10$ _____

4. Determine over what interval the function $f(x) = 3\left[\frac{1}{4}(x - 1)\right] + 6$ is positive. _____

5. Determine over what interval the function $f(x) = 5[x - 3] + 1$ is strictly negative. _____

6. Determine over what interval the function $f(x) = 3\left[\frac{1}{2}(x - 7)\right] + 6$ is increasing. _____

7. Consider the functions $f(x) = 2\left[\frac{1}{4}(x - 1)\right] + 2$ and $g(x) = -3\sqrt{x + 5} + 4$.

Determine $g \circ f(7) = $ _____

8. Determine the rule of the greatest integer function represented on the right.

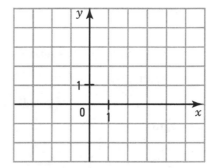

_____

_____

_____

_____

9. A salesman in a store receives a weekly base salary of $300 plus a commission of $40 for every 10 items he sells during that week.

a) Find the rule of the function which gives the salesman's salary y as a function of the number of items sold x. _____

b) What is this salesman's salary if he sold 84 items this week? _____

c) In what interval is the number of items sold if the salesman's salary is $500?

_____

d) Can this salesman earn a salary of $450? Justify your answer.

_____

10. The cost of parking in a lot is $8 for a duration of less than 30 min. Afterward, the cost increases by $4 for every 30 minutes or part thereof. The maximum cost is $20 per day.

a) What is the rule of the function which gives the cost y (in $) as a function of the parking duration x (in hours).

_____

b) Represent this situation in the Cartesian plane on the right.

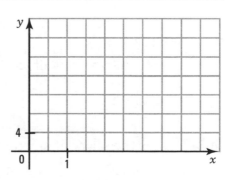

c) What is the cost for a parking duration of 1 h 40 min? _____

d) In what interval is the parking duration if the cost is $12?

_____

3.6 Piecewise function

ACTIVITY 1 Graph of a piecewise function

A function f is defined by three different rules, depending on
the interval over which x is located.
- Over the interval $]-\infty, -1]$, the function f is defined by the
  rule $f(x) = 2x + 3$.
- Over the interval $]-1, 1]$, the function f is defined by the rule
  $f(x) = -(x + 1)^2 + 1$.
- Over the interval $]1, +\infty]$, the function f is defined by the rule
  $f(x) = -3$.

a) Represent, in the Cartesian plane on the right, the function f.

b) Determine

   1. $f(-2) =$ _____ 2. $f(0) =$ _____ 3. $f(5) =$ _____

c) Find

   1. dom $f =$ _____ 2. ran $f =$ _____

d) Find

   1. the zero of f. _____ 2. the initial value of f. _____

e) Determine over what interval the function is positive. _____

f) Determine over what interval the function is

   1. strictly increasing. _____ 2. strictly decreasing. _____

   3. constant. _____

g) Does the function f have any extrema? If yes, what? _____

ACTIVITY 2 An employee's salary

The weekly salary $f(x)$ of an employee in an electronic games store
is calculated, according to the number x of games sold, using the
following rule:

$$f(x) = \begin{cases} 200 & \text{if } x < 2 \\ 50x + 200 & \text{if } 2 \leqslant x < 6 \\ 600 & \text{if } x \geqslant 6 \end{cases}$$

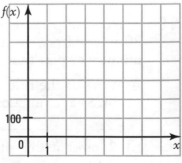

a) What is the salary of an employee who sells

   1. 2 games? _____ 2. 4 games? _____ 3. 12 games? _____

b) Determine the number of games sold by an employee whose salary is

   1. $200. _____ 2. $450. _____ 3. $600. _____

PIECEWISE FUNCTIONS

A piecewise function is a function whose rule differs depending on the interval over which the variable x is located.

Ex.: Consider the following function.

$$f(x) = \begin{cases} x - 1 & \text{if } x \leq 0 \\ x^2 & \text{if } 0 < x < 2 \\ -x + 2 & \text{if } x \geq 2 \end{cases}$$

The graph of this function is represented in the Cartesian plane on the right.
dom $f = \mathbb{R}$, ran $f =]-\infty, 4[$

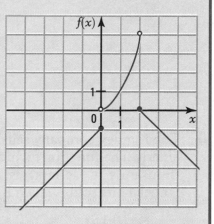

When we evaluate this function for a given value of the variable x, we find in which interval this value belongs to and we use the rule of the function defined over this interval.

Thus, $f(1.5) = (1.5)^2 = 2.25$; $f(3) = -(3) + 2 = -1$.

1. Graph the following functions.

a)
$$f_1(x) = \begin{cases} 1 & \text{if } x < -2 \\ -2x - 1 & \text{if } -1 \leq x < 1 \\ 2x - 5 & \text{if } x \geq 3 \end{cases}$$

b)
$$f_2(x) = \begin{cases} -(x+1)^2 + 2 & \text{if } -2 \leq x \leq 1 \\ \frac{1}{3}x + \frac{2}{3} & \text{if } 1 < x \leq 4 \end{cases}$$

c)
$$f_3(x) = \begin{cases} -2 & \text{if } x \leq -1 \\ x^2 & \text{if } 0 \leq x \leq 2 \\ -2x + 4 & \text{if } x > 2 \end{cases}$$

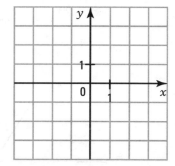
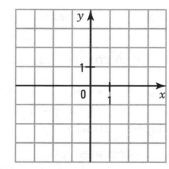
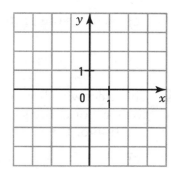

2. For each of the piecewise functions given in number 1, find

a) the domain and range.

_____

_____

_____

b) the image of 2.

_____

c) the initial value.

_____

3. Graph the following functions and determine their domain.

a)
$$f(x) = \begin{cases} x - 1 & \text{if } x \neq 2 \\ 3 & \text{if } x = 2 \end{cases}$$

b)
$$f(x) = \begin{cases} 2x + 1 & \text{if } x < -1 \\ -2 & \text{if } -1 < x < 1 \\ x^1 - 2 & \text{if } x \geq 2 \end{cases}$$

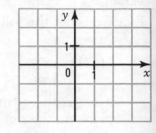

4. The Kandev company sells wheelchairs to residences for the elderly. The function f which gives the annual net profit y (in thousands of dollars) as a function of the number x of wheelchairs sold is given by the rule:

$$f(x) = \begin{cases} 0.15x & 0 \leq x \leq 1000 \\ 0.08x + 70 & 1000 < x < 3000 \\ 0.12x & 3000 \leq x \leq 4000 \end{cases}$$

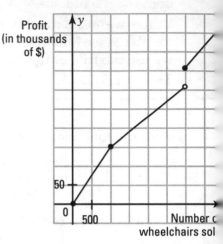

a) If the maximum number of wheelchairs sold per year is 4000, draw the graph of this function.

b) Find dom f. _____

c) What is the profit made from selling 2500 wheelchairs?

_____

d) Over what interval is the rate of change the greatest? _____

5. The piecewise function f represented on the right gives a company's accumulated profit $f(x)$ as a function of the number x of elapsed months.

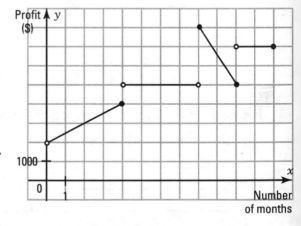

a) What is the company's accumulated profit after

1. 2 months? _____ 2. 4 months? _____
3. 6 months? _____ 4. 11 months? _____

b) Determine the number of elapsed months if the company's accumulated profit is

1. $3000. _____
2. $6500. _____

c) Determine the rule of the function f.

_____

_____

d) Over what interval is the function f

1. strictly increasing? _____
2. strictly decreasing? _____
3. constant? _____

3.7 Rational function

Consider the function f defined by the rule: $f(x) = \frac{1}{x}$.

a) What restriction must be imposed on the variable x?

_____

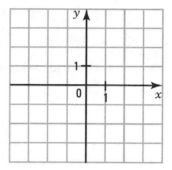

b) Complete the following table.

x	-4	-2	-1	$-\frac{1}{2}$	$-\frac{1}{4}$	0	$\frac{1}{4}$	$\frac{1}{2}$	1	2	4
$f(x)$											

c) Indicate what number the variable y approaches as
   1. the variable x takes positive values that are bigger and bigger. _____
   2. the variable x takes negative values that are smaller and smaller. _____

d) Indicate the behaviour of the variable y as
   1. the variable x takes positive values closer and closer to zero.

   _____

   2. the variable x takes negative values closer and closer to zero.

   _____

e) Graph the function in the Cartesian plane above.

f) Observe the branch of the hyperbola located in the 1st quadrant.
   1. When x takes positive values that are bigger and bigger, the branch gets closer and closer to the x-axis without ever touching it. *We say that the x-axis is a **horizontal asymptote** to the curve.* What is the equation of this asymptote? _____
   2. When x takes positive values closer and closer to zero, the branch gets closer and closer to the y-axis without ever touching it. *We say that the y-axis is a **vertical asymptote** to the curve.* What is the equation of this asymptote? _____

g) Observe the branch of the hyperbola located in the 3rd quadrant.
   1. Do we observe a horizontal asymptote? If yes, what is its equation?

   _____

   2. Do we observe a vertical asymptote? If yes, what is its equation?

   _____

The represented curve is called a **hyperbola**. This hyperbola consists of two branches. Place a random point M(x, y) on a branch and verify that the point M′($-x$, $-y$) is located on the other branch. The origin O, mid-point of the segment MM′, is therefore called the **symmetric centre** of the hyperbola.

h) Determine

1. dom $f =$ _____
2. ran $f =$ _____
3. the zero of f. _____
4. the initial value of f. _____
5. the sign of f. _____
6. the variation of f. _____
7. the extrema of f (if it exists). _____

BASIC RATIONAL FUNCTION

- Consider the rational function defined by the rule:

$$f(x) = \frac{1}{x}$$

This function is called the **basic rational function**.

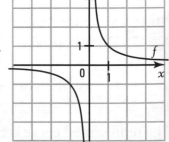

- We have:
  - dom $f = \mathbb{R}^*$, ran $f = \mathbb{R}^*$.
  - f has no zeros.
  - f is decreasing over $\mathbb{R}^*$.
  - The represented curve is called a **hyperbola**. This hyperbola consists of two branches.
  - The origin 0 is the **symmetrical centre** of the hyperbola.
  - The hyperbola has two **asymptotes**: the x-axis and the y-axis.

ACTIVITY 2 Role of the parameters a, b, h and k

The basic rational function $f(x) = \frac{1}{x}$ can be transformed into a rational function with the rule

$$g(x) = \frac{a}{b(x-h)} + k \quad \text{(standard form)}$$

a) Consider the basic rational function $f(x) = \frac{1}{x}$ and the rational function $g(x) = \frac{a}{x}$.

Represent, in the same Cartesian plane, the functions $g_1(x) = \frac{2}{x}$, $g_2(x) = \frac{0.5}{x}$ and $g_3(x) = \frac{-1}{x}$ and explain how to deduce the graph of g from the graph of f when

1. $a > 1$: _____
2. $0 < a < 1$: _____
3. $a = -1$: _____
4. Complete: From the graph of $f(x) = \frac{1}{x}$, we obtain the graph $g(x) = \frac{a}{x}$ by the transformation $(x, y) \rightarrow$ _____.

b) Consider the basic rational function $f(x) = \frac{1}{x}$ and the rational function $g(x) = \frac{1}{bx}$.

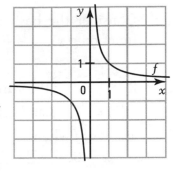

Represent, in the same Cartesian plane, the functions $g_1(x) = \frac{1}{2x}$, $g_2(x) = \frac{1}{0.5x}$ and $g_3(x) = \frac{1}{-x}$ and explain how to deduce the graph of g from the graph of f when

1. $b > 1$: _____

2. $0 < b < 1$: _____

3. $b = -1$: _____

4. Complete: From the graph of $f(x) = \frac{1}{x}$, we obtain the graph $g(x) = \frac{1}{bx}$ by the transformation $(x, y) \rightarrow$ _____.

5. Compare the graphs of f and g in each of the following cases and justify your answer.

    $f(x) = \frac{2}{x}$ and $g(x) = \frac{1}{0.5x}$: _____

    $f(x) = \frac{0.5}{x}$ and $g(x) = \frac{1}{2x}$: _____

    $f(x) = \frac{-1}{x}$ and $g(x) = \frac{1}{-x}$: _____

    _____

    _____

c) Consider the basic rational function $f(x) = \frac{1}{x}$ and the rational function $g(x) = \frac{1}{x - h}$.

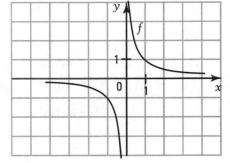

Represent, in the same Cartesian plane, the functions $g_1(x) = \frac{1}{x - 2}$, $g_2(x) = \frac{1}{x + 3}$ and explain how to deduce the graph of g from the graph of f when

1. $h > 0$: _____

2. $h < 0$: _____

3. What is the equation of the vertical asymptote of the function $g(x) = \frac{1}{x - h}$? _____

4. Complete: From the graph of $f(x) = \frac{1}{x}$, we obtain the graph $g(x) = \frac{1}{x - h}$ by the transformation $(x, y) \rightarrow$ _____.

d) Consider the basic rational function $f(x) = \frac{1}{x}$ and the rational function $g(x) = \frac{1}{x} + k$.

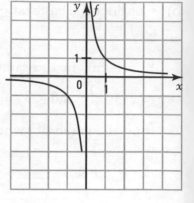

Represent, in the same Cartesian plane, the functions $g_1(x) = \frac{1}{x} + 1$, $g_2(x) = \frac{1}{x} - 3$ and explain how to deduce the graph of g from the graph of f when

1. $k > 0$: _____

2. $k < 0$: _____

3. What is the equation of the horizontal asymptote of the function $g(x) = \frac{1}{x} + k$? _____

4. Complete: From the graph of $f(x) = \frac{1}{x}$, we obtain the graph $g(x) = \frac{1}{x} + k$ by the transformation $(x, y) \rightarrow$ _____.

RATIONAL FUNCTION – STANDARD FORM

- The graph of the function

$$f(x) = \frac{a}{b(x - h)} + k$$

is deduced from the graph of the basic rational function $y = \frac{1}{x}$ by the transformation

$$(x, y) \rightarrow \left(\frac{x}{b} + h, \, ay + k \right)$$

- This hyperbola has two asymptotes, the vertical asymptote with equation $x = h$ and the horizontal asymptote with equation $y = k$.
- The point (h, k) is the symmetrical centre of the hyperbola.

Ex.: To graph the hyperbola $y = \frac{3}{2(x - 1)} + 2$,

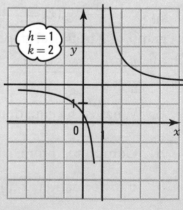

$h = 1$
$k = 2$

1. we draw the asymptotes.
   - vertical asymptote: $x = 1$.
   - horizontal asymptote: $y = 2$.
2. we complete a table of values.

x	–2	–1	0	1	2	3	4
y	1.5	1.25	0.5		3.5	2.75	2.5

3. we draw the hyperbola using the symmetrical centre (h, k).

---

1. Graph the following rational functions.

a) $f(x) = \frac{4}{x}$.

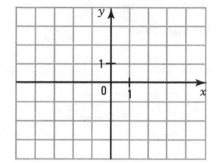

b) $f(x) = -\frac{3}{x}$.

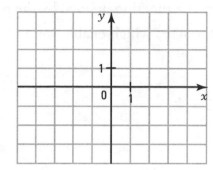

c) $f(x) = \frac{1}{x+3}$.

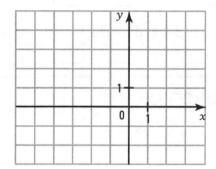

d) $f(x) = \frac{1}{x} + 2$.

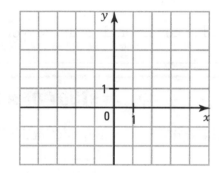

e) $f(x) = \frac{2}{x-3} + 1$.

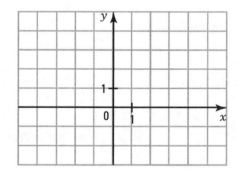

f) $f(x) = \frac{3}{-2(x+1)} + 2$.

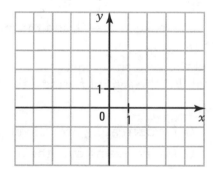

Consider the function f defined by the rule $y = \frac{3}{2(x-2)} + 1$.

a) Graph the function in the Cartesian plane on the right.

b) Determine

1. dom $f =$ _____ 2. ran $f =$ _____

3. the zero of f (if it exists). ____ 4. the initial value of f. _____

5. the sign of f. _____

6. the variation of f. _____

7. the extrema of f. _____

© Guérin, éditeur ltée

3.7 Rational function   123

ACTIVITY 4 Finding the zero of a rational function

a) Consider the function defined by the rule: $y = \dfrac{-3}{4(x-2)} + 5$.

Justify the steps which enable you to find the zero of this function.

$\dfrac{-3}{4(x-2)} + 5 = 0$ _____

$\dfrac{-3}{4(x-2)} = -5$ _____

$-20(x-2) = -3$ _____

$x - 2 = \dfrac{3}{20}$ _____

$x = \dfrac{43}{20}$ _____

b) Under what condition does the zero of a rational function defined by the rule $y = \dfrac{a}{b(x-h)} + k$ exist? _____

STUDY OF A RATIONAL FUNCTION

Consider the **rational function** f defined by the rule:

$$f(x) = \dfrac{a}{b(x-h)} + k \quad \text{(standard form)}$$

- $\text{dom } f = \mathbb{R}\backslash\{h\}$; $\text{ran } f = \mathbb{R}\backslash\{k\}$
- The **zero** of f exists if $k \neq 0$, and the initial value of f exists if $h \neq 0$.
- To study the **sign** of f,
  - we find the zero (if it exists);
  - we establish the sign of f using a sketch of the graph.

- **Variation**
  - If $ab > 0$, f is decreasing over the domain.
  - If $ab < 0$, f is increasing over the domain.
- The rational function has no **extrema**.

2. Determine the domain and range of the following functions.

a) $y = \dfrac{-2}{4(x+5)} - 7$

b) $y = \dfrac{3}{2(x-1)} + 4$

3. Determine the zero and initial value of the following functions.

a) $y = \dfrac{3}{x-5} + 4$

b) $y = \dfrac{-2}{3(x+1)}$

c) $y = \dfrac{-5}{4x} + 10$

4. Determine the interval over which the function $f(x) = \dfrac{-4}{5(x-1)} + 3$ is positive. _____

124 **Chapter 3** Real functions

5. Determine the interval over which the function $f(x) = \dfrac{3}{2(x+2)} - 1$ is strictly positive. _____

6. Study the variation of the function $f(x) = \dfrac{-2}{5(x-1)} + 4$. _____

7. Consider the functions $f(x) = -2|-x+4| + 5$, $g(x) = 3\sqrt{x-3} + 2$, $h(x) = \dfrac{6}{5(x-1)} + \dfrac{22}{5}$ and

$i(x) = 3\left|\dfrac{1}{4}(x-2)\right| + 1$. Determine $f \circ g \circ h \circ i\,(1) =$ _____

8. Given $f(x) = \dfrac{3}{2(x-4)} + 1$ and $g(x) = 3x - 1$. Determine, in standard form, the rule of the

function $f \circ g$. _____

ACTIVITY 5 Finding the rule of a rational function

Any rule of a rational function can be written in the form $y = \dfrac{a}{x-h} + k$.

a) Consider the function $y = \dfrac{-3}{6(x-2)} + 1$. Write the rule of this function in the form

$y = \dfrac{a}{x-h} + k$. _____

b) Consider a rational function whose graph passes through the point P(1, –2).

1. Identify h and k. _____

2. Determine a knowing that the coordinates of the point P(1, –2) verify the rule of the function.

We have:

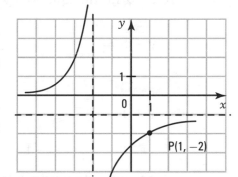

3. What is the rule of the function? _____

FINDING THE RULE OF A RATIONAL FUNCTION

Any rule of a rational function can be written in the form

$$y = \frac{a}{x-h} + k$$

The asymptotes and a point are known.

1. Identify the parameters h and k.

2. Find a after replacing, in the rule, x and y by the coordinates of the given point P.

3. Deduce the rule.

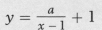

1. $h = 1$ and $k = 1$
$$y = \frac{a}{x-1} + 1$$

2. $3 = \dfrac{a}{2-1} + 1$

$a = 2$

3. $y = \dfrac{2}{x-1} + 1$

9. Find the rule of the following rational functions.

a)

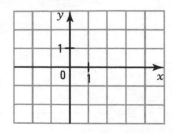

b)

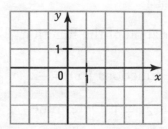

_____   _____

ACTIVITY 6 Inverse of a rational function – Standard form

a) Consider the rational function f defined by the rule: $y = \dfrac{-2}{3(x+1)} - 5$.

Justify the steps which enable you to determine the rule of the inverse function f^{-1}.

1. Isolate x in the equation $y = \dfrac{-2}{3(x+1)} - 5$

$$y + 5 = \frac{-2}{3(x+1)}$$ _____

$$3(x+1) = \frac{-2}{y+5}$$ _____

$$x + 1 = \frac{-2}{3(y+5)}$$ _____

$$x = \frac{-2}{3(y+5)} - 1$$ _____

2. Interchange the letters x and y to obtain the rule of the inverse. We get:

$$y = \frac{-2}{3(x+5)} - 1$$

b) Complete: The inverse of a rational function is a _____

c) 1. Determine

    1) dom $f =$ _____   2) ran $f =$ _____

    3) dom $f^{-1} =$ _____   4) ran $f^{-1} =$ _____

2. Verify that dom $f^{-1} =$ ran f and that ran $f^{-1} =$ dom f.

INVERSE OF A RATIONAL FUNCTION

The inverse of a rational function is a rational function.

Ex.: Given the rational function defined by the rule $y = \dfrac{-2}{3(x+1)} - 5$.

The inverse f^{-1} is a rational function defined by the rule $y = \dfrac{-2}{3(x+5)} - 1$.

(See activity 6 for finding the rule of f^{-1})

Note that $\operatorname{dom} f = \operatorname{ran} f^{-1} = \mathbb{R}\backslash\{1\}$ and that $\operatorname{ran} f = \operatorname{dom} f^{-1} = \mathbb{R}\backslash\{5\}$

10. Determine the inverse of the following rational functions.

a) $y = \dfrac{3}{x+5} - 1$ _____

b) $y = \dfrac{-1}{2(x-4)} + 3$ _____

11. A train travels a distance of 240 km. We consider the function f which gives the duration t (in h) of the trip as a function of the train's speed v (in km/h).

v (km/h)	40	60	80	120	160
t (h)					

a) Complete the table of values on the right.

b) Is the rate of change of the function f constant? _____

c) Verify that the product of the variables vt is constant. _____

We say that the duration of the trip is **inversely proportional** to the speed or that the speed is inversely proportional to the duration.

d) What is the rule of the function? _____

e) Graph the function f in the Cartesian plane.

f) Determine

1. dom f. _____ 2. ran f. _____

g) When one variable increases, does the other variable increase or decrease? _____

h) Is the function f increasing or decreasing? Justify your answer.

_____

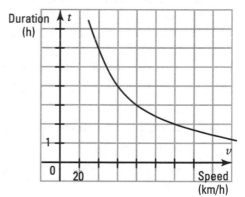

12. Renovations to a home require a total of 40 h of work for one employee. Consider the function f which gives the duration y (in h) of work per employee as a function of the number of employees x hired to do the renovations.

a) Complete the following table of values.

x	1	2	4	5	8	10
y						

b) What is the rule of function f? _____

c) Graph the function f in the Cartesian plane.

d) Is the function f increasing or decreasing? _____

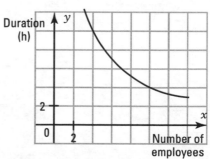

Consider the rational function defined by the rule $y = \dfrac{3}{2(x-5)} + 4$ (standard form).

a) Justify the steps which enable you to write the rule of this function in the form $y = \dfrac{ax+b}{cx+d}$.

$y = \dfrac{3}{2(x-5)} + 4 = \dfrac{3}{2(x-5)} + \dfrac{8(x-5)}{2(x-5)}$ _____

$= \dfrac{3+8(x-5)}{2(x-5)}$ _____

$= \dfrac{8x-37}{2x-10}$ _____

The form $y = \dfrac{ax+b}{cx+d}$ is called the **general form** of a rational function.

b) 1. Identify the parameters h and k of the standard form. _____

    2. Identify the parameters a, b, c and d of the general form. _____

    3. Verify that the vertical asymptote has the equation $x = -\dfrac{d}{c}$. _____

    4. Verify that the horizontal asymptote has the equation $y = \dfrac{a}{c}$. _____

c) Consider the rational function $y = \dfrac{5x-3}{2x+4}$ (general form).

To obtain the standard form from the general form $y = \dfrac{A(x)}{B(x)}$ where $A(x) = 5x - 3$ and $B(x) = 2x + 4$, we proceed in the following manner:

1° Determine the quotient $Q(x)$ and the remainder $R(x)$ from Euclidean division (i.e. long division) of $A(x)$ by $B(x)$.

$$\begin{array}{c|c} A(x) & B(x) \\ \hline R(x) & Q(x) \end{array}$$

2° From the Euclidean relation $A(x) = B(x) \cdot Q(x) + R(x)$, we deduce the standard form of the rule.

$\dfrac{A(x)}{B(x)} = Q(x) + \dfrac{R(x)}{Q(x)}$

    1. Perform the Euclidean division of $A(x) = 5x - 3$ by $B(x) = 2x + 4$ and determine the quotient $Q(x)$ and the remainder $R(x)$.

_____

    2. Deduce the standard form of the rule of the function $y = \dfrac{5x-3}{2x+4}$. _____

RATIONAL FUNCTION – GENERAL FORM

- The **general form** of a rational function is:

$$f(x) = \frac{ax+b}{cx+d}$$

- $\operatorname{dom} f = \mathbb{R} \setminus \left\{ -\frac{d}{c} \right\}$; $\operatorname{ran} f = \mathbb{R} \setminus \left\{ \frac{a}{c} \right\}$.

- Vertical asymptote: $x = -\frac{d}{c}$; horizontal asymptote: $y = \frac{a}{c}$.

Ex.: Given the rational function $f(x) = \frac{2x+3}{x-1}$.

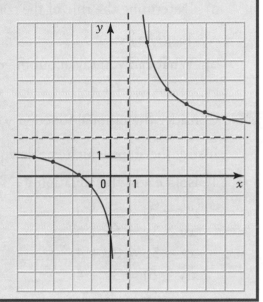

- $\operatorname{dom} f = \mathbb{R} \setminus \{1\}$; $\operatorname{ran} f = \mathbb{R} \setminus \{2\}$.
- Vertical asymptote: $x = 1$;
  horizontal asymptote: $y = 2$.
- Zero of f: $f(x) = 0 \Leftrightarrow 2x + 3 = 0 \Leftrightarrow x = -\frac{3}{2}$.
- Sign of f: $f(x) \geqslant 0 \Leftrightarrow x \in \left]-\infty, -\frac{3}{2}\right] \cup \left]1, +\infty\right[$

$$f(x) \leqslant 0 \Leftrightarrow x \in \left[-\frac{3}{2}, 1\right[.$$

- Variation of f: f is decreasing over $\mathbb{R} \setminus \{1\}$.
- f has no extrema.

---

13. Determine the domain and range of the following rational functions.

a) $y = \dfrac{3x+2}{x-5}$ b) $y = \dfrac{-2x+4}{3x-6}$ c) $y = \dfrac{5x+4}{2x-3}$

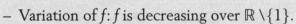

14. Determine the zero (if it exists) and the initial value (if it exists) of the following functions.

a) $y = \dfrac{3x-2}{x-4}$ b) $y = \dfrac{-5x+10}{2x-5}$ c) $y = \dfrac{-2x-6}{4x}$

15. Determine over which interval the following functions are positive.

a) $y = \dfrac{4x+2}{x-3}$ b) $y = \dfrac{-2x+8}{4x-2}$

16. Study the variation of the following functions.

a) $y = \dfrac{-4x+9}{x-3}$ b) $y = \dfrac{2x+5}{3x-2}$

17. Write the rule of the following rational functions in general form.

a) $y = \dfrac{3}{2(x-1)} + 4$ _____

b) $y = \dfrac{-2}{5(x-3)} - 1$ _____

18. Write the rule of the following rational functions in standard form.

a) $y = \dfrac{3x+2}{x-3}$

b) $y = \dfrac{4x+3}{2x-6}$

c) $y = \dfrac{-2x+5}{3x+4}$

_____   _____   _____

19. Consider the rational functions $f(x) = \dfrac{2x+3}{x-4}$ and $g(x) = \dfrac{3x+5}{x+3}$.

a) Determine the rule of the composite

    1. $g \circ f(x) =$ _____

    2. $f \circ g(x) =$ _____

b) What can you say about the composition of a rational function with a rational function?

_____

20. Consider the rational function $y = \dfrac{5x+4}{x-3}$ (general form).

Justify the steps which enable you to determine the rule of the inverse f^{-1}.

1. Isolate x in the equation $y = \dfrac{5x+4}{x-3}$.

$y(x-3) = 5x + 4$ _____

$xy - 3y = 5x + 4$ _____

$xy - 5x = 3y + 4$ _____

$x(y-5) = 3y + 4$ _____

$x = \dfrac{3y+4}{y-5}$ _____

2. Switch the letters x and y to obtain the rule of the inverse.

We get: $y = \dfrac{3x+4}{x-5}$.

21. Consider the rational function $f(x) = \dfrac{3x-2}{2x+5}$.

a) Determine the rule of the inverse f^{-1}. _____

b) Verify that

    1. $f \circ f^{-1}(x) = x$

    2. $f^{-1} \circ f(x) = x$

22. Consider the rational function $f(x) = \dfrac{-2x+3}{4x+1}$.

a) Determine the domain and range of f. _____

b) Determine the rule of the inverse f^{-1}. _____

c) Determine the domain and range of the inverse f^{-1} and verify that dom $f^{-1} =$ ran f and ran $f^{-1} =$ dom f.

_____

Evaluation 3

1. Determine the domain and range of each of the following functions.

   a) $y = -2x^2 + 4x - 9$ **b)** $y = 4|x - 5| + 8$ **c)** $y = \frac{1}{2}\sqrt{-(x - 4)} + 3$

   _____   _____   _____

   d) $y = -2\left|\frac{1}{3}(x - 5)\right| + 4$ **e)** $y = \frac{4}{3(x - 1)} + 2$ **f)** $y = -4x + 2$

   _____   _____   _____

2. Determine the zero(s) and the initial value of each of the following functions.

   a) $y = -2(x - 4)^2 + 8$ **b)** $y = 3x - 5$ **c)** $y = \frac{3}{4}\sqrt{x + 1} - 3$

   _____   _____   _____

   d) $y = 3\left|\frac{1}{2}(x - 5)\right| + 6$ **e)** $y = \frac{-2}{5(x - 1)} + 4$ **f)** $y = 3|2x - 1| - 6$

   _____   _____   _____

3. Determine over what interval each of the following functions is negative.

   a) $y = 2x^2 - 5x - 3$ **b)** $y = -7x + 63$ **c)** $y = 2|8 - x| - 12$

   _____   _____   _____

   d) $y = \frac{2}{x - 5} + 4$ **e)** $y = -2\sqrt{6 - x} + 4$ **f)** $y = -\left[\frac{x}{2}\right] - 3$

   _____   _____   _____

4. Determine over what interval each of the following functions is increasing.

   a) $y = -3(x - 5)(x + 1)$ **b)** $y = 2x - 5$ **c)** $y = -[6 - 3x] + 1$

   _____   _____   _____

   d) $y = -3\sqrt{-(x - 1)} + 4$ **e)** $y = 3|x - 5| + 2$ **f)** $y = \frac{3}{2(x - 1)} + 5$

   _____   _____   _____

5. Determine, if it exists, the extremum of each of the following functions.

   a) $y = -3x^2 + 12x - 7$ **b)** $y = -2|3 - 2x| + 5$ **c)** $y = -2\sqrt{x} + 7$

   _____   _____   _____

6. Find the rule of the inverse of each of the following functions.

   a) $y = -3x + 8$ **b)** $y = 3\sqrt{2 - x} + 4$ **c)** $y = \frac{3}{2(x - 1)} + 8$

   _____   _____   _____

7. Consider the following real functions.

$f(x) = 3x - 8$ $g(x) = 3\sqrt{2x+1} - 5$ $h(x) = -2|x-4| + 12$

$i(x) = 3(x-2)^2 + 4$ $k(x) = \dfrac{2}{x-5} + 1$ $l(x) = 3\left|\dfrac{1}{5}(x+4)\right| - 6$

Determine

a) $f \circ g(4) = $ _____   **b)** $l \circ h(3) = $ _____   **c)** $k \circ i(5) = $ _____

d) $f \circ l(0) = $ _____   **e)** $k \circ f \circ h(2) = $ _____   **f)** $l \circ h(-6) = $ _____

8. The path of a marble in a child's game can be represented by the graph in the Cartesian plane below. Initially, the marble is at a height of 7 dm from the ground.

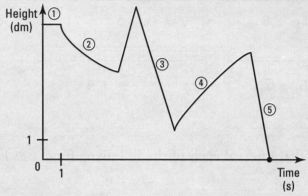

$$f(x) = \begin{cases} 7 & \text{if } 0 \leqslant x < 1 \\ \dfrac{3}{x} + 4 & \text{if } 1 \leqslant x \leqslant 4 \\ a|x-5| + 8 & \text{if } 4 \leqslant x \leqslant 7 \\ 2\sqrt{x-7} + k & \text{if } 7 \leqslant x \leqslant 11 \\ -5.5x + b & \text{if } 11 \leqslant x \leqslant t \end{cases}$$

Determine the duration t of the marble's path.

_____

_____

_____

9. Aaron is playing an electronic game. The height of a flashing dot on the screen can be modeled by a square root function f from 0 to 4 seconds and by an absolute value function g from 4 to 12 seconds as indicated by the graph on the right.

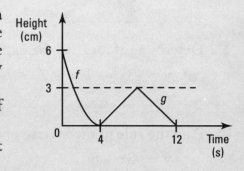

The starting point of the flashing dot is the vertex of the function f.

Determine at what times the flashing dot is at a height of 1.5 cm.

_____

_____

10. A company's logo was drawn using the graphs of three square root functions as indicated in the figure on the right.

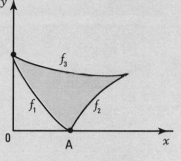

The rules of the functions f_1 and f_3 are respectively $f_1(x) = -\frac{4}{3}\sqrt{x} + 4$ and $f_3(x) = -\frac{1}{4}\sqrt{x} + 4$.

The x-coordinate of the intersection point of the functions f_2 and f_3 is 16. Knowing that point A is the vertex of the function f_2, what is the rule of the function f_2?

_____

_____

11. The value of one Kandev share fluctuated, over a one-month period, according to the rule of an absolute value function. At the opening of the market, this share was worth $3.50. Twelve days later, it reaches its maximum value of $8.

How many days go by between the moment the value of the share is worth $5 for the first time and the moment it is worth $2 on its descent?

_____

_____

12. The graph on the right illustrates a projectile's trajectory thrown from a height of 7 m. After 15 seconds, it reaches its maximum height of 40 m before descending onto the roof of an 18 m high building. The projectile bounces and, 4 seconds later, is at a height of 20 m. The first trajectory follows the model of an absolute value function and the second one follows the model of a square root function whose vertex corresponds to the point where it hits the roof of the building.

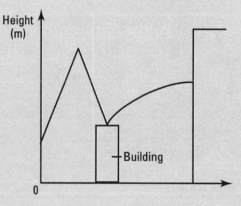

The projectile hits the wall of another building at a height of 25 m. How many seconds after the projectile was thrown does it hit the wall of the second building?

_____

_____

Chapter 4

Exponential and logarithmic functions

CHALLENGE 4

1. We are looking for the exponent x such that $2^x = 5$.

   a) Find an approximation of x, to the nearest tenth, by estimating. _____

   b) 1. What is the exact value of x? _____

   2. Use a calculator to approximate to the nearest thousandth the exact value of x.

   _____

2. A herd presently consists of 7 elephants. This herd doubles every 6 years. After how many years will this herd contain 100 elephants?

   _____

3. A $1000 capital is invested for 5 years at an annual interest rate of 10%, compounded twice per year. Determine the accumulated capital.

   _____

4. A ball bounces $\frac{3}{5}$ the height of its previous bounce. The ball is dropped from a 25 m high building. What height does the ball reach on the sixth bounce?

   _____

5. A full grocery cart for 4 people presently costs $125. If the rate of inflation remains constant at 3.6% over the next 10 years, in how many years will this cart cost $160?

   _____

6. Raphaelle pays $24 000 for a new car. Two years later, its value is evaluated at $13 500. After how many years will the car be worth $5695?

   _____

7. On January 1st 2000, a village had a population of 1500 residents. On January 1st 2007, this same village had a population of 1050 residents. If the rate of decay remains constant, in what year will the population of this village reach 800 residents?

   _____

8. The value of a house, bought for $150 000, has increased at a constant rate of 8% per year since its purchase. How long after its purchase will this house be worth more than $250 000?

   _____

4.1 Basic exponential function.

ACTIVITY 1 Exponential growth

The number of cells in a controlled environment doubles every day. Initially $(x = 0)$, we observed one million cells.

x	y
-2	
-1	
0	
1	
2	
3	

a) Complete the table of values for the function that gives the number y of cells (in millions) as a function of the number x of elapsed days since the beginning of the experiment.

b) What is the rule of this function? _____

c) How many cells are observed

   1. 5 days after the beginning? _____   2. 3 days prior to the beginning? _____

d) The number of cells grows rapidly. The growth is said to be **exponential**. At what moment do we observe

   1. 128 million cells? _____

   2. 62 500 cells? _____

ACTIVITY 2 Basic exponential function

Consider the functions $f(x) = 2^x$ and $g(x) = \left(\frac{1}{2}\right)^x$ where $x \in \mathbb{R}$.

a) Complete the corresponding table of values for each function.

1.

x	-2	-1	0	1	2	3
$y = 2^x$						

2.

x	-2	-1	0	1	2	3
$y = \left(\frac{1}{2}\right)^x$						

b) Graph each function in the Cartesian plane.

c) Complete the table below which gives the properties of these two functions.

	$f(x) = 2^x$	$f(x) = \left(\frac{1}{2}\right)^x$
Dom f		
Ran f		
Zero		
Initial value		
$f \geq 0$ over		
$f < 0$ over		
$f \nearrow$ over		
$f \searrow$ over		
Extrema		

We observe that each of the curves representing these functions gets closer and closer to the x axis without ever touching it.

*We say that the x-axis is an **asymptote** to the curve or that the curve is asymptotic to the x-axis.*

EXPONENTIAL FUNCTION $f(x) = c^x$

- The function $f(x) = c^x$, where c is a positive real number different from 1, is called the basic exponential function in **base c**.

  This function describes situations of **exponential growth** or **decay**, depending on the base being greater or less than 1.

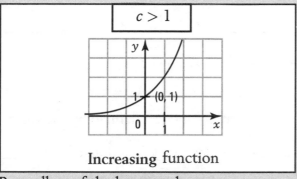

| $c > 1$ |
Increasing function

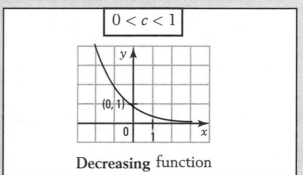

| $0 < c < 1$ |
Decreasing function

- Regardless of the base, we have:
  - dom $f = \mathbb{R}$ and ran $f = \mathbb{R}_+^*$.
  - The initial value is equal to 1 ($c^0 = 1$).
  - The function has no zero.
  - The function is positive over $\mathbb{R}$.
  - The x-axis is an **asymptote** to the curve.

- When the independent variable x increases by 1 unit, the dependent variable y is multiplied by the **multiplicative factor c** (basic exponential function) called **periodic multiplicative factor**.

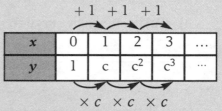

x	0	1	2	3	...
y	1	c	c^2	c^3	...

$\times c \quad \times c \quad \times c$

- The most common bases of the exponential function are the numbers 10 and e.

  e is an **irrational** number occurring in phenomena related to physics, biology, probability, ...

  $$e = 2.71828...$$

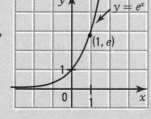

1. Given the exponential function $f(x) = c^x$. Explain why

  a) the base c is different from 1. _____

  _____

  b) the base c is different from 0. _____

  c) the base c cannot be negative. _____

2. For each of the following exponential functions,

    1. determine the base.   2. indicate if the function is increasing or decreasing.

    a) $f(x) = \left(\frac{4}{3}\right)^x$ _____

    b) $f(x) = \left(\frac{4}{5}\right)^x$ _____

    c) $f(x) = 2^{-x}$ _____

    d) $f(x) = \left(\frac{2}{3}\right)^{-x}$ _____

    e) $f(x) = 3^{2x}$ _____

    f) $f(x) = \left(\frac{9}{4}\right)^{-\frac{x}{2}}$ _____

3. In each of the following cases, the point A belongs to the graph of an exponential function defined by the rule $y = c^x$. Determine the rule of each function.

    a) $A(2, 9)$ _____

    b) $A\left(\frac{1}{2}, 2\right)$ _____

    c) $A\left(-\frac{1}{2}, \frac{3}{2}\right)$ _____

    d) $A\left(-\frac{1}{3}, \frac{1}{2}\right)$ _____

    e) $A\left(-\frac{1}{2}, \frac{5}{4}\right)$ _____

    f) $A\left(-\frac{3}{2}, \frac{8}{27}\right)$ _____

4. The point $A\left(-\frac{1}{2}, \frac{2}{3}\right)$ belongs to the graph of an exponential function defined by the rule $y = c^x$.

    a) A point B on this graph has an x-coordinate of -2. What is its y-coordinate? _____

    b) A point C on this graph has a y-coordinate of $\frac{4}{9}$. What is its x-coordinate? _____

5. On the right, we have represented the exponential functions defined by the rules:

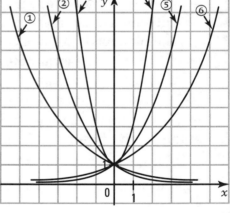

$$y = 2^x, y = \left(\frac{3}{2}\right)^x, y = 3^x, y = \left(\frac{1}{2}\right)^x, y = \left(\frac{2}{3}\right)^x, y = \left(\frac{1}{3}\right)^x.$$

    a) Associate each curve to its equation.

      1. _____   2. _____   3. _____

      4. _____   5. _____   6. _____

    b) Of the three increasing exponential functions, which one increases the fastest? Justify your answer.

    _____

    c) Of the three decreasing exponential functions, which one decreases the fastest? Justify your answer.

    _____

6. The functions $f(x) = 2^x$ and $g(x) = \left(\frac{1}{2}\right)^x$ are represented on the right.

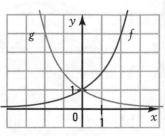

    a) Verify that $f(2) = g(-2)$. _____

    b) 1. Show that $f(x) = g(-x)$ for any real number x.

    _____

      2. What can be deduced from the curves of the exponential functions representing the functions f and g?

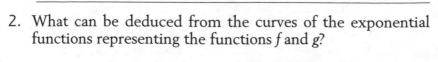

    _____

4.2 Exponential function

ACTIVITY 1 **Exponential function $f(x) = ac^x$ – Role of parameter a**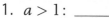

a) Consider the basic exponential function $f(x) = 2^x$ and the transformed exponential function $g(x) = a(2)^x$.

Represent, in the same Cartesian plane, the functions $g_1(x) = 2(2)^x$, $g_2(x) = \frac{1}{2}(2)^x$ and $g_3(x) = -2^x$ and explain how to deduce the graph of $g(x)$ from the graph of $f(x)$ when

1. $a > 1$: _____

2. $0 < a < 1$: _____

3. $a = -1$: _____

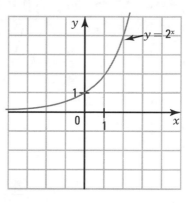

b) From the graph of $y = 2^x$, we get the graph of $y = a(2)^x$ by the transformation
$(x, y) \rightarrow$ _____ .

c) The accumulated value $c(t)$ after t years of an invested capital a at an interest rate i compounded annually is calculated using the rule:

$$\boxed{c(t) = a\,(1 + i)^t}$$

A capital of \$1000 is invested in a bank at an interest rate of 8% compounded annually.

1. Complete the table of values which associates the number t of years to the accumulated capital $c(t)$.

2. What is the rule of this exponential function? _____

3. What is the base of the exponential function? _____

4. Determine and interpret the role of the parameter a.

x	y
0	1000
1	1080
2	
3	
⋮	

EXPONENTIAL FUNCTION $f(x) = ac^x$ – ROLE OF PARAMETER a

- The exponential curve undergoes a **vertical stretch** when the absolute value of parameter a increases.
- The parameter a corresponds to the initial value of the function.

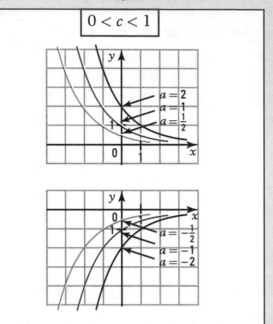

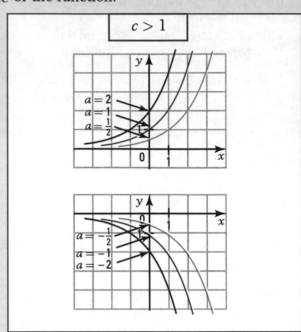

- The horizontal scale change $(x, y) \rightarrow (x, ay)$ transforms the graph of $y = c^x$ into a graph defined by the rule $y = ac^x$.

1. Consider the function $f(x) = ac^x$.

a) What is the domain of f? _____

b) What is the range of f when

1. $a > 0$? _____   2. $a < 0$? _____

c) Does the function f have a zero? _____

d) Does the function f have an asymptote? If yes, what is the equation of the asymptote?

_____

e) Indicate if the function is increasing or decreasing when

1. $a > 0$ and $c > 1$. _____   2. $a > 0$ and $0 < c < 1$. _____

3. $a < 0$ and $c > 1$. _____   4. $a < 0$ and $0 < c < 1$. _____

2. For each of the following functions, indicate if
1. the function is positive or negative.
2. the function is increasing or decreasing.

a) $y = -3\left(\frac{1}{4}\right)^x$ **b)** $y = 2\left(\frac{3}{2}\right)^x$ **c)** $y = -\frac{1}{4}(2)^x$ **d)** $y = 10\left(\frac{1}{2}\right)^x$

1. _____   1. _____   1. _____   1. _____

2. _____   2. _____   2. _____   2. _____

e) $y = 2(3)^{-x}$

1. _____

2. _____

f) $y = -2(5)^{-x}$

1. _____

2. _____

g) $y = \left(\frac{1}{3}\right)^{-x}$

1. _____

2. _____

h) $y = -\left(\frac{3}{2}\right)^{-x}$

1. _____

2. _____

3. Julie invests an amount of $1000 in a bank at an interest rate of 8% compounded annually. The capital, $C(t)$, accumulated after t months, is given by $C(t) = 1000(1.08)^t$. What is the accumulated capital after

a) 3 years? _____

b) 5 years? _____

4. A radioactive substance disintegrates over time. Its mass m (in grams) is expressed as a function of time t (in years) by the equation $m = 10(0.8)^t$. What is the mass of this substance

a) today $(t = 0)$? _____

b) in 2 years? _____

c) one year ago? _____

5. The value $v(t)$ of a car that depreciates by 20% per year is given by $v(t) = v_0(0.80)^t$ where v_0 represents the initial value of the car and t represents the number of years since its purchase.

a) What is the value of a new car 3 years after its purchase if it was bought for $30 000?

_____

b) How much did you pay for a car now worth $22 400 two years after its purchase? _____

ACTIVITY 2 Exponential function $f(x) = c^{bx}$ — Role of parameter b

a) Consider the basic exponential function $f(x) = 2^x$ and the transformed exponential function $g(x) = 2^{bx}$.

Represent, in the same Cartesian plane, the functions $g_1(x) = 2^{2x}$, $g_2(x) = 2^{\frac{1}{2}x}$ and $g_3(x) = 2^{-x}$ and explain how to deduce the graph of $g(x)$ from the graph of $f(x)$ when

1. $b > 1$: _____

2. $0 < b < 1$: _____

3. $b = -1$: _____

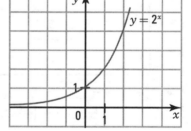

b) From the graph of $y = 2^x$, we get the graph of $y = 2^{bx}$ by the transformation $(x, y) \rightarrow$ _____.

c) The graph of the exponential function $y = 2^x$ is represented on the right.

1. Draw the graph of the function $y = \left(\frac{1}{2}\right)^x$.

2. Compare the graph of the function $y = \left(\frac{1}{2}\right)^x$ and that of the function $y = 2^{-x}$, found in a).

Justify algebraically. _____

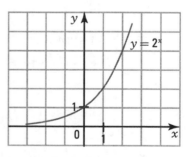

d) The value $c(t)$ of a capital a accumulated after t years invested at an interest rate i compounded n times per year is calculated according to the rule:

$$c(t) = a\left(1 + \frac{i}{n}\right)^{nt}$$

1. We invest \$1 at an interest rate of 12% compounded monthly. Establish the rule of the exponential function which gives the accumulated capital $c(t)$. _____

2. What is the base of the exponential function? _____

3. Determine and interpret the role of parameter b. _____

_____

EXPONENTIAL FUNCTION $f(x) = c^{bx}$ – ROLE OF PARAMETER b

- When we increase parameter b, the exponential curve undergoes a **horizontal reduction** regardless of its base.

- If x represents elapsed time, the parameter b corresponds to the number of periods per unit of time.

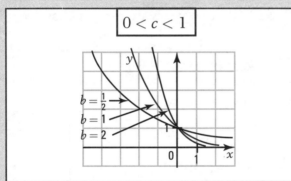
$0 < c < 1$

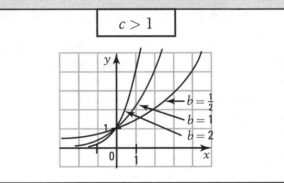
$c > 1$

- The vertical scale change $(x, y) \rightarrow \left(\frac{x}{b}, y\right)$ transforms the graph of $y = c^x$ into a graph defined by the rule $y = c^{bx}$.

6. Consider the following exponential functions:

$$f_1(x) = \left(\frac{1}{2}\right)^x, f_2(x) = 2\left(\frac{1}{2}\right)^x, f_3(x) = 2\left(\frac{1}{2}\right)^{\frac{x}{2}}$$

a) What geometric transformation applies

1. the graph of f_1 onto the graph of f_2?

_____

2. the graph of f_2 onto the graph of f_3?

_____

b) Using the geometric transformations established in a), draw the graphs of the functions f_2 and f_3.

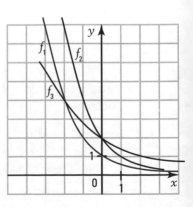

7. a) Among the four functions represented on the right, identify

1. $y = e^x$ _____
2. $y = -e^x$ _____
3. $y = e^{-x}$ _____
4. $y = -e^{-x}$ _____

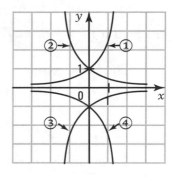

b) Complete the table below.

	$y = e^x$	$y = -e^x$	$y = e^{-x}$	$y = -e^{-x}$
Domain				
Range				
Sign				
Variation				

8. The number of bacteria, in a controlled environment, doubles on average every 15 minutes. Initially, this environment contains one thousand cells. Consider the function which gives the number $N(t)$ of cells as a function of the number t of hours elapsed since the beginning.

t	$N(t)$
0	
0.25	
0.50	
0.75	
1	
2	

a) Complete the table of values on the right.

b) What is the rule of the function? _____

c) What is the number of cells after 3 hours? _____

d) After how many hours does this environment contain 1024 thousand cells? _____

9. Mr. Desmond invests $30 000 in a bank that offers a 4.2% annual interest rate. Using the formula given in activity 4, determine the accumulated amount Mr. Desmond receives after 5 years if the interest is compounded

a) annually. _____

b) every 3 months. _____

c) every 4 months. _____

d) every 6 months. _____

e) monthly. _____

10. At the birth of his son Raphael, Alex invests $2000 in an education savings bond. This account's annual interest of 3.7% is compounded monthly. What will be the accumulated value of this bond when Raphael turns 20 years old?

_____

4.2 Exponential function

Activity 3 Exponential function $f(x) = c^{x-h} + k$ — Role of parameters h and k

a) The basic exponential function $y = 2^x$ is represented on the right..

1. Explain how to deduce the graph of
   1) $y = 2^{x-3}$ _____
   2) $y = 2^{x+1}$ _____

2. By applying the role of parameter h to the critical points $\left(-1, \frac{1}{2}\right)$,
   $(0, 1)$ and $(1, 2)$ of the basic function, graph the functions
   1) $y = 2^{x-3}$ 2) $y = 2^{x+1}$

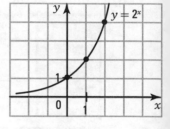

b) The basic exponential function $y = 2^x$ is represented on the right..

1. Explain how to deduce the graph of
   1) $y = 2^x - 3$ _____
   2) $y = 2^x + 1$ _____

2. By applying the role of parameter k to the critical points $\left(-1, \frac{1}{2}\right)$,
   $(0, 1)$ and $(1, 2)$ of the basic function, graph the functions
   1) $y = 2^x - 3$ 2) $y = 2^x + 1$

3. Determine the equation of the asymptote of the function
   1) $y = 2^x - 3$ _____   2) $y = 2^x + 1$ _____

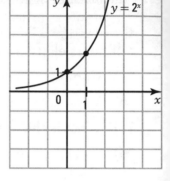

c) The basic exponential function $y = 2^x$ and the transformed exponential function $y = 2^{x-3} - 2$ are represented on the right.

Complete: The graph of the function $y = 2^{x-3} - 2$ is obtained from the graph of the function $y = 2^x$ by _____
_____
_____

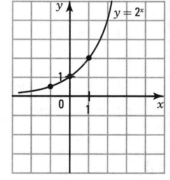

ACTIVITY 4 Exponential function $f(x) = ac^{b(x-h)} + k$

The basic exponential function $y = c^x$ can be transformed into an exponential function of the form $f(x) = ac^{b(x-h)} + k$.

Consider the exponential function $y = \left(\frac{1}{2}\right)^x$ and the exponential function $y = 3\left(\frac{1}{2}\right)^{2(x-1)} - 3$, each with the same base $\frac{1}{2}$.

a) Identify the parameters a, b, h and k. _____

b) The introduction of the parameters a, b, h and k in the rule of the basic exponential function causes a series of transformations to the graph. Complete the description of this process.

1. From the graph $y = \left(\frac{1}{2}\right)^x$, we obtain the graph of $y = 3\left(\frac{1}{2}\right)^x$

   by the transformation $(x, y) \to$ _____
   The parameter a causes _____

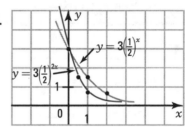

2. From the graph $y = 3\left(\frac{1}{2}\right)^x$, we obtain the graph of $y = 3\left(\frac{1}{2}\right)^{2x}$

   by the transformation $(x, y) \to$ _____
   The parameter b causes _____

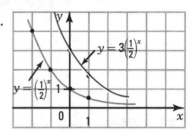

3. From the graph $y = 3\left(\frac{1}{2}\right)^{2x}$, we obtain the graph of

   $y = 3\left(\frac{1}{2}\right)^{2(x-1)}$ by the transformation $(x, y) \to$ _____
   The parameter h causes _____
   _____

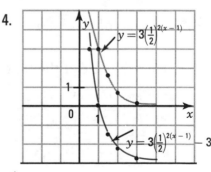

4. From the graph $y = 3\left(\frac{1}{2}\right)^{2(x-1)}$, we obtain the graph of

   $y = 3\left(\frac{1}{2}\right)^{2(x-1)} - 3$ by the transformation $(x, y) \to$ _____
   The parameter k causes _____
   _____

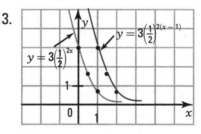

c) What does the line $y = -3$ represent for the function $y = 3\left(\frac{1}{2}\right)^{2(x-1)} - 3$?

_____

_____

d) Verify, using the tables of values, that the transformation $(x,y) \rightarrow \left[\frac{x}{b} + h, ay + k\right]$ directly applies the graph of $y = \left(\frac{1}{2}\right)^x$ onto the graph of $y = 3\left(\frac{1}{2}\right)^{2(x-1)} - 3$.

$$y = \left(\frac{1}{2}\right)^x \qquad y = 3\left(\frac{1}{2}\right)^{2(x-1)} - 3$$

x	y
−1	2
0	1
1	$\frac{1}{2}$

x	y
$\frac{1}{2}$	3
1	0
$\frac{3}{2}$	$-\frac{3}{2}$

_____

_____

_____

EXPONENTIAL FUNCTION $f(x) = ac^{b(x-h)} + k$

- The graph of the function $f(x) = ac^{b(x-h)} + k$ is deduced from the graph of the basic exponential function $y = c^x$ by the transformation

$$(x, y) \rightarrow \left[\frac{x}{b} + h, ay + k\right]$$

- The exponential function $f(x) = ac^{b(x-h)} + k$ has the horizontal line $y = k$ as an asymptote.
Ex.: See activity 4.

---

11. The following functions have a rule of the form $f(x) = a(2)^{b(x-h)} + k$.

$$f_1(x) = 3(2)^x; \quad f_2(x) = 2^{3x}; \quad f_3(x) = 2^{x+3}; \quad f_4(x) = 2^x + 3; \quad f_5(x) = -3(2)^{\frac{1}{2}(x+4)} - 5;$$

Complete the table on the right by determining, for each function, the parameters a, b, h and k and by giving the rule of the transformation which enables you to obtain the graph of the function from the graph of the basic function $f(x) = 2^x$.

	a	b	h	k	Rule
f_1					$(x, y) \rightarrow$
f_2					$(x, y) \rightarrow$
f_3					$(x, y) \rightarrow$
f_4					$(x, y) \rightarrow$
f_5					$(x, y) \rightarrow$

12. In each of the following cases, a transformation is applied to the basic exponential function $y = 5^x$.

Find the rule of the function whose graph is obtained by the following transformations.

a) $(x, y) \rightarrow (x, -y)$ _____

b) $(x, y) \rightarrow (x - 2, y - 3)$ _____

c) $(x, y) \rightarrow \left(\frac{x}{2}, y\right)$ _____

d) $(x, y) \rightarrow (2x, y)$ _____

e) $(x, y) \rightarrow (3x, -2y)$ _____

f) $(x, y) \rightarrow \left[\frac{x}{3} + 1, 2y - 1\right]$ _____

13. Write the rules of the following exponential functions in the form $y = ac^{b(x-h)} + k$.

a) $y = 2^{3x-6}$ _____

b) $y = 5^{-2x+6} + 1$ _____

c) $y = 5(3)^{2x+1}$ _____

d) $y = 3\left(\frac{1}{2}\right)^{4-2x} - 5$ _____

ACTIVITY 5 Exponential equation – Form $c^u = c^v$

a) Justify the steps in solving the equation $3(2)^{4x} = 768$.

$$3(2)^{4x} = 768$$
$$\Leftrightarrow \quad 2^{4x} = 256 \quad \rule{8cm}{0.4pt}$$
$$\Leftrightarrow \quad 2^{4x} = 2^8 \quad \rule{8cm}{0.4pt}$$
$$\Leftrightarrow \quad 4x = 8 \quad \rule{8cm}{0.4pt}$$
$$\Leftrightarrow \quad x = 2 \quad \rule{8cm}{0.4pt}$$

b) The number $P(t)$ of bacteria in a controlled environment is given by $P(t) = 100(2)^{3t}$ where t represents the number of elapsed days since the beginning.
How many days after the beginning do we observe 6400 cells?

EXPONENTIAL EQUATION – FORM $c^u = c^v$

When both sides of an exponential equation can be written as powers of the same base, we use the logical equivalence:

$$\boxed{c^u = c^v \Leftrightarrow u = v}$$

1. Isolate the power containing the unknown on one side.	**Ex.:** $5(2)^{3x} = 320$
2. Write the equation as powers of the same base.	$2^{3x} = 64$
3. Make the exponents equal.	$2^{3x} = 2^6$
4. Determine the value of the unknown.	$3x = 6$
5. Establish the solution set S.	$x = 2$
	Thus, S $= \{2\}$.

14. Solve the following exponential equations.

a) $3^x = 243$

b) $2^x = \dfrac{1}{8}$

c) $2(5)^x = 250$

d) $5^{2x} - 1 = 0$

e) $2(5)^x - 48 = 2$

f) $9^x - 27 = 0$

g) $3(4)^x - 96 = 0$

h) $\dfrac{1}{2}(8)^x - 16 = 0$

i) $27\left(\dfrac{4}{9}\right)^x - 8 = 0$

15. Determine the zero, if it exists, of the following exponential functions.

a) $y = 5(3)^{x-2} - 15$

b) $y = 2(3)^{-(x+2)} - 18$

c) $y = -3\left(\frac{1}{2}\right)^{-2(x+3)} + 12$

d) $y = -5\left(\frac{1}{5}\right)^{x-1} + 4$

e) $y = -4\left(\frac{2}{3}\right)^{x-1} + 9$

f) $y = 3\left(\frac{2}{5}\right)^{-2(x+1)} + \frac{12}{25}$

16. Solve the following exponential equations.

a) $2^{3x} \cdot 2^{2x} = \frac{1}{4}$

b) $\frac{3^x}{3^{2x}} = 27$

c) $\left(\frac{1}{2}\right)^x = 16$

d) $2^x \cdot 2^x = 64$

e) $(2^x)^2 = 16(2)^x$

f) $2^{x^2} = 16$

17. The growth of a herd of bison follows the rule $P(t) = P_0 \times 2^{\frac{t}{10}}$ where P_0 represents the initial population and $P(t)$ the population after t years. In how many years will the bison population quadruple its initial population?

18. A mosquito population doubles every seven days. If there were 5 mosquitoes initially, after how many days will the population contain 80 mosquitoes?

19. A 100 g radioactive mass disintegrates according to the rule $m(t) = 100\left(\frac{1}{2}\right)^{\frac{t}{4}}$ where $m(t)$ is the resulting mass after t hours.

a) Determine after how many hours the resulting mass is equal to 25 g. _____

b) We call the **half-life** of a radioactive substance the time necessary for its mass to be reduced by half by disintegration. What is the half-life of this mass? _____

ACTIVITY 6 Sketch of the graph and study of an exponential function

To sketch the graph of the function $f(x) = ac^{b(x-h)} + k$,
1. we draw the horizontal asymptote defined by the equation $y = k$.
2. we locate, using the rule, 2 points on the exponential curve.
3. we sketch the exponential curve.

a) Sketch the graphs of the following functions.

1. $f_1(x) = 2\left(\frac{1}{2}\right)^{2(x-1)} - 2$

2. $f_2(x) = -\frac{1}{4}(2)^{x+1} + 1$

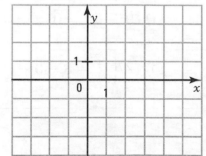

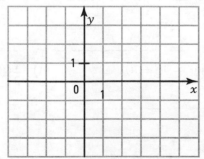

3. $f_3(x) = 2\left(\dfrac{1}{2}\right)^{2(x+1)} + 1$

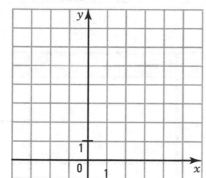

4. $f_4(x) = 3^{x-1} + 1$

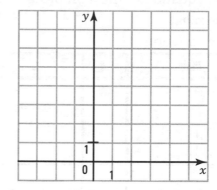

b) Find the zero, when it exists, of the preceding functions.

1. f_1: _____ 2. f_2: _____ 3. f_3: _____ 4. f_4: _____

c) Do a study of each of the preceding functions and complete the following table.

	a	b	h	k	Asymptote	Domain	Range	Zero	Sign	Variation
f_1										
f_2										
f_3										
f_4										

d) Verify that, for any exponential function, $f(x) = ac^{b(x-h)} + k$,
1. $\mathrm{dom}f = \mathbb{R}$ 2. the asymptote is the line $y = k$.
3. $\mathrm{ran}f =]k, +\infty[$ if $a > 0$ and $\mathrm{ran}f =]-\infty, k[$ if $a < 0$.
4. the zero of f exists if a and k are opposite signs.

STUDY OF AN EXPONENTIAL FUNCTION

- To sketch the graph of an exponential function,
  1. we draw the horizontal asymptote.
  2. we locate, using the rule, two points on the exponential curve.
  3. we sketch the exponential curve.
- We study an exponential function from the sketch of the graph. We have:
  – $\mathrm{dom}f = \mathbb{R}$.
  – $\mathrm{ran}f =]k, +\infty[$ if $a > 0$ and $\mathrm{ran}f =]-\infty, k[$ if $a < 0$.
  – The zero of f exists if a and k are opposite signs.
  – The sign of f is determined from the graph.
  – The variation of f is determined from the graph.
  – The function f has no extrema.
  Ex.: See activity 6.

20. For each of the following exponential functions, determine
   1. the equation of the asymptote.   2. a sketch of the graph.   3. the domain.
   4. the range.   5. the zero.   6. the sign.
   7. the variation.

Rule	1	2	3	4	5	6	7
$f_1(x) = 2^{x-1} - 4$							
$f_2(x) = 4\left(\frac{1}{2}\right)^{x+1} + 1$							
$f_3(x) = -2^{-(x-1)} - 1$							
$f_4(x) = 2^{-(x-1)} - 4$							

21. Consider the function $f(x) = 2(4)^{\frac{1}{2}(x-2)} - 2$.

   a) Represent the function f in the Cartesian plane using the table of values.

x	–2	–1	0	1	2	3	4
y							

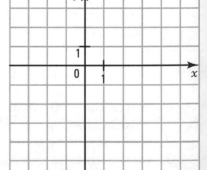

   b) Determine
   1. dom f _____   2. ran f _____   3. the zero of f _____
   4. the sign of f. _____
   5. the variation of f. _____   6. the equation of the asymptote. _____

22. Consider the function $f(x) = -2\left(\frac{1}{4}\right)^{-\frac{1}{2}(x-1)} + 2$.

   a) Represent the function f in the Cartesian plane using the table of values.

x	–3	–2	–1	0	1	2	3
y							

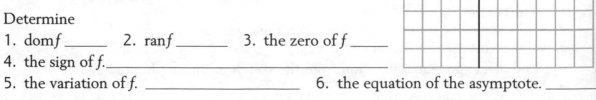

   b) Determine
   1. dom f _____   2. ran f _____   3. the zero of f _____
   4. the sign of f. _____
   5. the variation of f. _____   6. the equation of the asymptote. _____

23. Study the sign of the following exponential functions.

   a) $f(x) = \left(\frac{1}{2}\right)^{x+2} - 4$ **b)** $f(x) = -3(2)^{x-1} + 12$ **c)** $f(x) = -2(3)^{-2(x+1)} + 18$

   _____   _____   _____

   _____   _____   _____

24. Solve the following exponential inequalities.

    a) $-2^{x-2} + 8 \geq 0$ **b)** $6(3)^{x-2} - 2 > 0$ **c)** $3(2)^{\frac{1}{2}(x+1)} - 12 \leq 0$

_____   _____   _____

25. What is the range of the function $f(x) = -5(3)^{2(x-1)} + 10$? _____

26. Determine the initial value of $f(x) = -3(4)^{\frac{1}{2}(x+1)} + 10$. _____

27. Study the variation of the following functions.

    a) $f(x) = -2^{x-1} + 4$ **b)** $f(x) = -2\left(\frac{1}{3}\right)^{x+1} + 6$

_____   _____

ACTIVITY 7   Rule of an exponential function: $f(x) = ac^{bx}$

a) In a reforestation project, a company decides to double the number of trees it plants each year. Initially, the forest contained 25 trees.

    1. Find the rule of the function which gives the number y of trees in the forest as a function of the number x of elapsed years. _____

    2. How many trees will there be after 7 years? _____

b) A controlled environment contains 3 bacteria initially. The number of bacteria doubles every 15 minutes. We are trying to find the rule of the exponential function which gives the number y of bacteria as a function of the elapsed time in hours. The form of the rule is: $y = ac^{bx}$.

    1. Complete the table of values on the right.

    2. The initial value of the function represented by a is the value of y at the beginning $(x = 0)$. What is the initial value a? _____

    3. The number of bacteria doubles every 15 minutes. What is the multiplicative factor c? _____

    4. Since the elapsed time x is in hours, the parameter b represents the number of 15-minute periods per hour.

        1) What is the value of parameter b? _____

        2) What is the rule of the function in this situation? _____

    5. What would the rule be if the bacteria doubles

        1) every twenty minutes? _____   2) every two hours? _____

x	y
0	
$\frac{1}{4}$	
$\frac{1}{2}$	
$\frac{3}{4}$	
1	
2	

28. The tables of values below correspond to an exponential function with a rule of the form $y = ac^x$. Find the rule of each function.

a)

x	0	1
y	$\frac{1}{2}$	$\frac{3}{2}$

b)

x	0	−1
y	2	8

c)

x	0	2
y	−3	−12

d)

x	0	−2
y	−4	−9

29. Each of the following situations is described by an exponential function of the form $y = ac^{bx}$. After establishing the unit of time,

1. define the variables x and y. 2. determine the parameters a, b and c. 3. find the rule of the function.

a) In a controlled environment containing 1000 bacteria initially, the number of bacteria triples every 10 minutes.

b) In an environment initially containing 100 insects, the number of insects doubles every 3 days.

c) A car bought for $30 000 loses 20% of its value every year.

d) An initial population of 1000 deer increases by 15% each year.

e) A radioactive mass of 50 g loses half of its mass each period of 6 hours starting at noon.

_____

_____

f) An initial population of 100 birds increases by 15% every 2 years.

_____

_____

30. A capital c_0 is invested at a fixed annual interest rate i compounded n times per year. The accumulated capital $c(t)$ after t years is given by the formula

$$c(t) = c_0\left(1 + \frac{i}{n}\right)^{nt}.$$

a) Establish the rule of the function $c(t)$ that gives the accumulated capital of $1000 invested at a 6% interest rate compounded

1. annually. _____ 2. every 6 months. _____

3. each month. _____ 4. each day. _____

b) Calculate the accumulated capital after 5 years in each of the preceding cases.

1. _____ 2. _____ 3. _____ 4. _____

ACTIVITY 8 Finding the rule of an exponential function

a) Consider the exponential functions $f(x) = a(c)^{bx}$ and $g(x) = a(c^b)^x$.
1. Identify
    1) the base of f. _____ 2) the base of g. _____
2. Explain why the functions f and g have the same rule.

    _____

b) Consider the exponential functions $f(x) = ac^{x-h}$ and $g(x) = Ac^x$.
Determine A for which the functions f and g have the same rule.

_____

c) Write each of the following rules in the form $y = ac^x + k$.
1. $y = 5(2)^{3x} + 1$ _____
2. $y = 3(2)^{x+2} + 5$ _____
3. $y = 2(3)^{2x+1} - 4$ _____

Therefore, every exponential function can be represented by a rule of the form $y = ac^x + k$.

d) Find the rule of the following exponential functions knowing the asymptote and two points on the graph.

1.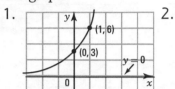

2.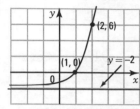

3.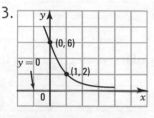

4.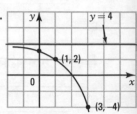

_____ _____ _____ _____

FINDING THE RULE OF AN EXPONENTIAL FUNCTION

Every rule of an exponential function can be written in the form $y = ac^x + k$.

Ex.: Consider the exponential function f on the right.

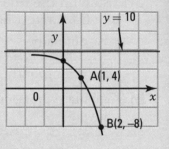

- Horizontal asymptote: $y = 10 \Rightarrow k = 10$.
- $f(1) = 4$
- $f(2) = -8$ $\Rightarrow \begin{cases} ac + 10 = 4 \\ ac^2 + 10 = -8 \end{cases} \Rightarrow \begin{cases} ac = -6 \\ ac^2 = -18 \end{cases}$

We deduce that $c = 3$ and $a = -2$. Therefore, $f(x) = -2(3)^x + 10$.

---

31. Find the rule of the following exponential functions knowing the asymptote and two points, A and B, on the graph.

a) Asymptote: $y = 0$
A(1, 6); B(2, 18)

b) Asymptote: $y = 0$
A(1, −10); B(2, −50)

c) Asymptote: $y = 2$
A(0, 1); B(1, −2)

d) Asymptote: $y = −10$
A(1, −4); B(2, 8)

_____ _____ _____ _____

32. A ping pong table is 70 cm high. A ball is dropped from above the table. The height reached by the ball relative to the floor is 100 cm on the first bounce and 88 cm on the second bounce.

a) Find the rule of the exponential function that gives the height y of the ball as a function of the number x of bounces.

x	1	2
y(cm)		

_____

b) Calculate, to the nearest tenth of cm, the height reached by the ball on the 6th bounce.

_____

4.3 Basic logarithmic function

ACTIVITY 1 Basic logarithmic function

a) The basic exponential function $y = 2^x$ is represented on the right.

1. Graph its inverse.
2. Explain why the inverse is a function.

_____

The inverse of an exponential function in base 2 is a function called logarithmic function in base 2, written $y = \log_2 x$.

3. The table of values for the exponential function $y = 2^x$ is represented on the right.

   Deduce the table of values for the logarithmic function $y = \log_2 x$.

4. Determine the following, and justify your answer.

   1) $\log_2 8 =$ _____

   2) $\log_2 \frac{1}{8} =$ _____

x	−2	−1	0	1	2
$y = 2^x$	$\frac{1}{4}$	$\frac{1}{2}$	1	2	4

x	$\frac{1}{4}$	$\frac{1}{2}$	1	2	4
$y = \log_2 x$					

5. For the function $y = \log_2 x$, determine

   1) the domain. _____ 2) the range. _____ 3) the zero. _____

   4) the sign _____

   5) the extrema, if it exists. _____ 6) the variation. _____

   7) the equation of the asymptote. _____

b) The basic exponential function $y = \left(\frac{1}{2}\right)^x$ is represented on the right.

1. Graph its inverse.
2. Explain why the inverse is a function.

_____

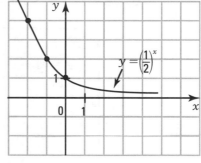

The inverse of an exponential function in base $\frac{1}{2}$ is a function called

logarithmic function in base $\frac{1}{2}$, written $y = \log_{\frac{1}{2}} x$.

3. The table of values for the exponential function $y = \left(\frac{1}{2}\right)^x$ is represented on the right.

   Deduce the table of values for the logarithmic function $y = \log_{\frac{1}{2}} x$.

x	−2	−1	0	1	2
$y = \left(\frac{1}{2}\right)^x$	4	2	1	$\frac{1}{2}$	$\frac{1}{4}$

x	4	2	1	$\frac{1}{2}$	$\frac{1}{4}$
$y = \log_{\frac{1}{2}} x$					

4. Determine the following, and justify your answer.

1) $\log_{\frac{1}{2}} \frac{1}{8} =$ _____

2) $\log_{\frac{1}{2}} 8 =$ _____

5. For the function $y = \log_{\frac{1}{2}} x$, determine

1) the domain. _____ 2) the range. _____ 3) the zero. _____

4) the sign _____

5) the extrema, if it exists. _____ 6) the variation. _____

7) the equation of the asymptote. _____

BASIC LOGARITHMIC FUNCTION $y = \log_c x$

- The inverse of the basic exponential function in base c, $y = c^x$, is a function called **logarithmic function** in base c written $y = \log_c x$.

$c > 1$	$0 < c < 1$
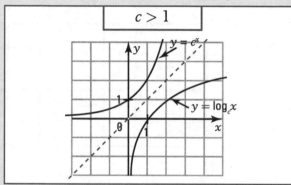	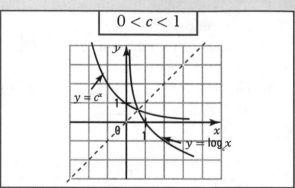

- We have: $\boxed{y = \log_c x \Leftrightarrow x = c^y}$.

- The graphical representation of $y = \log_c x$ depends on the base c.

$c > 1$	$0 < c < 1$
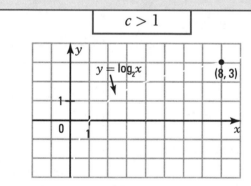	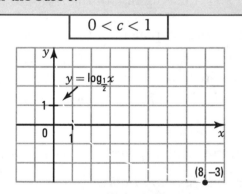
– Variation: increasing function.	– Variation: decreasing function.
– Sign: $\log_c x \leq 0$ if $0 < x \leq 1$ $\log_c x \geq 0$ if $x \geq 1$	– Sign: $\log_c x \geq 0$ if $0 < x \leq 1$ $\log_c x \leq 0$ if $x \geq 1$

Regardless of the base, we have:
- dom $= \mathbb{R}_+^*$ and ran $= \mathbb{R}$.
- the zero of the function is equal to 1.
- the function has no extrema.
- the function has a vertical asymptote: $x = 0$.

Activity 2 Definition of a logarithm

The logarithm in base c of a positive number p, written $\log_c p$, is the exponent q such that $c^q = p$. Thus, $\log_5 25 = 2$ since $5^2 = 25$.

We have the equivalence: $\boxed{\log_c p = q \Leftrightarrow c^q = p}$

Exponential form	Logarithmic form
$2^3 = 8$	$\log_2 8 = 3$
$3^2 = 9$	
	$\log_5 25 = 2$
$2^{-2} = \frac{1}{4}$	
	$\log_{\frac{2}{3}} \frac{27}{8} = -3$

a) Use this equivalence to complete the table on the right.

b) Calculate and justify your answer.

1. $\log_2 16 =$ _____
2. $\log_2 \frac{1}{8} =$ _____
3. $\log_2 1 =$ _____
4. $\log_{\frac{2}{3}} \frac{4}{9} =$ _____

c) The **logarithm in base 10** of a number x, called a common logarithm, is written **log x**. Mentally evaluate the following logarithms and then verify the value on your calculator.

1. $\log 10.$ _____
2. $\log 1000.$ _____
3. $\log 0.1.$ _____
4. $\log 0.01.$ _____

d) The logarithm in base e of a number x, called a natural logarithm, is written **ln x**. Mentally evaluate the following logarithms and then verify the value on your calculator.

1. $\ln e.$ _____
2. $\ln e^2.$ _____
3. $\ln e^{-1}.$ _____

DEFINITION OF A LOGARITHM

- The **logarithm in base** c of a positive number p, written $\log_c p$, is the exponent q such that $c^q = p$.

We have the equivalence: $\boxed{\log_c p = q \Leftrightarrow c^q = p}$

A logarithm is an exponent.

Ex.: $\log_2 8 = 3$ since $2^3 = 8$

- – The logarithm in base 10 of a number x is written $\log x$.
  – The logarithm in base e of a number x is written $\ln x$.
- The following formulas enable you to calculate $\log_c x$ using a calculator.

$$\log_c x = \frac{\log x}{\log c} \quad \text{or} \quad \log_c x = \frac{\ln x}{\ln c}$$

Use the log key or ln key on the calculator.

Thus, $\log_2 8 = \frac{\log 8}{\log 2} = 3$ or $\log_2 8 = \frac{\ln 8}{\ln 2} = 3$.

These formulas are established on page 178 (change of base law).

1. For each of the following exponential forms, write its equivalent logarithmic form.

a) $2^3 = 8$
b) $10^2 = 100$
c) $5^{-2} = \frac{1}{25}$
d) $\left(\frac{1}{2}\right)^2 = \frac{1}{4}$
e) $\left(\frac{2}{3}\right)^{-2} = \frac{9}{4}$

____ ____ ____ ____

2. For each of the following logarithmic forms, write its equivalent exponential form.

a) $\log_5 25 = 2$
b) $\log 1000 = 3$
c) $\log_3\left(\frac{1}{27}\right) = -3$
d) $\log_{\frac{1}{5}}\left(\frac{1}{25}\right) = 2$
e) $\log_{\frac{3}{2}}\left(\frac{8}{27}\right) = -3$

____ ____ ____ ____

3. Evaluate the following logarithms mentally, and then verify on your calculator.

a) $\log_2 16$ _____
b) $\log_5 25$ _____
c) $\log_{\frac{1}{2}} 2$ _____

d) $\log 0.001$ _____
e) $\log_{\frac{2}{3}}\left(\frac{4}{9}\right)$ _____
f) $\log_{\frac{2}{5}}\left(\frac{25}{4}\right)$ _____

g) $\log_{25} 5$ _____
h) $\log_8 2$ _____
i) $\log_{16}\left(\frac{1}{4}\right)$ _____

4. Evaluate the following logarithms mentally.

a) $\log_3 9 =$ _____
b) $\log_9 3 =$ _____
c) $\log_{\frac{2}{3}}\left(\frac{8}{27}\right) =$ _____

d) $\log_{\frac{2}{5}}\left(\frac{25}{4}\right) =$ _____
e) $\log_8 2 =$ _____
f) $\log_{\frac{4}{9}}\left(\frac{2}{3}\right) =$ _____

g) $\log_{\frac{16}{9}}\left(\frac{3}{4}\right) =$ _____
h) $\log_{\frac{2}{3}} 1 =$ _____
i) $\log_{\frac{2}{3}}\left(\frac{3}{2}\right) =$ _____

5. Evaluate the following logarithms mentally.

a) $\log 10\,000$ _____
b) $\log 0.01$ _____
c) $\log \frac{1}{10}$ _____

d) $\ln e^{-2}$ _____
e) $\log 10^5$ _____
f) $\ln 1$ _____

6. Explain why, for any base c, we have:

a) $\log_c 1 = 0.$ _____
b) $\log_c c = 1.$ _____

7. Determine x in each of the following.

a) $\log_2 x = 4$ _____
b) $\log_x 25 = 2$ _____
c) $\log_2\left(\frac{1}{8}\right) = x$ _____

d) $\log_x\left(\frac{4}{9}\right) = 2$ _____
e) $\log_3 x = -2$ _____
f) $\log_x \frac{25}{9} = -2$ _____

g) $\log_{\frac{3}{2}} x = -3$ _____
h) $\log_{\frac{2}{3}} \frac{3}{2} - x$ _____
i) $\log_5 x = 0$ _____

8. For each of the following logarithmic functions,
   1. indicate the base;   2. determine the variation;   3. determine the sign.

a) $y = \log_{\frac{3}{2}} x$ 1. _____   2. _____   3. _____

b) $y = \log_{\frac{2}{3}} x$ 1. _____   2. _____   3. _____

c) $y = \log x$ 1. _____   2. _____   3. _____

d) $y = \ln x$ 1. _____   2. _____   3. _____

9. In each of the following cases, the point A is on the graph of a logarithmic function defined by the rule $y = \log_c x$. Determine the rule of each function.

a) A(9, 2) _____
b) A(100, 2) _____
c) A(8, –3) _____

d) $A\left(\frac{27}{8}, 3\right)$ _____
e) A(e, 1) _____
f) $A\left(\frac{25}{4}, -2\right)$ _____

10. The point $A\left(2,\frac{1}{2}\right)$ is on the graph of a logarithmic function defined by the rule $y = \log_c x$.

a) A point B on this graph has an x-coordinate of 16. What is its y-coordinate? _____

b) A point C on this graph has a y-coordinate of 3. What is its x-coordinate? _____

11. The logarithmic functions $y = \log_2 x$, $y = \log_3 x$, $y = \log_{\frac{1}{2}} x$ and $y = \log_{\frac{1}{3}} x$ are represented on the right.

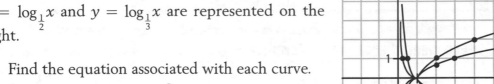

a) Find the equation associated with each curve.

1. _____ 2. _____

3. _____ 4. _____

b) True or False?
1. When considering two increasing logarithmic functions, the one that increases the fastest is the one with smallest base. _____
2. When considering two decreasing logarithmic functions, the one that decreases the fastest is the one with biggest base. _____

12. True or False?

a) $\log_c x$ is not defined when $x \leqslant 0$. _____

b) $y = \log_c x$ is increasing when $c > 1$. _____

c) For any base c, the curve defined by the rule $y = \log_c x$ passes through $(1, 0)$. _____

d) If $0 < c < 1$ and $x > 1$ then $\log_c x > 0$. _____

e) If $c > 1$ and $x < 1$ then $\log_c x < 0$. _____

13. Consider the function $y = \ln x$.

a) Complete the table of values.

x	e^{-1}	1	e	e^2
$y = \ln x$				

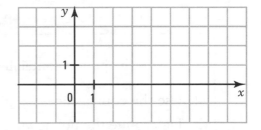

b) Graph $y = \ln x$ in the Cartesian plane.

14. a) Among the four functions represented on the right, identify

1. $y = \ln x$ _____ 2. $y = -\ln x$ _____

3. $y = \ln(-x)$ _____ 4. $y = -\ln(-x)$ _____

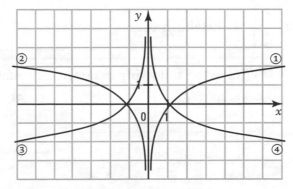

b) Complete the following table.

	$f(x) = \ln x$	$f(x) = -\ln x$	$f(x) = \ln(-x)$	$f(x) = -\ln(-x)$
Domain				
Range				
Sign				
Variation				

ACTIVITY 3 Exponential equation − Form $c^q = p$

The function $y = 2^x$ is represented on the right.

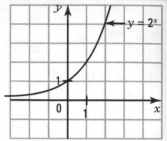

a) Complete the following table of values.

x						
y	$\frac{1}{4}$	$\frac{1}{2}$	1	2	4	8

b) We are trying to find the exponent x such that $2^x = 3$.

1. Use the graph of the function $y = 2^x$ or the table of values to determine between which consecutive integers the exponent x is located. _____

2. Use a calculator to approximate the exponent x to the nearest tenth. _____

3. Complete. $2^x = 3 \Leftrightarrow x$ _____

   Calculate the exponent x using a calculator (round to the nearest hundredth). _____

c) Solve the equation $2^x = 5$. Round the solution to the nearest hundredth.

_____

EXPONENTIAL EQUATION − FORM $c^q = p$

When solving an exponential equation, we use the following equivalence:

$$c^q = p \Leftrightarrow q = \log_c p$$

1. Isolate the power containing the unknown on one side.	$2(3)^{2x} - 10 = 0$ $2(3)^{2x} = 10$ $3^{2x} = 5$
2. Use the equivalence $c^q = p \Leftrightarrow q = \log_c p$.	$2x = \log_3 5$
3. Determine the unknown.	$x = \frac{1}{2}\log_3 5$
4. Establish the solution set.	$S = \left\{\frac{1}{2}\log_3 5\right\}$

15. Solve the following exponential equations (round solution to the nearest hundredth).

a) $3^x = 6$

b) $5^{2x} = 10$

c) $2^x + 1 = 4$

d) $(0,5)^x = 3$

e) $2^{2x} = 7$

f) $2(10)^x - 3 = 5$

16. Determine, if it exists, the zero of the following exponential functions.

a) $y = -2(3)^{x-1} + 1$

b) $y = 3\left(\frac{1}{2}\right)^{x+2} - 10$

c) $y = -2\left(\frac{2}{3}\right)^{2(x+1)} - 1$

_____   _____   _____

17. Given $f(x) = 2(5)^x - 1$. Determine, if possible, the value of x for which

a) $f(x) = 2$ _____   **b)** $f(x) = 0$_____   **c)** $f(x) = -2$_____

18. The bacterial growth within a culture is given by the rule $y = 10(2)^x$ where y represents the number of bacteria and x represents the elapsed time, in hours, since the beginning of the experiment.

a) What rule enables you to calculate the elapsed time as a function of a given number of bacteria in the culture? _____

b) Determine

1. the number of bacteria in the culture after 5 hours. _____
2. the elapsed time since the beginning of the experiment if we observe 1000 bacteria.

_____

19. The accumulated value $c(t)$ after t years of an initial capital c_0 invested at an interest rate i compounded n times per year is calculated according to the rule

$$c(t) = c_0\left(1 + \frac{i}{n}\right)^{nt}$$

a) What is the accumulated value of a $1000 capital invested at an interest rate of 10% after 7 years if the interest is compounded

1. annually. _____   2. every 3 months. _____

3. every month. _____   4. every day. _____

b) After how many years will the accumulated value of a $1000 capital, invested at an interest rate of 8%, be worth $2000 if the interest is compounded

1. annually. _____   2. every 3 months. _____

20. One litre of water evaporates by losing 1% of its volume each hour. After how long will the volume be 950 ml? _____

21. A grocery basket for 4 people cost $150 in the year 2000. The inflation rate remained at 3% for the following years.

a) How much did this same basket cost in 2005? _____

b) In what year will this basket cost $185? _____

22. A village of 1000 inhabitants increases at a rate of 10% per year. A neighbouring village of 2000 inhabitants decreases at a rate of 5% per year. After how many years will these two villages have the same population?

_____

23. A car loses 15% of its value for the first 3 years and 10% of its value for the following years. After how many years will a car purchased for $30 000 be worth $10 778? _____

4.4 Logarithmic function

ACTIVITY 1 Logarithmic function $f(x) = a \log_c b(x - h) + k$

The basic logarithmic function $y = \log_c x$ can be transformed into a logarithmic function defined by the rule $f(x) = a \log_c b(x - h) + k$.

Consider the logarithmic function $y = \log_2 x$ and the logarithmic function $y = 2 \log_2 2(x - 3) - 2$.

a) Identify the parameters a, b, h and k. _____

b) The introduction of the parameters a, b, h and k into the rule of the basic logarithmic function causes a series of transformations on the graph. Complete the description of this process.

1. From the graph of $y = \log_2 x$, we obtain the graph of $y = 2 \log_2 x$ by the transformation $(x, y) \rightarrow$ _____.

   The parameter a causes _____

   The function $y = 2 \log_2 x$ has a vertical asymptote with equation _____.

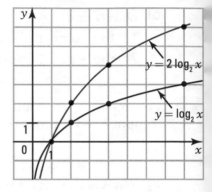

2. From the graph of $y = 2 \log_2 x$, we obtain the graph of $y = 2 \log_2 2x$ by the transformation

   $(x, y) \rightarrow$ _____.

   The parameter b causes _____

   _____

   The function $y = 2 \log_2 2x$ has a vertical asymptote with equation _____.

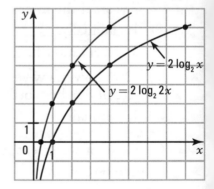

3. From the graph of $y = 2 \log_2 2x$, we obtain the graph of $y = 2 \log_2 2(x - 3)$ by the transformation
   $(x, y) \rightarrow$ _____.

   The parameter h causes _____

   _____

   The function $y = 2 \log_2 2(x - 3)$ has a vertical asymptote with equation _____.

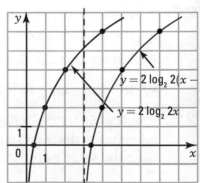

4. From the graph of $y = 2 \log_2 2(x - 3)$, we obtain the graph of $y = 2 \log_2 2(x - 3) - 2$ by the transformation $(x, y) \rightarrow$ _____.

The parameter k causes a _____

_____

The function $y = 2 \log_2 2(x - 3) - 2$ has a vertical asymptote with equation _____.

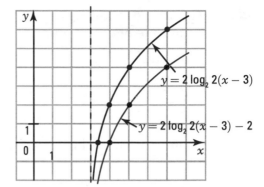

c) From the tables of values, verify that the transformation $(x, y) \rightarrow \left(\dfrac{x}{b} + h, ay + k \right)$ directly applies the graph of $y = \log_2 x$ onto the graph of $y = 2 \log_2 2(x - 3) - 2$.

_____

_____

_____

$y = \log_2 x$

x	y
1	0
2	1
4	2

$y = 2 \log_2 2(x - 3) - 2$

x	y
3.5	−2
4	0
5	2

LOGARITHMIC FUNCTION $f(x) = a \log_c b(x - h) + k$

- The graph of the function $f(x) = 2 \log_c b(x - h) + k$ can be deduced from the graph of the basic logarithmic function $y = \log_c x$ by the transformation

$$(x, y) \rightarrow \left(\frac{x}{b} + h, ay + k \right)$$

- The logarithmic function $f(x) = a \log_c b(x - h) + k$ has the vertical line $x = h$ as an asymptote.
Ex.: See activity 1.

---

1. The following functions are defined by a rule of the form $f(x) = a \log_2 b(x - h) + k$.

$f_1(x) = 5 \log_2 x$; $f_2(x) = \log_2 4x$; $f_3(x) = \log_2 (x + 1)$; $f_4(x) = \log_2 x + 1$; $f_5(x) = 2 \log_2 3(x - 1) - 5$.

Complete the table on the right by determining the parameters a, b, h and k and by giving the rule of the transformation which enables you to graph the function from the basic function $f(x) = \log_2 x$.

	a	b	h	k	Rule
f_1					$(x, y) \rightarrow$
f_2					$(x, y) \rightarrow$
f_3					$(x, y) \rightarrow$
f_4					$(x, y) \rightarrow$
f_5					$(x, y) \rightarrow$

2. In each of the following cases, a transformation is applied to the graph of the function $y = \log_5 x$. Find the rule of the function whose graph is obtained by applying the given transformation.

a) $(x, y) \rightarrow (x, -y)$ _____

b) $(x, y) \rightarrow (2x, y)$ _____

c) $(x, y) \rightarrow (x, 2y)$ _____

d) $(x, y) \rightarrow (x + 2, y)$ _____

e) $(x, y) \rightarrow (x, y - 5)$ _____

f) $(x, y) \rightarrow (x - 1, y + 3)$ _____

3. The function $f(x) = \log_{\frac{1}{2}} x$ is represented on the right.

a) Explain how to obtain the graph of $g(x) = 2 \log_{\frac{1}{2}}(x - 3)$, from the graph on the right, and represent the graph of function g.

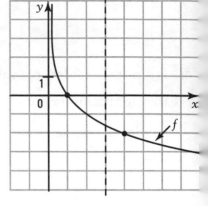

_____
_____
_____
_____

b) What is the equation of the asymptote of function g? _____

4. The function $f(x) = \log_2 x$ is represented on the right.

a) Explain how to obtain the graph of $g(x) = -\log_2\left(\frac{1}{2}x\right) + 1$ from the graph on the right, and represent the graph of function g.

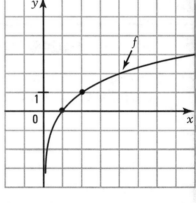

_____
_____
_____
_____
_____
_____

b) What is the equation of the asymptote of function g? _____

5. The functions represented below are defined by a rule of the form $y = \log_c (x - h)$. Find the rule of each function.

a)

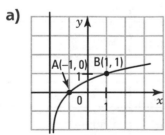

b)

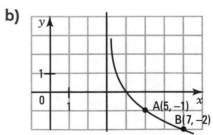

_____   _____

6. The functions represented below are defined by a rule of the form $y = \log_c (x - h) + k$. Find the rule of each function.

a)
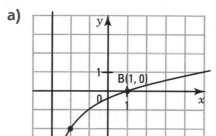

_____

b)
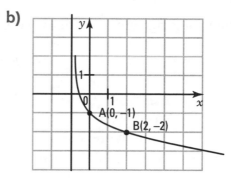

_____

ACTIVITY 2 Logarithmic equation – Form $\log_c p = q$

a) Consider the logarithmic equation: $5 \log_2 (2x + 1) - 3 = 12$.

1. What restriction must be placed on the variable x for $\log_2 (2x + 1)$ to exist?

_____

2. Justify the steps in solving equation.

$$5 \log_2 (2x + 1) - 3 = 12$$
$$5 \log_2 (2x + 1) = 15 \qquad \text{_____}$$
$$\log_2 (2x + 1) = 3 \qquad \text{_____}$$
$$2x + 1 = 2^3 \qquad \text{_____}$$
$$2x = 7 \qquad \text{_____}$$
$$x = 3.5 \qquad \text{_____}$$

3. Does the value found for x respect the restriction established in 1.? _____

4. Therefore, what is the solution to the equation? _____

b) A company has established that the required assembly time t for parts, in minutes, is given by $t = -20 \log_5 \left(\frac{n}{5} - 2\right) + 80$ where n represents the number of parts to be assembled.

1. What restriction must be placed on the variable n? _____

2. If an employee takes 40 minutes to assemble parts, how many parts did he assemble? (Verify if the number of parts found respects the restriction)

_____

_____

_____

_____

_____

LOGARITHMIC EQUATION – FORM $\log_c p = q$

When solving a logarithmic equation, we use the equivalence:

$$\log_c p = q \Leftrightarrow p = c^q$$

	Ex.: $3 \log_2 (2x - 4) - 5 = 4$
1. Determine the restrictions.	1. Restriction: $2x - 4 > 0 \Leftrightarrow x > 2$
2. Isolate the logarithm on one side.	2. $\log_2 (2x - 4) = 3$
3. Use the equivalence: $\log_c p = q \Leftrightarrow p = c^q$.	3. $(2x - 4) = 2^3$
4. Determine the unknown.	4. $x = 6$
5. Verify the validity of the solution.	5. The solution 6 respects the restriction.
6. Establish the solution set S.	6. $S = \{6\}$.

7. Solve the following logarithmic equations.

a) $\log_2 (x - 1) = 4$

b) $2 \log_3 (x + 1) - 3 = 1$

c) $\frac{1}{2} \log(5x + 10) - 1 = 0$

d) $2 \log_2 (x^2 - 1) - 5 = 1$

e) $5 \log_2 (x^2 + 3x - 2) - 10 = 5$

f) $\log_5 (x^2 + 9) = 2$

8. Find the zeros of the following logarithmic functions.

a) $f(x) = \log_5 (x + 10) - 2$

b) $f(x) = -2 \log_3 2(x + 5) - 4$

c) $f(x) = 2 \log_4 (x - 1) - 1$

d) $f(x) = 2 \log (x + 6) - 2$

9. The number of customers y (in thousands) willing to buy a product depending on its sale price x (in $) is estimated by the rule $y = 20 - 4 \ln(0.1x)$.

a) Estimate the number of customers willing to buy the product when the sale price is

1. $20. _____ 2. $50. _____ 3. $100. _____

b) Estimate the sale price of the product for the following number of customers.

1. 15 000 customers _____ 2. 4000 customers _____ 3. 0 customers _____

ACTIVITY 3 Sketch of the graph and study of a logarithmic function

To sketch the graph of the logarithmic function $f(x) = a \log_c b(x - h) + k$,
1. we draw the vertical asymptote with equation $x = h$.
2. we determine the domain of the function.
3. we locate, using the rule, 2 points on the logarithmic curve.
4. we sketch the logarithmic curve.

a) Sketch the graph of the following functions.

1. $f_1(x) = 2 \log_{\frac{1}{2}} 2(x - 1) + 4$

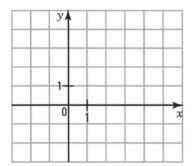

_____

_____

2. $f_2(x) = -2 \log_2 (x + 1) + 4$

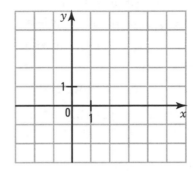

_____

_____

3. $f_3(x) = 2 \log_2 2(x + 2) - 4$

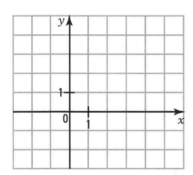

_____

_____

4. $f_4(x) = -\log_{\frac{1}{2}} -\frac{1}{2} (x - 2) + 1$

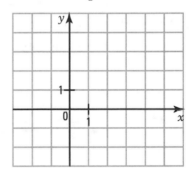

_____

_____

b) Find the zero of each of the preceding functions.

1. f_1 :_____ 2. f_2 :_____ 3. f_3 :_____ 4. f_4 :_____

c) Do a study of each of the preceding functions and complete the following table.

	a	b	h	k	Asymptote	Domain	Range	Zero	Sign	Variation
f_1										
f_2										
f_3										
f_4										

- To sketch the graph of a logarithmic function,
  1. we draw the vertical asymptote.
  2. we determine the domain of the function.
  3. we locate, using the rule, 2 points on the logarithmic curve.
  4. we sketch the logarithmic curve.

- We do a study of a logarithmic function using the sketch of the graph.
  - dom $f =]h, +\infty[$ if $b > 0$ and dom $f =]-\infty, h[$ if $b < 0$.
  - ran $f = \mathbb{R}$.
  - The sign of f is determined from the graph.
  - The variation of f is determined from the graph.
  - The function f has no extrema.

  Ex.: See activity 3.

10. For each of the following logarithmic functions, determine
1. the equation of the asymptote.   2. the domain.   3. a sketch of the graph.
4. the range.   5. the zero.   6. the sign.
7. the variation.

Rule	1	2	3	4	5	6	7
$f_1(x) = -3 \log_4 2(x + 1) + 3$							
$f_2(x) = 2 \log_2 2(x + 3)$							
$f_3(x) = \log_3 (-x + 1) - 2$							
$f_4(x) = -\log_2 (-x + 3) + 4$							

11. Consider the function $f(x) = 2 \log_2(x - 1) - 4$.

a) Determine
   1. the asymptote of f. _____   2. the domain f. _____

b) Represent the function f in the Cartesian plane.

x	$\frac{3}{2}$	2	3	5	9
y					

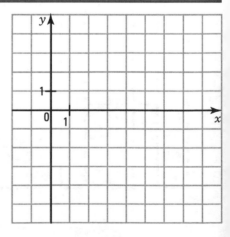

c) Determine
   1. ran f._____   2. the zero of f._____
   3. the sign of f. _____
   4. the variation of f._____

12. Consider the function $f(x) = 2\log_{\frac{1}{2}}(x+3) - 4$.

a) Determine

  1. the asymptote of f. _____

  2. the domain of f. _____

b) Represent the function f in the Cartesian plane.

x	$-\frac{5}{2}$	-2	-1	1	5
y					

c) Determine

  1. ran f. _____   2. the zero of f. _____

  3. the sign of f. _____

  4. the variation of f. _____

13. Find the domain of the following logarithmic functions.

a) $y = \log_3 2(x-1) + 5$

_____

b) $y = \log_5 -2(x+3) - 5$

_____

c) $y = \log(x^2 - 1)$

_____

d) $y = \ln(x^2 - 5x + 6)$

_____

e) $y = \log_2(x^2 + 1) + 5$

_____

f) $y = \ln(16 - x^2)$

_____

14. Study the sign of the following logarithmic functions.

a) $f(x) = \log_2(x-1) - 2$

_____

b) $f(x) = -2\log_3(x-1) + 2$

_____

c) $f(x) = 5\log_3 2(x-1) - 10$

_____

_____

d) $f(x) = -\frac{1}{2}\log_2 -2(x+1) + 2$

_____

_____

15. Solve the following logarithmic inequalities.

a) $2\log_3 x - 4 \geq 0$

_____

b) $-3\log_2 2(x-1) + 6 \geq 0$

_____

c) $2\log(x+1) - 4 \leq 0$

_____

16. Calculate, if it exists, the initial value of the following functions.

a) $f(x) = \frac{1}{2}\log_4 2(x+8) + 1$ _____

b) $f(x) = 2\log_{\frac{1}{2}}(x-1) + 1$ _____

17. Determine the variation of the following functions.

a) $f(x) = 2\log_{\frac{1}{2}} 2(x-1) + 4$

_____

b) $f(x) = \log_{\frac{1}{4}} -\frac{1}{2}(x+1) + 2$

_____

a) Consider the logarithmic function $y = 3 \log_2 4(x - 1) - 6$.
Justify the steps for finding the rule of the inverse.

1. Isolate x in the equation: $y = 3 \log_2 4(x - 1) - 6$

$$3 \log_2 4(x - 1) = y + 6$$ _____

$$\log_2 4(x - 1) = \tfrac{1}{3}(y + 6)$$ _____

$$4(x - 1) = 2^{\frac{1}{3}(y + 6)}$$ _____

$$x - 1 = \tfrac{1}{4}(2)^{\frac{1}{3}(y + 6)}$$ _____

$$x = \tfrac{1}{4}(2)^{\frac{1}{3}(y + 6)} + 1$$ _____

2. Interchange the letters x and y to get the rule of the inverse.
The inverse of the logarithmic function: $y = 3 \log_2 4(x - 1) - 6$ is the exponential function:
$y = \tfrac{1}{4}(2)^{\frac{1}{3}(x + 6)} + 1$.

b) Consider the exponential function $y = \tfrac{1}{2}(2)^{\frac{1}{4}(x + 3)} - 1$.

Justify the steps for finding the rule of the inverse.

1. Isolate x in the equation: $y = \tfrac{1}{2}(2)^{\frac{1}{4}(x + 3)} - 1$

$$y + 1 = \tfrac{1}{2}(2)^{\frac{1}{4}(x + 3)}$$ _____

$$2(y + 1) = 2^{\frac{1}{4}(x + 3)}$$ _____

$$\tfrac{1}{4}(x + 3) = \log_2 2(y + 1)$$ _____

$$x + 3 = 4 \log_2 2(y + 1)$$ _____

$$x = 4 \log_2 2(y + 1) - 3$$ _____

2. Interchange the letters x and y to get the rule of the inverse.
The inverse of the exponential function: $y = \tfrac{1}{2}(2)^{\frac{1}{4}(x + 3)} - 1$ is the logarithmic function:
$y = 4 \log_2 2(x + 1) - 3$.

c) Determine the domain and range of the preceding functions and verify that

1. $\operatorname{dom} f = \operatorname{ran} f^{-1}$

_____

2. $\operatorname{ran} f = \operatorname{dom} f^{-1}$

_____

d) Complete.
1. The inverse of an exponential function in base c is a _____
2. The inverse of a logarithmic function in base c is an _____

The inverse of an exponential (logarithmic) function in base c is a logarithmic (exponential) function in base c.

Ex.: See activity 4 for finding the rule.

18. For each of the following exponential functions,
   1. determine the inverse.
   2. verify that dom $f = \text{ran} f^{-1}$ and that $\text{ran} f = \text{dom } f^{-1}$.

   a) $f(x) = 3^{x+1} - 6$

   b) $f(x) = 5^{2(x-1)} - 25$

   c) $f(x) = -5(2)^{3(x+2)} + 10$

_____

_____

_____

19. Determine the inverse of each of the following logarithmic functions.

   a) $f(x) = \log_3 (x - 1) + 2$

   b) $f(x) = \log_2 -3(x + 1) - 4$

   c) $f(x) = \frac{1}{2} \log_5 2(x - 3) + 1$

_____

20. The population P (in millions of inhabitants) of a country varies according to the rule $P = 50(2)^{\frac{t}{25}}$ where t represents the number of elapsed years since the year 2000.

   a) Find the rule of the function which gives the number t of years since 2000 as a function of the population P.

   _____

   b) In what year will the population of this country reach 100 million inhabitants?

   _____

21. The time t (in years) required for a radioactive particle to disintegrate is given by: $t = 4 \log_{\frac{1}{2}}(m - 1)$ where m represents the mass (in g) of the particle at the beginning ($t = 0$).

   a) Find the rule of the function which gives the mass m of the radioactive particle as a function of the elapsed time t since the beginning.

   _____

   b) What was the mass of the particle
   1. at the beginning? _____   2. after 8 days? _____

4.5 Logarithmic calculations

a) 1. Complete the equivalence: $\log_a x = y \Leftrightarrow x = $ _____

2. Use the preceding equivalence to explain why

   1) $\log_a 1 = 0$ _____

   2) $\log_a a = 1$ _____

   3) $\log_a a^n = n$ _____

b) We know, by the definition of a logarithm, that the logarithm in base a of a positive number M is the exponent which must be given to the base a to get M. Therefore, deduce $a^{\log_a M}$. _____

c) Verify the preceding properties for logarithms in base 10.

   1. $\log_{10} 1 = 0$ 2. $\log_{10} 10 = 1$ 3. $\log_{10} 10^n = n$ 4. $10^{\log_{10} M} = M$

PROPERTIES OF LOGARITHMS

- $\boxed{\log_a 1 = 0}$ Ex.: $\log_2 1 = 0$

- $\boxed{\log_a a = 1}$ Ex.: $\log_5 5 = 1$

- $\boxed{\log_a a^n = n}$ Ex.: $\log_5 5^2 = 2$

- $\boxed{a^{\log_a M} = M}$ Ex.: $10^{\log_{10} 100} = 100$

---

1. Calculate, using the properties of logarithms.

a) $\log_5 1 = $ _____   b) $\log_{\frac{1}{2}} \frac{1}{2} = $ _____   c) $\log_2 2^3 = $ _____

d) $\log_{\frac{1}{3}}\left(\frac{1}{3}\right)^{-2} = $ _____   e) $\log_{\frac{2}{3}} 1 = $ _____   f) $2^{\log_2 3} = $ _____

g) $\left(\frac{3}{2}\right)^{\log_{\frac{3}{2}} 5} = $ _____   h) $\log_4 4^{\frac{3}{2}} = $ _____   i) $\log_{\frac{4}{9}}\left(\frac{4}{9}\right)^{\frac{1}{2}} = $ _____

2. Calculate the following real numbers.

a) $\log 10 = $ _____   b) $\ln e^2 = $ _____   c) $\log 10^{-3} = $ _____

d) $10^{\log 100} = $ _____   e) $e^{\ln 2} = $ _____   f) $10^{\log 10} = $ _____

g) $e^{\ln e^2} = $ _____   h) $10^{\log 10^{-1}} = $ _____   i) $\ln e^e = $ _____

3. Use the identity $M = a^{\log_a M}$ to write the real number 5 as a power of

a) 2 _____   b) 10 _____   c) e _____   d) $\frac{3}{2}$ _____

a) Verify that

   1. $\log_2 (8 \times 4) = \log_2 8 + \log_2 4$ _____

   2. $\log_2 \left(\frac{8}{4}\right) = \log_2 8 - \log_2 4$ _____

   3. $\log_2 2^3 = 3 \log_2 2$ _____

b) Justify the steps showing that $\log_a(xy) = \log_a x + \log_a y$.

	Steps	Justifications
1	$a^{\log_a (xy)} = a^{\log_a x} \times a^{\log_a y}$	
2	$a^{\log_a x} \times a^{\log_a y} = a^{\log_a x + \log_a y}$	
3	$a^{\log_a (xy)} = a^{\log_a x + \log_a y}$	
4	$\log_a (xy) = \log_a x + \log_a y$	

c) Justify the steps showing that $\log_a \left(\frac{x}{y}\right) = \log_a x - \log_a y$.

	Steps	Justifications
1	$a^{\log_a\left(\frac{x}{y}\right)} = a^{\log_a x} \div a^{\log_a y}$	
2	$a^{\log_a x} \div a^{\log_a y} = a^{\log_a x - \log_a y}$	
3	$a^{\log_a\left(\frac{x}{y}\right)} = a^{\log_a x - \log_a y}$	
4	$\log_a \left(\frac{x}{y}\right) = \log_a x - \log_a y$	

d) Justify the steps showing that $\log_a x^n = n \log_a x$.

	Steps	Justifications
1	$a^{\log_a x^n} = (a^{\log_a x})^n$	
2	$a^{\log_a x^n} = a^{n \log_a x}$	
3	$a^{\log_a x^n} = a^{n \log_a x}$	
4	$a^{\log_a x^n} = n \log_a x$	

        4.5 Logarithmic calculations   **175**

- Logarithm of a product.

$$\boxed{\log_a xy = \log_a x + \log_a y}$$

Ex.: $\log (100 \times 10) = \log 100 + \log 10$

- Logarithm of a quotient.

$$\boxed{\log_a \left(\frac{x}{y}\right) = \log_a x - \log_a y}$$

Ex.: $\log \left(\frac{100}{10}\right) = \log 100 - \log 10$

- Logarithm of a power.

$$\boxed{\log_a x^n = n \log_a x}$$

Ex.: $\log 10^2 = 2 \log 10$

4. **a)** True or false?

1. $\log_a x^n = (\log_a x)^n$ _____

2. $\log_a x^n = n \log_a x$ _____

b) Calculate

1. $(\log 10)^2$ _____

2. $\log 10^2$ _____

5. **a)** Show that $\log_a \sqrt[n]{x} = \frac{1}{n} \log_a x.$ _____

b) Simplify.

1. $\log_a \sqrt[3]{a}$ _____

2. $\log_a \sqrt[n]{a^m}$ _____

6. Knowing that $\log_2 3 \approx 1.5850$ and that $\log_2 5 \approx 2.3219$, determine

a) $\log_2 15$ _____

b) $\log_2 \left(\frac{5}{3}\right)$ _____

c) $\log_2 \left(\frac{3}{5}\right)$ _____

d) $\log_2 25$ _____

e) $\log_2 \sqrt{3}$ _____

f) $\log_2 \sqrt[3]{9}$ _____

7. Use the properties of logarithms to express the following logarithms as a sum or difference of logarithms.

a) $\log_2 (3 \times 5)$ _____

b) $\log_2 (3 \times 5 \times 7)$ _____

c) $\log_2 \left(\frac{5}{7}\right)$ _____

d) $\log_2 \left(\frac{2 \times 5}{7}\right)$ _____

e) $\log_2 \left(\frac{2 \times 5}{3 \times 7}\right)$ _____

f) $\log_2 (3^2 \times 5^3)$ _____

g) $\log_2 \left(\frac{3^2}{5^3}\right)$ _____

h) $\log_2 \left(\frac{3^2 \times 7^3}{5^2}\right)$ _____

8. Write the following expressions as a single logarithm.

a) $\log_2 3 + \log_2 5$ _____

b) $2 \log_2 3 + \log_2 5$ _____

c) $\log_3 7 - \log_3 2$ _____

d) $\log_5 2 + \log_5 3 - \log_5 7$ _____

e) $\log_2 7 + \log_2 5 - \log_2 6 - \log_2 3$ _____

f) $3 \log_5 2 + \log_5 3 - 2 \log_5 7$ _____

9. True or false?

a) $\log_2 8 + \log_2 16 = 7$ _____

b) $\log_3 25 = 2 \log_3 5$ _____

c) $\log_2 (2 + 4) = \log_2 2 + \log_2 4$ _____

d) $\log 2 \times \log 5 = \log (2 + 5)$ _____

e) $\log_2 \left(\frac{16}{8}\right) = \frac{\log_2 16}{\log_2 8}$ _____

f) $\log_3 12 - \log_3 6 = \log_3 2$ _____

g) $\log_2 (5^2)^3 = 2 \log_2 5^3$ _____

h) $\log_c \left(\frac{1}{c}\right)^n = -n$ _____

10. Write x in terms of a, b and c.

a) $\ln x = \ln a + \ln b - \ln c$ _____

b) $\ln x = 2 \ln a + 3 \ln b - \frac{1}{2} \ln c$ _____

11. Knowing that $x = \log_a 2$, $y = \log_a 3$ and $z = \log_a 5$, express the following logarithms in terms of x, y and z.

a) $\log_a 30$ _____

b) $\log_a \frac{6}{5}$ _____

c) $\log_a \frac{2}{15}$ _____

d) $\log_a 12$ _____

e) $\log_a 360$ _____

f) $\log_a \frac{72}{25}$ _____

12. Write the following expressions as a single logarithm.

a) $4 \ln 2x + \ln \left(\frac{6}{x}\right) - 2 \ln 2x =$ _____

b) $3 \log_2 a - 2 \log_2 b + 3 =$ _____

c) $2(\log x^2 - \log 2x) + 3 \log x =$ _____

d) $2 \log x - 3 \log y + \frac{1}{2} \log 4 =$ _____

13. Write the following expressions as a single logarithm.

a) $\log_2 (x + 3) + \log_2 (x - 3)$ _____

b) $\log_2 (x + 3) - \log_2 (x - 2)$ _____

c) $3 \log (x - 1) - 2 \log x$ _____

d) $\log (x^2 - 1) - \log (x - 1)$ _____

e) $\ln (x^2 + 5x + 6) - \ln (x + 3)$ _____

f) $\ln (2x^2 - 5x - 3) - \ln (x^2 - 9)$ _____

14. Calculate the numerical value of the following expressions.

a) $\log_{\frac{1}{2}} 8 + 3 \log_2 4^2 - 10 \log_3 \sqrt{3} + 2 \log_5 1$ _____

b) $8 \log_4 2 - 4 \log_2 \sqrt{8} - 2 \log_{\frac{1}{2}} 8 - \log_2 4^2$ _____

c) $3 \log_a a^2 + 2 \log_a \left(\frac{1}{a}\right) - 5 \log_a 1$ _____

15. Knowing that $\log_a 2 = 3$ and $\log_a 3 = 5$, calculate $\log_a 6a^3$.

_____

16. Knowing that $\log_a x = 2$ and $\log_a y = 6$, calculate $\log_a\left(\dfrac{ax^3}{\sqrt{y}}\right)$.

_____

17. Knowing that $\log_a 2 = x$ and $\log_a 3 = y$, express the following in terms of x and y.

a) $\log_a 18a$ _____

b) $\log_a \dfrac{12a^2}{\sqrt[3]{6}}$ _____

c) $\log_a\left(\dfrac{27}{4a^2}\right)$ _____

18. If $\log_a x = 2$, $\log_a y = 3$ and $\log_a z = 4$, find the numerical value of $\log_a\left(\dfrac{x^{-3}y^2\sqrt{z}}{a^2}\right)$.

_____

19. Show that: $\log_c\left(\dfrac{x}{y}\right) = -\log_c\left(\dfrac{y}{x}\right)$.

_____

20. Show that: $\log_{\frac{1}{c}}(x) = \log_c\left(\dfrac{1}{x}\right)$.

_____

_____

ACTIVITY 3 Change of base law

a) Given three positive numbers c, m and x different from 1.
Justify the steps showing that: $\log_c x = \dfrac{\log_m x}{\log_m c}$.

	Steps	Justifications
1	$y = \log_c x \Leftrightarrow c^y = x$	
2	$\log_m c^y = \log_m x$	
3	$y \log_m c = \log_m x$	
4	$y = \dfrac{\log_m x}{\log_m c}$	
5	Thus, $\log_c x = \dfrac{\log_m x}{\log_m c}$	

b) Use a calculator to verify that

1. $\log_2 8 = \dfrac{\log 8}{\log 2}$.

2. $\log_2 8 = \dfrac{\ln 8}{\ln 2}$.

CHANGE OF BASE LAW

- Given three positive numbers c, m and x different from 1, we have:

$$\log_c x = \frac{\log_m x}{\log_m c}$$

This law, called the **change of base law**, enables you to calculate the logarithm of a number in any base using the log and ln keys on the calculator.

Ex.: $\log_2 3 = \dfrac{\log 3}{\log 2} = 1.584\ 96$ or $\log_2 3 = \dfrac{\ln 3}{\ln 2} = 1.586\ 96$.

21. Use a calculator to evaluate the following (round to the nearest thousandth).

a) $\log_2 5$ _____

b) $\log_5 2$ _____

c) $\log_7 \sqrt{2}$ _____

22. Show that

a) $\log_a b \times \log_b a = 1$ _____

b) $\log_{\frac{1}{c}} x = -\log_c x$ _____

c) $\log_c \left(\frac{1}{x}\right) = \log_{\frac{1}{c}} x$ _____

23. True or false?

a) $\log (a \times b) = \log a \times \log b$ _____

b) $\log (a + b) = \log a + \log b$ _____

c) $\log \left(\frac{a}{b}\right) = \dfrac{\log a}{\log b}$ _____

d) $\log a^n = (\log a)^n$ _____

e) $\log a + \log b = \log ab$ _____

f) $\log a - \log b = \log \frac{a}{b}$ _____

g) $\log \frac{1}{a} = -\log a$ _____

h) $\dfrac{\log a}{\log b} = \log_b a$ _____

24. a) Determine the real number k such that for any real number x from $\mathbb{R}_+^*$, we have: $\log x = k \ln x$.

_____

b) Define the geometric transformation which enables you to obtain the graph of $y = \log x$ from the graph of $y = \ln x$.

_____

25. Use the properties of logarithms to calculate

a) $\log_2 2^4 + \log_2 2 - \log_2 8$ _____

b) $\log_2 (\log_2 2)$ _____

c) $\log_c (\log_c c^c) =$ _____

d) $\log_c \left(\frac{1}{c}\right) - \log_{\frac{1}{c}}(c)$ _____

26. Simplify.

a) $\ln e^x$ _____

b) $e^{\ln x}$ _____

c) $e^{x \ln x}$ _____

ACTIVITY 4 Equations involving logarithms – Form $log_c\ p = q$

Consider the equation $\log (x + 1) = 1 - \log (x - 2)$.

a) Determine the restrictions that the variable x must respect for both sides of the equation to be defined.

_____

b) Justify the steps in solving this equation.

	Steps	Justifications
	$\log (x + 1) = 1 - \log (x - 2)$	
1	$\log (x + 1) + \log (x - 2) = 1$	
2	$\log (x + 1)(x - 2) = 1$	
3	$(x + 1)(x - 2) = 10$	
4	$x^2 - x - 2 = 10$	
5	$x^2 - x - 12 = 0$	
6	$(x + 3)(x - 4) = 0$	
7	$x + 3 = 0$ or $x - 4 = 0$	
8	$x = -3$ or $x = 4$	
9	We reject the solution $x = -3$.	
10	Thus, S $= \{4\}$	

EQUATIONS INVOLVING LOGARITHMS – FORM $log_c\ p = q$

When solving an equation involving logarithms in the same base,

- determine the restrictions that the variable x must respect for both sides of the equation to be defined.
- use the properties of logarithms to get the form $\log_c p = q$.
- use the equivalence: $\boxed{\log_c p = q \Leftrightarrow c^q = p}$
- determine the solutions that respect the restrictions.
  Ex.: See activity 4.

27. Solve the following equations.

a) $\log_6 (x - 5) = 2 - \log_6 x$

b) $\log (x + 3) = 1 - \log x$

c) $\log_2 (x + 1) + \log_2 (x - 1) = 3$

d) $\log_2 (x + 2) = 2 - \log_2 (x - 1)$

Activity 5 Equation involving logarithms – Form $log_c u = log_c v$

a) Justify the steps showing the equivalence $\log_c u = \log_c v \Leftrightarrow u = v$.

$\log_c u = \log_c v \Leftrightarrow c^{\log_c u} = c^{\log_c v}$ _____

$\qquad\qquad \Leftrightarrow \quad u \ = \ v$ _____

b) Consider the logarithmic equation $\ln (x + 2) = \ln (-x + 6) + \ln (x - 1)$.

What restrictions must the variable x respect for both sides of the equation to be defined?

_____

c) Justify the steps in solving the equation $\ln (x + 2) = \ln (-x + 6) + \ln (x - 1)$.

	Steps	Justifications
	$\ln (x + 2) = \ln (-x + 6) + \ln (x - 1)$	
1	$\ln (x + 2) = \ln (-x + 6)(x - 1)$	
2	$(x + 2) = (-x + 6)(x - 1)$	
3	$x + 2 = -x^2 + 7x - 6$	
4	$x^2 - 6x + 8 = 0$	
5	$(x - 4)(x - 2) = 0$	
6	$x = 4$ or $x = 2$	
7	The solutions are valid. Thus, $S = \{2, 4\}$	

EQUATIONS INVOLVING LOGARITHMS – FORM $log_c u = log_c v$

When solving an equation involving logarithms in the same base,
- determine the restrictions that the variable x must respect for both sides of the equation to be defined.
- use the properties of logarithms to get the form $\log_c u = \log_c v$.
- use the equivalence: $\boxed{\log_c u = \log_c v \Leftrightarrow u = v}$
- determine the solutions that respect the restrictions.
  Ex.: See activity 5.

28. Solve the following equations.

a) $\log (x + 1) = \log 6 - \log x$

_____

_____

b) $\ln (x - 2) + \ln 3 = \ln (x + 1)$

_____

_____

c) $\log_2 (x + 1) - \log_2 2 = \log_2 5 - \log_2 (x - 2)$

_____

_____

d) $\ln (x + 3) - \ln (x + 1) = \ln (x - 3) - \ln (x - 2)$

_____

_____

29. Solve the following equations.

a) $\log_5 (x + 2) + \log_5 (x - 2) - \log_5 4 = \log_5 3$ **b)** $\log_5 (x^2 - 4) - \log_5 4 = \log_5 3$

_____

_____

c) $\log_5 (x + 2) = 1 - \log_5 (x - 2)$ **d)** $\log_5 (x^2 - 4) = 1$

_____

_____

30. **a)** Solve the equation $\log_2 (x + 1) + \log_2 (x - 1) = 3$.

_____

b) Solve the equation $\log_2 (x^2 - 1) = 3$.

_____

c) Explain why the equations $\log_2 (x + 1) + \log_2 (x - 1) = 3$ and $\log_2 (x^2 - 1) = 3$ are not equivalent.

_____

ACTIVITY 6 Exponential equation – Form $a^u = b^v$

The exponential equation $3^{x-1} = 2^{x+1}$ contains powers with different bases.
Justify the steps to find the solution.

	Steps	Justifications
	$3^{x-1} = 2^{x+1}$	
1	$\ln 3^{x-1} = \ln 2^{x+1}$	
2	$(x - 1) \ln 3 = (x + 1) \ln 2$	
3	$x \ln 3 - \ln 3 = x \ln 2 + \ln 2$	
4	$x(\ln 3 - \ln 2) = \ln 3 + \ln 2$	
5	$x \ln \left(\frac{3}{2}\right) = \ln 6$	
6	$x = \dfrac{\ln 6}{\ln \frac{3}{2}}$	
7	$x = \log_{\frac{3}{2}} 6$	
	Thus, $S = \left\{ \log_{\frac{3}{2}} 6 \right\}$	

EXPONENTIAL EQUATION — FORM $a^u = b^v$

The use of logarithms enables you to solve an exponential equation involving powers of different bases.

Ex.: Solve the equation $3^{x-1} = 2^{x+1}$.

1. Use the equivalence $\quad a = b \Leftrightarrow \ln a = \ln b$	$3^{x-1} = 2^{x+1}$ $\ln 3^{x-1} = \ln 2^{x+1}$
2. Apply the property: $\log_a b^n = n \log_a b$.	$(x-1)\ln 3 = (x+1)\ln 2$
3. Distribute and isolate the terms with x.	$x \ln 3 - \ln 3 = x \ln 2 + \ln 2$ $x(\ln 3 - \ln 2) = \ln 2 + \ln 3$
4. Apply, if necessary, the properties: $\quad \ln a + \ln b = \ln ab$ and $\ln a - \ln b = \ln \frac{a}{b}$.	$x \ln\left(\frac{3}{2}\right) = \ln 6$
5. Determine x.	$x = \dfrac{\ln 6}{\ln \frac{3}{2}}$
6. Use the change of base law if necessary. $\quad \dfrac{\ln a}{\ln b} = \log_b a$.	$x = \log_{\frac{3}{2}} 6$ Thus, $S = \left\{ \log_{\frac{3}{2}} 6 \right\}$

31. Solve the following exponential equations.

a) $3^{2x-1} = 2^{x+2}$ 　　　　b) $2^{x+1} = 5^{1-x}$ 　　　　c) $\dfrac{2^{x+1}}{5^x} = 3$

_____   _____   _____

32. Solve the following equations.

a) $5^{2x} + 5^x - 6 = 0$ (hint: let $y = 5^x$)

_____

b) $9^x - 5(3^x) + 6 = 0$ (hint: let $y = 3^x$)

_____

33. Julian invests $1000 at an interest rate of 8% compounded annually. One year later, Julie also invests $1000 at an interest rate of 10% compounded annually. After how many years, since the beginning of Julian's investment, will Julian and Julie's accumulated capital be equal? (Round your answer to the nearest tenth.)

_____

_____

Evaluation 4

1. Consider the function $f(x) = -2\left(\frac{1}{2}\right)^{x-2} + 4$.

   a) Represent the function f in the Cartesian plane.

x					
y					

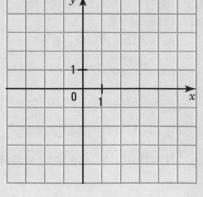

   b) Determine

      1. dom f._____ 2. ran f. _____ 3. zero of f. _____

      4. sign of f. _____

      _____

      5. variation of f. _____ 6. the initial value of f. _____

      7. the equation of the asymptote. _____

2. Consider the function $f(x) = 3\log_2 \frac{1}{2}(x+3) - 3$.

   a) Represent the function f in the Cartesian plane.

x					
y					

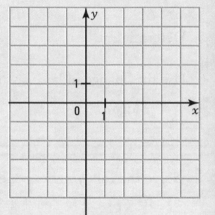

   b) Determine

      1. dom f. _____ 2. ran f. ____ 3. zero of f. _____

      4. sign of f. _____

      _____

      5. variation of f. _____

      6. the initial value of f. _____

      7. the equation of the asymptote. _____

3. Find the domain of the following functions.

   a) $f(x) = -2\left(\frac{3}{2}\right)^{x-1} + 1$ _____ **b)** $f(x) = 2\ln(2x-1) + 3$ _____

   c) $f(x) = \log_2(-2x+6) - 1$ _____ **d)** $f(x) = -5\log_2(x^2 - 9)$ _____

4. Solve the following equations.

   a) $3(2)^x - 24 = 0$ **b)** $3(5)^x - 6 = 0$ **c)** $2(3)^x + 1 = 0$

   _____   _____   _____

   d) $3\log_2 x - 6 = 0$ **e)** $2\log_3 x + 4 = 0$ **f)** $3\log_2(x-1) - 4 = 0$

   _____   _____   _____

5. Solve the following equations.

   a) $\log_2 (x - 3) + \log_2 x = 2$

   _____

   _____

   b) $\ln (x - 1) + \ln (x + 6) = \ln (10 - x)$

   _____

   _____

   c) $3^{x-1} = 2^{x+1}$

   _____

   d) $2(5^{2x}) - 3(5^{2x}) + 1 = 0$

   _____

6. Determine the equation of the asymptote of the following functions.

   a) $f(x) = 2^{3(x-1)} - 4$ _____

   b) $f(x) = -2 \ln (2x - 6) + 1$ _____

7. Determine the range of the following functions.

   a) $f(x) = -3(2)^{2(x+1)} + 5$ _____

   b) $f(x) = -2 \log (2x - 5) + 1$ _____

8. Determine the zero of the following functions.

   a) $f(x) = 2(3)^{(x-2)} - 4$ _____

   b) $f(x) = -2 \log_2 (2x + 1) + 6$ _____

9. Study the sign of the following functions.

   a) $f(x) = -3(2)^{(x-3)} + 12$

   _____

   _____

   b) $f(x) = 3 \log_{\frac{1}{2}} (x - 2) + 3$

   _____

   _____

10. Study the variation of the following functions.

   a) $f(x) = -5\left(\dfrac{1}{2}\right)^{2x+1} + 2$ _____

   b) $f(x) = -2 \log_{\frac{1}{2}} (-2x + 1) + 6$ _____

11. Find the inverse of the following functions.

   a) $y = -2(3)^{2(x-1)} + 4$

   _____

   b) $y = 5 \log_2 3(x - 1) - 10$

   _____

12. Find the rule of the exponential function passing through the points A(1, −5) and B(2, −11) and having the line $y = 1$ for an asymptote.

   _____

13. A logarithmic function has a rule of the form $y = \log_c (x - h) + k$. Its graph passes through the points A(4, 2) and B(10, 3) and has the line $x = 1$ for an asymptote. Find the rule of this function.

   _____

14. Knowing that $x = \log_a 2$; $y = \log_a 3$ and $z = \log_a 5$, express the following logarithms in terms of x, y and z.

a) $\log_a 60$ _____

b) $\log_a \frac{72}{25}$ _____

15. Knowing that $\log_a x = 2$ and $\log_a y = 3$; calculate the numerical value of the following logarithms.

a) $\log_a x^3 y^2$ _____

b) $\log_a \left(\frac{a^3 x^2}{y^2} \right)$ _____

16. Write the following expressions as a single logarithm.

a) $2 \log 3 + \log 2 - \log 6 - \log 4$ _____

b) $3 \ln x - 2 \ln x^2 + \ln x^3$ _____

c) $\log (x^2 - 1) - \log (x^2 - 3x + 2)$ _____

d) $\ln (2x^2 - 3x - 2) - 2 \ln (x - 2)$ _____

17. In a laboratory experiment, there are initially 12 insects. We notice that the number of insects doubles every 3 days.

a) What is the rule which gives the resulting number y of insects as a function of the number t of days since the beginning of the experiment? _____

b) After how many days will there be at least 6144 insects? _____

18. The formula $c(t) = c_0 \left(1 + \frac{i}{n} \right)^{nt}$ gives the accumulated capital after t years of an initial capital c_0 invested at an annual interest rate i compounded n times per year.

a) A capital of \$2500 is invested at an annual interest rate of 6% compounded monthly. What will the accumulated capital be after 5 years? _____

b) How long will it take for a capital invested at an annual interest rate of 8% compounded twice per year to double its value? _____

_____

19. The population of a village decreased by approximately 2% per year since 1990. In the year 2000, the village had a population of 2500.

a) What was the population of this village in

1. 1995? _____   2. 2007? _____

b) If the rate of decay is maintained, in what year will the population of this village be equal to half the population recorded in the year 2000? _____

20. The number of bacteria triples every thirty minutes in a culture. Four hours after the beginning of the experiment, we observe 32 805 bacteria. How many bacteria are there in the culture 1 hour and 15 minutes after the beginning of the experiment?

_____

_____

Chapter 5

Trigonometry

1. If $P(t) = (a, b)$ is a trigonometric point, what are the coordinates of the trigonometric point $P(2t)$?

_____

2. If $P(t) = (a, b)$ is a trigonometric point, what are the coordinates of the following trigonometric points?

   a) $P(t + \pi)$ _____   **b)** $P\left(t + \frac{\pi}{2}\right)$ _____

3. If $P(t) = (a, b)$ is a trigonometric point, determine

   a) $\tan t$ _____ **b)** $\cotan t$ _____ **c)** $\sec t$ _____ **d)** $\csc t$_____

4. Determine the exact coordinates of the following trigonometric points.

   a) $P\left(\frac{25\pi}{6}\right)$ _____   **b)** $P\left(-\frac{19\pi}{4}\right)$ _____   **c)** $P\left(-\frac{16\pi}{3}\right)$ _____

5. If $\tan t = \frac{12}{5}$ and $\pi \leqslant t \leqslant \frac{3\pi}{2}$, determine

   a) $\sin t$ _____ **b)** $\cos t$_____ **c)** $\sec t$ _____ **d)** $\csc t$_____

6. Solve the equation $2 \sin \pi(x + 1) + 1 = 0$ in $\mathbb{R}$.

_____

7. Given the function $f(x) = -2 \cos \frac{\pi}{3}(x + 1) + 1$.

   a) Determine

      1. the amplitude of f._____   2. the period of f. _____

      3. the domain of f._____   4. the range of f. _____

   b) Graph the function f in the Cartesian plane.

   c) Determine in $\mathbb{R}$

      1. the zeros of f._____

      2. the sign of f._____

      3. the variation of f._____

   d) Determine over $[11, 17]$

      1. the zeros of f._____

      2. the sign of f. _____

      _____

      3. the variation of f.

      _____

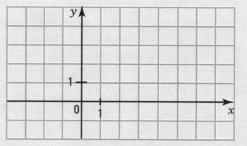

5.1 Trigonometric ratios in a right triangle

ACTIVITY 1 Trigonometric ratios

Consider the triangle ABC on the right.

a) 1. What is the length of the hypotenuse? _____

    2. What can we say about the acute angles A and B? _____

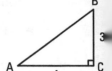

b) Determine the ratios

    1. $\sin A$ _____   2. $\cos A$ _____   3. $\tan A$ ___

c) By inverting each of the preceding ratios, we define the ratios

    $\sec A = \dfrac{1}{\cos A}$, $\csc A = \dfrac{1}{\sin A}$ and $\cot A = \dfrac{1}{\tan A}$. Determine

    1. $\sec A$ _____   2. $\csc A$ _____   3. $\cot A$ _____

d) Verify the following trigonometric identities.

    1. $\sin^2 A + \cos^2 A = 1$ _____

    2. $1 + \tan^2 A = \sec^2 A$ _____

    3. $1 + \cot^2 A = \csc^2 A$ _____

TRIGONOMETRIC RATIOS

- All right triangles verify the Pythagorean theorem:

$$a^2 + b^2 = c^2$$

- The acute angles of a right triangle are complementary.

$$m \angle A + m \angle B = 90°$$

- We define the following ratios for the angle A.

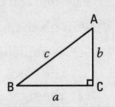

$\overline{AB}$ is the hypotenuse.
$\overline{BC}$ is the opposite side to $\angle A$.
$\overline{AC}$ is the adjacent side to $\angle A$.

$$\sin A = \frac{\text{measure of the opposite side}}{\text{measure of the hypotenuse}} = \frac{a}{c}$$

$$\cos A = \frac{\text{measure of the adjacent side}}{\text{measure of the hypotenuse}} = \frac{b}{c}$$

$$\tan A = \frac{\text{measure of the opposite side}}{\text{measure of the adjacent side}} = \frac{a}{b}$$

By inverting the preceding ratios, we get:

$$\sec A = \frac{1}{\cos A} = \frac{c}{b} \qquad \csc A = \frac{1}{\sin A} = \frac{c}{a} \qquad \cot A = \frac{1}{\tan A} = \frac{b}{a}$$

1. Consider the right triangle ABC.

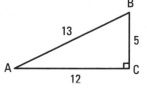

a) Determine the following ratios.

    1. $\sin A$ _____   2. $\cos A$ _____   3. $\tan A$ _____

    4. $\sec A$ _____   5. $\csc A$ _____   6. $\cot A$ _____

b) Verify the trigonometric identities.

    1. $\sin^2 A + \cos^2 A = 1$ _____

    2. $1 + \tan^2 A = \sec^2 A$ _____

    3. $1 + \cot^2 A = \csc^2 A$ _____

c) Verify that

    1. $\tan A = \dfrac{\sin A}{\cos A}$ _____   2. $\cot A = \dfrac{\cos A}{\sin A}$ _____

d) Verify that

    1. $\sin A = \cos B$ 2. $\cos A = \sin B$ 3. $\tan A = \cot B$

2. Solve the following triangles (round the measures of the sides and angles to the nearest tenth).

a)

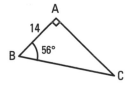

b)

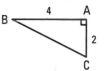

c)

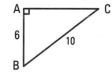

    _____   _____   _____

    _____   _____   _____

    _____   _____   _____

ACTIVITY 2   Remarkable angles: 0°, 30°, 45°, 60°, 90°

a) The triangle ABC on the right is equilateral, with each side measuring 1 unit. We have drawn the altitude AH.

    1. Explain why $m\overline{BH} = 0.5$ u.

    _____

    2. Explain why $m \angle ABC = m \angle BAC = m \angle ACB = 60°$.

    _____

    3. Explain why $m \angle BAH = 30°$.

    _____

    4. Refer to the triangle ABH to show that $\sin 30° = \frac{1}{2}$.

    _____

5. Explain why $m\overline{AH} = \dfrac{\sqrt{3}}{2}$.

_____

6. Refer to the triangle ABH to show that $\sin 60° = \dfrac{\sqrt{3}}{2}$.

_____

_____

7. Explain why $\cos 60° = \dfrac{1}{2}$ and $\cos 30° = \dfrac{\sqrt{3}}{2}$.

_____

8. Explain why $\tan 30° = \dfrac{\sqrt{3}}{3}$ and $\tan 60° = \sqrt{3}$.

_____

_____

b) The given right triangle is isosceles. The hypotenuse measures 1 unit. 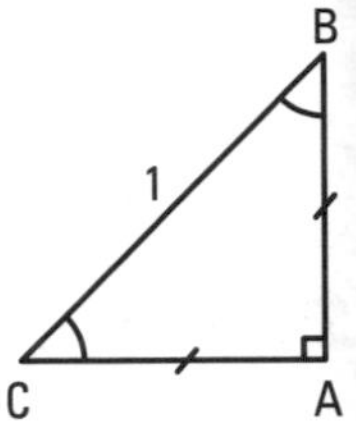
1. What is the measure of the sides of the right angle?

_____

_____

2. What is the measure of each acute angle? _____

3. Show that $\sin 45° = \dfrac{\sqrt{2}}{2}$ and that $\cos 45° = \dfrac{\sqrt{2}}{2}$.

_____

_____

4. Explain why $\tan 45° = 1$. _____

c) Using a calculator, verify that $\sin 0° = 0$; $\sin 90° = 1$; $\cos 0° = 1$ and $\cos 90° = 0$.

d) Explain why $\tan 90°$ is not defined.

_____

REMARKABLE ANGLES

Angles	0°	30°	45°	60°	90°
Sine	0	$\dfrac{1}{2}$	$\dfrac{\sqrt{2}}{2}$	$\dfrac{\sqrt{3}}{2}$	1
Cosine	1	$\dfrac{\sqrt{3}}{2}$	$\dfrac{\sqrt{2}}{2}$	$\dfrac{1}{2}$	0
Tangent	0	$\dfrac{\sqrt{3}}{3}$	1	$\sqrt{3}$	

Memorize the sine line.

From the sine line, we deduce the cosine line, since $\cos x = \sin(90° - x)$.

From the sine and cosine lines, we deduce the tangent line, since $\tan x = \dfrac{\sin x}{\cos x}$.

3. Complete the following table by giving the exact ratios.

Angles	0°	30°	45°	60°	90°
Secant					
Cosecant					
Cotangent					

4. Determine the exact measures of x and y.

a)

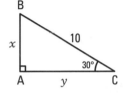

_____

b)

_____

c)

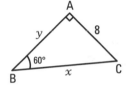

_____

d)

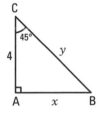

_____

e)

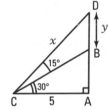

_____

5.2 Arc length

A **turn** is a natural unit for measuring angles. Certain fractions of turns define units of angle measures.
– a **degree** (°) corresponds to the fraction $\frac{1}{360}$ of a turn. Therefore: 1 turn = 360°.

– a **gradian** (grad) corresponds to the fraction $\frac{1}{400}$ of a turn. Therefore: 1 turn = 400 grad.

– a **radian** (rad) corresponds to the fraction $\frac{1}{2\pi}$ of a turn (0.159... turn). Therefore: 1 turn = 2π rad.

a) Convert $\frac{1}{4}$ turn in

1. degrees _____ 2. gradians _____ 3. radians _____

b) Convert 180° in

1. turns _____ 2. gradians _____ 3. radians _____

RADIANS

- In a circle, a **radian** (rad) corresponds to the measure of the central angle that subtends an arc whose length is equal to the circle's radius.

  We have: 1 turn = 360° = 2π rad.

  Remember that:

  $$\boxed{\pi \text{ rad} = 180°}$$

  Therefore: $1 \text{ rad} = \frac{180°}{\pi}$ and $1° = \frac{\pi}{180°}$ rad.

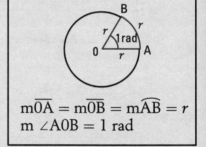

$$m\overline{OA} = m\overline{OB} = m\widehat{AB} = r$$
$$m \angle AOB = 1 \text{ rad}$$

  These relations enable you to convert radians into degrees and vice-versa.

  Ex.: $3 \text{ rad} = 3\left(\frac{180°}{\pi}\right) = \frac{540°}{\pi}$.

  $$120° = 120\left(\frac{\pi}{180°} \text{ rad}\right) = \frac{2\pi}{3} \text{ rad}.$$

- When the unit measure of an angle is not indicated, it is implied that the angle measure is in radians.

---

1. Express, in radians, the measures of the following angles.

a) 30°_____ **b)** 45°_____ **c)** 60°_____ **d)** 90° _____

e) 120°_____ **f)** 135° _____ **g)** 300° _____ **h)** 390°_____

2. Express, in degrees, the measures of the following angles.

a) 2 rad _____ **b)** $\frac{\pi}{3}$ rad _____ **c)** $\frac{7\pi}{6}$ rad _____ **d)** $\frac{4\pi}{3}$ rad _____

e) 5 rad _____ **f)** $\frac{2\pi}{5}$ rad _____ **g)** $\frac{11\pi}{6}$ rad _____ **h)** $\frac{5\pi}{2}$ rad _____

3. Convert according to the desired unit.

a) 0.5 turn = _____ rad   b) 60° = _____ turn   c) $\frac{5\pi}{6}$ rad = _____ °

d) $\frac{3\pi}{2}$ rad = _____ turn   e) 150° = _____ rad   f) $\frac{2\pi}{3}$ rad = _____ turn

g) 2 turns = _____ °   h) 240° = _____ rad   i) 405° = _____ rad

4. Express, in radians and in terms of π, the measures of the angles that are multiples of 45°.

a) 45°_____   b) 90°_____   c) 135°_____   d) 180°_____

e) 225°_____   f) 270°_____   g) 315°_____   h) 360°_____

5. The following angles, in radians, are expressed in terms of $\frac{\pi}{6}$. Express them in degrees.

a) $\frac{\pi}{6}$ rad _____   b) $\frac{5\pi}{6}$ rad _____   c) $\frac{7\pi}{6}$ rad _____   d) $\frac{11\pi}{6}$ rad _____

6. The following angles, in radians, are expressed in terms of $\frac{\pi}{3}$. Express them in degrees.

a) $\frac{\pi}{3}$ rad _____   b) $\frac{2\pi}{3}$ rad _____   c) $\frac{4\pi}{3}$ rad _____   d) $\frac{5\pi}{3}$ rad _____

ACTIVITY 2 Arc length

Consider the circle on the right with radius r and central angle AOB.

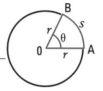

a) What is the measure of the arc AB if the central angle AOB measures

1. 1 radian?_____   2. 2 radians?_____   3. 3 radians?_____

b) If we let θ represent the measure, in radians, of the central angle AOB and s represent the measure of the arc AB, express s as a function of r and θ. _____

c) If the circle has a radius of $r = 1$, what can be said of the measure s of the arc subtended by the central angle measuring θ radians?

_____

ARC LENGTH

- Consider a circle with radius r and a central angle AOB which subtends the arc AB.
  If θ represents the measure, in radians, of the central angle and s represents the length of the subtended arc, then

$$s = r\theta$$

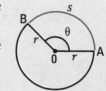

- Note that r and s are expressed in the same units.
  Ex.: On the right, we have: $r = 2$ cm and $\theta = \frac{\pi}{3}$ rad.

  The arc AB measures $s = \frac{2\pi}{3}$ cm ≈ 2.09 cm.

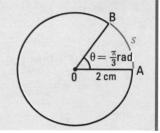

- In a circle with a radius of 1 unit, the length of an arc is equal to the central angle which subtends this arc.

$$r = 1 \Rightarrow s = \theta$$

Ex.: $r = 1$ cm and $\theta = \dfrac{\pi}{3}$ rad $\Rightarrow s = \dfrac{\pi}{3}$ cm ≈ 1.05 cm.

7. By referring to the figure on the right, calculate the length of

a) $\overset{\frown}{AB}$ _____ b) $\overset{\frown}{CD}$ _____ c) $\overset{\frown}{EF}$ _____

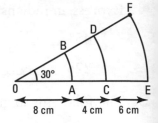

8. In a circle with radius r, a central angle A0B measuring θ subtends the arc AB of length s.

Complete the table of values on the right.

r	θ	s
2 cm	$\dfrac{2\pi}{3}$ rad	
	$\dfrac{5\pi}{6}$ rad	5π cm
12 cm		10π cm

9. The radius of curvature of a railroad track is equal to 600 m. What is the central angle of a train's trajectory if it travels 1.8 km along this track? _____

10. The minute hand of a watch measures 0.8 cm. What is the distance traveled by the end of the minute hand in

a) 2 h 15 min? _____ b) 1 day? _____ c) 1 year? _____

11. The wheel of a bicycle turns at a speed of 150 turns per minute.

a) Express the speed in radians per second. _____

b) What is the distance traveled in 30 minutes if the radius of the wheel measures 40 cm? _____

12. A circular segment is the surface on a disk between an arc and the chord which subtends this arc. Let r represent the radius of the circle on the right and θ represent the central angle that defines the circular segment.

a) Show that the area A of the circular segment is: $A = \dfrac{r^2}{2}(\theta - \sin\theta)$.

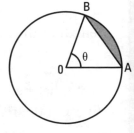

_____

_____

_____

b) Calculate the area A of a circular segment when $r = 10$ cm and $\theta = \dfrac{\pi}{6}$.

_____

5.3 Trigonometric circle

ACTIVITY 1 Trigonometric angle

In the Cartesian plane on the right, the angle AOB is obtained by having the initial side 0A undergo a rotation with centre 0, angle of 145° in a positive direction (counter-clockwise). Such an angle is called a trigonometric angle. The side 0B is called the terminal side.

Define a clockwise rotation which applies the initial side 0A onto the terminal side 0B.

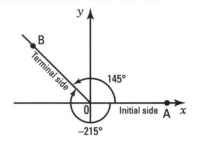

TRIGONOMETRIC ANGLE

In a **trigonometric angle**, we distinguish:
- the vertex, located at the centre 0 of the Cartesian plane.
- the side of the angle, called **initial side**, that is along the positive x-axis.
- the other side of the angle, called **terminal side**, obtained by a rotation centered at 0 of the initial side.

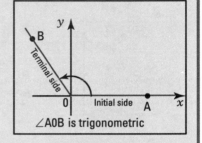

$\angle$AOB is trigonometric

- If the rotation is performed in a positive direction (counter-clockwise), then the measure of the trigonometric angle is positive.

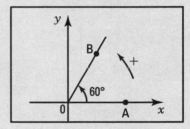

- If the rotation is performed in a negative direction (clockwise), then the measure of the trigonometric angle is negative.

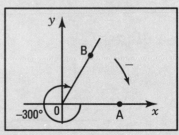

---

1. Consider the trigonometric angle AOB. What conditions must be met when considering

a) the vertex 0 of the angle? _____

b) the point A if $\overline{0A}$ is the initial side of the angle?

_____

c) the point B if $\overline{0B}$ is the terminal side of the angle? _____

---

2. Determine the measure *t*, in degrees and radians, of each of the following trigonometric angles.

a)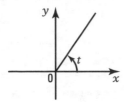

b)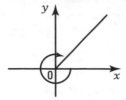

c)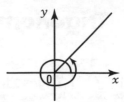

d)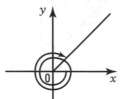

e)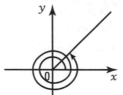

f)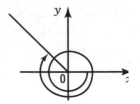

3. Represent each of the following trigonometric angles with the given measure.

a) $\frac{\pi}{6}$ rad

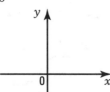

b) 120°

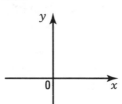

c) 420°

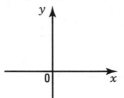

d) $\frac{7\pi}{3}$ rad

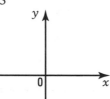

e) −120°

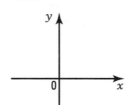

f) −450°

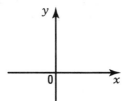

g) $-\frac{5\pi}{6}$ rad

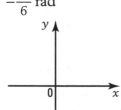

h) $\frac{13\pi}{6}$ rad

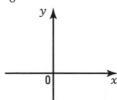

i) −3π rad

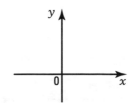

ACTIVITY 2 Trigonometric circle and trigonometric points

A circle centered at 0 with radius 1 has been drawn in the Cartesian plane on the right. This circle is called the **trigonometric circle**. Any point P(x, y) on this circle is called a **trigonometric point**.

Any trigonometric point P(x, y) verifies the equation $x^2 + y^2 = 1$ and, conversely, any point P(x, y) that verifies the equation $x^2 + y^2 = 1$ is trigonometric.

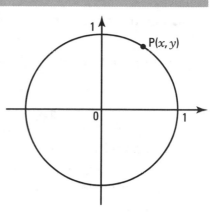

Determine if the following points are trigonometric.

a) $\left(\frac{1}{2}, \frac{1}{2}\right)$ _____

b) $(1, 0)$ _____

c) $\left(\frac{\sqrt{2}}{2}, \frac{\sqrt{2}}{2}\right)$ _____

d) $\left(\frac{1}{2}, \frac{\sqrt{3}}{2}\right)$ _____

e) $\left(\frac{\sqrt{3}}{2}, \frac{-1}{2}\right)$ _____

f) $(0, -1)$ _____

TRIGONOMETRIC CIRCLE AND TRIGONOMETRIC POINTS

- The **trigonometric circle** is a circle centered at 0, the origin of the Cartesian plane, with a radius of 1.

- Any point P(x, y) on the unit circle is called a **trigonometric point**. We have:

$$P(x, y) \text{ is trigonometric} \Leftrightarrow x^2 + y^2 = 1$$

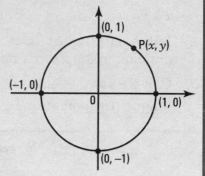

4. The point $\left(\frac{a-4}{13}, \frac{a+3}{13}\right)$ is a trigonometric point. Determine the possible values for a.

_____

5. Determine the possible values for x if the following points are trigonometric.

a) P$(x, 1)$ _____

b) P$\left(x, \frac{1}{2}\right)$ _____

c) P$(x, 0.6)$ _____

d) P$\left(x, \frac{5}{13}\right)$ _____

6. In each of the following cases, determine the coordinates of the trigonometric point P.

a) P$\left(\frac{1}{2}, y\right) \in$ 4th quadrant. _____

b) P$(-0.6, y) \in$ 2nd quadrant. _____

c) P$\left(\frac{\sqrt{3}}{2}, y\right) \in$ 1st quadrant. _____

d) P$\left(-\frac{1}{2}, y\right) \in$ 3rd quadrant. _____

Consider the trigonometric circle on the right, a trigonometric point $P(x, y)$ and the measure t, in radians, of the trigonometric angle A0P. $(0 \leqslant t \leqslant 2\pi)$

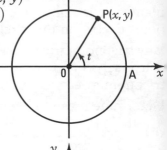

a) What is the length of arc AP? Justify your answer.

_____

_____

b) Let $P(t)$ represent the trigonometric point associated with the trigonometric angle t. $(t \in \mathbb{R})$

Determine the Cartesian coordinates (x, y) of the following trigonometric points $P(t)$.

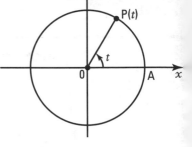

1. $P(0)$ _____ 2. $P\left(\frac{\pi}{2}\right)$ _____ 3. $P(\pi)$ _____

4. $P\left(\frac{3\pi}{2}\right)$ _____ 5. $P(2\pi)$ _____ 6. $P\left(-\frac{\pi}{2}\right)$ _____

7. $P(-\pi)$ _____ 8. $P\left(-\frac{3\pi}{2}\right)$ _____ 9. $P(-2\pi)$ _____

c) Is it true to say that for each real number t, there is a unique corresponding trigonometric point on the trigonometric circle? _____

d) Can we say that each trigonometric point $P(x, y)$ on the trigonometric circle corresponds to a unique trigonometric angle t? _____

LOCATING A TRIGONOMETRIC POINT

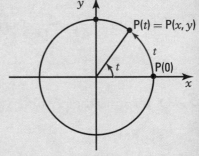

- Each real number t corresponds to a unique point on the unit circle written as $P(t)$.

  $P(t)$ is the extremity of the arc whose origin is the point $P(0)$ and whose directed measure is equal to t.

  $P(x, y)$ is the Cartesian notation of this point.

  Ex.: $P(0°) = P(1, 0)$
  $P(90°) = P(0, 1)$

- If t is positive, we locate the point $P(t)$ by moving in a counter-clockwise direction.

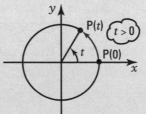

- If t is negative, we locate the point $P(t)$ by moving in a clockwise direction.

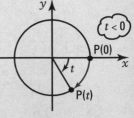

Ex.:

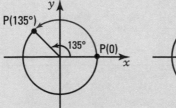

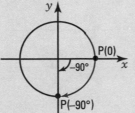

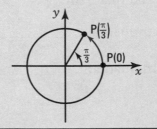

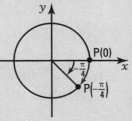

7. Indicate in which quadrant each of the following trigonometric points is located.

a) P(120°) _____ b) P(300°) _____ c) P(400°) _____ d) P(−120°) _____

e) $P\left(\frac{5\pi}{6}\right)$ _____ f) $P\left(\frac{4\pi}{3}\right)$ _____ g) $P\left(\frac{11\pi}{6}\right)$ _____ h) $P\left(-\frac{3\pi}{4}\right)$ _____

8. If P(*t*) is a trigonometric point located in the 1st quadrant, deduce the quadrant that each of following trigonometric points will be located in.

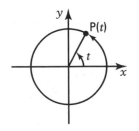

a) P(*t* + π) _____ b) $P\left(t + \frac{\pi}{2}\right)$ _____ c) $P\left(t + \frac{3\pi}{2}\right)$ _____

d) P(−*t*) _____ e) P(π − *t*) _____ f) $P\left(t - \frac{\pi}{2}\right)$ _____

g) P(*t* + 2π) _____ h) P(*t* − 2π) _____ i) P(*t* + 6π) _____

ACTIVITY 4 **Cartesian coordinates of a trigonometric point**

a) Consider a trigonometric point P(*t*) located in the 1st quadrant; $\left(0 \leqslant t \leqslant \frac{\pi}{2}\right)$.

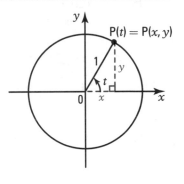

Which trigonometric ratio enables you to calculate

1. the *x*-coordinate of the point P(*t*)? _____
2. the *y*-coordinate of the point P(*t*)? _____

b) Determine, without using a calculator, the coordinates of the trigonometric points

1. P(0) = _____

2. $P\left(\frac{\pi}{2}\right) =$ _____

c) The points $P\left(\frac{\pi}{6}\right)$, $P\left(\frac{\pi}{4}\right)$ and $P\left(\frac{\pi}{3}\right)$ are trigonometric points in the 1st quadrant called remarkable trigonometric points. Determine the exact coordinates of these points without using a calculator.

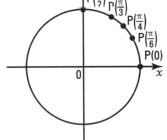

1. $P\left(\frac{\pi}{6}\right) =$ _____

2. $P\left(\frac{\pi}{4}\right) =$ _____

3. $P\left(\frac{\pi}{3}\right) =$ _____

d) The points P(1 rad) and P(40°) are trigonometric points located in the 1st quadrant. Using a calculator, determine the coordinates of these points to the nearest hundredth. Use the appropriate mode, rad or deg, which applies.

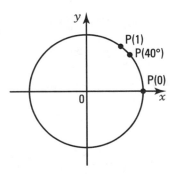

1. P(1) = _____
2. P(40°) = _____

e) The results observed in a), valid for any trigonometric point in the 1st quadrant, are generalized and bring us to the definition of the Cartesian coordinates of any trigonometric point P(t).

We have: P(t) = (cos t, sin t) where $0 \leqslant t \leqslant 2\pi$.

Calculate, using a calculator, the Cartesian coordinates of

1. P(100°) _____ 2. P(200°) _____ 3. P(300°) _____

CARTESIAN COORDINATES OF A TRIGONOMETRIC POINT

- Given a trigonometric point P(t). ($0 \leqslant t \leqslant 2\pi$)
  - the x-coordinate of P(t) is equal to cos t.
  - the y-coordinate of P(t) is equal to sin t.

  Note that:

  $$\boxed{P(t) = (\cos t,\ \sin t)}$$

  By convention, we call the x-axis the cosine axis, and the y-axis the sine axis.

  Ex.: $P\left(\dfrac{\pi}{3}\right) = \left(\cos\dfrac{\pi}{3},\ \sin\dfrac{\pi}{3}\right) = \left(\dfrac{1}{2},\ \dfrac{\sqrt{3}}{2}\right)$

  P(140°) = (cos 140°, sin 140°) = (−0.7660, 0.6428)

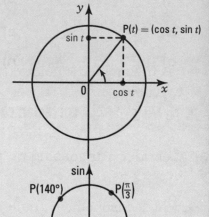

---

9. For each of the following trigonometric points P(t), indicate
  1. the quadrant in which the trigonometric point is located.
  2. the sign of cos t and the sign of sin t.

a) P(160°)   **b)** P(350°)   **c)** P(−150°)   **d)** P(750°)
  1. _____   1. _____   1. _____   1. _____
  2. _____   2. _____   2. _____   2. _____

e) $P\left(\dfrac{5\pi}{6}\right)$ **f)** $P\left(\dfrac{5\pi}{3}\right)$.   **g)** $P\left(-\dfrac{2\pi}{3}\right)$ **h)** $P\left(\dfrac{10\pi}{3}\right)$
  1. _____   1. _____   1. _____   1. _____
  2. _____   2. _____   2. _____   2. _____

10. Using a calculator, determine the coordinates of the following trigonometric points to the nearest thousandth.

a) P(175°) _____   **b)** P(625°) _____

c) $P\left(\dfrac{11\pi}{5}\right)$ _____   **d)** $P\left(-\dfrac{29\pi}{6}\right)$ _____

11. Knowing that $P(t) = \left(\dfrac{3}{5},\ \dfrac{-4}{5}\right)$ is a trigonometric point, determine

a) cos t = _____   **b)** sin t = _____   **c)** tan t = _____

d) sec t = _____   **e)** csc t = _____   **f)** cotan t = _____

12. Knowing that $P(t) = \left(\cos t, \frac{5}{13}\right)$ is a trigonometric point located in the 2nd quadrant, determine

a) $\cos t =$ _____

b) $\sec t =$ _____

c) $\csc t =$ _____

d) $\tan t =$ _____

e) $\cot t =$ _____

13. For each of the following trigonometric points, give the two possible values for the missing coordinate.

a) $P\left(\frac{1}{2}, \ldots\right)$ _____

b) $P\left(\ldots, \frac{\sqrt{3}}{2}\right)$ _____

c) $P(\ldots, 0.6)$ _____

d) $P\left(\frac{-5}{13}, \ldots\right)$ _____

e) $P\left(\frac{2}{3}, \ldots\right)$ _____

f) $P\left(\ldots, \frac{\sqrt{2}}{2}\right)$ _____

14. A trigonometric point $P(t)$ has an x-coordinate of $\cos t = 0.8$.

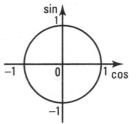

a) If the point $P(t)$ is located in the 1st quadrant,

    1. determine the y-coordinate $\sin t$. _____

    2. deduce, in degrees, the value of t knowing that $0 \leqslant t \leqslant 90°$.

    _____

    3. deduce, in degrees, the value of t knowing that $360° \leqslant t \leqslant 450°$.

    _____

b) If the point $P(t)$ is located in the 4th quadrant,

    1. determine the y-coordinate $\sin t$. _____

    2. deduce, in degrees, the value of t knowing that $270° \leqslant t \leqslant 360°$. _____

    3. deduce, in degrees, the value of t knowing that $630° \leqslant t \leqslant 720°$. _____

15. A trigonometric point $P(t)$ has an x-coordinate of $\cos t = -0.6$.

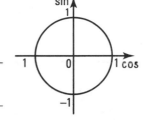

a) If the point $P(t)$ is located in the 2nd quadrant,

    1. determine the y-coordinate $\sin t$. _____

    2. deduce, in degrees, the value of t knowing that $90° \leqslant t \leqslant 180°$.

    _____

    3. deduce, in degrees, the value of t knowing that $450° \leqslant t \leqslant 540°$.

    _____

b) If the point $P(t)$ is located in the 3rd quadrant,

    1. determine the y-coordinate $\sin t$. _____

    2. deduce, in degrees, the value of t knowing that $180° \leqslant t \leqslant 270°$. _____

    3. deduce, in degrees, the value of t knowing that $540° \leqslant t \leqslant 630°$. _____

16. A trigonometric point $P(t)$ has a y-coordinate of $\sin t = \frac{5}{13}$.

a) If the point $P(t)$ is located in the 1st quadrant,

    1. determine the x-coordinate $\cos t$. _____

    2. deduce, in degrees, the value of t knowing that $0° \leqslant t \leqslant 90°$. _____

b) If the point $P(t)$ is located in the 2nd quadrant,

    1. determine the x-coordinate $\cos t$. _____

    2. deduce, in degrees, the value of t knowing that $90° \leqslant t \leqslant 180°$. _____

17. A trigonometric point $P(t)$ has a y-coordinate of $\sin t = \frac{-4}{5}$.

a) If the point $P(t)$ is located in the 3rd quadrant,

    1. determine the x-coordinate $\cos t$. _____

    2. deduce, in degrees, the value of t knowing that $180° \leqslant t \leqslant 270°$. _____

b) If the point $P(t)$ is located in the 4th quadrant,

    1. determine the x-coordinate $\cos t$. _____

    2. deduce, in degrees, the value of t knowing that $270° \leqslant t \leqslant 360°$. _____

ACTIVITY 5   Properties of trigonometric points

a) Consider the trigonometric points represented on the unit circle on the right.

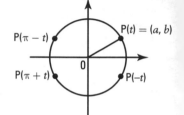

    1. Name the geometric transformation that applies the point $P(t)$ onto the trigonometric point

      1) $P(\pi - t)$ _____

      2) $P(-t)$ _____

      3) $P(\pi + t)$ _____

    2. Deduce the Cartesian coordinates of the points

      1) $P(\pi - t)$ _____   2) $P(-t)$ _____   3) $P(\pi + t)$ _____

b) Consider the trigonometric points on the right.

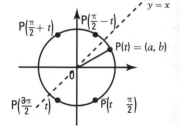

    1. Find the image of the point $P(t)$ by the reflection about the line $y = x$, and deduce the coordinates of this image.

    _____

    2. Deduce the coordinates of the trigonometric points

      1) $P\left(\frac{\pi}{2} + t\right)$ _____   2) $P\left(\frac{3\pi}{2} - t\right)$ _____   3) $P\left(t - \frac{\pi}{2}\right)$ _____

PROPERTIES OF TRIGONOMETRIC POINTS

Given a trigonometric point $P(t) = (a, b)$, geometric transformations enable you to deduce the Cartesian coordinates of the following trigonometric points.

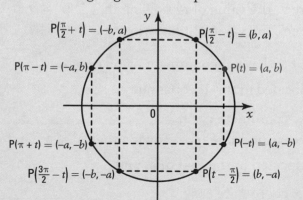

---

18. Consider the trigonometric point $P(t) = \left(\frac{5}{13}, \frac{12}{13}\right)$.

  a) Deduce the coordinates of the following trigonometric points.

  1. $P(-t)$ _____   2. $P(\pi - t)$ _____   3. $P(\pi + t)$ _____

  b) Deduce

  1. $\cos t$ _____   2. $\sin t$ _____   3. $\cos(-t)$ _____

  4. $\sin(-t)$ _____   5. $\cos(\pi - t)$ _____   6. $\sin(\pi + t)$ _____

19. In each of the following cases, choose the correct answer from the following 4 possible answers: $\cos t$, $\sin t$, $-\cos t$ and $-\sin t$.

  a) $\cos(-t)$ _____   **b)** $\sin(-t)$ _____   **c)** $\cos(\pi + t)$ _____   **d)** $\sin(\pi + t)$ _____

  e) $\cos(\pi + t)$ _____   **f)** $\sin(\pi - t)$ _____   **g)** $\cos\left(\frac{\pi}{2} - t\right)$ _____   **h)** $\sin\left(\frac{\pi}{2} - t\right)$ _____

  i) $\cos\left(\frac{\pi}{2} + t\right)$ _____   **j)** $\sin\left(\frac{\pi}{2} + t\right)$ _____   **k)** $\cos\left(t - \frac{\pi}{2}\right)$ _____   **l)** $\sin\left(t - \frac{\pi}{2}\right)$ _____

ACTIVITY 6 Periodicity of trigonometric points

Given the trigonometric point $P(t) = (a, b)$.

a) Determine the coordinates of the following trigonometric points.

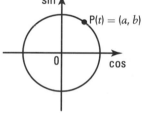

  1. $P(t + 2\pi)$ _____   2. $P(t + 4\pi)$ _____   3. $P(t + 6\pi)$ _____
  4. $P(t - 2\pi)$ _____   5. $P(t - 4\pi)$ _____   6. $P(t - 6\pi)$ _____

b) 1. What can we say about the 6 trigonometric points defined in a)?

  _____

  2. What is the smallest positive real number a such that $P(t) = P(t + a)$? _____
  3. Is it true to say that $P(t) = P(t + 2\pi n), n \in \mathbb{Z}$? _____

c) If $n \in \mathbb{Z}$, is it true to say that

  1. $\cos t = \cos(t + 2\pi n)$? _____   2. $\sin t = \sin(t + 2\pi n)$? _____

PERIODICITY OF TRIGONOMETRIC POINTS

- Given a trigonometric point $P(t)$. The smallest positive real number p such that $P(t + p) = P(t)$ is called the period.
  This period is equal to 2π, that is

  $$\boxed{P(t + 2\pi) = P(t), \forall\, t \in \mathbb{R}}$$

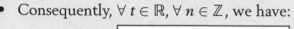

- Note that $P(t) = P(t + 2\pi n), n \in \mathbb{Z}$.
  Thus, $...P(t - 4\pi) = P(t - 2\pi) = P(t) = P(t + 2\pi) = P(t + 4\pi) ...$
- Consequently, $\forall\, t \in \mathbb{R}, \forall\, n \in \mathbb{Z}$, we have:

  $$\boxed{\cos(t + 2\pi n) = \cos t} \quad \text{and} \quad \boxed{\sin(t + 2\pi n) = \sin t}$$

  Ex.: If $P(t) = (0.6; 0.8)$ then $P(t + 10\pi) = (0.6; 0.8)$,
  $\cos(t + 10\pi) = 0.6$ and $\sin(t + 10\pi) = 0.8$.

20. Write each of the following trigonometric points in the form $P(t)$ where $0 \leqslant t < 2\pi$.

a) $P\left(\dfrac{13\pi}{6}\right)$ _____

b) $P(2\pi)$ _____

c) $P\left(\dfrac{17\pi}{4}\right)$ _____

d) $P\left(\dfrac{-5\pi}{3}\right)$ _____

e) $P\left(\dfrac{-10\pi}{3}\right)$ _____

f) $P\left(\dfrac{121\pi}{6}\right)$ _____

ACTIVITY 7 Cartesian coordinates of the remarkable trigonometric points

The three remarkable trigonometric points of the 1st quadrant $P\left(\dfrac{\pi}{6}\right)$, $P\left(\dfrac{\pi}{4}\right)$ and $P\left(\dfrac{\pi}{3}\right)$ are represented on the right.

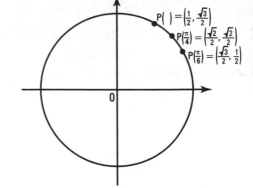

a) Locate on the unit circle the remarkable points of the 2nd quadrant and give the Cartesian coordinates of these points.

1. $P\left(\dfrac{2\pi}{3}\right)$ _____

2. $P\left(\dfrac{3\pi}{4}\right)$ _____

3. $P\left(\dfrac{5\pi}{6}\right)$ _____

b) Locate on the trigonometric circle the remarkable points of the 3rd quadrant and give the Cartesian coordinates of these points.

1. $P\left(\dfrac{7\pi}{6}\right)$ _____

2. $P\left(\dfrac{5\pi}{4}\right)$ _____

3. $P\left(\dfrac{4\pi}{3}\right)$ _____

c) Locate on the trigonometric circle the remarkable points of the 4th quadrant and give the Cartesian coordinates of these points.

1. $P\left(\dfrac{5\pi}{3}\right)$ _____

2. $P\left(\dfrac{7\pi}{4}\right)$ _____

3. $P\left(\dfrac{11\pi}{6}\right)$ _____

REMARKABLE TRIGONOMETRIC POINTS

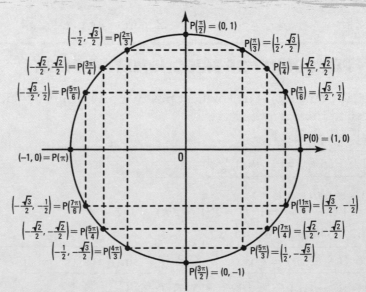

From the coordinates of the remarkable points of the 1st quadrant, we deduce by symmetry the coordinates of the remarkable points of the three other quadrants.

21. Determine the Cartesian coordinates of the following trigonometric points.

a) $P\left(-\dfrac{\pi}{6}\right)$ _____

b) $P\left(-\dfrac{3\pi}{4}\right)$ _____

c) $P\left(-\dfrac{4\pi}{3}\right)$ _____

d) $P\left(\dfrac{7\pi}{3}\right)$ _____

e) $P\left(\dfrac{31\pi}{6}\right)$ _____

f) $P\left(-\dfrac{13\pi}{4}\right)$ _____

22. From the Cartesian coordinates of the remarkable trigonometric points, determine the exact value of

a) $\sin\left(\dfrac{2\pi}{3}\right)$ _____

b) $\cos\left(\dfrac{7\pi}{6}\right)$ _____

c) $\sin\left(\dfrac{3\pi}{4}\right)$ _____

d) $\sin\left(\dfrac{3\pi}{2}\right)$ _____

e) $\cos\left(\dfrac{11\pi}{6}\right)$ _____

f) $\cos\left(\dfrac{4\pi}{3}\right)$ _____

23. Determine the exact value of

a) $\sin\left(-\dfrac{\pi}{6}\right)$ _____

b) $\cos\left(-\dfrac{\pi}{3}\right)$ _____

c) $\sin\left(\dfrac{13\pi}{6}\right)$ _____

d) $\cos\left(\dfrac{19\pi}{4}\right)$ _____

e) $\sin\left(-\dfrac{7\pi}{3}\right)$ _____

f) $\cos\left(-\dfrac{17\pi}{4}\right)$ _____

24. Determine the exact value of

a) $\tan\left(\dfrac{2\pi}{3}\right)$ _____

b) $\cot\left(\dfrac{5\pi}{6}\right)$ _____

c) $\sec\left(\dfrac{7\pi}{6}\right)$ _____

d) $\csc\left(\dfrac{11\pi}{6}\right)$ _____

25. Knowing that $0 \leqslant t \leqslant 2\pi$, determine the two values of t such that

a) $\cos t = \dfrac{1}{2}$ _____

b) $\sin t = \dfrac{\sqrt{3}}{2}$ _____

c) $\cos t = \dfrac{-\sqrt{3}}{2}$ _____

d) $\sin t = -\dfrac{1}{2}$ _____

26. Find t if

a) $\sin t = \dfrac{1}{2}$ and $\dfrac{\pi}{2} \leqslant t \leqslant \dfrac{3\pi}{2}$ _____

b) $\cos t = \dfrac{-1}{2}$ and $\pi \leqslant t \leqslant \dfrac{3\pi}{2}$ _____

c) $\sin t = \dfrac{-\sqrt{3}}{2}$ and $\dfrac{3\pi}{2} \leqslant t \leqslant 2\pi$ _____

d) $\cos t = \dfrac{1}{2}$ and $0 \leqslant t \leqslant \dfrac{\pi}{2}$ _____

27. Knowing that $0 \leqslant t \leqslant 360°$, find the two values of t (to the nearest tenth) such that

a) $\cos t = 0.8$ _____

b) $\cos t = -0.6$ _____

c) $\sin t = 0.2$ _____

d) $\sin t = -0.4$ _____

28. Knowing that $0 \leqslant t \leqslant 2\pi$, find the two values of t (to the nearest hundredth) such that

a) $\sin t = 0.7$ _____

b) $\sin t = -0.6$ _____

c) $\cos t = 0.2$ _____

d) $\cos t = -0.8$ _____

a) On the trigonometric circle on the right, line l is drawn perpendicular to the x-axis at the point $A(1, 0)$.

Given a trigonometric point $P(t)$ of the first quadrant, we designate C as the intersection of the extension of the radius $0P$ and the line l.

Explain why $\tan t = m\overline{AC}$.

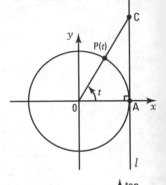

_____

b) On the trigonometric circle on the right, we have directed and scaled the line l. The chosen scale corresponds to the radius of the unit circle. The resulting line l, scaled and directed, is called the **tangent axis**.

Given a trigonometric point $P(t)$, we locate $\tan t$ on the tangent axis by extending the radius $\overline{0P}$ (see a)).

1. Locate the point $P\left(\dfrac{\pi}{4}\right)$ and verify by construction that $\tan \dfrac{\pi}{4} = 1$.

2. Locate the point $P\left(\dfrac{-\pi}{4}\right)$ and verify by construction that $\tan\left(-\dfrac{\pi}{4}\right) = -1$.

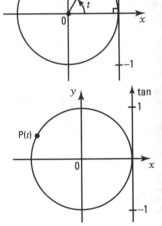

c) Given a trigonometric point $P(t)$ in the 2nd quadrant, explain how to locate $\tan t$ on the tangent axis and deduce the sign of $\tan t$.

_____

_____

TRIGONOMETRIC CIRCLE AND THE TANGENT AXIS

- The trigonometric circle and **tangent axis** are represented on the right.

  Given a trigonometric point $P(t)$, to locate $\tan t$ on the tangent axis, we extend the radius $0P$. The intersection of the extension of the radius $0P$ and the tangent axis enables you to locate $\tan t$.

- Note that

  $0 \leqslant t < \dfrac{\pi}{2} \Rightarrow \tan t \geqslant 0.$

  $\dfrac{\pi}{2} < t \leqslant \pi \Rightarrow \tan t \leqslant 0.$

  $\pi \leqslant t < \dfrac{3\pi}{2} \Rightarrow \tan t \geqslant 0.$

  $\dfrac{3\pi}{2} < t \leqslant 2\pi \Rightarrow \tan t \leqslant 0.$

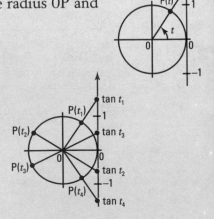

29. a) Consider the trigonometric point P(t).

Determine in which quadrant(s) P(t) is located if

1. $\tan t > 0.$ _____

2. $\tan t < 0.$ _____

b) If $0 \leqslant t \leqslant 2\pi$, determine t in each of the following cases.

1. $\tan t = 1$ _____ 2. $\tan t = -1$ _____

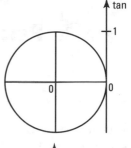

30. Consider the trigonometric circle on the right.

a) Randomly place a trigonometric point P(t).

b) Deduce the location of the trigonometric point P(t + π).

c) Locate on the tangent axis $\tan t$ and $\tan (t + \pi)$ and compare $\tan t$ and $\tan (t + \pi)$. _____

d) Is it true to say that for any real t, we have: $\tan (t + \pi) = \tan t$? _____

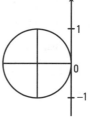

31. Consider the trigonometric point P(t).

If $0 \leqslant t \leqslant 2\pi$, determine the two possible solutions for t in each of the following cases.

a) $\tan t = \sqrt{3}$ _____

b) $\tan t = -\sqrt{3}$ _____

c) $\tan t = \dfrac{\sqrt{3}}{3}$ _____

d) $\tan t = \dfrac{-\sqrt{3}}{3}$ _____

e) $\tan t = 0$ _____

f) $\tan t = 0.7$ _____

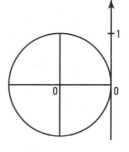

32. a) The trigonometric circle and a trigonometric point P(t) in the 1st quadrant are represented on the right.

As t approaches $\dfrac{\pi}{2}$, what can we say about $\tan t$?

_____

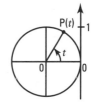

b) The trigonometric circle and a trigonometric point P(t) in the 4th quadrant are represented on the right.

As t approaches $\dfrac{-\pi}{2}$, what can we say about $\tan t$?

_____

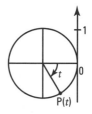

33. a) Place the trigonometric points P(t) and P(–t) on the unit circle.

b) Compare $\tan(-t)$ and $\tan t$. _____

c) Is it true to say that for any real t, we have: $\tan (-t) = -\tan t$. _____

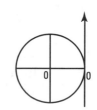

5.4 Periodic functions

ACTIVITY 1 Movement of a swing

Initially ($t = 0$), the seat of a swing is in position A. We notice that it takes 8 seconds for the swing to go back and forth 5 times.

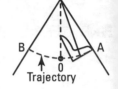

Trajectory

a) Does the seat periodically follow the same trajectory? _____
If yes, each return is called a **cycle**.

b) The required time p to return to point A for the first time, ie the duration of one cycle, is called the **period** of the movement. Determine the period p of the movement.

_____

c) Complete the table below which gives the position $P(t)$ (A, 0 or B) of the movement as a function of elapsed time t since the start.

t	0	0.4	0.8	1.2	1.6	2	2.4	2.8	3.2	4.8	6.4	8
$P(t)$												

d) Verify that for any value of t ($0 \leqslant t \leqslant 8$), we have: $P(t) = P(t + p)$ where p is the period of the movement.

_____

e) The **frequency** of the movement is the number of cycles per unit of time. Given that we observe here 5 cycles in 8 seconds, calculate the frequency F, ie the number of cycles per second.

_____

f) The trajectory of the swing's seat is represented by the arc AB in the Cartesian plane on the right. The points A, 0 and B have x-coordinates 1, 0 and –1 respectively.

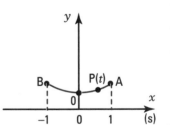

1. In what interval is the x-coordinate of a point $P(t)$ on the trajectory? _____

2. Complete the table of values below which gives the x-coordinate of a point $P(t)$ on the trajectory as a function of elapsed time t since the start.

t	0	0.4	0.8	1.2	1.6	2	2.4	2.8	3.2	4.8	6.4	8
x												

3. We have represented two cycles of the function f which gives the x-coordinate of a point $P(t)$ on the trajectory as a function of elapsed time t since the start. Draw 3 other cycles.

PERIODIC FUNCTIONS

- A function f is called **periodic** if there exists a real number a such that for any value x of the domain of f, we have:

$$f(x + a) = f(x)$$

The smallest positive value of a for which $f(x + a) = f(x)$ is called the **period** (denoted p) of the function.

- One **cycle** of a periodic function is the smallest portion of the graph that, by repetition, forms the curve representing the function. The distance between the extremities of the cycle is equal to the period p of the function.

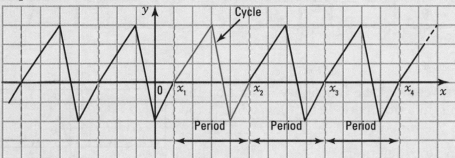

$$p = x_2 - x_1 = x_3 - x_2 = x_4 - x_3 = \ldots$$

- The frequency, denoted F, is the reciprocal of the period.

$$F = \frac{1}{p}$$

In a situation where the variable x represents time, the period represents the **duration of one cycle** and the frequency represents the **number of cycles** per unit of time.

---

1. Indicate if the following functions are periodic. If yes, indicate the period p of the function.

a)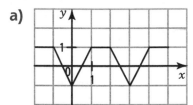

b)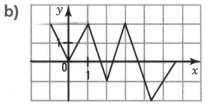

c)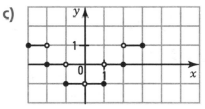

_____   _____   _____

2. One cycle of a periodic function f is represented on the right.

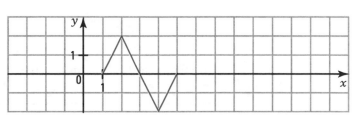

a) Determine the period p and the frequency F of this function.

_____

b) Complete the graph of this function for $x \in [-3, 13]$.

c) Determine
1. ran f. _____   2. min f. _____   3. max f. _____

d) Determine
1. $f(15)$. _____   2. $f(25)$. _____   3. $f(42)$. _____   4. $f(32)$. _____

e) What are the zeros of f over the interval $[0, 10]$? _____

5.5 Sine function

The basic sine function, denoted sin, has the rule $y = \sin t$.

a) Complete the table of values below when t varies from -2π to 4π.

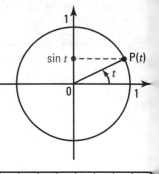

t	-2π	$-\dfrac{3\pi}{2}$	$-\pi$	$-\dfrac{\pi}{2}$	0	$\dfrac{\pi}{2}$	π	$\dfrac{3\pi}{2}$	2π	$\dfrac{5\pi}{2}$	3π	$\dfrac{7\pi}{2}$	4π
$\sin t$													

b) We have represented the function $y = \sin t$ on the right. Is this function periodic? If yes, what is the period p of the function? _____

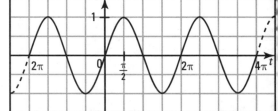

c) For this function, determine

   1. the domain. _____   2. the range. _____

   3. the maximum. _____   4. the minimum. _____

d) The amplitude A of a function f is equal to half the difference between the maximum and the minimum of the function, i.e. $A = \dfrac{\max f - \min f}{2}$.

What is the amplitude A of the sine function? _____

e) When $t \in [0, 2\pi]$, determine, for the sine function,

   1. the zeros. _____

   2. the sign. _____

   3. the variation. _____

f) Verify the property $\forall\, t \in \mathbb{R}: \sin(-t) = -\sin t$, using the graph or trigonometric circle.

BASIC SINE FUNCTION

- The sine function, denoted sin, is defined by
$$\sin: \mathbb{R} \to \mathbb{R}$$
$$x \mapsto y = \sin x$$

- The sine function is a periodic function with period 2π. $\boxed{\sin(x + 2\pi) = \sin x}$

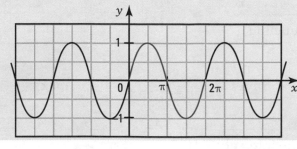

One cycle of the basic sine function is represented in blue over $[0, 2\pi]$

- The **amplitude** of a sine function f is given by $A = \dfrac{\max f - \min f}{2}$.

  The amplitude of the basic sine function is: $A = 1$.

- We have:
  - domain $= \mathbb{R}$, range $= [-1, 1]$.
  - zeros over $[0, 2\pi]$: 0, π and 2π.
  - sign over $[0, 2\pi]$: $\sin x \geqslant 0$ if $x \in [0, \pi]$ and $\sin x \leqslant 0$ if $x \in [\pi, 2\pi]$.
  - variation over $[0, 2\pi]$: $\sin \nearrow$ if $x \in \left[0, \dfrac{\pi}{2}\right] \cup \left[\dfrac{3\pi}{2}, 2\pi\right]$; $\sin \searrow$ if $x \in \left[\dfrac{\pi}{2}, \dfrac{3\pi}{2}\right]$.
  - extrema: $\max = 1$; $\min = -1$.

- For any real x, we have: $\sin(-x) = -\sin x$. The basic sine function is therefore considered to be an **odd** function.

1. Consider the function $f(x) = \sin x$.

  a) Find the zeros of f when
  1. $x \in [-2\pi, 4\pi]$. _____
  2. $x \in \mathbb{R}$. _____

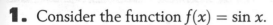

  b) Solve the inequality $\sin x \geqslant 0$ when
  1. $x \in [-2\pi, 4\pi]$. _____
  2. $x \in \mathbb{R}$. _____

  c) Find the values of x for which the function f is increasing when

  1. $x \in [-2\pi, 4\pi]$. _____

  2. $x \in \mathbb{R}$. _____

Activity 2 Equation $sin\ \theta = k$

The function $y = \sin x$ is represented on the right when $x \in [-2\pi, 4\pi]$.

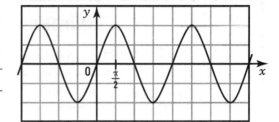

a) 1. By referring to the trigonometric circle, solve the equation $\sin \theta = \dfrac{1}{2}$ when $\theta \in [0, 2\pi]$.

  _____

  2. Explain how to find, from the solutions in 1, the solutions to the equation $\sin \theta = \dfrac{1}{2}$ when

  1) $\theta \in [2\pi, 4\pi]$. _____
  2) $\theta \in [-2\pi, 0]$. _____

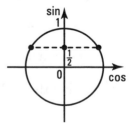

  3. Verify that the solution set S to the equation $\sin \theta = \dfrac{1}{2}$ over $\mathbb{R}$ is described by

  $$S = \left\{ \ldots, -\dfrac{11\pi}{6}, -\dfrac{7\pi}{6}, \dfrac{\pi}{6}, \dfrac{5\pi}{6}, \dfrac{13\pi}{6}, \dfrac{17\pi}{6}, \ldots \right\} \text{ (enumeration)}.$$

  or by

  $$S = \left\{ \dfrac{\pi}{6} + 2\pi n \right\} \cup \left\{ \dfrac{5\pi}{6} + 2\pi n \right\} \text{ where } n \in \mathbb{Z} \text{ (set-builder notation)}.$$

b) By referring to the trigonometric circle and using a calculator, solve the equation $\sin \theta = 0.4$ wher

    1. $\theta \in [0, 2\pi]$. _____

    2. $\theta \in [4\pi, 6\pi]$. _____

    3. $\theta \in \mathbb{R}$. _____

c) Solve the inequality $\sin \theta \geqslant \dfrac{1}{2}$ when

    1. $\theta \in [0, 2\pi]$. _____

    2. $\theta \in [0, 4\pi]$. _____

    3. $\theta \in \mathbb{R}$. _____

EQUATION $sin\ \theta = k, \quad -1 \leqslant k \leqslant 1$

- When $\theta \in [0, 2\pi[$, the equation $\sin \theta = k$ yields 2 solutions θ_1 and θ_2.

$$\boxed{\theta_1 = \sin^{-1} k \ \text{ and } \ \theta_2 = \pi - \theta_1}$$

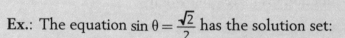

- When $\theta \in \mathbb{R}$, the equation $\sin \theta = k$ yields an infinite number of solutions.

$$\boxed{S = \{\theta_1 + 2\pi n\} \cup \{\theta_2 + 2\pi n\} \text{ where } n \in \mathbb{Z}}$$

Ex.: The equation $\sin \theta = \dfrac{\sqrt{2}}{2}$ has the solution set:

- $S = \left\{\dfrac{\pi}{4}, \dfrac{3\pi}{4}\right\}$ when $\theta \in [0, 2\pi[$

- $S = \left\{\dfrac{\pi}{4} + 2\pi n\right\} \cup \left\{\dfrac{3\pi}{4} + 2\pi n\right\}, n \in \mathbb{Z}$ when $\theta \in \mathbb{R}$.

---

2. Solve the following equations over

    1. $[0, 2\pi]$ 2. $[2\pi, 4\pi]$ 3. $\mathbb{R}$

  a) $\sin x = \dfrac{\sqrt{3}}{2}$ 1. _____ 2. _____ 3. _____

  b) $\sin x = 1$ 1. _____ 2. _____ 3. _____

  c) $\sin x = -\dfrac{1}{2}$ 1. _____ 2. _____ 3. _____

  d) $\sin x = 0.6$ 1. _____ 2. _____ 3. _____

3. Solve the following inequalities over

    1. $[0, 2\pi]$ 2. $\mathbb{R}$

  a) $\sin x \geqslant \dfrac{\sqrt{2}}{2}$ 1. _____ 2. _____

  b) $\sin x \leqslant \dfrac{1}{2}$ 1. _____ 2. _____

c) $\sin x \leqslant -\dfrac{1}{2}$ 1. _____   2. _____

d) $\sin x \leqslant 1$ 1. _____   2. _____

ACTIVITY 3   Function $y = a \sin x$

a) For each of the following functions,

1. determine the value of parameter a.
2. indicate how to obtain the graph of the function from the graph of $y = \sin x$.
3. determine the amplitude.

$$f_1(x) = 2 \sin x \qquad\qquad f_2(x) = \frac{1}{2} \sin x \qquad\qquad f_3(x) = -\sin x$$

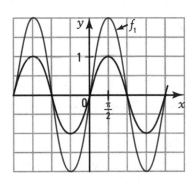 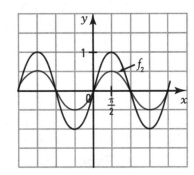 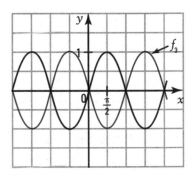

_____   _____   _____

_____   _____   _____

_____   _____   _____

b) 1. From the graph of the function $y = \sin x$ ($0 \leqslant x \leqslant 2\pi$), deduce the graph of $y = -2 \sin x$. Explain the procedure.

_____

_____

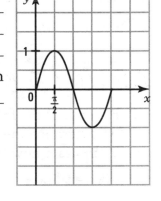

2. What is the amplitude of the function $y = -2 \sin x$? _____

c) What is the relationship between the parameter a of the function $y = -2 \sin x$ and the amplitude of the function? _____

Activity 4 Function $y = \sin bx$

a) For each of the following functions,
   1. determine the value of parameter b.
   2. indicate how to obtain the graph of the function from the graph of $y = \sin x$.
   3. determine the period.

$f_1(x) = \sin 2x$

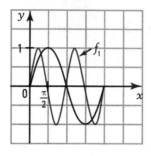

$f_2(x) = \sin \frac{1}{2}x$

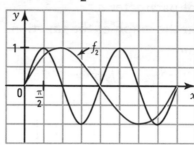

$f_3(x) = \sin(-x)$

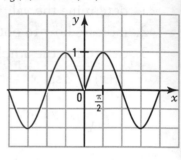

_____
_____
_____

b) 1. From the graph of the function $y = \sin x$ $(0 \leqslant x \leqslant 4\pi)$, deduce the graph of $y = \sin\left(-\frac{1}{2}x\right)$. Explain the procedure.

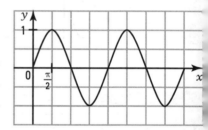

   _____
   _____
   _____

   2. What is the period of the function $y = \sin\left(-\frac{1}{2}x\right)$? _____

c) What is the relationship between the parameter b of the function $y = \sin bx$ and the period of the function? _____

Activity 5 Function $y = \sin(x - h)$

a) For each of the following functions,
   1. determine the value of parameter h.
   2. indicate how to obtain the graph of the function from the graph of $y = \sin x$.

$f_1(x) = \sin(x - \pi)$

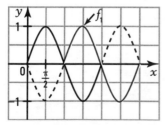

$f_2(x) = \sin\left(x + \frac{\pi}{2}\right)$

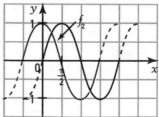

_____

_____

b) From the graph of the function $y = \sin x$ $(0 \leqslant x \leqslant 2\pi)$, deduce the graph of $y = \sin\left(x - \dfrac{\pi}{2}\right)$. Explain the procedure.

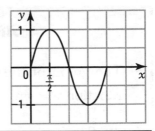

PHASE SHIFT

The graph of the function $y = \sin(x - h)$ is deduced from the graph of the function $y = \sin x$ by a horizontal translation of

- $|h|$ units to the right if $h > 0$.
- $|h|$ units to the left if $h < 0$.

Such a shift of the basic function is called the **phase shift**.

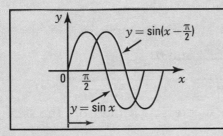 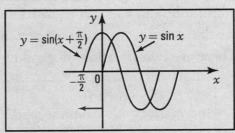

– The curve $y = \sin x$ is phase shifted $|h|$ units to the **right**.

– The curve $y = \sin x$ is phase shifted $|h|$ units to the **left**.

ACTIVITY 6 Function $y = \sin x + k$

From the graph of $y = \sin x$ $(0 \leqslant x \leqslant 2\pi)$, deduce, explaining the procedure, the graph of

a) $y = \sin x + 1$.

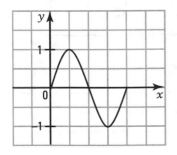

b) $y = \sin x - \dfrac{1}{2}$.

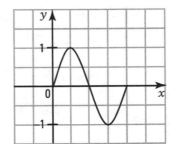

SINUSOIDAL FUNCTION $y = a \sin b(x - h) + k$

- The graph of the function $y = a \sin b(x - h) + k$ is deduced from the graph of the basic function $y = \sin x$ by the transformation $(x, y) \to \left(\dfrac{x}{b} + h, ay + k\right)$.

- We have:

  period: $p = \dfrac{2\pi}{|b|}$; amplitude: $A = |a|$;

  domain $= \mathbb{R}$;

  range $= [k - A, k + A]$.

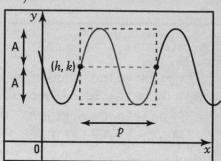

- To draw one cycle of the graph of $y = a \sin b(x - h) + k$,
  1. we identify the point (h, k), starting point of one cycle.
  2. we draw a rectangle with a height equal to 2A, twice the amplitude, and a length equal to the period p.
  3. we draw one cycle inside the rectangle.

  There are two situations depending on the signs of a and b.

| $ab > 0$ Increasing cycle from the start. | $ab < 0$ Decreasing cycle from the start. |

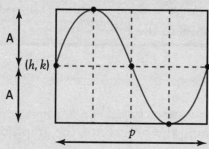

The dotted lines make it easier to use symmetry to draw the graph.

Ex.: Draw one cycle of the function

$$y = -2 \sin \frac{\pi}{4}(x - 3) + 1.$$

We have: $a = -2$, $b = \frac{\pi}{4}$, $h = 3$, $k = 1$

- starting point of the cycle: $(h, k) = (3, 1)$.
- amplitude: $A = |a| = 2$.
- period: $p = \dfrac{2\pi}{|b|} = 8$.

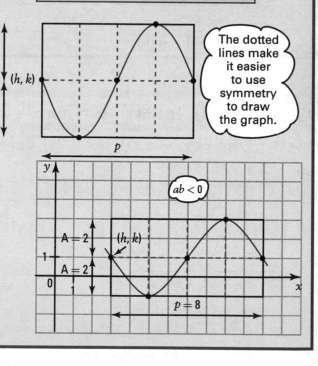

---

4. Consider the functions $f(x) = a \sin b(x - h) + k$ and $g(x) = -a \sin -b(x - h) + k$. Explain why the functions f and g are equal.

---

5. Draw one cycle of each of the following functions.

a) $y = 2 \sin \frac{\pi}{2}(x - 1) - 1$

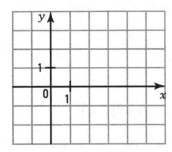

b) $y = -2 \sin \frac{\pi}{3}(x + 1) + 1$

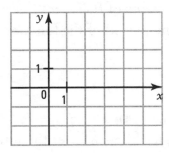

c) $y = 3 \sin 2\left(x - \frac{\pi}{2}\right) + 1$

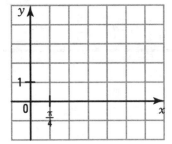

d) $y = -3 \sin -2(x - \pi) + \frac{3}{2}$

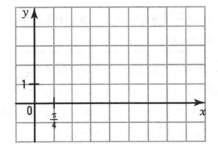

ACTIVITY 7 Finding the zeros of the function $y = a \sin b(x - h) + k$

A portion of the graph of the function
$f(x) = -2 \sin \frac{\pi}{3}(x - 1) + 1$ is represented on the right.

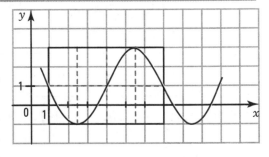

a) What is the period p of the function? _____

b) 1. How many zeros does the function f have?
_____

   2. How many zeros does the function f have when $x \in [1, 7]$? _____

c) Justify the steps for finding the zeros of f when $x \in [1, 7]$.

   1. $-2 \sin \frac{\pi}{3}(x - 1) + 1 = 0$ _____

   2. $\sin \frac{\pi}{3}(x - 1) = \frac{1}{2}$ _____

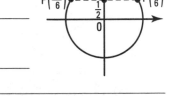

   3. $\frac{\pi}{3}(x - 1) = \frac{\pi}{6}$ or $\frac{\pi}{3}(x - 1) = \frac{5\pi}{6}$ _____

   4. $x = 1.5$ or $x = 3.5$ _____

d) From the zeros of f obtained over $[1, 7]$, explain how to deduce the zeros of f located on the next cycle, i.e. when $x \in [7, 13]$.

_____

e) Verify that the set of zeros of f is $\{\ldots; -4.5; -2.5; 1.5; 3.5; 7.5; 9.5; \ldots\}$

   or $\{1.5 + 6n\} \cup \{3.5 + 6n\}, n \in \mathbb{Z}$.

FINDING THE ZEROS OF THE FUNCTION $f(x) = a \sin b(x - h) + k$

To determine the zeros of $f(x) = a \sin b(x - h) + k$,

1. we establish the period of the function.

$$p = \frac{2\pi}{|b|}$$

2. we solve the equation $f(x) = 0$.

- Isolate $\sin b(x - h)$.
- Find the angles $b(x - h)$ over the interval $[0, 2\pi]$ that verify the equation.

- Isolate x.

- Determine the solution set, taking the period into consideration.

Ex.: $f(x) = 2 \sin \frac{\pi}{2}(x - 1) - 1$

$p = 4$

$$2 \sin \frac{\pi}{2}(x - 1) - 1 = 0$$

$$\sin \frac{\pi}{2}(x - 1) = \frac{1}{2}$$

$$\frac{\pi}{2}(x - 1) = \frac{\pi}{6} \text{ or } \frac{\pi}{2}(x - 1) = \frac{5\pi}{6}$$

$$x = \frac{4}{3} \text{ or } \qquad x = \frac{8}{3}$$

$$S = \left\{\frac{4}{3} + 4n\right\} \cup \left\{\frac{8}{3} + 4n\right\}$$

6. The following functions have the rule $f(x) = a \sin b(x - h) + k$.

Find the zeros of each function over

1. the interval $[h, h + p]$ where p is the period of the function.
2. the set of all real numbers.

a) $f(x) = 2 \sin \frac{\pi}{6}(x - 2) + 1$

b) $f(x) = -2 \sin \frac{\pi}{3}(x + 1) + \frac{1}{2}$

c) $f(x) = \sin 2(x - \pi) + 1$

d) $f(x) = 6 \sin\left(x + \frac{\pi}{2}\right) - 3$

e) $f(x) = -3 \sin \frac{\pi}{4}x + 6$

f) $f(x) = -2 \sin \frac{\pi}{8}(x + 2) + \sqrt{2}$

7. Determine the zeros of the function $f(x) = -2 \sin \frac{\pi}{12}(x+5) - 1$ over the interval $[90, 150]$.

_____

_____

_____

_____

ACTIVITY 8 Study of the function $f(x) = a \sin b(x - h) + k$

One cycle of the function $f(x) = 2 \sin \frac{\pi}{6}(x-1) + 1$ is represented below.

a) Determine

   1. the period. _____   2. the amplitude. ____

b) Determine

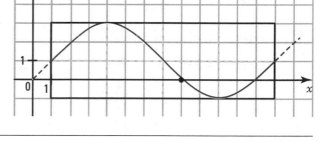

   1. dom f. _____   2. ran f. _____

   3. the zeros of f over $[1, 13]$. _____

   4. the zeros of f over $\mathbb{R}$. _____

   5. the sign of f over $[1, 13]$. _____

   6. the sign of f over $\mathbb{R}$. _____

         _____

   7. the variation of f over $[1, 13]$. _____

   8. the variation of f over $\mathbb{R}$. _____

         _____

   9. the maximum and minimum of f. _____

STUDY OF THE FUNCTION $f(x) = a \sin b(x - h) + k$

Given $f(x) = -2 \sin 2\left(x - \frac{\pi}{6}\right) + 1$. We have:

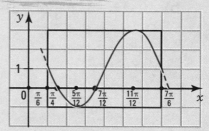

- dom $f = \mathbb{R}$; ran $f = [-1, 3]$
- period $p = \pi$; amplitude $A = 2$
- zeros of f: $\left\{\frac{\pi}{4} + \pi n\right\} \cup \left\{\frac{7\pi}{12} + \pi n\right\}$
- sign of f.

$$f(x) \geqslant 0 \text{ over } \left[\frac{\pi}{6} + \pi n, \frac{\pi}{4} + \pi n\right] \cup \left[\frac{7\pi}{12} + \pi n, \frac{7\pi}{6} + \pi n\right]$$

$$f(x) \leqslant 0 \text{ over } \left[\frac{\pi}{4} + \pi n, \frac{7\pi}{12} + \pi n\right]$$

- variation of f.

$$f \searrow \text{ over } \left[\frac{\pi}{6} + \pi n, \frac{5\pi}{12} + \pi n\right] \cup \left[\frac{11\pi}{12} + \pi n, \frac{7\pi}{6} + \pi n\right]$$

$$f \nearrow \text{ over } \left[\frac{5\pi}{12} + \pi n, \frac{11\pi}{12} + \pi n\right]$$

- min $f = -1$; max $f = 3$.

           5.5 Sine function

8. For each of the following functions, determine

    1. the period,   2. the amplitude,   3. the range of the function.

  a) $f(x) = -2 \sin \frac{\pi}{8}(x - 5) + 3$

    1. _____

    2. _____

    3. _____

  b) $f(x) = 3 \sin 12\left(x + \frac{\pi}{2}\right) + 5$

    1. _____

    2. _____

    3. _____

  c) $f(x) = 5 \sin \frac{4\pi}{3}(x + 1) - 4$

    1. _____

    2. _____

    3. _____

  d) $f(x) = 10 \sin \frac{6}{5}\left(x - \frac{\pi}{4}\right) + 4$

    1. _____

    2. _____

    3. _____

9. Determine the initial value of the following functions.

  a) $f(x) = 4 \sin \frac{\pi}{6}(x + 1) - 3$ _____

  b) $f(x) = -2 \sin \frac{\pi}{3}(x - 2) + 2$ _____

  c) $f(x) = 2 \sin 2\left(x - \frac{\pi}{4}\right) + 4$ _____

  d) $f(x) = 3 \sin \pi(x + 5) - 1$ _____

10. For each of the following functions, determine, over $\mathbb{R}$, the interval over which the function is positive.

  a) $f(x) = 2 \sin \frac{\pi}{6}(x - 1) - 1$

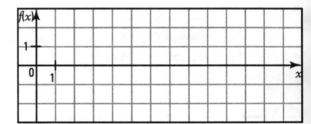

  b) $f(x) = -3 \sin \frac{\pi}{4}(x + 3) + 3$

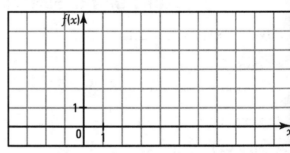

  c) $f(x) = 2 \sin \frac{1}{3}\left(x - \frac{\pi}{2}\right) + 1$

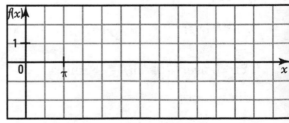

11. For each of the following functions, determine the interval over which the function is decreasing.

a) $f(x) = \sin \frac{\pi}{3}(x + 4) + 1$ dans $[-4, 2]$.

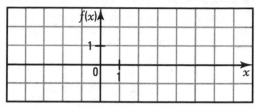

_____

b) $f(x) = -2 \sin \frac{\pi}{4}x + 1$ over $[0.8]$

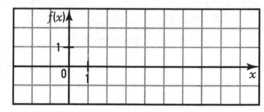

_____

12. In an experiment, we define a function I which gives the electrical current across a cable, expressed in amperes, as a function of time x, expressed in seconds. The function I is defined by the rule: $I(x) = 4 \sin \frac{\pi}{6}(x + 8) + 4$.

A light bulb lights up when the intensity of the current is equal to 6 amperes.

Determine at what times the light bulb lights up during the first 30 seconds of the experiment.

_____

_____

_____

_____

13. In a company, the number of parts assembled varies according to a sinusoidal function defined by the rule: $f(x) = 200 \sin\left(\frac{\pi}{24}x\right) + 15$ where x represents the number of days elapsed since the beginning of the year.

Over the course of the first 50 days, for how many days was the number of parts assembled greater than or equal to 115?

_____

_____

_____

_____

ACTIVITY 9 Finding the rule $y = a \sin b(x - h) + k$

Consider the function f represented on the right.

a) Determine

    1. the period of f. _____   2. the amplitude of f. _____

b) Determine the rule of the function f when we choose a cycle starting at the point $(h, k) = (2, 1)$.

    Explain your procedure: _____

    _____

    _____

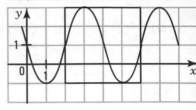

c) Determine the rule of the function f when we choose a cycle starting at the point $(h, k) = (0, 1)$.

    Explain your procedure: _____

    _____

    _____

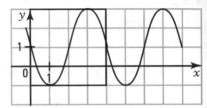

d) Is it true to say that the writing of the rule varies depending on the chosen cycle but that all of the resulting rules represent the same function? _____

FINDING THE RULE $y = a \sin b(x - h) + k$

From the graph of the function on the right, we deduce that: $|a| = 1.5$ and $|b| = 2$.

The writing of the function's rule depends on your choice of the starting point (h, k) of one cycle.

Consider two cases:

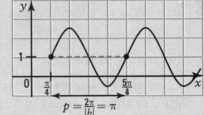

$p = \frac{2\pi}{|b|} = \pi$

1st case: $(h, k) = \left(\frac{\pi}{4}, 1\right)$

The cycle is increasing from the start $\Rightarrow ab > 0$.

Thus, $a = 1.5$ and $b = 2$ or $a = -1.5$ and $b = -2$.

The rule is written in two ways:

$y = 1.5 \sin 2\left(x - \frac{\pi}{4}\right) + 1$ or $y = -1.5 \sin -2\left(x - \frac{\pi}{4}\right) + 1$.

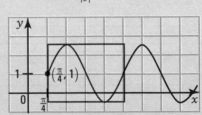

2nd case: $(h, k) = \left(\frac{3\pi}{4}, 1\right)$

The cycle is decreasing from the start $\Rightarrow ab < 0$.

Thus, $a = 1.5$ and $b = -2$ or $a = -1.5$ and $b = 2$.

The rule is written in two ways:

$y = 1.5 \sin -2\left(x - \frac{3\pi}{4}\right) + 1$ or $y = -1.5 \sin 2\left(x - \frac{3\pi}{4}\right) + 1$.

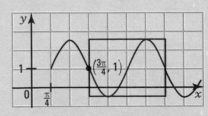

Note that the different ways of writing the rule represent the same function.

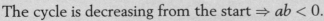

14. Find a rule of the form $y = a \sin b(x - h) + k$ for each of the following functions.

a)

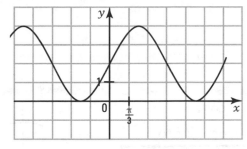

_____

b)

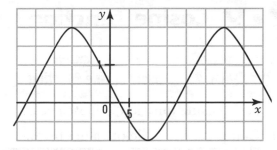

_____

c)

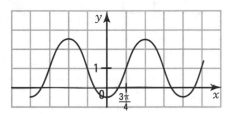

_____

d)

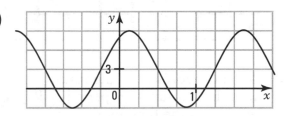

_____

15. The waves of an artificial lake are observed in a laboratory setting as indicated in the figure on the right. The graph represents the movement of one wave where t is time, expressed in seconds, and $h(t)$ is the height of the wave, in metres.

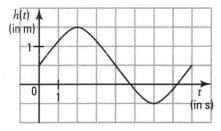

What is the height of the wave after 3 seconds?

_____

16. Raphael is playing with a yo-yo for 30 seconds. The height of the yo-yo, in metres, varies as a function of time t, in seconds, according to the rule of a sinusoidal function.
Initially, the yo-yo is at its maximum height of 2 m. After 4 seconds, the yo-yo reaches its minimum height of 1 m for the first time.
After how many seconds does Raphael's yo-yo reach a height of 1.8 m for the first time?

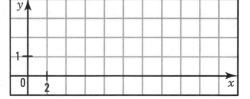

_____

_____

_____

17. The flashing light of an electronic game follows the trajectory of a sinusoidal function as indicated in the graph on the right. If t represents the time (in seconds) and $h(t)$ represents the height (in dm) of the light, determine at what height the light is at the moment $t = 6$ s?

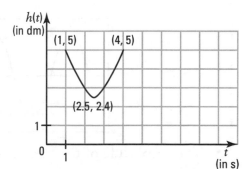

_____

_____

_____

5.6 Cosine function

ACTIVITY 1 Basic cosine function

The basic cosine function, denoted cos, has the rule $y = \cos t$.

a) Complete the table of values below when t varies from -2π to 4π.

t	-2π	$-\dfrac{3\pi}{2}$	$-\pi$	$-\dfrac{\pi}{2}$	0	$\dfrac{\pi}{2}$	π	$\dfrac{3\pi}{2}$	2π	$\dfrac{5\pi}{2}$	3π	$\dfrac{7\pi}{2}$	4π
$\cos t$													

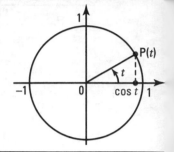

b) We have represented the function $y = \cos t$ on the right. Is this function periodic? If yes, what is the period p of the function? _____

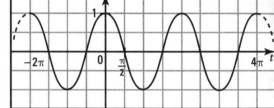

c) For this function, determine
1. the domain. _____ 2. the range. _____
3. the maximum. _____ 4. the minimum. _____

d) What is the amplitude A of the cosine function? _____

e) When $t \in [0, 2\pi]$, determine, for the basic cosine function,

1. the zeros. _____

2. the sign. _____
3. the variation. _____

f) Verify, using the graph or the trigonometric circle, the property: $\forall\, t \in \mathbb{R}: \cos(-t) = \cos(t)$.

BASIC COSINE FUNCTION

- The cosine function, denoted cos, is defined by
$$\cos: \mathbb{R} \to \mathbb{R}$$
$$x \mapsto y = \cos x$$

- The cosine function is a periodic function with period 2π. $\boxed{\cos(x + 2\pi) = \cos x}$

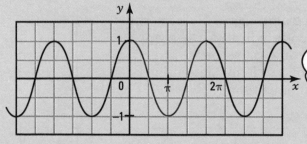

One cycle of the basic cosine function is represented in blue over $[0, 2\pi]$.

- The amplitude of the basic cosine function is: $A = 1$.

- We have:
  - domain $= \mathbb{R}$, range $= [-1, 1]$.
  - zeros over $[0, 2\pi]$: $\frac{\pi}{2}$ and $\frac{3\pi}{2}$.
  - sign over $[0, 2\pi]$: $\cos x \geqslant 0$ if $x \in \left[0, \frac{\pi}{2}\right] \cup \left[\frac{3\pi}{2}, 2\pi\right]$ and $\cos x \leqslant 0$ if $x \in \left[\frac{\pi}{2}, \frac{3\pi}{2}\right]$.
  - variation over $[0, 2\pi]$: $\cos \searrow$ if $x \in [0, \pi]$; $\cos \nearrow$ if $x \in [\pi, 2\pi]$.
  - extrema: max $= 1$; min $= -1$.
- For any real x, we have: $\cos(-x) = \cos x$. The basic cosine function is therefore considered to be an even function.

1. Consider the function $f(x) = \cos x$.

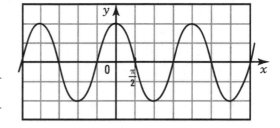

  a) Find the zeros of f when

   1. $x \in [-2\pi, 4\pi]$. _____

   2. $x \in \mathbb{R}$. _____

  b) Solve the inequality $\cos x \geqslant 0$ when

   1. $x \in \left\{-\frac{5\pi}{2}, \frac{5\pi}{2}\right\}$. _____

   2. $x \in \mathbb{R}$. _____

  c) Find the values of x for which the function f is increasing when
   1. $x \in [-2\pi, 4\pi]$. _____
   2. $x \in \mathbb{R}$. _____

2. The functions $y = \sin x$ and $y = \cos x$ are represented on the right.

  a) Verify that $\sin\left(x + \frac{\pi}{2}\right) = \cos x$.

  b) Complete.

   The graph of the function $y = \cos x$ is deduced from the graph
   of $y = \sin x$ by _____

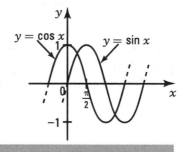

ACTIVITY 2 Equation $cos\ \theta = k$

The function $y = \cos x$ is represented on the right when
$x \in [-2\pi, 4\pi]$.

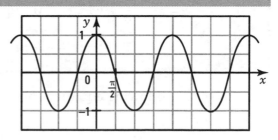

 a) 1. By referring to the trigonometric circle, solve the
   equation $\cos \theta = \frac{1}{2}$ when $\theta \in [0, 2\pi]$.

   _____

2. Explain how to find, from the solutions in 1, the solutions to the equation $\cos \theta = \frac{1}{2}$ when

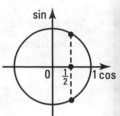

1) $\theta \in [2\pi, 4\pi]$. _____

2) $\theta \in [-2\pi, 0]$. _____

3. Verify that the solution set S to the equation $\cos \theta = \frac{1}{2}$ over $\mathbb{R}$ is described by

$$S = \left\{ ..., -\frac{5\pi}{3}, -\frac{\pi}{3}, \frac{\pi}{3}, \frac{5\pi}{3}, \frac{7\pi}{3}, \frac{11\pi}{3}, ... \right\} \text{ (enumeration)}.$$

or by

$$S = \left\{ \frac{\pi}{3} + 2\pi n \right\} \cup \left\{ \frac{5\pi}{3} + 2\pi n \right\} \text{ where } n \in \mathbb{Z} \text{ (set-builder notation)}.$$

b) By referring to the trigonometric circle and using a calculator, solve the equation $\cos \theta = 0.4$ when

1. $\theta \in [0, 2\pi]$. _____

2. $\theta \in [4\pi, 6\pi]$. _____

3. $\theta \in \mathbb{R}$. _____

c) Solve the inequality $\cos \theta \geqslant \frac{1}{2}$ when

1. $\theta \in [0, 2\pi]$. _____

2. $\theta \in [0, 4\pi]$. _____

3. $\theta \in \mathbb{R}$. _____

EQUATION $cos \theta = k$, $-1 \leqslant k \leqslant 1$

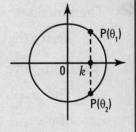

- When $\theta \in [0, 2\pi[$, the equation $\cos \theta = k$ yields 2 solutions θ_1 and θ_2.

$$\boxed{\theta_1 = \cos^{-1} k \text{ and } \theta_2 = 2\pi - \theta_1}$$

- When $\theta \in \mathbb{R}$, the equation $\cos \theta = k$ yields an infinite number of solutions. The solution set S is defined in set-builder notation by

$$\boxed{S = \{\theta_1 + 2\pi n\} \cup \{\theta_2 + 2\pi n\} \text{ where } n \in \mathbb{Z}}$$

Ex.: The equation $\cos \theta = \frac{\sqrt{3}}{2}$ has the solution set:

- $S = \left\{ \frac{\pi}{6}, \frac{11\pi}{6} \right\}$ when $\theta \in [0, 2\pi[$

- $S = \left\{ \frac{\pi}{6} + 2\pi n \right\} \cup \left\{ \frac{11\pi}{6} + 2\pi n \right\}, n \in \mathbb{Z}$ when $\theta \in \mathbb{R}$.

---

3. Solve the following equations over

    1. $[0, 2\pi]$ 2. $[2\pi, 4\pi]$ 3. $\mathbb{R}$

a) $\cos x = \frac{\sqrt{3}}{2}$ 1. _____   2. _____   3. _____

b) $\cos x = 1$ 1. _____   2. _____   3. _____

c) $\cos x = -\dfrac{\sqrt{2}}{2}$ 1. _____ 2. _____ 3. _____

d) $\cos x = 0.6$ 1. _____ 2. _____ 3. _____

4. Solve the following inequalities over
1. $[0, 2\pi]$ 2. $\mathbb{R}$

a) $\cos x \geqslant \dfrac{\sqrt{3}}{2}$ 1. _____ 2. _____

b) $\cos x \leqslant \dfrac{1}{2}$ 1. _____ 2. _____

c) $\cos x \leqslant -\dfrac{1}{2}$ 1. _____ 2. _____

d) $\cos x \leqslant 1$ 1. _____ 2. _____

ACTIVITY 3 Sinusoidal function $y = a \cos b(x - h) + k$

Consider the function $y = 2 \cos \dfrac{\pi}{2}(x - 1) - 1$.

a) Identify the parameters a, b, h and k.

_____

b) For this function, determine

1. the period. _____ 2. the amplitude. _____

c) Draw one cycle of this function using the point $(h, k + A)$ as the starting point.

FONCTION SINUSOÏDALE $y = a \cos b(x - h) + k$

- The graph of the function $y = a \cos b(x - h) + k$ is deduced from the graph of the basic function $y = \cos x$ by the transformation $(x, y) \rightarrow \left(\dfrac{x}{b} + h, ay + k \right)$.

- We have:

  period: $p = \dfrac{2\pi}{|b|}$; amplitude: $A = |a|$;

  domain $= \mathbb{R}$;

  range $= [k - A, k + A]$

- To draw one cycle of the graph of $y = a \cos b(x - h) + k$,
  1. we identify the point (h, k).
  2. we draw a rectangle with a height equal to 2A, twice the amplitude, and a length equal to the period p.
  3. we draw one cycle inside the rectangle.

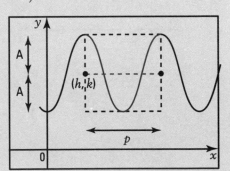

There are two situations depending on the sign of a.

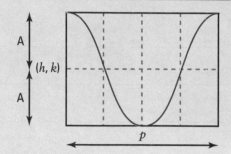

$a > 0$
Decreasing cycle from the start.
Starting point: $(h, k + A)$.

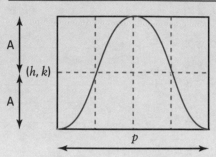

$a < 0$
Increasing cycle from the start.
Starting point: $(h, k - A)$.

Ex.: Draw one cycle of the function

$$y = -2 \cos \frac{-\pi}{4}(x - 3) + 1.$$

We have: $a = -2$, $b = \frac{-\pi}{4}$, $h = 3$, $k = 1$

– starting point of the cycle: $(h, k - A) = (3, -1)$.
– amplitude: $A = |a| = 2$.
– period: $p = \frac{2\pi}{|b|} = 8$.

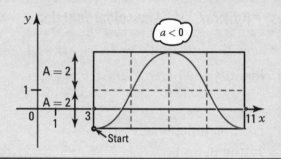

5. Consider the functions $f(x) = a \cos b(x - h) + k$ and $g(x) = a \cos -b(x - h) + k$.
Explain why the functions f and g are equal.

6. Draw one cycle of each of the following functions.

a) $y = 2 \cos \frac{\pi}{2}(x - 1) - 1$

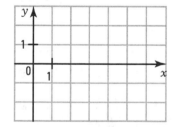

b) $y = -2 \cos \frac{\pi}{3}(x + 1) + 1$

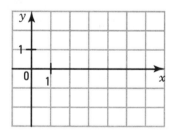

c) $y = 3 \cos 2\left(x - \frac{\pi}{2}\right) + 1$

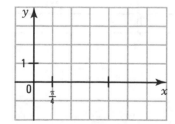

d) $y = -2 \cos - (x + \pi) + 1$

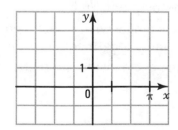

ACTIVITY 4   Finding the zeros of the function $y = a\cos b(x - h) + k$

A portion of the graph of the function $f(x) = -2\cos\frac{\pi}{3}(x-1)+1$ is represented on the right.

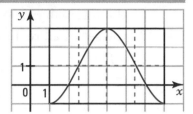

a) What is the period p of the function? _____

b) 1. How many zeros does the function f have? _____

     2. How many zeros does the function f have when $x \in [1, 7]$?

_____

c) Justify the steps for finding the zeros of f when $x \in [1, 7]$.

1. $-2\cos\frac{\pi}{3}(x-1)+1=0$ _____

2. $\qquad \cos\frac{\pi}{3}(x-1)=\frac{1}{2}$ _____

3. $\frac{\pi}{3}(x-1)=\frac{\pi}{3}$ or $(x-1)=\frac{5\pi}{3}$ _____

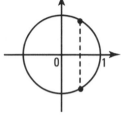

4. $\qquad x=2$ or $\qquad x=6$ _____

d) From the zeros of f obtained over $[1, 7]$, explain how to deduce the zeros of f located on the next cycle, i.e. when $x \in [7, 13]$.

_____

e) Verify that the set of zeros of f is $\{\ldots, -4, 0, 2, 6, 8, 12, \ldots\}$

or $\{2 + 6n\} \cup \{6 + 6n\}, n \in \mathbb{Z}$.

FINDING THE ZEROS OF THE FUNCTION $f(x) = a\cos b(x - h) + k$

To determine the zeros of $f(x) = a\cos b(x - h) + k$,

1. we establish the period p of the function.

$$p = \frac{2\pi}{|b|}$$

2. we solve the equation $f(x) = 0$.

– Isolate $\cos b(x - h)$.

– Find the angles $b(x - h)$ over the interval $[0, 2\pi]$ that verify the equation.

– Isolate x.

– Determine the solution set, taking the period into consideration.

Ex.: $f(x) = 2\cos\frac{\pi}{2}(x-1)-1$

$p = 4$

$2\cos\frac{\pi}{2}(x-1)-1=0$

$\cos\frac{\pi}{2}(x-1)=\frac{1}{2}$

$\frac{\pi}{2}(x-1)=\frac{\pi}{3}$ or $\frac{\pi}{2}(x-1)=\frac{5\pi}{3}$

$x=\frac{5}{3}$ or $\qquad x=\frac{13}{3}$

$S=\left\{\frac{5}{3}+4n\right\}\cup\left\{\frac{13}{3}+4n\right\}$

---

7. The following functions have the rule $f(x) = a \cos b(x - h) + k$.

Find the zeros of each function over

1. the interval $[h, h + p]$ where p is the period of the function.
2. the set of all real numbers.

a) $f(x) = 2 \cos \frac{\pi}{6}(x - 2) + 1$

b) $f(x) = -2 \cos \frac{\pi}{3}(x + 1) + \frac{1}{2}$

c) $f(x) = \cos 2(x - \pi) + 1$

d) $f(x) = 2 \cos\left(x + \frac{\pi}{2}\right) - \sqrt{3}$

e) $f(x) = -3 \cos \frac{\pi}{4}x + 6$

f) $f(x) = -2 \cos \frac{\pi}{8}(x + 2) - \sqrt{2}$

8. Determine the zeros of the function $f(x) = -2 \cos \frac{\pi}{12}(x + 5) - 1$ over the interval $[66, 126]$.

ACTIVITY 5 Study of the function $f(x) = a \cos b(x - h) + k$

One cycle of the function $f(x) = 2 \cos \frac{\pi}{6}(x - 1) + 1$ is represented below.

a) Determine

   1. the period. _____ 2. the amplitude. ____

b) Determine

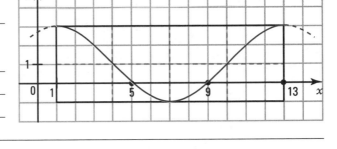

   1. dom f. _____ 2. ran f. _____

   3. the zeros of f over $[1, 13]$. _____

   4. the zeros of f over $\mathbb{R}$. _____

   5. the sign of f over $[1, 13]$. _____

   6. the sign of f over $\mathbb{R}$. _____

   _____

   7. the variation of f over $[1, 13]$. _____

   8. the variation of f over $\mathbb{R}$. _____

   9. the maximum and minimum of f. _____

STUDY OF THE FUNCTION $f(x) = a \cos b(x - h) + k$

Given $f(x) = -2 \cos 2\left(x - \dfrac{\pi}{6}\right) + 1$. We have:

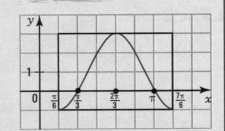

- dom $f = \mathbb{R}$; ran $f = [-1, 3]$
- period $p = \pi$; amplitude $A = 2$
- zeros of f: $\left\{\dfrac{\pi}{3} + \pi n\right\} \cup \left\{\pi + \pi n\right\}$
- sign of f.

$$f(x) \leqslant 0 \text{ over } \left[\frac{\pi}{6} + \pi n, \frac{\pi}{3} + \pi n\right] \cup \left[\pi + \pi n, \frac{7\pi}{6} + \pi n\right]$$

$$f(x) \geqslant 0 \text{ over } \left[\frac{\pi}{3} + \pi n, \pi + \pi n\right]$$

- variation of f.

$$f \nearrow \text{ over } \left[\frac{\pi}{6} + \pi n, \frac{2\pi}{3} + \pi n\right]; f \searrow \text{ over } \left[\frac{2\pi}{3} + \pi n, \frac{7\pi}{6} + \pi n\right]$$

- min $f = -1$; max $f = 3$.

9. For each of the following functions, determine

   1. the period,   2. the amplitude,   3. the range of the function.

   a) $f(x) = 2 \cos \dfrac{3\pi}{4}(x - 1) + 5$ **b)** $f(x) = 5 \cos 4(x + 2) - 12$

   1. _____   1. _____

   2. _____   2. _____

   3. _____   3. _____

10. Determine the initial value of the following functions.

a) $f(x) = 2 \cos \frac{\pi}{3}(x+1) + 1$ _____

b) $f(x) = 5 \cos 2\left(x - \frac{\pi}{2}\right) + 1$ _____

11. Determine, over $\mathbb{R}$, the interval over which the function $f(x) = \cos \frac{\pi}{4}(x+2) + 1$ is increasing.

_____

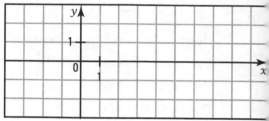

12. Determine, over $\mathbb{R}$, the interval over which the function $f(x) = 2 \cos \frac{\pi}{3}(x-3) + 1$ is negative.

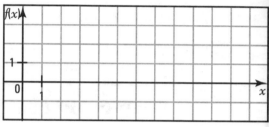

13. On a boat, a sailor observes the movement of the waves while on a sailing expedition. The height of a wave (in m) can be expressed as a function of the time (in s) since the start of the observation by the rule:

$$h(t) = 2 \cos \frac{\pi}{6}(t-4) + 1$$

The sailor observes a wave for 30 seconds. Determine at which moments the wave will be at a height of 2 metres.

_____

_____

_____

_____

ACTIVITY 6 Finding the rule $y = a \cos b(x - h) + k$

Consider the function f represented on the right.

a) Determine

   1. the period of f. _____   2. the amplitude of f. _____

b) Determine the rule of the function f when we choose a cycle starting at the point $(h, k + \mathrm{A}) = (0, 3)$.

   Explain your procedure: _____

   _____

   _____

   _____

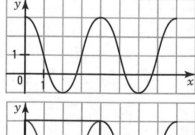

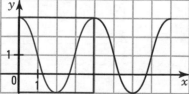

c) Determine the rule of the function f when we choose a cycle starting at the point $(h, k - A) = (2, -1)$.

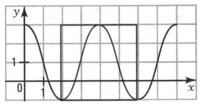

_____

d) Write the rule of the function in the form $y = a \sin b(x - h) + k$.

_____

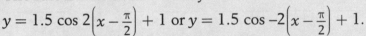

FINDING THE RULE $\quad y = a \cos b(x - h) + k$

From the graph of the function on the right, we deduce that: $|a| = 1.5$, $|b| = 2$ and $k = 1$.

The writing of the function's rule depends on your choice of the starting point of one cycle.

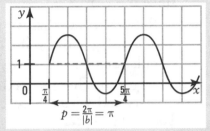

Consider two cases:

1st case: starting point: $\left(h, k + A\right) = \left(\dfrac{\pi}{2}, 2.5\right)$

The cycle is decreasing from the start $\Rightarrow a > 0$.

Thus, $a = 1.5$ and $b = 2$ or $a = 1.5$ and $b = -2$.

The rule is written in two ways:

$y = 1.5 \cos 2\left(x - \dfrac{\pi}{2}\right) + 1$ or $y = 1.5 \cos -2\left(x - \dfrac{\pi}{2}\right) + 1$.

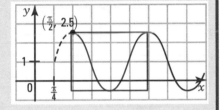

2nd case: starting point: $(h, k - A) = (\pi, -0.5)$.

The cycle is increasing from the start $\Rightarrow a < 0$.

Thus, $a = -1.5$ and $b = 2$ or $a = -1.5$ and $b = -2$.

The rule is written in two ways:

$y = -1.5 \cos 2(x - \pi) + 1$ or $y = -1.5 \cos -2(x - \pi) + 1$.

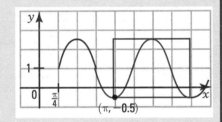

Note that this function can be described by a rule written in the form $y = a \sin b(x - h) + k$.

For example, $y = 1.5 \sin 2\left(x - \dfrac{\pi}{4}\right) + 1$.

Thus, any sinusoidal function can be described by a rule written in the form $y = a \sin b(x - h) + k$ or $y = a \cos b(x - h) + k$.

14. Find a rule of the form $y = a \cos b(x - h) + k$ for each of the following functions.

a)

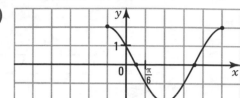

b)

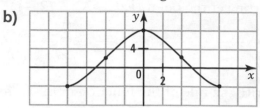

_____   _____

15. The populations of two neighboring villages A and B vary according to the model of a sinusoidal function which gives the population P of the village as a function of time t, in years, since the year 2000.

In the year 2000, the two villages had 3000 and 2500 inhabitants respectively.

The graph on the right shows the progression of the population of each village.

Village A reaches its maximum population of 4125 after 2 years and village B reaches its minimal population of 1000 after 3 years.

What will be the difference in population between these two villages in the year 2005?

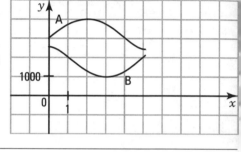

_____

_____

_____

_____

_____

_____

_____

_____

5.7 Tangent function

ACTIVITY 1 Basic tangent function

The basic tangent function, denoted tan, has the rule $y = \tan t$.

a) Complete the table of values below when t varies from $-\dfrac{3\pi}{2}$ to $\dfrac{3\pi}{2}$.

t	$-\dfrac{3\pi}{2}$	$-\dfrac{5\pi}{4}$	$-\pi$	$-\dfrac{3\pi}{4}$	$-\dfrac{\pi}{2}$	$-\dfrac{\pi}{4}$	0	$\dfrac{\pi}{4}$	$\dfrac{\pi}{2}$	$\dfrac{3\pi}{4}$	π	$\dfrac{5\pi}{4}$	$\dfrac{3\pi}{2}$
tan t													

b) Explain why tan t does not exist when $t = \dfrac{\pi}{2}$.

_____

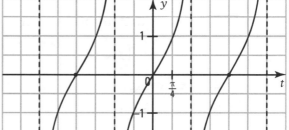

c) We have represented the function $y = \tan t$ on the right. Is this function periodic? If yes, what is the period p of the function? _____

d) The graph of the tangent function has vertical asymptotes. What are the equations of the tangent function's asymptotes when

$-\dfrac{\pi}{2} \le t \le \dfrac{\pi}{2}$? _____

e) When $t \in \left[-\dfrac{\pi}{2}, \dfrac{\pi}{2}\right]$, determine, for the basic tangent function,

1. the domain. _____   2. the range. _____   3. the zero. _____

4. the sign. _____

5. the variation. _____

f) Does the basic tangent function have any extrema? _____

BASIC TANGENT FUNCTION

- The **tangent** function, denoted tan, is defined by
$$\tan : \mathbb{R} \to \mathbb{R}$$
$$x \mapsto y = \tan x$$

- The basic tangent function is a **periodic** function with **period** π.

$$\boxed{\tan(x + \pi) = \tan x}$$

- The tangent function has an infinite number of vertical asymptotes with equations:

$x = \dfrac{\pi}{2} + \pi n \; (n \in \mathbb{Z})$.

Note that the distance separating two consecutive asymptotes is the period π.

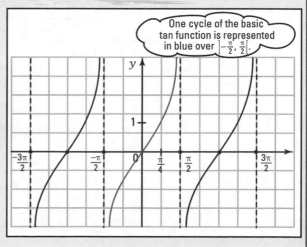

One cycle of the basic tan function is represented in blue over $\left]-\dfrac{\pi}{2}, \dfrac{\pi}{2}\right[$.

- We have:
  - domain $= \mathbb{R} \setminus \left\{ \frac{\pi}{2} + \pi n \right\};$ range $= \mathbb{R}.$
  - zero over $\left] -\frac{\pi}{2}, \frac{\pi}{2} \right[: 0.$
  - sign over $\left] -\frac{\pi}{2}, \frac{\pi}{2} \right[: \tan x \leqslant 0$ if $-\frac{\pi}{2} < x \leqslant 0$ and $\tan x \geqslant 0$ if $0 \leqslant x < \frac{\pi}{2}.$
  - variation: $\tan \nearrow$ over $\left] -\frac{\pi}{2}, \frac{\pi}{2} \right[.$
  - extrema: none
- For any real x, we have: $\tan (-x) = -\tan x.$ The basic tangent function is therefore considered to be an **odd** function.

1. Consider the function $y = \tan x.$

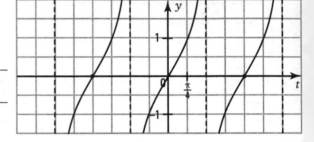

   a) Find the equations of the asymptotes when

      1. $x \in \left] -\frac{\pi}{2}, \frac{\pi}{2} \right[.$ _____

      2. $x \in \mathbb{R}.$ _____

   b) Find the zeros of f when

      1. $x \in \left] -\frac{3\pi}{2}, \frac{3\pi}{2} \right[.$ _____

      2. $x \in \mathbb{R}.$ _____

   c) Solve the inequality $\tan x \geqslant 0$ when

      1. $x \in \left] -\frac{3\pi}{2}, \frac{3\pi}{2} \right[.$ _____   2. $x \in \mathbb{R}.$ _____

Activity 2 Equation $tan\,\theta = k$

The function $y = \tan x$ is represented on the right when
$x \in \left] -\frac{3\pi}{2}, \frac{3\pi}{2} \right[.$

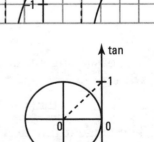

  a) 1. By referring to the trigonometric circle, solve
      the equation $\tan \theta = 1$ when

      $\theta \in \left] -\frac{\pi}{2}, \frac{\pi}{2} \right[.$ _____

     2. Explain how to find, from the solutions in 1,
     the solution to $\tan \theta = 1$ when

      1) $\theta \in \left] \frac{\pi}{2}, \frac{3\pi}{2} \right[.$ _____

      2) $\theta \in \left] -\frac{3\pi}{2}, -\frac{\pi}{2} \right[.$ _____

3. Verify that the solution set S to the equation $\tan \theta = 1$ over $\mathbb{R}$ is described by

$$S = \left\{ \ldots, -\frac{7\pi}{4}, -\frac{3\pi}{4}, \frac{\pi}{4}, \frac{5\pi}{4}, \frac{9\pi}{4}, \ldots \right\} \text{ (enumeration).}$$

or $S = \left\{ \frac{\pi}{4} + \pi n \right\}$ where $n \in \mathbb{Z}$ (set-builder notation).

b) Using a calculator, solve the equation $\tan \theta = 2$ when

1. $\theta \in \left] -\frac{\pi}{2}, \frac{\pi}{2} \right[$. _____

2. $\theta \in \left] \frac{3\pi}{2}, \frac{5\pi}{2} \right[$. _____

3. $\theta \in \mathbb{R}$. _____

c) Solve the inequality $\tan \theta \geqslant 2$ when

1. $\theta \in \left] -\frac{\pi}{2}, \frac{\pi}{2} \right[$. _____

2. $\theta \in \left] \frac{3\pi}{2}, \frac{5\pi}{2} \right[$. _____

3. $\theta \in \mathbb{R}$. _____

EQUATION $tan\ \theta = k, k \in \mathbb{R}$

- When $\theta \in \left] -\frac{\pi}{2}, \frac{\pi}{2} \right[$, the equation $\tan \theta = k$ yields one unique solution

$$\boxed{\theta_1 = \tan^{-1} k}$$

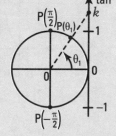

- When $\theta \in \mathbb{R}$, the equation $\tan \theta = k$ yields an infinite number of solutions. The solution set S is defined in set-builder notation by

$$\boxed{S = \{ \theta_1 + \pi n \} \text{ where } n \in \mathbb{Z}}$$

Ex.: The equation $\tan \theta = \sqrt{3}$ has the solution set:

- $S = \left\{ \frac{\pi}{3} \right\}$ when $\theta \in \left] -\frac{\pi}{2}, \frac{\pi}{2} \right[$.

- $S = \left\{ \frac{\pi}{3} + \pi n \right\}$ when $\theta \in \mathbb{R}$.

---

2. Solve the following equations over

1. $\left] -\frac{\pi}{2}, \frac{\pi}{2} \right[$ 2. $\left] \frac{\pi}{2}, \frac{3\pi}{2} \right[$ 3. $\mathbb{R}$

a) $\tan x = \frac{\sqrt{3}}{3}$ 1. _____   2. _____   3. _____

b) $\tan x = -1$ 1. _____   2. _____   3. _____

c) $\tan x = -\sqrt{3}$ 1. _____   2. _____   3. _____

d) $\tan x = 5$ 1. _____   2. _____   3. _____

5.7 Tangent function   **239**

3. Solve the following inequalities over

1. $\left] -\dfrac{\pi}{2}, \dfrac{\pi}{2} \right[$ 2. $\mathbb{R}$

a) $\tan x \geqslant \sqrt{3}$ 1. _____ 2. _____

b) $\tan x \leqslant \dfrac{\sqrt{3}}{3}$ 1. _____ 2. _____

c) $\tan x \leqslant -1$ 1. _____ 2. _____

d) $\tan x \geqslant -\sqrt{3}$ 1. _____ 2. _____

ACTIVITY 3 **Function** $y = \tan bx$

a) For each of the following functions,
   1. determine the value of parameter b.
   2. find the period p.

a) $y = \tan 2x$

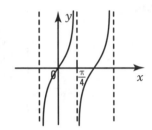

_____

b) $y = \tan (-2x)$

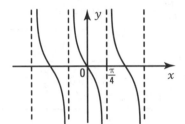

_____

c) $y = \tan \dfrac{1}{2}x$

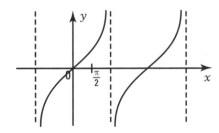

_____

d) $y = \tan \left(-\dfrac{1}{2}x \right)$

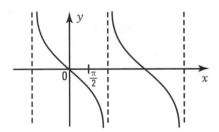

_____

b) What is the period p of the function $y = \tan bx$? _____

ACTIVITY 4 Tangent function $y = a \tan b(x - h) + k$

a) Consider the function $y = 2 \tan \frac{1}{2}\left(x - \frac{\pi}{2}\right) + 1$.

   1. Identify the parameters a, b, h and k. _____

   2. What is the period p of the function? _____

b) To determine the equation of an asymptote, solve the equation $b(x - h) = \frac{\pi}{2}$.

   1. Find the equation of an asymptote. _____
   2. What distance separates two consecutive asymptotes? _____

c) In the Cartesian plane on the right, the point (h, k) has been located and 2 consecutive asymptotes are drawn.

Complete the following table of values and draw one cycle of the function.

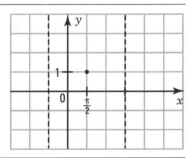

x	$-\frac{\pi}{2}$	0	$\frac{\pi}{2}$	π	$\frac{3\pi}{2}$
y					

TANGENT FUNCTION $y = a \tan b(x - h) + k$

- The graph of the function $y = a \tan b(x - h) + k$ is deduced from the graph of the basic function $y = \tan x$ by the transformation $(x, y) \rightarrow \left(\frac{x}{b} + h, ay + k\right)$.

- The function is periodic with period: $p = \frac{\pi}{|b|}$.

- The function has an infinite number of vertical asymptotes.

  – To determine the equation of an asymptote, we solve the equation $b(x - h) = \frac{\pi}{2}$.

  – Equation of an asymptote: $x = h - \frac{p}{2}$ or $x = h + \frac{p}{2}$.

  – The distance separating two consecutive asymptotes is equal to the period p of the function.

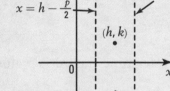

- To draw one cycle of the function $y = a \tan b(x - h) + k$,
  1. we locate the point (h, k).
  2. we draw, equal distance from the point (h, k), two consecutive asymptotes.

   We have two possible situations depending on the signs of a and b.

$ab > 0$ Increasing function	$ab < 0$ Decreasing function
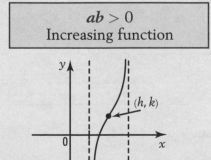	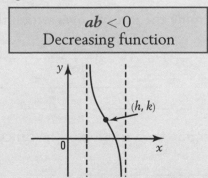

---

4. For each of the following functions, determine
   1. the period.   2. the equations of 2 consecutive asymptotes.   3. the domain.

   a) $f(x) = 2 \tan \frac{\pi}{4}(x-1) + 1$

   1. _____
   2. _____
   3. _____

   b) $f(x) = -3 \tan \frac{2\pi}{3}(x+2) - 5$

   1. _____
   2. _____
   3. _____

5. Draw one cycle of each of the following functions.

   a) $f(x) = 3 \tan \frac{\pi}{4}(x+2) - 1$

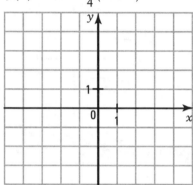

   b) $f(x) = -2 \tan \frac{1}{2}\left(x - \frac{\pi}{2}\right) + 1$

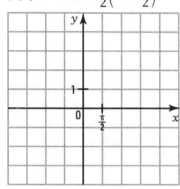

6. Determine the zeros of the following functions over $\mathbb{R}$.

   a) $f(x) = -2 \tan \frac{\pi}{6}(x-1) + 2$

   _____

   _____

   _____

   _____

   b) $f(x) = 3 \tan \frac{\pi}{3}(x+2) + \sqrt{3}$

   _____

   _____

   _____

   _____

7. Determine the initial value of the following functions.

   a) $f(x) = 3 \tan \frac{\pi}{2}\left(x + \frac{1}{2}\right) - 1$

   _____

   b) $f(x) = 3 \tan \frac{1}{2}\left(x - \frac{\pi}{2}\right) + 2$

   _____

8. Determine the interval over which the function $f(x) = 4 \tan \frac{\pi}{4}(x-1) + 4$ is positive.

   _____

   _____

   _____

9. Determine the variation of the function $f(x) = -2 \tan \frac{\pi}{6}(x+4) - 1$.

   _____

5.8 Trigonometric identities

ACTIVITY 1 Trigonometric identities

Consider the trigonometric point P(t) and the right triangle 0PC.

a) Prove the identity $\sin^2 t + \cos^2 t = 1$.

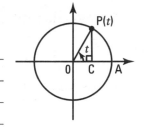

_____

_____

_____

_____

b) Justify the steps proving the identity $\tan^2 t + 1 = \sec^2 t$.

Steps	Justifications
1. $\sin^2 t + \cos^2 t = 1$	
2. $\dfrac{\sin^2 t + \cos^2 t}{\cos^2 t} = \dfrac{1}{\cos^2 t}$	
3. $\dfrac{\sin^2 t}{\cos^2 t} + \dfrac{\cos^2 t}{\cos^2 t} = \dfrac{1}{\cos^2 t}$	
4. $\tan^2 t + 1 = \sec^2 t$	

c) Prove the identity: $1 + \cot^2 t = \csc^2 t$.

_____

d) Consider the trigonometric circle on the right and the right triangle 0AC.
Justify the steps showing that $m\overline{0C} = \sec t$.

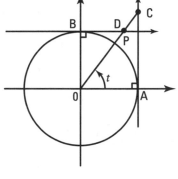

Steps	Justifications
1. $m\overline{0C}^2 = m\overline{0A}^2 + m\overline{AC}^2$	
2. $m\overline{0C}^2 = 1 + \tan^2 t$	
3. $m\overline{0C}^2 = \sec^2 t$	
4. $m\overline{0C} = \sec t$	

e) Refer to the trigonometric circle and right triangle 0BD above to show that $m\overline{0D} = \csc t$.

_____

_____

_____

_____

BASIC TRIGONOMETRIC IDENTITIES

- If $P(t)$ is a trigonometric point, then
  $m\overline{OE} = \cos t$, $m\overline{PE} = \sin t$.
  $m\overline{AC} = \tan t$, $m\overline{BD} = \cot t$.
  $m\overline{OC} = \sec t$, $m\overline{OD} = \csc t$.

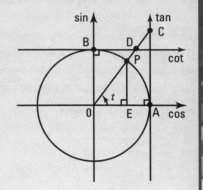

- 1st basic identity:

$$\sin^2 t + \cos^2 t = 1$$

- Other basic identities:

$$1 + \tan^2 t = \sec^2 t$$

$$1 + \cot^2 t = \csc^2 t$$

1. Verify the three basic identities when $t = \frac{\pi}{6}$.

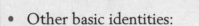

2. Using an angle measure t of your choice, expressed in radians or in degrees, verify the three basic identities.

3. Use the appropriate basic identity to calculate

    a) $\sin t$, knowing that $\cos t = \frac{3}{5}$ and $270° \leqslant t \leqslant 360°$.

    b) $\cos t$, knowing that $\sin t = \frac{40}{41}$ and $90° \leqslant t \leqslant 180°$.

    c) $\tan t$, knowing that $\sec t = \frac{-5}{4}$ and $180° \leqslant t \leqslant 270°$.

    d) $\cot t$, knowing that $\csc t = -\frac{13}{12}$ and $270° \leqslant t \leqslant 360°$.

    e) $\sec t$, knowing that $\tan t = \frac{7}{24}$ and $180° \leqslant t \leqslant 270°$.

    f) $\csc t$, knowing that $\cot t = \frac{4}{3}$ and $0° \leqslant t \leqslant 90°$.

4. Reduce the following expressions to a single term.

a) $1 - \sin^2 t$ _____

b) $\sec^2 t - \tan^2 t$ _____

c) $\cot^2 t - \csc^2 t$ _____

d) $\sin t \sec t$ _____

e) $\tan x \cdot \csc x$ _____

f) $(1 - \sin^2 x) \sec^2 x$ _____

g) $(1 + \tan^2 x) \sin^2 x$ _____

h) $\csc^2 x(1 - \cos^2 x)$ _____

i) $(\sec^2 x - 1) \cot^2 x$ _____

j) $\csc^2 x - \cot^2 x - \sin^2 x$ _____

5. Express each of the following trigonometric ratios in terms of $\sin x$ knowing that $0 \leqslant x \leqslant \frac{\pi}{2}$.

a) $\cos x$ _____

b) $\tan x$ _____

c) $\cot x$ _____

d) $\sec x$ _____

6. If $\sin t = 0.6$ and $\frac{\pi}{2} \leqslant t \leqslant \pi$, deduce the other 5 trigonometric ratios.

_____

7. If $\cos t = \frac{12}{13}$ and $\frac{3\pi}{2} \leqslant t \leqslant 2\pi$, deduce the other 5 trigonometric ratios.

_____

8. If $\tan t = \frac{3}{4}$ and $0 \leqslant t \leqslant \frac{\pi}{2}$, deduce the other 5 trigonometric ratios.

_____

9. If $\cot t = \frac{-5}{12}$ and $\frac{3\pi}{2} \leqslant t \leqslant 2\pi$, deduce the other 5 trigonometric ratios.

_____

10. Simplify the following expressions.

a) $\dfrac{\sin^2 x + \cos^2 x}{1 - \cos^2 x}$ _____

b) $\dfrac{1 + \tan^2 x}{1 + \cot^2 x}$ _____

c) $\dfrac{\sec^2 x - \tan^2 x}{1 - \sin^2 x}$ _____

d) $\dfrac{\sec^2 x - 1}{\csc^2 x} \cdot \dfrac{\cot^2 x}{\sin^2 x}$ _____

11. Simplify the following expressions.

a) $\dfrac{1 - \cos^2 x}{1 - \sin^2 x}$ _____

b) $\dfrac{1 + \tan^2 x}{1 + \cot^2 x}$ _____

c) $(1 + \sec x)(1 - \sec x)$ _____

d) $\dfrac{\csc^2 x - \cot^2 x}{\cos^2 x}$ _____

12. Perform the following operations.

a) $\dfrac{1}{1 + \sin x} + \dfrac{1}{1 - \sin x} =$ _____

b) $\dfrac{\cos x}{\sec x + 1} + \dfrac{\cos x}{\sec x - 1} =$ _____

Justify the steps which prove the identity: $\sin x + \cos x \cot x = \csc x$ according to the following procedures.

1st procedure: Transform the left side using algebraic manipulations to make it identical to the right side.

Steps	Justifications
$\sin x + \cos x \cot x = \csc x$	
1. $\sin x + \cos x \cdot \dfrac{\cos x}{\sin x} = \csc x$	
2. $\dfrac{\sin^2 x + \cos^2 x}{\sin x} = \csc x$	
3. $\dfrac{1}{\sin x} = \csc x$	
4. $\csc x = \csc x$	

2nd procedure: Transform the right side using algebraic manipulations to make it identical to the left side.

Steps	Justifications
$\sin x + \cos x \cot x = \csc x$	
1. $\sin x + \cos x \cot x = \dfrac{1}{\sin x}$	
2. $\sin x + \cos x \cot x = \dfrac{\sin^2 x + \cos^2 x}{\sin x}$	
3. $\sin x + \cos x \cot x = \sin x + \dfrac{\cos^2 x}{\sin x}$	
4. $\sin x + \cos x \cot x = \sin x + \cos x \cot x$	

PROVING A TRIGONOMETRIC IDENTITY

To prove an identity, we simplify one side (usually the more complex side) to make it identical to the other side. The algebraic manipulations used consist of
- substituting expressions by other known identities.
- using the definitions of the trigonometric ratios.
- multiplying or dividing by the same trigonometric expression.
- factoring.
- reducing to a common denominator.

...

Ex.: See activity 2.

13. Prove the following trigonometric identities.

a) $\cot^2 x \sin^2 x + \sin^2 x = 1$

---

b) $\dfrac{1}{\csc^2 x} + \dfrac{1}{\sec^2 x} = 1$

---

c) $\dfrac{1 + \tan^2 x}{\cot^2 x + 1} = \tan^2 x$

---

d) $\dfrac{\cos^2 x \cdot \tan x}{\cot x} - 1 = -\cos^2 x$

---

e) $\dfrac{\sec x}{\cos x} - 1 = \tan^2 x$

---

f) $(1 + \cot^2 x)(1 - \cos^2 x) = 1$

---

g) $2 \cos^2 a - 1 = 1 - 2 \sin^2 a$

---

h) $\tan x + \cot x = \sec x \csc x$

---

14. Prove the following trigonometric identities.

a) $\sec x - \cos x = \sin x \tan x$

---

b) $\dfrac{1 + \sin x}{\cos x} = \dfrac{\cos x}{1 - \sin x}$

---

c) $\dfrac{\sin^2 x}{1 - \cos x} = 1 + \cos x$

---

d) $(1 + \tan x)^2 + (1 - \tan x)^2 = 2 \sec^2 x$

---

e) $(1 + \tan x)(1 - \tan x) - (1 + \cot x)(1 - \cot x) = \dfrac{1 - \tan^4 x}{\tan^2 x}$

5.9 Trigonometric equations

ACTIVITY 1 Solving a trigonometric equation

A marble is hanging at the end of a spring that oscillates over a table. The height h (in cm) of the marble, relative to the table, as a function of elapsed time t (in sec) since the start of the movement is given by $h = 10 \sin \pi t + 15$.

a) What is the period of the function that describes the movement of the spring? _____

b) Justify the steps in solving the equation that enables you to calculate at what moments, during the first period of the movement, the marble is located 20 cm above the table.

   1. $10 \sin \pi t + 15 = 20$ _____

   2. $ 10 \sin \pi t = 5$ _____

   3. $ \sin \pi t = 0.5$ _____

   4. $ \pi t = \dfrac{\pi}{6}$ or $\pi t = \dfrac{5\pi}{6}$ _____

   5. $ t = \dfrac{1}{6}$ or $t = \dfrac{5}{6}$ _____

c) Keeping the periodicity of the movement in mind, determine the moments during the first 5 seconds when the marble is located 20 cm above the table.

_____

_____

ACTIVITY 2 Solving more complex trigonometric equations

Consider the equation $3 \sin \theta - 2 \cos^2 \theta = 0$ where $\theta \in [0, 2\pi[$.

a) Express the non-zero side in terms of only $\sin \theta$.

_____

_____

b) Factor the non-zero side and then apply the zero product principle to determine the possible values of $\sin \theta$.

_____

_____

_____

c) Of the two values found for $\sin \theta$, indicate which one must be rejected and explain why.

_____

d) What are the solutions to the equation?

_____

TRIGONOMETRIC EQUATIONS

Let us illustrate the procedure for solving: $\tan^2\theta + 3\sec\theta\tan\theta - \sec^2\theta = 1$.

	$\tan^2\theta + 3\sec\theta\tan\theta - \sec^2\theta = 1$		
1	$\dfrac{\sin^2\theta}{\cos^2\theta} + \dfrac{3\sin\theta}{\cos^2\theta} - \dfrac{1}{\cos^2\theta} = 1$	1	Use the definitions of the trigonometric ratios.
2	$\cos^2\theta \neq 0 \Leftrightarrow \cos\theta \neq 0$ $\theta \neq \dfrac{\pi}{2} + 2\pi n$ and $\theta \neq \dfrac{3\pi}{2} + 2\pi n,\ n \in \mathbb{Z}$	2	Set the restrictions on θ.
3	$\sin^2\theta + 3\sin\theta - 1 = \cos^2\theta$	3	Multiply each side by $\cos^2\theta$.
4	$\sin^2\theta + 3\sin\theta - 1 = 1 - \sin^2\theta$ $2\sin^2\theta + 3\sin\theta - 2 = 0$	4	Use identities so that the equation uses the same trigonometric ratio ($\sin\theta$ here).
5	$(2\sin\theta - 1)(\sin\theta + 2) = 0$	5	Factor the non-zero side.
6	$2\sin\theta - 1 = 0$ or $\sin\theta + 2 = 0$	6	Apply the zero product principle.
7	$\sin\theta = \dfrac{1}{2}$ or $\sin\theta = -2\,(\text{reject})$	7	Deduce the values for $\sin\theta$ and reject some, if necessary.
8	$\theta = \dfrac{\pi}{6}$ or $\theta = \dfrac{5\pi}{6}$	8	Deduce the value of θ over $[0, p[$ where $p = 2\pi$ is the period of $\sin\theta$.
9	$S = \left\{\dfrac{\pi}{6} + 2\pi n\right\} \cup \left\{\dfrac{5\pi}{6} + 2\pi n\right\}, n \in \mathbb{Z}$	9	Deduce the solution set S over $\mathbb{R}$, from the resulting solutions and period.

1. Solve the following trigonometric equations over $[0, 2\pi[$.

a) $\cos x \cdot (2\sin x + 1) = 0$ _____

b) $(\sin x - 2)(2\cos x - 1) = 0$ _____

2. Solve the following trigonometric equations over $\mathbb{R}$.

a) $(2\sin x + 1)(\sin x - 1) = 0$ _____

b) $(3\sin x - 1) \cdot \cos x = 0$ _____

3. Solve the following trigonometric equations over $[0, 2\pi[$.

a) $4\cos^2\theta - 1 = 0$

b) $2\sin^2\theta - \sin\theta - 1 = 0$

c) $\tan^2\theta - 3 = 0$

d) $2\sin^2 2x - \sin 2x = 0$

e) $2\sin^2\theta - \cos\theta - 1 = 0$

f) $\sec^2\theta + \sec\theta - 2 = 0$

g) $\sec^2\theta - \tan\theta\sec\theta - 2 = 0$

h) $4\tan^2 2\theta = \sec^2 2\theta$

5.10 Trigonometric formulas

ACTIVITY 1 Opposite angle formulas

The trigonometric points $P(t)$ and $P(-t)$ are symmetrical about the x-axis.

a) Compare

1. $\cos(-t)$ and $\cos t$ _____
2. $\sin(-t)$ and $\sin t$ _____

b) Prove that, $\forall\, t \in \mathbb{R}$,

1. $\tan(-t) = -\tan t$ _____

2. $\cot(-t) = -\cot t$ _____

3. $\sec(-t) = \sec t$ _____

4. $\csc(-t) = -\csc t$ _____

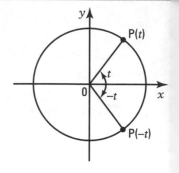

OPPOSITE ANGLE FORMULAS

For any real t, we have:

$\sin(-t) = -\sin t;$ $\cos(-t) = \cos t$

$\tan(-t) = -\tan t;$ $\cot(-t) = -\cot t$

$\csc(-t) = -\csc t;$ $\sec(-t) = \sec t$

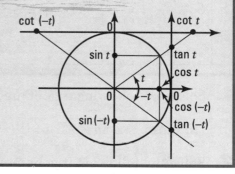

ACTIVITY 2 Addition formulas

On the right, we have represented the points $P(a)$, $P(b)$, $P(a-b)$ and $P(0)$ on the trigonometric circle.

a) The following steps enable you to prove the formula:
$\cos(a-b) = \cos a \cos b + \sin a \sin b$.

1. Calculate $d(P(a), P(b))^2$.

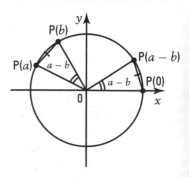

_____

_____

_____

_____

2. Calculate $d(P(a-b), P(0))^2$.

_____

_____

_____

_____

_____

3. Knowing that $d(P(a), P(b)) = d(P(a - b), P(0))$, justify the formula.

_____

_____

b) Use the formula: $\cos(a - b) = \cos a \cos b + \sin a \sin b$, and the opposite angle formulas (Activity 1) to prove the formula:

$\cos(a + b) = \cos a \cos b - \sin a \sin b$.

_____

c) Justify the steps in proving the formula: $\sin(a + b) = \sin a \cos b + \sin b \cos a$.

Steps	Justifications
1. $\sin(a + b) = \cos\left[\frac{\pi}{2} - (a + b)\right]$	
2. $= \cos\left[\left(\frac{\pi}{2} - a\right) - b\right]$	
3. $= \cos\left(\frac{\pi}{2} - a\right)\cos b + \sin\left(\frac{\pi}{2} - a\right)\sin b$	
4. $= \sin a \cos b + \sin b \cos a$	

d) Use the formula: $\sin(a + b) = \sin a \cos b + \sin b \cos a$ and the opposite angle formulas to prove the formula: $\sin(a - b) = \sin a \cos b - \sin b \cos a$.

_____

e) Justify the steps in proving the formula: $\tan(a + b) = \frac{\tan a + \tan b}{1 - \tan a \tan b}$.

Steps	Justifications
1. $\tan(a + b) = \frac{\sin(a + b)}{\cos(a + b)}$	
2. $= \frac{\sin a \cos b + \sin b \cos a}{\cos a \cos b - \sin a \sin b}$	
3. $= \frac{(\sin a \cos b + \sin b \cos a) \div \cos a \cos b}{(\cos a \cos b - \sin a \sin b) \div \cos a \cos b}$	
4. $= \frac{\tan a + \tan b}{1 - \tan a \tan b}$	

f) Use the formula: $\tan(a + b) = \frac{\tan a + \tan b}{1 - \tan a \tan b}$ and the opposite angle formulas to prove the formula:

$\tan(a - b) = \frac{\tan a - \tan b}{1 + \tan a \tan b}$. _____

ADDITION FORMULAS

$$\sin (a + b) = \sin a \cos b + \sin b \cos a$$
$$\cos (a + b) = \cos a \cos b - \sin a \sin b$$
$$\tan (a + b) = \frac{\tan a + \tan b}{1 - \tan a \tan b}$$

The opposite angle formulas enable you to deduce that

$$\sin (a - b) = \sin a \cos b - \sin b \cos a$$
$$\cos (a - b) = \cos a \cos b + \sin a \sin b$$
$$\tan (a - b) = \frac{\tan a - \tan b}{1 + \tan a \tan b}$$

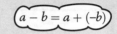

$a - b = a + (-b)$

ACTIVITY 3 Double-angle formulas

a) Knowing that $2a = a + a$, use the addition formulas to show that

1. $\sin 2a = 2 \sin a \cos a$.

_____

2. $\cos 2a = \cos^2 a - \sin^2 a$.

_____

3. $\tan 2a = \frac{2 \tan a}{1 - \tan^2 a}$ _____

b) Knowing that $\sin^2 a + \cos^2 a = 1$, prove that

1. $\cos 2a = 2 \cos^2 a - 1$.

_____

2. $\cos 2a = 1 - 2 \sin^2 a$.

_____

DOUBLE-ANGLE FORMULAS

$$\sin 2a = 2 \sin a \cos a$$
$$\cos 2a = \cos^2 a - \sin^2 a$$
$$\ldots = 2 \cos^2 a - 1$$
$$\ldots = 1 - 2 \sin^2 a$$
$$\tan 2a = \frac{2 \tan a}{1 - \tan^2 a}$$

ACTIVITY 4 Supplementary angle formulas

a) Use the addition formulas to show that

1. $\sin(\pi - x) = \sin x$.

_____

_____

_____

2. $\cos(\pi - x) = -\cos x$.

_____

_____

_____

3. $\tan(\pi - x) = -\tan x$.

_____

b) Deduce that

1. $\sec(\pi - x) = -\sec x$.

_____

2. $\csc(\pi - x) = \csc x$.

_____

3. $\cot(\pi - x) = -\cot x$.

_____

SUPPLEMENTARY ANGLE FORMULAS

$$\sin(\pi - t) = \sin t$$
$$\cos(\pi - t) = -\cos t$$
$$\tan(\pi - t) = -\tan t$$

$$\sec(\pi - t) = -\sec t$$
$$\csc(\pi - t) = \csc t$$
$$\cot(\pi - t) = -\cot t$$

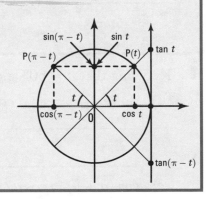

a) Use the addition formulas to show that

1. $\sin\left(\dfrac{\pi}{2} - x\right) = \cos x$.

2. $\cos\left(\dfrac{\pi}{2} - x\right) = \sin x$.

_____

_____

_____

_____

_____

_____

b) Deduce that

1. $\tan\left(\dfrac{\pi}{2} - x\right) = \cot x$.

2. $\sec\left(\dfrac{\pi}{2} - x\right) = \csc x$.

_____

_____

3. $\csc\left(\dfrac{\pi}{2} - x\right) = \sec x$.

4. $\cot\left(\dfrac{\pi}{2} - x\right) = \tan x$.

_____

_____

COMPLEMENTARY ANGLE FORMULAS

$$\sin\left(\dfrac{\pi}{2} - t\right) = \cos t$$

$$\cos\left(\dfrac{\pi}{2} - t\right) = \sin t$$

$$\tan\left(\dfrac{\pi}{2} - t\right) = \cot t$$

$$\sec\left(\dfrac{\pi}{2} - t\right) = \csc t$$

$$\csc\left(\dfrac{\pi}{2} - t\right) = \sec t$$

$$\cot\left(\dfrac{\pi}{2} - t\right) = \tan t$$

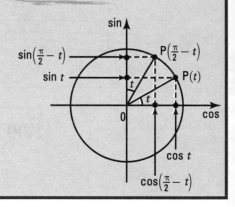

---

1. Knowing that $a = 60°$ and $b = 30°$, verify that

a) $\sin(a + b) = \sin a \cos b + \sin b \cos a$

b) $\sin(a - b) = \sin a \cos b - \sin b \cos a$

_____

_____

_____

_____

c) $\cos(a + b) = \cos a \cos b - \sin a \sin b$

d) $\cos(a - b) = \cos a \cos b + \sin a \sin b$

_____

_____

_____

_____

2. Knowing that $a = 30°$, verify that

a) $\sin 2a = 2 \sin a \cos a$

b) $\cos 2a = \cos^2 a - \sin^2 a$

c) $\cos 2a = 2 \cos^2 a - 1$

d) $\cos 2a = 1 - 2 \sin^2 a$

3. Use the addition formulas to simplify

a) $\sin (\pi + x)$ _____

b) $\cos (\pi + x)$ _____

c) $\sin \left(\dfrac{\pi}{2} + x \right)$ _____

d) $\cos \left(\dfrac{\pi}{2} + x \right)$ _____

4. Knowing that $\sin a = \dfrac{3}{5}$ and $\sin b = \dfrac{12}{13}$ and that $0 \leqslant a \leqslant \dfrac{\pi}{2}$ and $0 \leqslant b \leqslant 2$, calculate

a) $\sin (a + b)$

b) $\cos (a + b)$

c) $\tan (a + b)$

d) $\sin 2a$

e) $\cos 2a$

5. Prove the following identities.

a) $\sin 2x = \dfrac{2 \tan x}{1 + \tan^2 x}$

b) $\cos 2x = \dfrac{1 - \tan^2 x}{1 + \tan^2 x}$

c) $\tan 2x = \dfrac{2 \tan x}{1 - \tan^2 x}$

6. Show that $\tan 75°$ has the exact value: $2 + \sqrt{3}$.

5.11 Inverse trigonometric functions

a) The sine function is represented below. Explain why the inverse of the sine function is not a function.

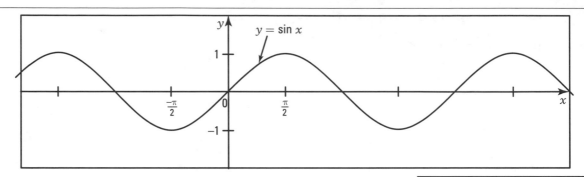

b) A portion of the sine function, when the variable x varies between $-\frac{\pi}{2}$ and $\frac{\pi}{2}$ is represented on the right.

This new graph represents the function called **principal sine** denoted Sin.

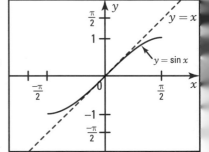

1. Determine

   1) dom Sin _____ 2) ran Sin _____

2. Is the inverse of the Sin function a function? _____

3. Deduce the graph of the inverse Sin^{-1} by a reflection about the line $y = x$.

4. Complete

   $Sin\,\frac{\pi}{6} = \frac{1}{2} \Leftrightarrow Sin^{-1}\,\frac{1}{2} =$ _____

5. Determine

   1) dom Sin^{-1} _____ 2) ran Sin^{-1} _____

ARCSINE FUNCTION

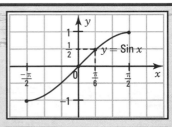

- The **principal sine** function, denoted Sin, is defined by

$$Sin: \left[-\frac{\pi}{2}, \frac{\pi}{2}\right] \rightarrow [-1, 1]$$

$$x \mapsto y = Sin\,x$$

- The inverse Sin^{-1} of the principal sine function is a function called **arcsine function**, denoted arcsin.

$$arcsin: [-1, 1] \rightarrow \left[-\frac{\pi}{2}, \frac{\pi}{2}\right]$$

$$x \mapsto y = arcsin\,x$$

Ex.: $arcsin\left(\frac{1}{2}\right) = \frac{\pi}{6}$ since $Sin\,\frac{\pi}{6} = \frac{1}{2}$

- We have: dom arcsin $= [-1, 1]$ and ran arcsin $= \left[-\frac{\pi}{2}, \frac{\pi}{2}\right]$

ACTIVITY 2 Arccosine function

a) The cosine function is represented below. Explain why the inverse of the cosine function is not a function.

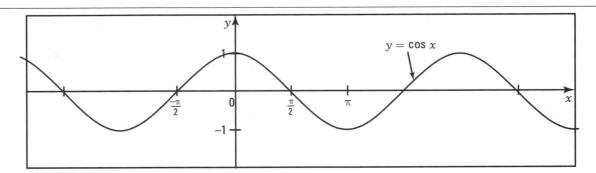

b) A portion of the cosine function, when the variable x varies between 0 and π is represented on the right.

This new graph represents the function called **principal cosine** denoted Cos.

1. Determine
   1) dom Cos _____ 2) ran Cos _____

2. Is the inverse of the Cos function a function?

   _____

3. Deduce the graph of the inverse Cos^{-1} by a reflection about the line $y = x$.

4. Complete

$$\text{Cos}\,\frac{\pi}{3} = \frac{1}{2} \Leftrightarrow \text{Cos}^{-1}\,\frac{1}{2} = \rule{3cm}{0.4pt}$$

5. Determine
   1) dom Cos^{-1} _____ 2) ran Cos^{-1} _____

ARCCOSINE FUNCTION

- The **principal cosine** function, denoted Cos, is defined by

  $$\text{Cos}: [0, \pi] \rightarrow [-1, 1]$$

  $$x \mapsto y = \text{Cos}\,x$$

- The inverse Cos^{-1} of the principal cosine function is a function called **arccosine function**, denoted arccos.

  $$\text{arccos}: [-1, 1] \rightarrow [0, \pi]$$

  $$x \mapsto y = \text{arccos}\,x$$

  Ex: $\text{arccos}\,\frac{1}{2} = \frac{\pi}{3}$ since $\text{Cos}\,\frac{\pi}{3} = \frac{1}{2}$

- We have: dom arccos $= [-1, 1]$ and ran arccos $= [0, \pi]$.

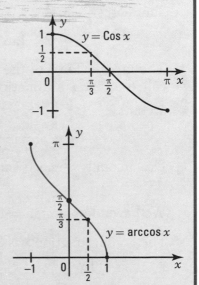

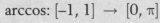

ACTIVITY 3 Arctangent function

a) The tangent function is represented below. Explain why the inverse of the tangent function is not a function.

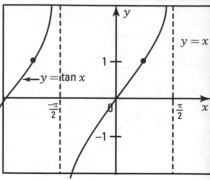

_____

_____

b) A portion of the tangent function, when the variable x varies between $-\frac{\pi}{2}$ and $\frac{\pi}{2}$ is represented on the right. This new graph represents the function called **principal tangent** denoted Tan.

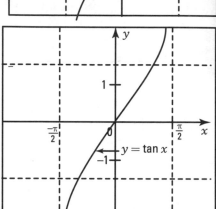

  1. Determine
     1) dom Tan _____ 2) ran Tan _____
  2. Is the inverse of the Tan function a function?

     _____

  3. Deduce the graph of the inverse Tan^{-1} by a reflection about the line $y = x$.
  4. Complete

     $Tan \frac{\pi}{4} = 1 \Leftrightarrow Tan^{-1} 1 =$ _____

  5. Determine
     1) dom Tan^{-1} _____ 2) ran Tan^{-1} _____
  6. Does the inverse Tan^{-1} have any asymptotes? If yes, give their equations.

     _____

ARCTANGENT FUNCTION

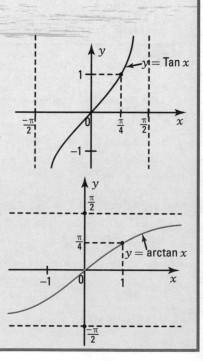

- The **principal tangent** function, denoted Tan, is defined by

  $Tan: \left]-\frac{\pi}{2}, \frac{\pi}{2}\right[\rightarrow \mathbb{R}$

  $\qquad x \mapsto y = Tan\ x$

- The inverse Tan^{-1} of the principal tangent function is a function called **arctangent** function, denoted arctan.

  $arctan: \mathbb{R} \rightarrow \left]-\frac{\pi}{2}, \frac{\pi}{2}\right[$

  $\qquad x \mapsto y = arctan\ x$

  Ex.: $arctan\ 1 = \frac{\pi}{4}$ since $Tan \frac{\pi}{4} = 1$

- We have: dom arctan $= \mathbb{R}$ and ran arctan $= \left]-\frac{\pi}{2}, \frac{\pi}{2}\right[$.

- The arctan function has 2 horizontal asymptotes:

  $y = -\frac{\pi}{2}$ and $y = \frac{\pi}{2}$.

1. Without using a calculator, determine the exact value of

    a) $\sin^{-1}\dfrac{\sqrt{2}}{2}$ _____
    b) $\cos^{-1}\dfrac{\sqrt{3}}{2}$ _____
    c) $\tan^{-1}\sqrt{3}$ _____
    d) $\arcsin\left(-\dfrac{1}{2}\right)$ _____

    e) $\arccos\left(-\dfrac{1}{2}\right)$ _____
    f) $\arctan\dfrac{\sqrt{3}}{3}$ _____
    g) $\arcsin 1$ _____
    h) $\arccos(-1)$ _____

2. Find the zeros of the following functions.

    a) arcsine _____
    b) arccosine _____
    c) arctangent _____

3. Study the sign of the following functions.

    a) arcsine _____

    b) arccosine _____

    c) arctangent _____

4. Calculate

    a) $\sin\left(\cos^{-1}\dfrac{1}{2}\right)$ _____
    b) $\cos\left(\sin^{-1}\dfrac{\sqrt{3}}{2}\right)$ _____
    c) $\tan\left(\sin^{-1}\dfrac{\sqrt{2}}{2}\right)$ _____

    d) $\sin(\tan^{-1}1)$ _____
    e) $\cos\left(\tan^{-1}\sqrt{3}\right)$ _____
    f) $\tan\left(\cos^{-1}\left(-\dfrac{1}{2}\right)\right)$ _____

    g) $\cos\left(\sin^{-1}\left(-\dfrac{1}{2}\right)\right)$ _____
    h) $\sin^{-1}\left(\tan\dfrac{\pi}{4}\right)$ _____
    i) $\tan\left(\sin^{-1}\left(-\dfrac{\sqrt{2}}{2}\right)\right)$ _____

5. True or false?

    a) The arcsine function is always increasing. _____

    b) The arccosine function is always decreasing. _____

    c) The arctangent function is always increasing. _____

    d) The arcsine and arccosine functions have the same domain. _____

    e) The arcsine and arccosine functions have the same range. _____

6. Solve the following equations.

    a) $\arcsin x = \dfrac{\pi}{4}$ _____
    b) $\arccos x = \dfrac{5\pi}{6}$ _____
    c) $\arctan x = \dfrac{-\pi}{4}$ _____

    d) $\arctan x = -\dfrac{\pi}{3}$ _____
    e) $\arcsin x = \dfrac{-\pi}{4}$ _____
    f) $\arccos x = \dfrac{\pi}{2}$ _____

7. Solve the following equations.

    a) $\sin(\arccos x) = \dfrac{1}{2}$ _____
    b) $\tan(\arcsin x) = 1$ _____

    c) $\cos(\arctan x) = 1$ _____
    d) $\sin(\arctan x) = \dfrac{-\sqrt{2}}{2}$ _____

8. True or false?

    a) $\arcsin x + \arccos x = \dfrac{\pi}{2}$ _____

    b) $\tan(\arcsin x) = \dfrac{x}{\sqrt{1-x^2}}$ _____

Evaluation 5

1. a) Convert $\frac{5\pi}{36}$ into degrees. _____

b) Convert 75° into radians. _____

2. A central angle measuring 54° sub-tends an arc on the circle.
If the circle has a radius of 12 cm, calculate the length of the sub-tended arc (round to the nearest tenth). _____

3. What are the coordinates of the trigonometric point $P(t)$ located in the 3rd quadrant if $\cos t = -\frac{15}{17}$? _____

4. Evaluate $\sin\left(t - \frac{\pi}{4}\right)$ if $\frac{\pi}{2} < t < \pi$ and $\sin t = \frac{\sqrt{3}}{2}$.

_____

_____

5. Evaluate $\cos 2t$ if $\cos t = \frac{4}{5}$.

_____

6. Find the coordinates of the point $P(t)$, located in the 3rd quadrant, if $\tan t = \frac{8}{15}$?

_____

7. If $P(t) = \left(-\frac{3}{5}, \frac{4}{5}\right)$, find the coordinates of the point $P(2t)$.

_____

8. Find the exact Cartesian coordinates of the trigonometric point $P\left(-\frac{19\pi}{6}\right)$.

_____

9. Knowing that $\sin a = \frac{3}{5}$, $\cos a = \frac{4}{5}$, $\sin b = \frac{5}{13}$, $\cos b = \frac{12}{13}$, find the value of

a) $\sin(a + b)$ _____

b) $\cos(a - b)$ _____

c) $\tan(a + b)$ _____

10. Simplify $\frac{\sin 2\theta}{1 + \cos 2\theta}$. _____

11. Simplify $\frac{\sin 4a \cos 2a - \sin 2a \cos 4a}{\cos 2a \cos a + \sin 2a \sin a}$. _____

12. Given the trigonometric point $P(t)=\left(\frac{3}{5},\frac{4}{5}\right)$, find the coordinates of the following trigonometric points.

a) $P\left(t+\frac{\pi}{2}\right)$ _____

b) $P\left(t-\frac{\pi}{2}\right)$ _____

c) $P(t+\pi)$ _____

d) $P(\pi-t)$ _____

13. If $P\left(\frac{a+2}{5},\frac{a+1}{5}\right)$ is a trigonometric point located in the 3rd quadrant, determine a.

_____

_____

14. If $\sin t=\frac{15}{17}$ and $\frac{\pi}{2}\leqslant t\leqslant\pi$, find

a) $\cos t$ _____ **b)** $\tan t$ _____ **c)** $\cot t$ _____ **d)** $\sec t$ _____ **e)** $\csc t$ _____

15. The function f is given by the rule $f(x)=-4\cos\frac{\pi}{6}(x-2)+2$. Determine

a) the amplitude. _____ **b)** the period of f. _____ **c)** ran f. _____

d) the zeros of f. _____

e) the sign of f over $[2, 14]$. _____

16. Determine the zeros of the following trigonometric functions over $\mathbb{R}$.

a) $f(x)=2\sin\frac{\pi}{2}(x-3)-1$ _____

b) $f(x)=-6\cos\frac{\pi}{3}(x+1)+3$ _____

c) $f(x)=2\tan\frac{\pi}{4}(x-1)+2$ _____

d) $f(x)=5\sin\frac{2\pi}{3}(x+1)+2$ _____

e) $f(x)=-2\cos 2(x+1)+1$ _____

17. Find the rule of the sinusoidal function represented on the right.

_____

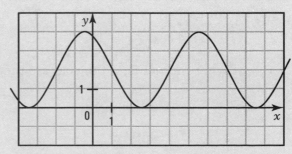

18. Solve the following trigonometric equations over $\mathbb{R}$.

a) $2 \sin x(\cos x - 1) = 0$ _____

b) $(2 \sin x + 1)(2 \cos x - 1) = 0$ _____

c) $2 \sin^2 x - 5 \sin x + 2 = 0$ _____

d) $\tan^2 x - 1 = 0$ _____

19. Solve the following equations over $[0, 2\pi[$.

a) $2 \sin^2 x - 1 = 0$ _____

b) $(2 \cos x + 1)(\sin x - 3) = 0$ _____

c) $25 \sin^2 x - 9 = 0$ _____

d) $(5 \cos x + 2)(2 \sin x - 1) = 0$ _____

20. True of false?

a) $\sin (a + b) = \sin a + \sin b$ _____   **b)** $\sin 2a = 2 \sin a$ _____

c) $\sin x^2 = \sin^2 x$ _____   **d)** $\cos 2a = \cos^2 a - \sin^2 a$ _____

21. A metal ball is attached to the end of a vertical spring. The spring is stretched to a length of 5 cm in relation to its equilibrium point and then released.

The function which gives the ball's position (in sec) relative to its equilibrium point, as a function of time t (in cm) since the release of the spring is given by the rule: $p(t) = 5 \cos \pi t, 0 \leqslant t \leqslant 10$.

At what moments over the first 5 seconds is the spring's position even with its equilibrium point?

_____

_____

22. The bird population of a certain region varies throughout the year. The population $P(t)$, in thousands, as a function of time t since January 1st is described by the rule: $P(t) = -6.4 \cos\left(\frac{\pi}{6} t\right) + 10$.

At what moments in the year are there 6800 birds in this region?

_____

_____

23. The current I (in amperes) produced by a generator is given by the rule $I = 20 \sin 30\pi\, t$ where t represents the time (in seconds) since the moment the generator was turned on. How long, after turning the generator on, do we observe an intensity of 10 amperes

   a) the first time? _____

   b) the second time? _____

24. Prove the following identities.

   a) $\dfrac{1 - \sin t}{\cos t} = \dfrac{\cos t}{1 + \sin t}$

   _____

   b) $\dfrac{\sin 2t}{1 + \cos 2t} = \tan t$

   _____

   c) $\cos^4 t - \sin^4 t = \cos 2t$

   _____

   d) $\dfrac{\sec t - 1}{\tan t} = \csc t - \cot t$

   _____

25. Calculate

   a) $\sin\left(\cos^{-1}\dfrac{\sqrt{3}}{2}\right)$ _____ **b)** $\cos\left(\sin^{-1}\dfrac{1}{2}\right)$ _____ **c)** $\tan\left(\sin^{-1} 0\right)$ _____

   d) $\cos\left(\tan^{-1}\dfrac{\sqrt{3}}{3}\right)$ _____ **e)** $\tan\left(\sin^{-1}\left(\dfrac{-1}{2}\right)\right)$ _____ **f)** $\sec\left(\tan^{-1}\sqrt{3}\right)$ _____

26. Solve the following equations.

   a) $\sin\left(\arccos x\right) = \dfrac{\sqrt{3}}{2}$ _____ **b)** $\tan\left(\arcsin x\right) = -1$ _____

   c) $\sec\left(\arcsin x\right) = \dfrac{2}{\sqrt{3}}$ _____ **d)** $\csc\left(\arctan x\right) = 2$ _____

Chapter 6

Vectors

1. Consider the line segment AB with endpoints A(–1, 3) and B(5, 6).

Find the coordinates of the point P located on line segment AB if $\dfrac{m\overline{AP}}{m\overline{AB}} = \dfrac{2}{3}$.

_____

2. Two perpendicular forces applied to an object give a resultant force of 30 N. If the resultant has an orientation of 60°, determine, rounded to the nearest unit, the norms of the two forces.

_____

_____

3. Amelia and Ben are pulling on an object. They apply respectively forces of 100 N and 80 N, with respective orientation of 40° and 120°. Claudio claims he is able, by himself, to cause the same effect on the object.

Determine the force (magnitude and orientation) that
Claudio must apply to the object.

_____

4. Calculate the acute angle formed by the lines $l_1 : y = 2x + 1$ and $l_2 : y = \frac{1}{2}x - 3$.

_____

_____

6.1 Geometric vectors

ACTIVITY 1 Concept of vector

Four archaeologists Alex, Bridget, Celia and Dennis are conducting an archaeological excavation. They leave the research centre located at point 0. Alex moves 20 m eastwards and Bridget moves 15 m southwards. Each motion is represented by a directed arrow with length proportional to the distance traveled.

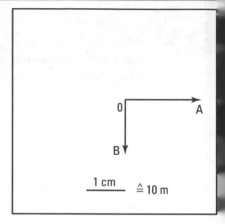

a) Represent, using an arrow, the following motions.

1. Celia moves 30 m westwards.

2. Dennis moves 20 m northwards.

b) Alex and Dennis travel the same distance. Explain why, however, the arrows representing Alex's and Dennis' motions are not the same.

---

*Some observations can be described by a single number, like the number of passengers on a train, while describing the motion of the train requires **2 characteristics**, namely the **direction** of the motion and its **magnitude** (speed of the train).*

VECTOR AND SCALAR

- A number that can, by itself, describe a quantity is called a **scalar**.
  Ex.: The age, height, weight of a person are scalars.

- The two characteristics, direction and magnitude, required to describe an observation are called a **vector**.
  Ex.: The observation of a moving train, the blowing wind or the flow of a river is described by a vector indicating the direction and magnitude of the motion.

1. For each of the following observations, indicate if it can be described by a scalar or a vector.

a) Temperature _____

b) Speed of a plane _____

c) Volume of a solid _____

d) Earth's gravity _____

e) Mass of an atom _____

f) Motion of a boat _____

ACTIVITY 2 Description of a geometric vector

a) The arrow on the right is the geometric representation of vector AB. This vector is written $\vec{AB}$.

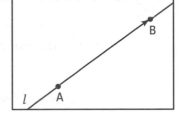

 - A is called the **origin** and B is called the **endpoint** of the vector.
 - The arrow gives the **direction** of the vector.
 - The **norm** of the vector corresponds to the length of the line segment AB.

1. Draw vector $\vec{BA}$.

2. What is the origin of vector $\vec{BA}$? _____

3. What is the endpoint of vector $\vec{BA}$? _____

4. Is it true that $\vec{AB}$ and $\vec{BA}$ have opposite directions?

_____

5. Do vectors $\vec{AB}$ and $\vec{BA}$ have the same norm? _____

b) Consider vector $\vec{AA}$ represented on the right, having its origin equal to its endpoint.

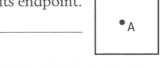

What is the norm of vector $\vec{AA}$? _____

This vector, written $\vec{0}$, is called **zero vector**.

c) To describe vector $\vec{AB}$ on the right, we proceed in two steps.

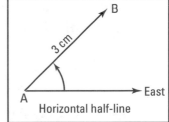

1st step:

We measure the norm or length of vector $\vec{AB}$.

The norm of vector $\vec{AB}$ is written $\|\vec{AB}\|$. Here, we have $\|\vec{AB}\| = 3$ cm.

2nd step:

We draw the horizontal half-line oriented eastwards and passing through the origin A of the vector, then we measure the directed angle (counterclockwise direction) having initial side the horizontal half-line and terminal side the vector $\vec{AB}$.

This directed angle, written $\theta_{\vec{AB}}$, gives the orientation of vector $\vec{AB}$ and thus defines the direction of $\vec{AB}$. Here, we have $\theta_{\vec{AB}} = 45°$.

Vector $\vec{AB}$ is described by giving its norm, $\|\vec{AB}\|$, and its orientation, $\theta_{\vec{AB}}$.

1. Describe vector $\vec{CD}$ represented on the right.

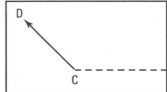

_____

2. Represent vector $\vec{EF}$ having norm 2.5 cm and orientation 60°.

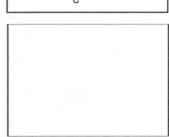

d) Vector $\overrightarrow{AB}$ on the right has a norm of 2 cm and an orientation $\theta_{\overrightarrow{AB}} = 60°$.

This vector is located 30° East of North.

It is written $\overrightarrow{AB}$: 2 cm [N 30° E].

Vector $\overrightarrow{AC}$ on the right has norm 1.5 cm and orientation $\theta_{\overrightarrow{AC}} = 210°$.

Vector $\overrightarrow{AC}$ is written $\overrightarrow{AC}$: 1.5 cm [W 30° S] or $\overrightarrow{AC}$: 1.5 cm [S 60° W].

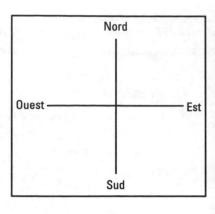

1. Interpret the notation $\overrightarrow{AC}$: 1.5 cm [W 30° S].

_____

2. Interpret the notation $\overrightarrow{AC}$: 1.5 cm [S 60° W].

_____

DESCRIPTION OF A GEOMETRIC VECTOR

- A **geometric vector** is described by:
  - its **direction**,
  - its **norm** (or length).
  - **Ex.:** On the figure on the right,
    - vectors $\overrightarrow{AB}$ and $\overrightarrow{CD}$ do not have the same direction.
    - vectors $\overrightarrow{AB}$ and $\overrightarrow{EF}$ have same the direction.
    - vectors $\overrightarrow{AB}$ and $\overrightarrow{GH}$ have opposite directions.

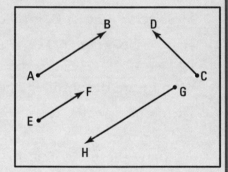

- Vector $\overrightarrow{AB}$ with origin A and endpoint B can be written using a letter $u, v, \ldots$ with an arrow above it.

  $\vec{u}$ and $\overrightarrow{AB}$ are two different notations representing the same geometric vector.

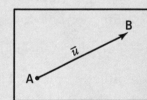

- Vector $\overrightarrow{AB}$ on the right, with norm 2 cm, has an orientation of 60°.
  - The **norm** of vector $\overrightarrow{AB}$ is written $\|\overrightarrow{AB}\|$.
  - The **orientation** of vector $\overrightarrow{AB}$ is written $\theta_{\overrightarrow{AB}}$.

  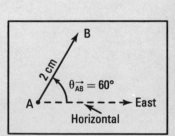

  This angle, directed in the counterclockwise direction, has for initial side the horizontal half-line directed eastwards and terminal side the vector $\overrightarrow{AB}$.

  The orientation $\theta_{\overrightarrow{AB}}$ of a vector $\overrightarrow{AB}$ gives the direction of this vector.

  We have: $\boxed{0° \leqslant \theta_{\overrightarrow{AB}} < 360°}$

- The vector $\overrightarrow{AA}$, with origin and endpoint A, is called zero vector. It is written $\vec{0}$.

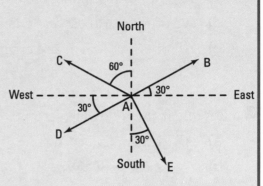

We have: $\|\vec{0}\| = 0$. The zero vector has every direction.

- A vector $\vec{u}$ is called unit vector if $\|\vec{u}\| = 1$.

  Ex.: Vectors $\overrightarrow{AB}, \overrightarrow{AC}, \overrightarrow{AD}$ and $\overrightarrow{AE}$ on the right all have the same norm, 2 cm, but different orientations. We have:

  $\theta_{\overrightarrow{AB}} = 30°, \theta_{\overrightarrow{AC}} = 150°, \theta_{\overrightarrow{AD}} = 210°$ and $\theta_{\overrightarrow{AE}} = 300°$.

- We usually describe a vector by giving its norm and a rotation angle spanning two consecutive cardinal points.

  Ex.: – Vector $\overrightarrow{AB}$ on the right, with norm 2 cm, is oriented 60° East of North. We write: 2 cm [N 60° E].

  – Vector $\overrightarrow{AC}$, with norm 2 cm, is oriented 60° West of North. $\overrightarrow{AC}$: 2 cm [N 60° W].

  – Vector $\overrightarrow{AD}$, with norm 2 cm, is oriented 30° South of West. $\overrightarrow{AD}$: 2 cm [W 30° S].

  – Vector $\overrightarrow{AE}$, with norm 2 cm, is oriented 30° East of South. $\overrightarrow{AE}$: 2 cm [S 30° E].

2. Lines l_1, l_2, l_3 and l_4 on the right are parallel.
Compare each vector on the right with vector $\overrightarrow{AB}$ according to direction and norm.

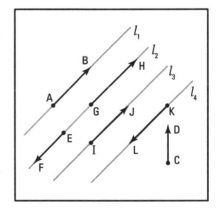

	Same direction as $\overrightarrow{AB}$	Direction opposite to $\overrightarrow{AB}$	Same norm as $\overrightarrow{AB}$
$\overrightarrow{CD}$			
$\overrightarrow{EF}$			
$\overrightarrow{GH}$			
$\overrightarrow{IJ}$			
$\overrightarrow{KL}$			

3. Represent the following vectors.

a) $\overrightarrow{AB}$ of norm 2 cm and orientation 45°.

b) $\overrightarrow{AC}$ of norm 3 cm and orientation 120°.

c) $\overrightarrow{AD}$ of norm 2 cm and orientation 180°.

d) $\overrightarrow{AE}$ of norm 1.5 cm and orientation 225°.

e) $\overrightarrow{AF}$ of norm 2.5 cm and orientation 330°.

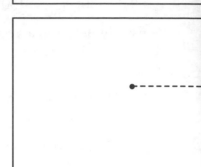

4. Represent the following vectors.

a) $\overrightarrow{AB}$: 1.5 cm [N 30° W].

b) $\overrightarrow{AC}$: 2 cm [S 30° W].

c) $\overrightarrow{AD}$: 3 cm [W].

d) $\overrightarrow{AE}$: 2 cm [E 30° S].

e) $\overrightarrow{AF}$: 1.5 cm [N 30° E].

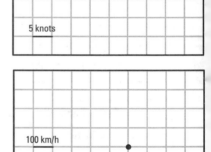

5. Represent the following situations.

a) A boat crosses a river perpendicularly. The speed of the boat is 10 knots and the speed of the current is 15 knots.

_____

b) A plane is moving at 400 km/h 30° West of North and the wind blows at 100 km/h 45° in the East of North.

_____

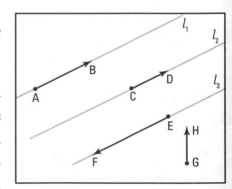

5 knots

100 km/h

Activity 3 Comparison of vectors

a) Lines l_1, l_2 and l_3 on the right are parallel.

Two vectors are called **collinear** or **parallel** when they have the same direction or opposite directions.

1. Which vectors are collinear with vector $\overrightarrow{AB}$?

_____

2. Which vector collinear with $\overrightarrow{AB}$ has the same direction as $\overrightarrow{AB}$? _____

3. Which vector collinear with $\overrightarrow{AB}$ has the direction opposite to $\overrightarrow{AB}$? _____

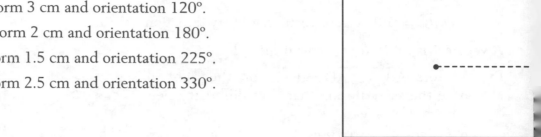

b) Consider lines l_1, l_2, l_3 and l_4 such that $l_1 /\!/ l_2$, $l_3 /\!/ l_4$ and $l_1 \perp l_3$.
Two vectors are called **perpendicular** or **orthogonal** when they have perpendicular directions.

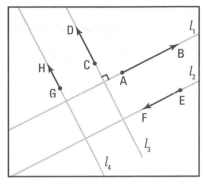

1. Find the vectors orthogonal to vector $\overrightarrow{AB}$. _____

2. Find the vectors orthogonal to vector $\overrightarrow{CD}$. _____

3. What can be said of vectors $\overrightarrow{AB}$ and $\overrightarrow{EF}$?

_____

4. What can be said of vectors $\overrightarrow{CD}$ and $\overrightarrow{GH}$? _____

c) Lines l_1, l_2 and l_3 on the right are parallel.

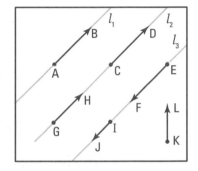

1. Two vectors are called **equal** or **equipollent** if they have same direction and same norm. Which vector, among the vectors on the right, is equal to vector $\overrightarrow{AB}$? _____

2. Two vectors are **opposite** if they have opposite directions and same norm. Which vector, among the vectors on the right, is opposite to vector $\overrightarrow{AB}$? _____

COMPARISON OF VECTORS

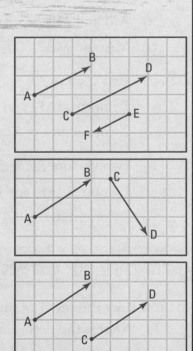

- Two vectors $\vec{u}$ and $\vec{v}$ are called **collinear** or **parallel** if they have the same direction or opposite directions. We write: $\vec{u} /\!/ \vec{v}$.

  Ex.: Vectors $\overrightarrow{AB}$, $\overrightarrow{CD}$ and $\overrightarrow{EF}$ on the right are collinear.
  We have: $\overrightarrow{AB} /\!/ \overrightarrow{CD} /\!/ \overrightarrow{EF}$.

- Two vectors $\vec{u}$ and $\vec{v}$ are called **orthogonal** if they have perpendicular directions. We write: $u \perp \vec{v}$.

  Ex.: Vectors $\overrightarrow{AB}$ and $\overrightarrow{CD}$ on the right are orthogonal.
  We have: $\overrightarrow{AB} \perp \overrightarrow{CD}$.

- Two vectors $\vec{u}$ and $\vec{v}$ are called **equal** or **equipollent** if they have the same direction and the same norm.
  We write: $\vec{u} = \vec{v}$.

- Two vectors $\vec{u}$ and $\vec{v}$ are called **opposite** if they have opposite directions and same norm.
  We write: $\vec{u} = -\vec{v}$ or $\vec{v} = -\vec{u}$.

  Ex.: Vectors $\overrightarrow{AB}$ and $\overrightarrow{CD}$ on the right are equal and vectors $\overrightarrow{AB}$ and $\overrightarrow{EF}$ are opposite. We have: $\overrightarrow{AB} = \overrightarrow{CD}$ and $\overrightarrow{AB} = -\overrightarrow{EF}$

- Given two points A and B, vectors $\overrightarrow{AB}$ and $\overrightarrow{BA}$ are opposite. We have: $\overrightarrow{AB} = -\overrightarrow{BA}$.

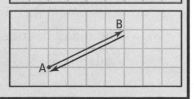

6. Two vectors $\vec{AB}$ and $\vec{CD}$ are opposite. Compare $\|\vec{AB}\|$ and $\|\vec{CD}\|$. _____

7. Consider parallelogram ABCD on the right.

a) Complete:
   1. $\vec{AB} =$ _____ 2. $\vec{AD} =$ _____

b) What can be said of vectors
   1. $\vec{AB}$ and $\vec{CD}$? _____ 2. $\vec{AD}$ and $\vec{CB}$? _____ 3. $\vec{AD}$ and $\vec{DA}$? _____

8. Consider rectangle ABCD on the right. Answer true or false.

a) $\vec{AB} \perp \vec{AD}$ _____ b) $\vec{AD} /\!/ \vec{BC}$ _____

c) $\vec{AD} = \vec{BC}$ _____ d) $\vec{AB} = -\vec{CD}$ _____

e) $\vec{AC} = \vec{BD}$ _____ f) $\|\vec{AC}\| = \|\vec{BD}\|$ _____

9. a) If $\vec{AB}$ is a vector of length 2 cm and orientation 60°, describe $\vec{BA}$.

_____

b) Let $\vec{CD}$: 3 cm [N 30° E], define $\vec{DC}$. _____

10. Consider a line segment AB and its midpoint M.
What can be said of vectors

a) $\vec{AM}$ and $\vec{MB}$? _____

b) $\vec{MA}$ and $\vec{MB}$? _____

11. a) Two vectors $\vec{AB}$ and $\vec{CD}$ are equal. Compare
   1. norms $\|\vec{AB}\|$ and $\|\vec{CD}\|$. _____
   2. orientations $\theta_{\vec{AB}}$ and $\theta_{\vec{CD}}$. _____

b) Two vectors $\vec{EF}$ and $\vec{GH}$ are opposite. Compare
   1. norms $\|\vec{EF}\|$ and $\|\vec{GH}\|$. _____
   2. orientations $\theta_{\vec{EF}}$ and $\theta_{\vec{GH}}$. _____

ACTIVITY 4 Representative of a geometric vector

a) Consider the set $\mathbb{Q}$ of rational numbers.
   1. What is the definition of a rational number? _____

   _____

   2. The fraction $\frac{1}{2}$ is a representative of the rational number 0.5.
      How many representatives does the rational number 0.5 have? _____
   3. Complete: $0.5 = \frac{1}{2} = \frac{}{4} = \frac{}{6} = \frac{4}{} = \frac{5}{} = ...$

   4. How many fractions are there with denominator equal to 100 representing the rational number 0.5? _____

b) By analogy with the set $\mathbb{Q}$ of rational numbers, consider the set $\mho$ of geometric vectors.

Let $\vec{u}$ be the geometric vector on the right.

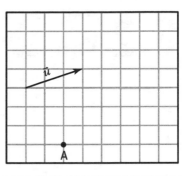

1. How many arrows can represent $\vec{u}$? _____

2. Draw 3 arrows representing the geometric vector $\vec{u}$.

3. Given a point A, how many arrows with origin A represent vector $\vec{u}$? _____

4. Draw the representative of vector $\vec{u}$ having its origin at point A.

REPRESENTATIVE OF A GEOMETRIC VECTOR

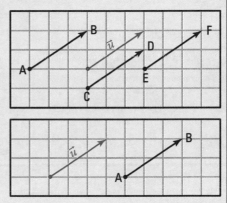

- A geometric vector $\vec{u}$ has an infinite number of representatives. Ex.: $\overrightarrow{AB}$, $\overrightarrow{CD}$, $\overrightarrow{EF}$ are 3 representatives of vector $\vec{u}$ on the right.

- Given a geometric vector $\vec{u}$ and a point A, there exists only one arrow with origin A representing vector $\vec{u}$.

- Every arrow represents only one vector but a vector can be represented by an infinite number of arrows.

  Speaking loosely, we identify a vector with the arrow representing it, in the same way we identify a rational number with the fraction representing it.

12. Consider vectors $\vec{u}$ and $\vec{v}$ on the right.

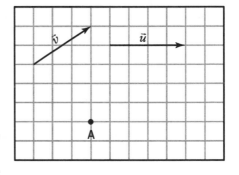

  a) Starting from point A, draw

1. the vector $\overrightarrow{AB}$ representing $\vec{u}$.

2. the vector $\overrightarrow{AC}$ representing $\vec{v}$.

3. the vector $\overrightarrow{BD}$ representing $\vec{v}$.

  b) What is the representative of vector $\vec{u}$ having origin C?

  _____

  c) Vector $-\vec{u}$ is the opposite of vector $\vec{u}$. Find two representatives of vector $-\vec{u}$.

  _____

6.2 Operations on geometric vectors

ACTIVITY 1 Vector addition

Starting from point A, David travels 3 m east until he reaches point B then travels 4 m north until he reaches point C.

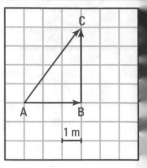

The first motion is represented by vector $\vec{AB}$ and the second motion is represented by vector $\vec{BC}$.

The result of these two motions is equivalent to a single motion represented by vector $\vec{AC}$.

Vector $\vec{AC}$ is called vector sum or resultant of vectors $\vec{AB}$ and $\vec{BC}$. We write: $\vec{AB} + \vec{BC} = \vec{AC}$.

a) Find the norm of vector $\vec{AC}$. _____

b) Find the orientation $\theta_{\overrightarrow{AC}}$ of vector $\vec{AC}$. _____

VECTOR ADDITION

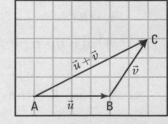

- There are two methods for adding two vectors $\vec{u}$ and $\vec{v}$.

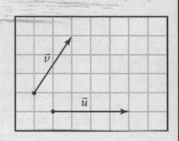

  - **Triangle method**
    Starting from any point A in the plane,
    1. we draw vector $\vec{AB}$ representing vector $\vec{u}$.
    2. we draw vector $\vec{BC}$ representing vector $\vec{v}$.
    3. we draw vector $\vec{AC}$ representing vector $\vec{u} + \vec{v}$.

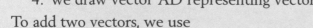

  - **Parallelogram method**
    Starting from any point A in the plane,
    1. we draw vector $\vec{AB}$ representing vector $\vec{u}$.
    2. we draw vector $\vec{AC}$ representing vector $\vec{v}$.
    3. we locate the point D such that ABDC is a parallelogram.
    4. we draw vector $\vec{AD}$ representing vector $\vec{u} + \vec{v}$.

- To add two vectors, we use
  - the triangle method if the origin of one vector corresponds to the endpoint of the other.
  - the parallelogram method if both vectors have the same origin.

1. In each of the following cases, represent starting from point A the sum $\vec{u} + \vec{v}$ using the given method.

a) Triangle method.

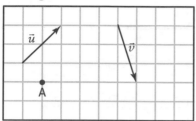

b) Parallelogram method.

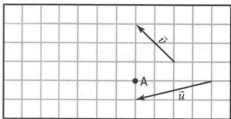

c) Triangle method.

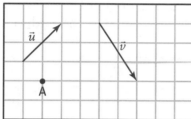

d) Parallelogram method.

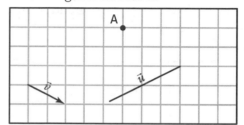

2. An object is acted upon by two perpendicular forces of 30 N [E] and 40 N [N]. Determine the resultant force $\vec{F_r}$ acting on this object.

3. Two perpendicular forces $\vec{F_1}$ and $\vec{F_2}$ are applied to an object. The resultant $\vec{R}$ of these two forces has norm 200 N and orientation 60°. Find the norm of each of the forces applied to the object.

ACTIVITY 2 Chasles' relation

a) Consider the sum of vectors $\overrightarrow{PQ}$ and $\overrightarrow{QR}$ where the endpoint Q of the first vector is the origin of the second vector.

Complete: $\overrightarrow{PQ} + \overrightarrow{QR}$ = _____

b) Consider the sum of vectors $\overrightarrow{PQ}$, $\overrightarrow{QR}$ and $\overrightarrow{RS}$ where the endpoint of the first vector is the origin of the second one and the endpoint of the second one is the origin of the third one.

Complete: $\overrightarrow{PQ} + \overrightarrow{QR} + \overrightarrow{RS}$ = _____

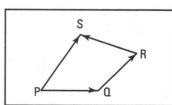

c) Consider any two vectors $\overrightarrow{AB}$ and $\overrightarrow{BC}$ where the endpoint B of the first vector is the origin B of the second vector.

Complete: $\overrightarrow{AB} + \overrightarrow{BC} =$ _____

CHASLES' RELATION

For any points A, B and C, we have:

$$\overrightarrow{AB} + \overrightarrow{BC} = \overrightarrow{AC}$$

The sum of 2 vectors with the endpoint of the first one equal to the origin of the second one is a vector whose origin is the origin of the first vector and whose endpoint is the endpoint of the second vector.

---

4. Consider triangle ABC on the right.

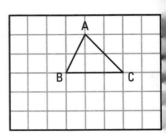

a) Locate
1. Point D knowing that $\overrightarrow{AD} = \overrightarrow{AB} + \overrightarrow{AC}$.
2. Point E knowing that $\overrightarrow{BE} = \overrightarrow{BA} + \overrightarrow{BC}$.
3. Point F knowing that $\overrightarrow{CF} = \overrightarrow{CA} + \overrightarrow{CB}$.

b) What can be said of triangles ABC, BCD, ACE and ABF?

_____

5. Consider parallelogram ABCE and triangle CDE.

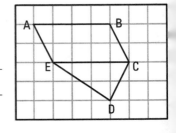

a) Justify the steps to simplify the sum $\overrightarrow{AB} + \overrightarrow{CD}$.

$\overrightarrow{AB} + \overrightarrow{CD} = \overrightarrow{EC} + \overrightarrow{CD}$ _____

$\qquad\qquad = \overrightarrow{ED}$ _____

b) Simplify the sum $\overrightarrow{AE} + \overrightarrow{CD}$.

_____

6. Consider triangle ABC and line segment MN joining the midpoints of sides AB and AC.

a) Explain why
1. $\overrightarrow{BM} = \overrightarrow{MA}$. _____

_____

2. $\overrightarrow{AN} = \overrightarrow{NC}$. _____

_____

b) Simplify the sum $\overrightarrow{BM} + \overrightarrow{NC}$.

_____

ACTIVITY 3 Properties of vector addition

a) 1. Given two vectors $\vec{u}$ and $\vec{v}$, verify that $\vec{u} + v = \vec{v} + \vec{u}$.

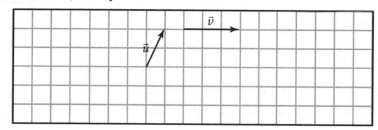

2. Refer to the parallelogram on the right to show that:

$\vec{u} + v = \vec{v} + \vec{u}$. _____

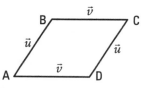

b) 1. Given three vectors $\vec{u}$, $\vec{v}$ and $\vec{w}$, verify that $(\vec{u} + \vec{v}) + \vec{w} = \vec{u} + (\vec{v} + \vec{w})$.

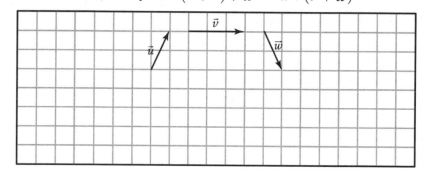

2. Use Chasles' relation to show that $\left(\overrightarrow{AB} + \overrightarrow{BC}\right) + \overrightarrow{CD} = \overrightarrow{AB} + \left(\overrightarrow{BC} + \overrightarrow{CD}\right)$.

_____

_____

c) Justify the steps showing that:

1. $\overrightarrow{AB} + \vec{0} = \overrightarrow{AB}$

$\overrightarrow{AB} + \vec{0} = \overrightarrow{AB} + \overrightarrow{BB}$ _____

$\qquad = \overrightarrow{AB}$ _____

2. $\vec{0} + \overrightarrow{AB} = \vec{0}$

$\vec{0} + \overrightarrow{AB} = \overrightarrow{AA} + \overrightarrow{AB}$ _____

$\qquad = \overrightarrow{AB}$ _____

d) 1. What can be said of vectors $\overrightarrow{AB}$ and $\overrightarrow{BA}$? _____

2. What can be said of the sum $\overrightarrow{AB} + \overrightarrow{BA}$? Justify your answer.

_____

_____

PROPERTIES OF VECTOR ADDITION

- The addition of vectors is **commutative**.
  $$\vec{u} + \vec{v} = \vec{v} + \vec{u}$$

- The addition of vectors is **associative**.
  $$(\vec{u} + \vec{v}) + \vec{w} = \vec{u} + (\vec{v} + \vec{w})$$

- $\vec{0}$ is the **neutral element** for the addition of vectors.
  $$\vec{u} + \vec{0} = \vec{u} \text{ and } \vec{0} + \vec{u} = \vec{u}$$

- For any vector $\vec{u}$, there exists an **opposite vector** $-\vec{u}$ such that:
  $$\vec{u} + (-\vec{u}) = \vec{0} \text{ and } (-\vec{u}) + \vec{u} = \vec{0}$$

7. Quadrilateral ABCD on the right is a parallelogram. Simplify

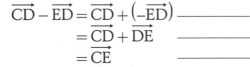

a) $\overrightarrow{AB} + \overrightarrow{BC}$ _____

b) $\overrightarrow{AD} + \overrightarrow{DB}$ _____

c) $\overrightarrow{AD} + \overrightarrow{DC} + \overrightarrow{CB}$ _____

d) $\overrightarrow{AC} + \overrightarrow{CD} + \overrightarrow{DA}$ _____

e) $\overrightarrow{AB} + \overrightarrow{CD}$ _____

f) $\overrightarrow{AD} + \overrightarrow{CB} + \overrightarrow{DC}$ _____

g) $\overrightarrow{AC} + \overrightarrow{BD} + \overrightarrow{CB}$ _____

h) $\overrightarrow{CB} + \overrightarrow{AB} + \overrightarrow{BD} + \overrightarrow{DC}$ _____

ACTIVITY 4 Vector subtraction

Subtracting a vector $\vec{v}$ from a vector $\vec{u}$ consists in adding vector $\vec{u}$ to the opposite of $\vec{v}$.

$$\vec{u} - \vec{v} = \vec{u} + (-\vec{v})$$

a) Given vectors $\vec{u}$ and $\vec{v}$ on the right, represent vector $\vec{u} - \vec{v}$.

b) Justify the steps of the following subtraction.

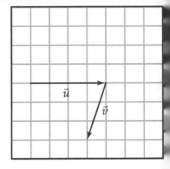

$$\overrightarrow{CD} - \overrightarrow{ED} = \overrightarrow{CD} + (-\overrightarrow{ED}) \rule{4cm}{0.4pt}$$
$$= \overrightarrow{CD} + \overrightarrow{DE} \rule{4cm}{0.4pt}$$
$$= \overrightarrow{CE} \rule{4cm}{0.4pt}$$

VECTOR SUBTRACTION

For any vectors $\vec{u}$ and $\vec{v}$, we have: $\vec{u} - \vec{v} = \vec{u} + (-\vec{v})$

Thus, $\overrightarrow{AB} - \overrightarrow{CB} = \overrightarrow{AB} + (-\overrightarrow{CB})$ Subtraction rule.

$\qquad\qquad = \overrightarrow{AB} + \overrightarrow{BC}$ $\overrightarrow{BC}$ is the opposite of $\overrightarrow{CB}$.

$\qquad\qquad = \overrightarrow{AC}$ Chasles' relation.

---

8. Consider vectors $\vec{u}$ and $\vec{v}$ on the right.
Construct the vectors

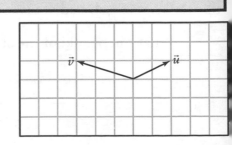

a) $\overrightarrow{w_1} = u + \vec{v}$

b) $\overrightarrow{w_2} = \vec{u} - \vec{v}$

c) $\overrightarrow{w_3} = \vec{v} - \vec{u}$

d) $\overrightarrow{w_4} = -\vec{u} - \vec{v}$

9. Consider vectors $\vec{u}$, $\vec{v}$ and $\vec{w}$ and point A.

Draw vector $\overrightarrow{AB}$ knowing that $\overrightarrow{AB} = \vec{u} - \vec{v} + \vec{w}$.

10. Consider parallelogram ABCD and vectors $\vec{u}$ and $\vec{v}$ represented by $\overrightarrow{AB}$ and $\overrightarrow{BC}$ respectively. Express, as a function of $\vec{u}$ and $\vec{v}$, the vector

a) $\overrightarrow{AC}$ _____ **b)** $\overrightarrow{BD}$ _____ **c)** $\overrightarrow{DB}$ _____

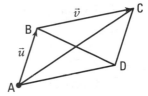

11. Simplify the following expressions.

a) $\overrightarrow{AB} - \overrightarrow{CB} + \overrightarrow{CD}$ _____ **b)** $\overrightarrow{BC} - \overrightarrow{ED} - \overrightarrow{DC}$ _____

c) $\overrightarrow{BC} - \overrightarrow{BA} - \overrightarrow{DC}$ _____ **d)** $\overrightarrow{BA} - \overrightarrow{CB} + \overrightarrow{AB}$ _____

e) $\overrightarrow{CD} + \overrightarrow{BC} - \overrightarrow{BD}$ _____ **f)** $\overrightarrow{AD} - \overrightarrow{BD} - \overrightarrow{AB}$ _____

𝖠ᴄᴛɪᴠɪᴛʏ 5 Calculating the length and orientation of the sum vector

a) An object located at 0 is subjected to a force $\vec{F_1}$ of 3 N oriented northwards and a force $\vec{F_2}$ of 4 N oriented eastwards.

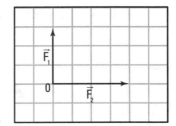

1. Draw the force $\vec{F}$ resultant of the sum of forces $\vec{F_1}$ and $\vec{F_2}$.

2. Calculate the norm of $\vec{F}$.

_____

3. Calculate the orientation of $\vec{F}$.

_____

_____

b) Consider triangle ABC on he right.

1. State the sine law. _____

2. State the cosine law.

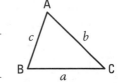

_____

_____

_____

c) Consider vector $\vec{AB}$ of length 4 cm and orientation 15°, vector $\vec{AC}$ of length 3 cm and orientation 60° and vector $\vec{AD}$ representing the sum of vectors $\vec{AB}$ and $\vec{AC}$.

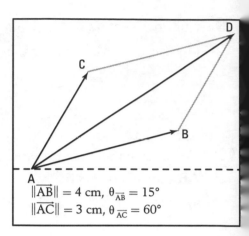

$\|\vec{AB}\| = 4$ cm, $\theta_{\overline{AB}} = 15°$
$\|\vec{AC}\| = 3$ cm, $\theta_{\overline{AC}} = 60°$

1. Explain why $\angle BAC$ measures 45°.

_____

2. Explain why $\angle ABD$ measures 135°.

_____

_____

3. Consider triangle ABD and use the cosine law to calculate $\|\vec{AD}\|$.

_____

_____

4. Consider triangle ABD and use the sine law to calculate m $\angle BAD$.

_____

_____

5. Deduce the orientation of vector $\vec{AD}$. _____

6. Describe vector $\vec{AD}$, sum of vectors $\vec{AB}$ and $\vec{AC}$.

_____

NORM AND ORIENTATION OF THE SUM VECTOR

We use the sine law and the cosine law to determine the sum vector.

- **Sine law**

$$\frac{\sin A}{a} = \frac{\sin B}{b} = \frac{\sin C}{c}$$

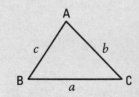

- **Cosine law**

- $a^2 = b^2 + c^2 - 2bc \cos A$
- $b^2 = a^2 + c^2 - 2ac \cos B$
- $c^2 = a^2 + b^2 - 2ab \cos C$

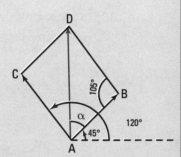

Ex.: Let us determine the norm and orientation of vector $\vec{AD}$ if

$$\vec{AD} = \vec{AB} + \vec{AC}$$

$\|\vec{AB}\| = 2$; $\theta_{\overline{AB}} = 45°$; $\|\vec{AC}\| = 3$; $\theta_{\overline{AC}} = 120°$ and $\theta_{\overline{AB}} = 45°$.

1. m $\angle BAC = \theta_{\overline{AC}} - \theta_{\overline{AB}} = 120° - 45° = 75°$

2. m $\angle ABD = 105°$ because angles BAC and ABD are two consecutive angles of the parallelogram ABDC.

3. $\left\|\overrightarrow{AD}\right\|^2 = \left\|\overrightarrow{AB}\right\|^2 + \left\|\overrightarrow{BD}\right\|^2 - 2\left\|\overrightarrow{AB}\right\| \times \left\|\overrightarrow{BD}\right\| \times \cos 105°$.

   We get: $\left\|\overrightarrow{AD}\right\|^2 = 16.10$ and so $\left\|\overrightarrow{AD}\right\| = 4.01$.

4. We apply the sine law to triangle ABD to find α.

   $\dfrac{\sin \alpha}{\left\|\overrightarrow{BD}\right\|} = \dfrac{\sin 105°}{\left\|\overrightarrow{AD}\right\|} \Rightarrow \sin \alpha = 0.7226 \Rightarrow \alpha = 46.3°$.

5. We deduce $\theta_{\overrightarrow{AD}}$.

   $\theta_{\overrightarrow{AD}} = \theta_{\overrightarrow{AB}} + \alpha = 45° + 46.3° = 91.3°$

Thus, vector $\overrightarrow{AD}$ has norm 4.01 and orientation 91.3°.

12. A boat is traveling north at a speed of 25 knots. A current of 10 knots and orientation 150° acts on the boat.

a) Represent the situation.

b) Determine the actual speed of the boat and its orientation.

_____

_____

_____

13. An object is subjected to two forces $\overrightarrow{F_1}$ and $\overrightarrow{F_2}$.

$\overrightarrow{F_1}$ has an intensity of 3 newtons and an orientation of 30°.

$\overrightarrow{F_2}$ has an intensity of 2 newtons and an orientation of 60°.

Find the force $\overrightarrow{F}$ that must be applied to the object in order to cancel the effect of forces $\overrightarrow{F_1}$ and $\overrightarrow{F_2}$.

_____

_____

_____

_____

_____

14. Rafael travels 2 km on foot 30° East of North then 1 km 30° West of North. Determine the length and the orientation of the resulting motion.

_____

_____

_____

_____

_____

6.2 Operations on geometric vectors

15. Nomi and Karen are pulling an object. The forces $\vec{F_N}$ and $\vec{F_K}$ applied to the object are, respectively, of 150 N and 200 N with orientations 60° and 135°.

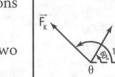

a) What is the intensity of the resultant force $\vec{R}$, sum of the two forces $\vec{F_N}$ and $\vec{F_K}$?

_____

b) Find the orientation of the resultant force $\vec{R}$.

_____

16. Vectors $\vec{u}$ and $\vec{v}$ on the right form an angle of 120° and have norm $\|\vec{u}\| = 3.6$ and $\|\vec{v}\| = 4$ respectively. Calculate the norm, rounded to the nearest tenth of a unit, of

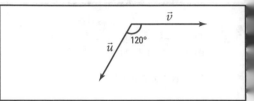

a) $\vec{u} + \vec{v}$

_____

b) $\vec{u} - \vec{v}$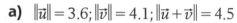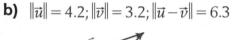

17. Determine the measure, rounded to the nearest tenth of a unit, of the angle θ between $\vec{u}$ and $\vec{v}$ if

a) $\|\vec{u}\| = 3.6; \|\vec{v}\| = 4.1; \|\vec{u} + \vec{v}\| = 4.5$

b) $\|\vec{u}\| = 4.2; \|\vec{v}\| = 3.2; \|\vec{u} - \vec{v}\| = 6.3$

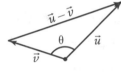

_____   _____

_____   _____

_____   _____

18. A force of 20 N and another force of 30 N applied to the same object yield a resultant of 40 N. What is, rounded to the nearest tenth of a unit, the angle between the two forces?

_____

_____

19. Valerie travels 3 km North on a sailboat. She then changes her route by turning 60° westwards and traveling 2 km. Determine at what distance Valerie is from her starting point and how she is oriented at the end of her trip.

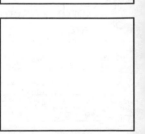

_____

_____

_____

ACTIVITY 6 Multiplication of a vector by a real number

Consider a vector $\vec{u}$ and a point 0.

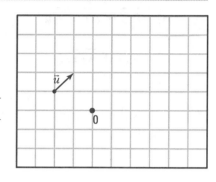

a) 1. Draw the vector $\overrightarrow{OA}$ if $\overrightarrow{OA} = 3\vec{u}$. (Note: $3\vec{u} = \vec{u} + \vec{u} + \vec{u}$).

    2. Compare vectors $\vec{u}$ and $3\vec{u}$ according to

       1) direction; _____

       2) norm. _____

b) 1. Draw the vector $\overrightarrow{OB}$ if $\overrightarrow{OB} = -2\vec{u}$. (Note: $-2\vec{u} = -\vec{u} + -\vec{u}$).

    2. Compare vectors $\vec{u}$ and $-2\vec{u}$ according to

       1) direction; _____

       2) norm. _____

c) Let k be a real number. ($k \neq 0$).

    1. Complete by indicating the sign of k, vectors $\vec{u}$ and $k\vec{u}$ have

       1) the same direction. _____ 2) opposite directions. _____

    2. Compare $\|k\vec{u}\|$ and $\|\vec{u}\|$. _____

d) Determine the value of the real number k if $k\vec{u} = \vec{0}$. _____

MULTIPLICATION OF A VECTOR BY A REAL NUMBER

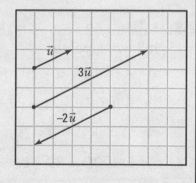

- The product of a non-zero vector $\vec{u}$ by a real number k is a vector written $k\vec{u}$. Thus

$$k \times \vec{u} = k\vec{u}$$

   – $k\vec{u}$ and $\vec{u}$ have **same direction** if $k > 0$,

     $k\vec{u}$ and $\vec{u}$ have **opposite directions** if $k < 0$.

   – $\|k\vec{u}\| = |k| \times \|\vec{u}\|$.

- Note that: $0 \times \vec{u} = \vec{0}$; $1 \times \vec{u} = \vec{u}$; $(-1) \times \vec{u} = -\vec{u}$.

- Vectors $\vec{u}$ and $k\vec{u}$ are called **collinear** or **parallel**.

- Two vectors $\vec{u}$ and $\vec{v}$ are **collinear** if and only if there exists a nonzero real number k such that $\vec{v} = k\vec{u}$.

$$\vec{u} /\!/ \vec{v} \Leftrightarrow \exists\, k \in \mathbb{R}^* : \vec{v} = k\vec{u}$$

---

20. Consider vector $\vec{u}$ and point A on the right. Draw the following vectors.

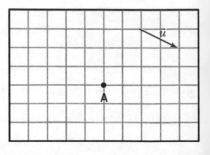

   a) $\overrightarrow{AB}$ if $\overrightarrow{AB} = \frac{3}{2}\vec{u}$.
      b) $\overrightarrow{AC}$ if $\overrightarrow{AC} = \frac{1}{2}\vec{u}$.

   c) $\overrightarrow{AD}$ if $\overrightarrow{AD} = (-1) \times \vec{u}$.
     d) $\overrightarrow{AE}$ if $\overrightarrow{AE} = -2\vec{u}$.

21. Consider vectors $\overrightarrow{OA}$ and $\overrightarrow{OB}$ in the plane on the right.

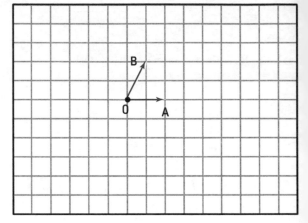

   a) Draw the vector

      1. $\overrightarrow{OA'}$ if $\overrightarrow{OA'} = 3\overrightarrow{OA}$.

      2. $\overrightarrow{OB'}$ if $\overrightarrow{OB'} = 2\overrightarrow{OB}$.

      3. $\overrightarrow{OC}$ if $\overrightarrow{OC} = 3\overrightarrow{OA} + 2\overrightarrow{OB}$.

   b) Draw the vector $\overrightarrow{OD}$ if $\overrightarrow{OD} = -3\overrightarrow{OA} + 2\overrightarrow{OB}$.

   c) Draw the vector $\overrightarrow{OE}$ if $\overrightarrow{OE} = -2\overrightarrow{OA} - \overrightarrow{OB}$.

   d) Draw the vector $\overrightarrow{OF}$ if $\overrightarrow{OF} = 3\overrightarrow{OA} - 2\overrightarrow{OB}$.

22. Consider 2 vectors $\vec{u}$ and $\vec{v}$ and a point 0. Locate the following points.

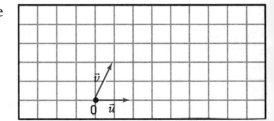

   a) A if $\overrightarrow{OA} = 3\vec{u}$.

   b) B if $\overrightarrow{OB} = 2\vec{v}$.

   c) C if $\overrightarrow{OC} = 3\vec{u} + 2\vec{v}$.

23. Consider 2 vectors $\vec{u}$ and $\vec{v}$ and a point 0. Locate the following points.

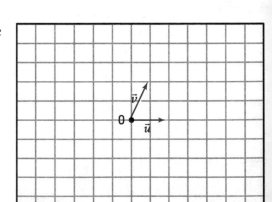

   a) A if $\overrightarrow{OA} = \vec{u} + 2\vec{v}$.

   b) B if $\overrightarrow{OB} = -2\vec{u} + 2\vec{v}$.

   c) C if $\overrightarrow{OC} = -\vec{u} - 2\vec{v}$.

   d) D if $\overrightarrow{OD} = 3\vec{u} - 2\vec{v}$.

24. Consider vectors $\vec{a}, \vec{b}, \vec{c}$ and $\vec{d}$ on the right.

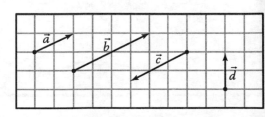

   a) 1. Does there exist a real number k such that $\vec{b} = k\vec{a}$? _____

      2. What can be said of vectors $\vec{a}$ and $\vec{b}$?

      _____

b) Does there exist real number k such that $\vec{c} = k\vec{a}$? If so, what can we conclude?

_____

c) Does there exist a real number k such that $\vec{d} = k\vec{a}$? If so, what can we conclude?

_____

25. Consider a vector $\vec{u}$ and a real number k. Complete:

    a) $k \neq 0$ and $k\vec{u} = \vec{0} \Rightarrow$ ____
    b) $\vec{u} \neq \vec{0}$ and $k\vec{u} = \vec{0} \Rightarrow$ ____
    c) $k\vec{u} = \vec{0} \Leftrightarrow$ _____

26. Let $\vec{u}$ be a vector such that $\|\vec{u}\| = 6$. Find the norm of

    a) $3\vec{u}$ _____
    b) $-5\vec{u}$ _____
    c) $-\frac{1}{2}\vec{u}$ _____
    d) $\frac{\vec{u}}{3}$ _____
    e) $\frac{\vec{u}}{\|\vec{u}\|}$ _____

ACTIVITY 7   Properties of multiplication of a vector by a real number

a) Consider vector $\vec{u}$ on the right.

    1. Verify that $2(3\,\vec{u}) = (2 \times 3)\,\vec{u}$.

    2. If a and b are two real numbers, is it true that $a(b\vec{u}) = (ab)\vec{u}$? **Yes**

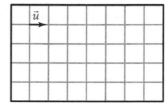

b) Which real number is the neutral element when we multiply a vector by a real number? Justify your answer. _____

c) Consider vectors $\vec{u}$ and $\vec{v}$ on the right.

    1. Compare $2(\vec{u} + \vec{v})$ and $2\vec{u} + 2\vec{v}$. _____

    2. If a is any real number, is it true that $a(\vec{u} + \vec{v}) = a\vec{u} + a\vec{v}$? **Yes**

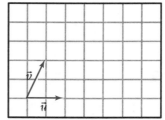

d) Consider vector $\vec{u}$ on the right.

    1. Verify that $(3 + 2)\vec{u} = 3\vec{u} + 2\vec{u}$.

    2. If a and b are two real numbers, is it true that $(a + b)\vec{u} = a\vec{u} + b\vec{u}$?

    _____

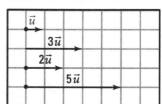

PROPERTIES OF MULTIPLICATION OF A VECTOR BY A REAL NUMBER

Consider two vectors $\vec{u}$ and $\vec{v}$ and two real numbers a and b.
Multiplication of a vector by a real number has the following properties:

  – Associativity :
      $\boxed{a(b\vec{u}) = (ab)\vec{u}}$

  – 1 is the neutral element:
      $\boxed{1 \times \vec{u} = \vec{u}}$

  – Distributivity over the sum of vectors:
      $\boxed{a(\vec{u} + \vec{v}) = a\vec{u} + a\vec{v}}$

  – Distributivity over the sum of real numbers:
      $\boxed{(a + b)\vec{u} = a\vec{u} + b\vec{u}}$

27. Reduce the following expressions.

   a) $2\vec{u} + 6\vec{u}$ _____

   b) $-2(5\vec{u})$ _____

   c) $5\vec{u} - 7\vec{u}$ _____

   d) $3(2\vec{u} + 3\vec{v})$ _____

   e) $3(2\vec{u}) - 2(3\vec{u})$ _____

   f) $-(\vec{u} - 2\vec{v})$ _____

28. Reduce the following expressions.

   a) $-2\vec{u} + 3\vec{v} + 5\vec{u} - 4\vec{v}$ _____

   b) $-(\vec{u} + 2\vec{v}) + 2(\vec{u} - \vec{v})$ _____

   c) $3(2\vec{u} - \vec{v}) - (2\vec{u} - 3\vec{v})$ _____

   d) $-2(2\vec{u} - 3\vec{v}) - 3(\vec{u} + 2\vec{v})$ _____

29. Justify the steps to reduce: $2\overrightarrow{AB} - 2\overrightarrow{DC} + 2\overrightarrow{BC} - 2\overrightarrow{BD}$.

Steps	Justifications
$2\overrightarrow{AB} - 2\overrightarrow{DC} + 2\overrightarrow{BC} - 2\overrightarrow{BD}$	
$= 2\overrightarrow{AB} + 2\overrightarrow{CD} + 2\overrightarrow{BC} + 2\overrightarrow{DB}$	
$= 2\overrightarrow{AB} + 2\overrightarrow{BC} + 2\overrightarrow{CD} + 2\overrightarrow{DB}$	
$= 2\left(\overrightarrow{AB} + 2\overrightarrow{BC}\right) + 2\left(\overrightarrow{CD} + 2\overrightarrow{DB}\right)$	
$= 2\overrightarrow{AC} + 2\overrightarrow{CB}$	
$= 2\left(\overrightarrow{AC} + \overrightarrow{CB}\right)$	
$= 2\overrightarrow{AB}$	

30. Reduce the following expression. $5\overrightarrow{AC} + \overrightarrow{BC} - 2\overrightarrow{AC} - 4\overrightarrow{BC} + \overrightarrow{BE} - 2\overrightarrow{CE} + 2\overrightarrow{BE} - \overrightarrow{CE}$.

_____

_____

6.3 Vector basis

Consider 2 vectors $\vec{u_1}$ and $\vec{u_2}$.

Any expression of the form $c_1\vec{u_1} + c_2\vec{u_2}$ where c_1 and c_2 are real numbers is called **linear combination** of vectors $\vec{u_1}$ and $\vec{u_2}$.

a) Explain why a linear combination of vectors always yields a vector. _____

_____

_____

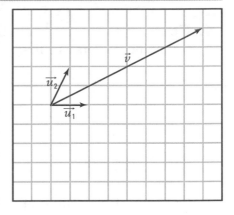

b) Represent the vector $\vec{u}$ knowing that $\vec{u} = 3\vec{u_1} - 2\vec{u_2}$.

c) Express vector $\vec{v}$ on the right as a linear combination of the vectors $\vec{u_1}$ and $\vec{u_2}$.

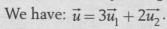

$\vec{v} = 3\vec{u_1} + 2\vec{u_2}$

LINEAR COMBINATION OF VECTORS

- Given a sequence of vectors $\vec{u_1}$, $\vec{u_2}$, ..., $\vec{u_n}$, any expression of the form
  $c_1\vec{u_1} + c_2\vec{u_2} + ..., + c_n\vec{u_n}$ where $c_i \in \mathbb{R}$ is a **linear combination** of the vectors $\vec{u_1}$, $\vec{u_2}$, ..., $\vec{u_n}$.
- Note that a linear combination of vectors is a vector.

  Ex.: Given the vectors $\vec{u_1}$ and $\vec{u_2}$, $3\vec{u_1} + 2\vec{u_2}$ is a linear combination of the vectors $\vec{u_1}$ and $\vec{u_2}$.

  We have: $\vec{u} = 3\vec{u_1} + 2\vec{u_2}$.

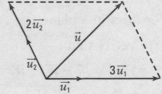

- A vector $\vec{u}$ is a linear combination of the vectors $\vec{u_1}, \vec{u_2}, ... \vec{u_n}$ if there exist real numbers $c_1, c_2, ..., c_n$ such that $\vec{u} = c_1\vec{u_1} + c_2\vec{u_2} + \cdots + c_n\vec{u_n}$.

---

1. Consider vectors $\vec{u_1}, \vec{u_2}$ and $\vec{u_3}$ on the right. Represent the following linear combinations.

a) $2\vec{u_1} + \vec{u_2}$

b) $\vec{u_1} - \vec{u_2}$

c) $\vec{u_2} + \vec{u_3}$

d) $\vec{u_1} + \vec{u_2} + \vec{u_3}$

e) $2\vec{u_1} + 3\vec{u_2} - 3\vec{u_3}$

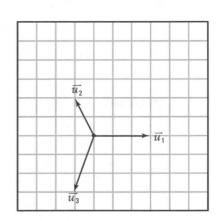

2. Consider vectors $\vec{u_1}$, $\vec{u_2}$ and $\vec{u_3}$ on the right.

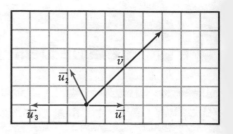

a) Express vector $\vec{v}$ as a linear combination of the vectors
  1. $\vec{u_1}$ and $\vec{u_2}$ _____
  2. $\vec{u_2}$ and $\vec{u_3}$ _____

b) Can we express vector $\vec{v}$ as a linear combination of $\vec{u_1}$ and $\vec{u_3}$? _____

3. Consider the vectors on the right. Express each of the following vectors as a linear combination of vectors $\vec{u}$ and $\vec{v}$.

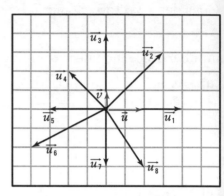

a) $\vec{u_1}$ _____

b) $\vec{u_2}$ _____

c) $\vec{u_3}$ _____

d) $\vec{u_4}$ _____

e) $\vec{u_5}$ _____

f) $\vec{u_6}$ _____

g) $\vec{u_7}$ _____

h) $\vec{u_8}$ _____

4. Consider the points of the right. Express each of the following vectors as a linear combination of vectors $\vec{u}$ and $\vec{v}$.

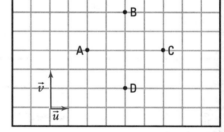

a) $\overrightarrow{AB}$ _____

b) $\overrightarrow{BA}$ _____

c) $\overrightarrow{AC}$ _____

d) $\overrightarrow{CA}$ _____

e) $\overrightarrow{AD}$ _____

f) $\overrightarrow{DA}$ _____

g) $\overrightarrow{BD}$ _____

h) $\overrightarrow{CD}$ _____

Aᴄᴛɪᴠɪᴛʏ 2 **Vector basis**

Consider in a plane the vectors $\vec{u_1}$, $\vec{u_2}$ and $\vec{u_3}$ and the vector $\vec{v}$.

a) Verify that

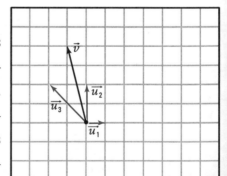

  1. $\vec{v} = \vec{u_1} + \vec{u_2} + \vec{u_3}$
  2. $\vec{v} = 5\vec{u_1} - \vec{u_2} + 3\vec{u_3}$

b) Is the expression of $\vec{v}$ as a linear combination of vectors $\vec{u_1}$, $\vec{u_2}$ and $\vec{u_3}$ unique? _____

c) Express vector $\vec{v}$ as a linear combination of vectors $\vec{u_1}$ and $\vec{u_2}$.
_____

d) Is the expression of $\vec{v}$ as a linear combination of vectors $\vec{u_1}$ and $\vec{u_2}$ unique? _____

e) Can we say that for any vector $\vec{v}$ in that plane, there exist two unique real numbers a and b such that $\vec{v} = a\vec{u_1} + b\vec{u_2}$? _____

*If so, we say that vectors $\vec{u_1}$ and $\vec{u_2}$ form a **vector basis** of the plane.*

VECTOR BASIS

In a plane, two vectors $\vec{u_1}$ and $\vec{u_2}$ that are not parallel (not collinear) form a vector basis.

The two vectors $\vec{u_1}$ and $\vec{u_2}$ of this basis can generate any vector $\vec{v}$ in the plane, meaning that given any vector $\vec{v}$ in the plane, there exist two unique real numbers c_1 and c_2 such that:

$$\vec{v} = c_1 \vec{u_1} + c_2 \vec{u_2}$$

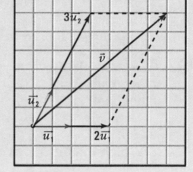

The real numbers c_1 and c_2 are called components of vector $\vec{v}$ relative to the basis $\{\vec{u_1}, \vec{u_2}\}$.

Ex.: Vector $\vec{v}$ above can be written in a unique way as a linear combination of the basis vectors $\vec{u_1}$ and $\vec{u_2}$.

We have: $\vec{v} = 2\vec{u_1} + 3\vec{u_2}$.

5. True or false?

a) Three vectors in the plane can form a vector basis. _____

b) Two vectors in the plane always form a vector basis. _____

c) Two vectors that are not parallel always form a vector basis. _____

d) If $\vec{u_1}$ and $\vec{u_2}$ form a vector basis of the plane then any vector $\vec{v}$ in the plane can be written in a unique way as a linear combination of the vectors $\vec{u_1}$ and $\vec{u_2}$. _____

6. Consider the vectors on the right.

a) Explain why $\vec{u_1}, \vec{u_2}$ and $\vec{u_4}$ do not form a vector basis.

_____

b) Explain why $\vec{u_1}$ and $\vec{u_3}$ do not form a vector basis.

_____

c) Explain why $\vec{u_1}$ and $\vec{u_2}$ form a vector basis.

_____

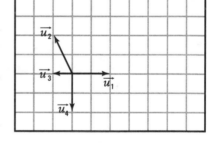

7. Consider the vectors on the right.

a) Express vector $\vec{v}$ as a linear combination of the vectors in the vector basis.

1. $\{\vec{u_1}, \vec{u_2}\}$ _____

2. $\{\vec{u_1}, \vec{u_3}\}$ _____

3. $\{\vec{u_2}, \vec{u_3}\}$ _____

b) Do the components of vector $\vec{v}$ relative to a basis depend on the basis? _____

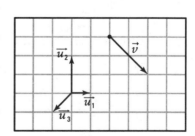

a) Explain why two orthogonal vectors in a plane form a vector basis of the plane.

<u>*Two orthogonal vectors are not parallel.*</u>

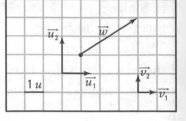

b) A basis is orthogonal when the two vectors of the basis are orthogonal. If, in addition, the vectors are unit vectors then the orthogonal basis is called orthonormal.

1. Find, in the plane on the right, the two orthogonal bases. _____

2. Which one of the two bases is orthonormal? _____

c) Express vector $\vec{w}$ as a linear combination of the vectors of the basis.

1. $\left\{ \vec{u_1}, \vec{u_2} \right\}$ _____   2. $\left\{ \vec{v_1}, \vec{v_2} \right\}$ _____

ORTHOGONAL BASIS – ORTHONORMAL BASIS

- A vector basis with orthogonal vectors is called **orthogonal**. If, in addition, the vectors are unit vectors, then the basis is called **orthonormal**.

- The Cartesian plane usually uses an orthonormal basis. We denote by $\vec{i}$ and $\vec{j}$ the vectors of an orthonormal basis.

  We have: $\vec{i} \perp \vec{j}$; $\|\vec{i}\| = 1$ and $\|\vec{j}\| = 1$.

  Ex.: Vector $\vec{u}$, in the orthonormal basis $\left\{ \vec{i}, \vec{j} \right\}$ on the right, is written: $\vec{u} = 3\vec{i} + 2\vec{j}$.

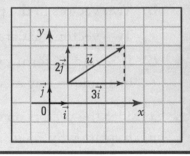

---

8. Consider the Cartesian plane on the right.

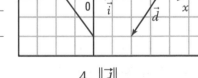

a) Express, as a linear combination of vectors $\vec{i}$ and $\vec{j}$, the vector

1. $\vec{a}$ _____   2. $\vec{b}$ _____

3. $\vec{c}$ _____   4. $\vec{d}$ _____

b) Determine

1. $\|\vec{a}\|$ _____   2. $\|\vec{b}\|$ _____   3. $\|\vec{c}\|$ _____   4. $\|\vec{d}\|$ _____

9. Consider the Cartesian plane on the right. Represent, starting from the origin 0, the vector

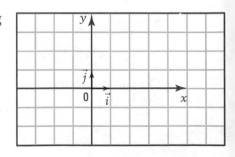

a) $\vec{a} = 3\vec{i} + 2\vec{j}$.

b) $\vec{b} = 3\vec{i} - 2\vec{j}$.

c) $\vec{c} = -3\vec{i} - 2\vec{j}$.

d) $\vec{d} = -2\vec{i} + 3\vec{j}$.

6.4 Algebraic vectors

Consider the geometric vector $\vec{v}$ located in the Cartesian plane on the right.

a) Write vector $\vec{v}$ as a linear combination of vectors $\vec{i}$ and $\vec{j}$.

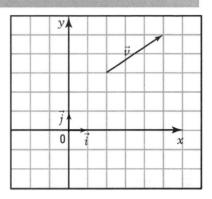

_____

b) 1. Is it true that to any geometric vector $\vec{u}$ located in the Cartesian plane corresponds a unique couple (a, b) such that $\vec{u} = a\vec{i} + b\vec{j}$ where $a \in \mathbb{R}$ and $b \in \mathbb{R}$? _____

2. The couple (a, b) defines algebraically the vector $\vec{u}$. What is the couple defining vector $\vec{v}$? _____

c) 1. Draw vector $\overrightarrow{OM}$, representative with origin 0 of vector $\vec{v}$.

2. Verify that the coordinates of point M are equal to the components of vector $\vec{v}$.

ALGEBRAIC VECTORS

- Consider the Cartesian plane and the orthonormal basis $\{\vec{i}, \vec{j}\}$.
  An **algebraic vector** $\vec{u}$ in the Cartesian plane is defined by a couple (a, b) where $a \in \mathbb{R}$ and $b \in \mathbb{R}$. We write: $\vec{u} = (a, b)$.

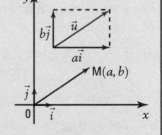

- We have the equivalence:

$$\vec{u} = (a, b) \Leftrightarrow \vec{u} = a\vec{i} + b\vec{j}$$

  a is called **horizontal component** and b **vertical component**.

- If $\overrightarrow{OM}$ is the representative with origin 0 of the vector $\vec{u}$, then the coordinates (a, b) of point M correspond to the components (a, b) of vector $\vec{u}$.

  Ex.: Consider the vector $\vec{u} = (-3, 2)$.

  – We have: $\vec{u} = -3\vec{i} + 2\vec{j}$.
  – $\overrightarrow{OM}$ is the representative with origin 0 of vector $\vec{u}$.
    We have: $M(-3, 2)$.

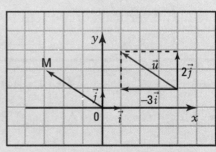

- The zero vector $\vec{0}$ is defined by $\vec{0} = (0, 0)$.

- Vectors $\vec{u} = (a, b)$ and $\vec{v} = (c, d)$ are **equal** if and only if the corresponding components of the two vectors are equal.

$$\vec{u} = \vec{v} \Leftrightarrow a = c \text{ and } b = d$$

1. Consider, in the Cartesian plane on the right, point A(3, 2). Draw the representative with origin A of each of the following vectors.

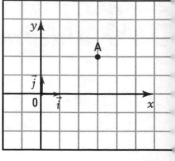

a) $\vec{u_1} = (-2, 1)$ b) $\vec{u_2} = (3, 2)$ c) $\vec{u_3} = (2, -3)$

d) $\vec{u_4} = (-2, -4)$ e) $\vec{u_5} = (2, 0)$ f) $\vec{u_6} = (0, -4)$

2. Represent vector $\vec{u}(-1, 2)$ by an arrow with origin

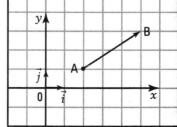

a) A(3, 1)   b) B(2, -1)   c) 0(0, 0)

3. Determine the orientation of the following vectors.

a) $\vec{a} = (3, 0)$ _____   b) $\vec{b} = (0, 2)$ _____   c) $\vec{c} = (2, 2)$ _____   d) $\vec{d} = (-2, 0)$ _____

e) $\vec{e} = (1, \sqrt{3})$ _____   f) $\vec{f} = (-1, -\sqrt{3})$ ___   g) $\vec{g} = (-1, -1)$ _____   h) $\vec{h} = (3, 4)$ _____

i) $\vec{i} = (-3, -4)$ _____   j) $\vec{j} = (-3, 4)$ _____   k) $\vec{k} = (3, -4)$ _____   l) $\vec{l} = (3, -3)$ _____

ACTIVITY 2   Calculating the components of a vector

Consider vector $\vec{AB}$ on the right with origin A(2, 1) and endpoint B(5,3).

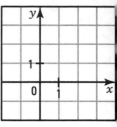

a) 1. Write vector $\vec{AB}$ as a linear combination of vectors $\vec{i}$ and $\vec{j}$.

_____

2. What are the components of vector $\vec{AB}$? _____

b) Verify that

1. the horizontal component of vector $\vec{AB}$ is equal to the difference of the x-coordinates: $(x_B - x_A)$. _____

2. the vertical component of vector $\vec{AB}$ is equal to the difference of the y-coordinates: $(y_B - y_A)$. _____

CALCULATING THE COMPONENTS OF A VECTOR

- Given two points A(x_A, y_A) and B(x_B, y_B), the vector $\vec{AB}$ has components:

$$\vec{AB} = \left(x_B - x_A, y_B - y_A\right)$$

- Note that the horizontal component of a vector is equal to the difference between the x-coordinate of the endpoint and the x-coordinate of the origin and that the vertical component of a vector is equal to the difference between the y-coordinate of the endpoint and the y-coordinate of the origin.

Ex.: Consider the points A(2, 1), B(4, 4), C(4, –1), D(–2, –1) and E(–1, 3).

We have:

$\overrightarrow{AB} = (4 - 2, 4 - 1) = (2, 3)$

$\overrightarrow{AC} = (4 - 2, -1 - 1) = (2, -2)$

$\overrightarrow{AD} = (-2 - 2, -1 - 1) = (-4, -2)$

$\overrightarrow{AE} = (-1 - 2, 3 - 1) = (-3, 2)$

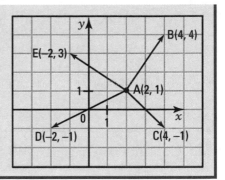

4. Consider points A(1, –2), B(–2, 5) and C(–3, –1). Find the components of

a) $\overrightarrow{AB}$ _____

b) $\overrightarrow{AC}$ _____

c) $\overrightarrow{BC}$ _____

d) $\overrightarrow{CB}$ _____

5. Consider A(–1, 2) and B(x, y). Find the coordinates of B if $\overrightarrow{AB} = (2, -3)$.

_____

6. Consider points A(0, 3), B(4, 6), C(–2, –3) and D(7, 2).

a) Find P(x, y) if $\overrightarrow{CP} = \overrightarrow{AB}$. _____

b) Find Q(x, y) if $\overrightarrow{QC} = \overrightarrow{CD}$. _____

7. Consider points A(–1, 2), B(3, 4) and C(2, –3).

a) Find the point D(x, y) if $\overrightarrow{AB} = \overrightarrow{CD}$. _____

b) What can be said of the quadrilateral ABDC? Justify your answer.

_____

c) Verify that $\overrightarrow{AC} = \overrightarrow{BD}$. _____

ACTIVITY 3 Norm of an algebraic vector

a) 1. Consider the vector $\vec{u} = (2, 1)$. Calculate $\|\vec{u}\|$. _____

2. Consider the vector $\vec{u} = (a, b)$. Establish a formula to calculate

$\|\vec{u}\|$. _____

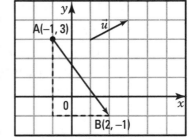

b) Consider the vector $\overrightarrow{AB}$ such that A(–1, 3) and B(2, –1).

1. Calculate the components of $\overrightarrow{AB}$. _____

2. Calculate $\|\overrightarrow{AB}\|$. _____

c) Let $\overrightarrow{AB}$ be a vector such that $A(x_A, y_A)$ and $B(x_B, y_B)$. Establish a formula to calculate the norm of $\overrightarrow{AB}$. _____

NORM OF AN ALGEBRAIC VECTOR

- If $\vec{u} = (a, b)$, then $\boxed{\|\vec{u}\| = \sqrt{a^2 + b^2}}$.

- If $A(x_A, y_A)$ and $B(x_B, y_B)$, then $\boxed{\|\overrightarrow{AB}\| = \sqrt{(x_B - x_A)^2 + (y_B - y_A)^2}}$.

Ex.: Consider $A(1, 3)$ and $B(3, -1)$. We have:

$$\vec{AB} = (2, -4).$$

$$\|\vec{AB}\| = \sqrt{(2)^2 + (-4)^2} = \sqrt{4 + 16} = \sqrt{20}.$$

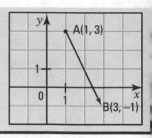

8. Consider $A(-1, 2)$ and $B(3, 4)$. Calculate

a) $\|\vec{AB}\|$ _____ b) $\|\vec{BA}\|$ _____ c) $\|\vec{AA}\|$ _____

9. Given any three points A, B and C, answer true or false.

a) $\|\vec{AB}\| = \|\vec{BA}\|$ _____ b) $\|\vec{AB} + \vec{BC}\| = \|\vec{AB}\| + \|\vec{BC}\|$ _____

c) $\|\vec{AB} - \vec{CB}\| = \|\vec{AC}\|$ _____ d) $\|\vec{AB} + \vec{BC} + \vec{CA}\| = 0$ _____

ACTIVITY 4 Operations between algebraic vectors

Consider points $A(1, 2)$, $B(3, 5)$ and $C(6, 3)$.

a) 1. Calculate the components of

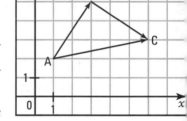

    1) $\vec{AB}$ _____ 2) $\vec{BC}$ _____ 3) $\vec{AC}$ _____

   2. What is the sum vector $\vec{AB} + \vec{BC}$? _____

   3. Verify that

     1) the horizontal component of the sum vector is equal to the sum of the horizontal components. _____

     2) the vertical component of the sum vector is equal to the sum of the vertical components. _____

b) If $\vec{u} = (a, b)$ and $\vec{v} = (c, d)$, what are the components of the sum $\vec{u} + \vec{v}$? _____

c) 1. What is the difference vector $\vec{AC} - \vec{BC}$? _____

   2. Verify that

     1) the horizontal component of the difference vector is equal to the difference of the horizontal components. _____

     2) the vertical component of the difference vector is equal to the difference of the vertical components. _____

d) If $\vec{u} = (a, b)$ and $\vec{v} = (c, d)$, what are the components of the difference $\vec{u} - \vec{v}$? _____

e) Let $\vec{u} = (2, 1)$ be the vector represented on the right.

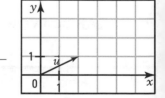

   1. Draw the vector $\vec{v} = 2\vec{u}$.

   2. What are the components of $\vec{v}$? _____

f) 1. If $\vec{u} = (a, b)$, find the components of the vector $\vec{v}$ if $\vec{v} = k\vec{u}$ $(k \in \mathbb{R})$.

_____

   2. If $\vec{u} = (a, b)$ and $\vec{v} = (c, d)$, under what conditions are vectors $\vec{u}$ and $\vec{v}$ parallel?

_____

OPERATIONS BETWEEN ALGEBRAIC VECTORS

Given vectors $\vec{u} = (a, b)$ and $\vec{v} = (c, d)$, we have:

$\vec{u} + \vec{v} = (a + c, b + d)$
$\vec{u} - \vec{v} = (a - c, b - d)$
$k\vec{u} = (ka, kb)$ $(k \in \mathbb{R})$

10. Consider the vectors $\vec{u} = (-3, 4)$, $\vec{v} = (2, -3)$ and $\vec{w} = (1, -2)$. Calculate

a) $-2\vec{u}$ _____

b) $\vec{u} + \vec{v} - \vec{w}$ _____

c) $-\vec{w}$ _____

d) $\|-3\vec{u}\|$ _____

e) $2\vec{u} + 3\vec{v}$ _____

f) $3\vec{u} - 2\vec{v} + \vec{w}$ _____

g) $\|\vec{u} + \vec{v}\|$ _____

h) $\|\vec{u} - \vec{v} + 5\vec{w}\|$ _____

i) $0\vec{u}$ _____

11. Consider the points A(-1, 2), B(1,3), C(2, -3) and D(3, -4). Calculate

a) $2\overrightarrow{AB}$ _____

b) $\overrightarrow{AB} + \overrightarrow{AC}$ _____

c) $\overrightarrow{AD} - \overrightarrow{BC}$ _____

d) $3\overrightarrow{AB} - 2\overrightarrow{AC}$ _____

e) $\|2\overrightarrow{AB} - 4\overrightarrow{CD}\|$ _____

f) $\|\overrightarrow{AB} + \overrightarrow{BC} - \overrightarrow{DC}\|$ _____

12. In each of the following cases, indicate if vectors $\vec{u}$ and $\vec{v}$ are parallel. If so, justify your answer.

a) $\vec{u} = (-1, 2)$ and $\vec{v} = (3, -6)$ _____

b) $\vec{u} = (2, -3)$ and $\vec{v} = (4, -5)$ _____

c) $\vec{u} = (6, -9)$ and $\vec{v} = (4, -6)$ _____

d) $\vec{u} = (0, 1)$ and $\vec{v} = (2, 0)$ _____

e) $\vec{u} = (2, 0)$ and $\vec{v} = (-4, 0)$ _____

f) $\vec{u} = (1, 2)$ and $\vec{v} = (-1, -2)$ _____

13. Determine the unit vectors among the following vectors.

$\overrightarrow{u_1} = \left(-\dfrac{3}{5}, \dfrac{4}{5}\right)$, $\overrightarrow{u_2} = \left(\dfrac{1}{2}, \dfrac{1}{2}\right)$, $\overrightarrow{u_3} = \left(-\dfrac{1}{2}, \dfrac{\sqrt{3}}{2}\right)$, $\overrightarrow{u_4} = (-1, 0)$, $\overrightarrow{u_5} = (\cos \theta, \sin \theta)$

14. a) Consider $\vec{u} = (3, 4)$, verify that $\dfrac{\vec{u}}{\|\vec{u}\|}$ is a unit vector.

b) Let $\vec{u} = (a, b)$ be a nonzero vector. Show that $\dfrac{\vec{u}}{\|\vec{u}\|}$ is a unit vector.

15. Consider $\vec{u} = (a, b)$. Show that $\|k\vec{u}\| = |k| \cdot \|\vec{u}\|$ $(k \in \mathbb{R})$.

16. Consider $\vec{v} = (3, 4)$.

a) 1. Find the unit vector $\vec{u_1}$ having the same direction as $\vec{v}$.

_____

2. Find the vector $\vec{v_1}$, with norm equal to 2, having the same direction as $\vec{v}$.

_____

b) 1. Find the unit vector $\vec{u_2}$ having the direction opposite to $\vec{v}$.

_____

2. Find the vector $\vec{v_2}$, with norm equal to 7, having direction opposite to $\vec{v}$.

_____

17. Determine the direction and the norm of each of the following vectors.

a) $\vec{a} = (-1, -1)$_____

b) $\vec{b} = (0, 2)$_____

c) $\vec{c} = (2, 3)$_____

d) $\vec{d} = (-2, 2)$_____

e) $\vec{e} = \left(1, -\sqrt{3}\right)$_____

18. Find the components of the vectors opposite to the following vectors.

a) $\vec{a}(-1, 2)$ _____ **b)** $\vec{b}(2, -3)$_____ **c)** $\vec{c}(2, 3)$ _____

19. In each of the following cases, find the components of vector $\vec{v}$.

a) $\vec{u} = (-1, 2), \vec{w} = (2, -3)$ and $\vec{u} + \vec{v} = \vec{w}$_____

b) $\vec{u} = (2, -3), \vec{w} = (3, -1)$ and $\vec{u} - \vec{v} = \vec{w}$_____

c) $\vec{w} = (4, -2)$ and $\vec{w} = -2\vec{v}$_____

d) $\vec{u} = (2, -1), \vec{w} = (2, 1)$ and $\vec{w} = 3\vec{u} + 2\vec{v}$_____

e) $\vec{u} = (1, 2), \vec{w} = (-1, -2)$ and $\vec{w} = 2\vec{u} - 3\vec{v}$_____

20. Write each of the following vectors as a linear combination of vectors $\vec{i}$ and $\vec{j}$.

a) $\vec{AB}$ if A$(-1, 2)$ and B$(3, -1)$ _____

b) $\vec{CD}$ if C$(2, -3)$ and D$(-3, 1)$ _____

c) $\vec{EF}$ if E$(0, 2)$ and F$(-1, 0)$ _____

d) $\vec{GH}$ if G$(2, -4)$ and H$(2, 1)$ _____

21. Consider vectors $\vec{u_1} = (1, 2)$ and $\vec{u_2} = (2, 4)$.

a) Do vectors $\vec{u_1}$ and $\vec{u_2}$ form a vector basis? Justify your answer.

_____

b) Is it possible to write any vector $\vec{v}$ of the plane as linear combination of vectors $\vec{u_1}$ and $\vec{u_2}$?

_____

22. Consider vectors $\vec{u_1} = (1, 2)$ and $\vec{u_2} = (-1, 1)$.

a) Do vectors $\vec{u_1}$ and $\vec{u_2}$ form a basis? Justify your answer.

_____

b) Is it possible to write any vector $\vec{v}$ of the plane as linear combination of vectors $\vec{u_1}$ and $\vec{u_2}$?

_____

c) Express vector $\vec{v} = (1, 8)$ as a linear combination of vectors $\vec{u_1}$ and $\vec{u_2}$.

_____

23. Consider vectors $\vec{u_1} = (-1, 2)$ and $\vec{u_2} = (3, 2)$ in the plane.

a) Explain why vectors $\vec{u_1}$ and $\vec{u_2}$ form a vector basis of the plane.

_____

b) Find the components of vector $\vec{v}$ if $\vec{v} = 3\vec{u_1} + 2\vec{u_2}$. _____

c) Write vector $\vec{w} = (1, 6)$ as a linear combination of vectors $\vec{u_1}$ and $\vec{u_2}$.

_____

24. Consider, in the Cartesian plane, the basis formed by the vectors $\vec{u_1} = (2, 1)$ and $\vec{u_2} = (-1, 2)$. Express each of the following vectors as a linear combination of vectors $\vec{u_1}$ and $\vec{u_2}$.

a) $\vec{u} = (4, 7)$ _____

b) $\vec{v} = (-7, 4)$ _____

c) $\vec{w} = (5, 0)$ _____

ACTIVITY 5 Midpoint of a line segment

A line segment AB and its midpoint M are represented on the right.

a) 1. What can be said of vectors $\overrightarrow{MA}$ and $\overrightarrow{MB}$? _____

2. Complete: $\overrightarrow{MA} + \overrightarrow{MB} =$ _____

b) Complete using the appropriate real number.

1. $\overrightarrow{AB} = \boxed{}\overrightarrow{AM}$
2. $\overrightarrow{AM} = \boxed{}\overrightarrow{AB}$

MIDPOINT OF A LINE SEGMENT

The following propositions are equivalent.
1. M is the midpoint of AB.
2. $\overrightarrow{MA} + \overrightarrow{MB} = \vec{0}$.
3. $\overrightarrow{AM} = \overrightarrow{MB}$.
4. $\overrightarrow{AM} = \frac{1}{2}\overrightarrow{AB}$.
5. $\overrightarrow{AB} = 2\overrightarrow{AM}$.

---

25. Let $A(x_A, y_A)$ and $B(x_B, y_B)$ be the endpoints of a line segment AB. Let M be the midpoint of line segment AB.

Show that the coordinates of M are: $\left(\dfrac{x_A + x_B}{2}, \dfrac{y_A + y_B}{2} \right)$.

26. Let A(3, 4), B(–1, 0) and C(5, 2) be the vertices of a triangle ABC.
Let M and N denote the midpoints of sides AB and AC. Verify the following theorem: The line segment joining the midpoints of 2 sides of a triangle measures half the length of the 3rd side and is parallel to the 3rd side.

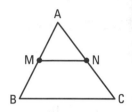

ACTIVITY 6 Dividing point of a line segment

Consider the line segment AB on the right having endpoints A(1, 2) and B(7, 5).

a) Locate the point P such that $\overrightarrow{AP} = \dfrac{2}{3}\overrightarrow{AB}$.

b) Determine the coordinates of P.

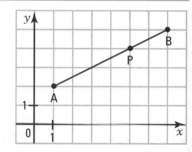

DIVIDING POINT OF A LINE SEGMENT

Point P on the right divides the line segment AB

– in a 3:2 ratio or $\dfrac{3}{2}$ from A.

or

– in a 2:3 ratio or $\dfrac{2}{3}$ from B.

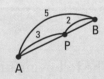

We can also say that P is located at $\dfrac{3}{5}$ of the line segment AB from point A or at $\dfrac{2}{5}$ of line segment AB from B.

This situation is translated by the vector equality:

$\overrightarrow{AP} = \dfrac{3}{5}\overrightarrow{AB}$ or $\overrightarrow{BP} = \dfrac{2}{5}\overrightarrow{BA}$.

Ex.: Consider A(1, 4) and B(7, 1).

Let us find point P if $\overrightarrow{AP} = \frac{2}{3}\overrightarrow{AB}$.

$P(x, y)$; $\overrightarrow{AP} = (x - 1, y - 4)$; $\overrightarrow{AB} = (6, -3)$

$\overrightarrow{AP} = \frac{2}{3}\overrightarrow{AB} \Rightarrow (x - 1, y - 4) = \frac{2}{3}(6, -3)$

$(x - 1, y - 4) = (4, -2)$

We deduce that $x - 1 = 4$ and $y - 4 = -2$

$x = 5$ and $y = 2$

Thus, we obtain P(5, 2).

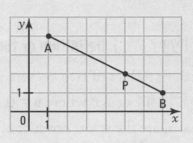

27. Consider A(–2, 1) and B(2, 9). Find the coordinates of points P and Q if

a) $\overrightarrow{AP} = \frac{3}{4}\overrightarrow{AB}$ _____

b) $\overrightarrow{BQ} = \frac{3}{4}\overrightarrow{BA}$ _____

28. Consider A(–1, 5) and B(5, 2). Find the following points.

a) P if $\overrightarrow{AP} = \frac{1}{3}\overrightarrow{AB}$ _____

b) Q if $\overrightarrow{AQ} = \frac{2}{3}\overrightarrow{AB}$ _____

c) R if $\overrightarrow{AR} = \frac{1}{2}\overrightarrow{AB}$ _____

d) S if $\overrightarrow{BS} = \frac{5}{6}\overrightarrow{BA}$ _____

29. Consider triangle ABC on the right whose vertices are A(–5, 6), B(–2, 2) and C(4, 4).

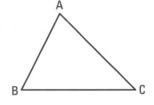

a) Determine the coordinates of point M, if $\overrightarrow{AM}$ is the median relative to side BC. _____

b) Determine the coordinates of the centre of gravity G of the triangle knowing that G divides each median in a 2:1 ratio from the corresponding vertex.

_____

c) Verify the following property: If G is the centre of gravity of a triangle ABC then $\overrightarrow{GA} + \overrightarrow{GB} + \overrightarrow{GC} = \vec{0}$.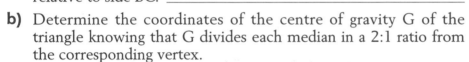

30. Consider the line l passing through points A(–1, 2) and B(5, –1).

a) Find the coordinates of points P_1, P_2, P_3, P_4 and P_5 knowing that

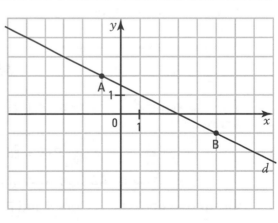

1. $\overrightarrow{AP_1} = -\frac{2}{3}\overrightarrow{AB}$ _____

2. $\overrightarrow{BP_2} = \frac{4}{3}\overrightarrow{BA}$ _____

3. $\overrightarrow{AP_3} = \frac{1}{3}\overrightarrow{AB}$ _____

4. $\overrightarrow{AP_4} = \frac{2}{3}\overrightarrow{AB}$ _____

5. $\overrightarrow{BP_5} = -\frac{1}{3}\overrightarrow{BA}$

b) Locate points P_1, P_2, P_3, P_4 and P_5 on line l.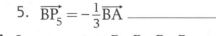

6.5 Scalar product

ACTIVITY 1 Definition of the scalar product

The scalar product of two vectors $\vec{u}$ and $\vec{v}$ written $\vec{u} \cdot \vec{v}$ is defined by:

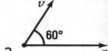

$\vec{u} \cdot \vec{v} = \|\vec{u}\| \times \|\vec{v}\| \times \cos\theta$ where $\theta \in [0, \pi]$ is the angle formed by vectors $\vec{u}$ and $\vec{v}$.

a) Calculate the scalar product of vectors $\vec{u}$ and $\vec{v}$ on the right if $\|\vec{u}\| = 4$ and $\|\vec{v}\| = 3$. _____

b) Explain why the scalar product of any two vectors $\vec{u}$ and $\vec{v}$ is a real number and not a vector. _____

c) What can be said about the angle θ between two vectors if
1. $\vec{u} \cdot \vec{v} > 0$? _____
2. $\vec{u} \cdot \vec{v} < 0$? _____
3. $\vec{u} \cdot \vec{v} = 0$? _____

d) Complete:
1. $\vec{u} \cdot \vec{v} = 0 \Rightarrow$ _____
2. $\vec{u} = \vec{0}$ or $\vec{v} = \vec{0}$ or $\vec{u} \perp \vec{v} \Rightarrow \vec{u} \cdot \vec{v} =$ _____

e) $\vec{u}$ and $\vec{v}$ being two nonzero vectors, complete:
1. $\vec{u} \cdot \vec{v} = 0 \Leftrightarrow$ _____
2. $\vec{u} \cdot \vec{v} \neq 0 \Leftrightarrow$ _____

f) A force $\vec{F}$ of 10 newtons is applied to an object 0, which then moves 5 m in direction $\vec{d}$.

In physics, the work W performed by this force is defined by the scalar product $W = \vec{F} \cdot \vec{d}$ where force $\vec{F}$ is in newtons, the displacement $\vec{d}$ is in metres and work W is in joules. Calculate the work W. _____

SCALAR PRODUCT

- The scalar product of two vectors $\vec{u}$ and $\vec{v}$, written $\vec{u} \cdot \vec{v}$, is the real number defined by

$$\vec{u} \cdot \vec{v} = \|\vec{u}\| \times \|\vec{v}\| \times \cos\theta$$

where $\theta \in [0, \pi]$ is the angle formed by vectors $\vec{u}$ and $\vec{v}$.

- Given two nonzero vectors $\vec{u}$ and $\vec{v}$ we have the equivalence:

$$\vec{u} \cdot \vec{v} = 0 \Leftrightarrow \vec{u} \perp \vec{v}$$

Ex.: Vectors $\vec{u}$ and $\vec{v}$ form a 30° angle and have norms $\|\vec{u}\| = 4$ and $\|\vec{v}\| = 3$.
We have: $\vec{u} \cdot \vec{v} = 4 \times 3 \times \cos 30° = 6\sqrt{3}$.

---

1. Calculate the following scalar products.

    a) $\vec{i} \cdot \vec{j}$ _____ **b)** $\vec{i} \cdot \vec{i}$ _____ **c)** $\vec{j} \cdot \vec{j}$ _____

2. Let $\vec{u}$ be a vector such that $\|\vec{u}\| = 5$. Calculate $\vec{u} \cdot \vec{u}$. _____

3. Calculate, in each case, $\vec{u} \cdot \vec{v}$ if

    a) $\|\vec{u}\| = 3, \|\vec{v}\| = 2$ **b)** $\|\vec{u}\| = 3, \|\vec{v}\| = 2$ **c)** $\|\vec{u}\| = 4, \|\vec{v}\| = 3$

_____   _____   _____

4. Show that, for any vector $\vec{u}$, we have: $\|\vec{u}\| = \sqrt{\vec{u} \cdot \vec{u}}$.

_____

5. Show that the scalar product is commutative.

_____

_____

ACTIVITY 2   Scalar product in the Cartesian plane

a) Consider vectors $\vec{u} = (a_1, b_1); \vec{v} = (a_2, b_2)$ and $\vec{u} - \vec{v}$ represented by the arrows $\overrightarrow{OA}, \overrightarrow{OB}$ and $\overrightarrow{BA}$ respectively. Justify the steps showing that $\vec{u} \cdot \vec{v} = a_1 a_2 + b_1 b_2$.

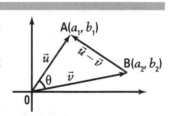

Steps	Justifications
1. $\|\vec{u} - \vec{v}\|^2 = \|\vec{u}\|^2 + \|\vec{v}\|^2 - 2\|\vec{u}\|\|\vec{v}\| \cos \theta$	
2. $\|\vec{u}\|\|\vec{v}\| \cos \theta = \frac{1}{2}\left[\|\vec{u}\|^2 + \|\vec{v}\|^2 - \|\vec{u} - \vec{v}\|^2 \right]$	
3. $\vec{u} \cdot \vec{v} = \frac{1}{2}\left[\|\vec{u}\|^2 + \|\vec{v}\|^2 - \|\vec{u} - \vec{v}\|^2 \right]$	

    4. Reduce the right hand side of the last equality to show that $\vec{u} \cdot \vec{v} = a_1 a_2 + b_1 b_2$.

_____

_____

b) Consider vectors $\vec{u} = \left(1, \sqrt{3}\right)$ and $\vec{v} = \left(-1, \sqrt{3}\right)$.

    1. Calculate $\vec{u} \cdot \vec{v}$. _____

    2. Determine, using the definition of the scalar product, the cosine of the angle θ formed by vectors $\vec{u}$ and $\vec{v}$.

    3. What is the angle θ formed by vectors $\vec{u}$ and $\vec{v}$? _____

SCALAR PRODUCT IN THE CARTESIAN PLANE

- Let $\vec{u} = (a_1, b_1)$ and $\vec{v} = (a_2, b_2)$, we have:

$$\vec{u} \cdot \vec{v} = a_1 a_2 + b_1 b_2$$

- Let θ be the angle formed by vectors $\vec{u}$ and $\vec{v}$, we have:

$$\cos \theta = \frac{\vec{u} \cdot \vec{v}}{\|\vec{u}\|\|\vec{v}\|}$$

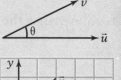

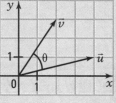

Ex.: Let $\vec{u} = (4, 1)$ and $\vec{v} = (2, 3)$. We have:

$$\vec{u} \cdot \vec{v} = 4 \times 2 + 1 \times 3 = 11$$

$$\cos \theta = \frac{\vec{u} \cdot \vec{v}}{\|\vec{u}\|\|\vec{v}\|} = \frac{11}{\sqrt{17}\sqrt{13}} = \frac{11}{\sqrt{221}}$$

hence $\quad \theta = \cos^{-1} \frac{11}{\sqrt{221}} = 42.3°$

---

6. Calculate the scalar product $\vec{u} \cdot \vec{v}$ in each of the following cases.

    a) $\vec{u} = (2, 3)$ and $\vec{v} = (4, -1)$ _____
    b) $\vec{u} = 3\vec{i} - 2\vec{j}$ and $\vec{v} = -2\vec{i} + \vec{j}$ _____

7. Determine, in each case, whether vectors $\vec{u}$ and $\vec{v}$ are perpendicular.

    a) $\vec{u} = (2, -3)$ and $\vec{v} = (3, 2)$ _____
    b) $\vec{u} = 2\vec{i} + 5\vec{j}$ and $\vec{v} = 7\vec{i} - 3\vec{j}$ _____

8. Find, in each of the following cases, the value of a if vectors $\vec{u}$ and $\vec{v}$ are perpendicular.

    a) $\vec{u} = (a + 1, 2)$ and $\vec{v} = (-3, a - 2)$
    b) $\vec{u} = (a + 2, -1)$ and $\vec{v} = (a - 2, 5)$

9. Consider points A(1, 3), B(2, 5), C(2, 2) and D(4, 1).
Show that the lines AB and CD are perpendicular.

a) Consider vectors $\vec{u} = (1, 2)$, $\vec{v} = (2, 1)$ and $\vec{w} = (3, 2)$.

1. Verify that $\vec{u} \cdot \vec{v} = \vec{v} \cdot \vec{u}$.

_____

2. Verify that $2\vec{u} \cdot 3\vec{v} = (2 \times 3)\,\vec{u} \cdot \vec{v}$.

_____

3. Verify that $\vec{u} \cdot (\vec{v} + \vec{w}) = \vec{u} \cdot \vec{v} + \vec{u} \cdot \vec{w}$.

_____

b) Consider vectors $\vec{u} = (a_1, b_1)$, $\vec{v} = (a_2, b_2)$ and $\vec{w} = (a_3, b_3)$.

1. Show that $\vec{u} \cdot \vec{v} = \vec{v} \cdot \vec{u}$.

_____
_____
_____

2. Show that $r\vec{u} \cdot s\vec{v} = (rs)\vec{u} \cdot \vec{v}$.

_____
_____
_____
_____

3. Show that $\vec{u} \cdot (\vec{v} + \vec{w}) = \vec{u} \cdot \vec{v} + \vec{u} \cdot \vec{w}$.

_____
_____
_____
_____
_____

PROPERTIES OF THE SCALAR PRODUCT

Let $\vec{u}$, $\vec{v}$ and $\vec{w}$ be any three vectors, we have:

– $\boxed{\vec{u} \cdot \vec{v} = \vec{v} \cdot \vec{u}}$

– $\boxed{r\vec{u} \cdot s\vec{v} = (rs)\vec{u} \cdot \vec{v}}$ $(r \in \mathbb{R},\ s \in \mathbb{R})$

– $\boxed{\vec{u} \cdot (\vec{v} + \vec{w}) = \vec{u} \cdot \vec{v} + \vec{u} \cdot \vec{w}}$

10. Knowing that $\vec{u} \cdot \vec{v} = 3$ and $\vec{u} \cdot \vec{w} = 2$, calculate

a) $(2\vec{u}) \cdot \vec{v}$ _____

b) $\vec{u} \cdot (5\vec{v})$ _____

c) $(-2\vec{u}) \cdot (3\vec{v})$ _____

d) $\vec{u} \cdot (\vec{v} + \vec{w})$ _____

e) $\vec{u} \cdot (\vec{v} - \vec{w})$ _____

f) $2\vec{u} \cdot (3\vec{v} - 2\vec{w})$ _____

11. Knowing that $\vec{u} \perp \vec{v}$ and that $\|\vec{u}\| = 3$ and $\|\vec{v}\| = 2$, calculate

a) $\vec{u} \cdot (\vec{u} + \vec{v})$ _____

b) $(\vec{u} + \vec{v}) \cdot (\vec{u} - \vec{v})$ _____

c) $(2\vec{u} + 3\vec{v}) \cdot (3\vec{u} - 2\vec{v})$ _____

12. Consider three points A, B and C on a triangle.
Determine if triangle ABC is right. If, so indicate the right angle.

a) A(–1, 2), B(2, 3) and C(–2, 5)

_____

b) A(2, 3), B(–1, 4) and C(0, 7)

_____

c) A(1, 2), B(2, –1) and C(–1, 1)

_____

13. Consider two vectors $\vec{u}$ and $\vec{v}$ such that $\|\vec{u}\| = 2$ and $\|\vec{v}\| = 3$. Calculate $\vec{u} \cdot \vec{v}$ if

a) $\vec{u}$ and $\vec{v}$ have the same direction. _____

b) $\vec{u}$ and $\vec{v}$ have opposite directions. _____

14. Consider the vector $\vec{w} = (3, -4)$.

a) Find the two unit vectors $\vec{u_1}$ and $\vec{u_2}$ which are perpendicular to $\vec{w}$.

_____

b) Find the two vectors $\vec{v_1}$ and $\vec{v_2}$ with norm equal to 10 and which are perpendicular to $\vec{w}$.

_____

15. Calculate, in each case, the angle θ formed by vectors $\vec{u}$ and $\vec{v}$.

a) $\vec{u} = (-3, 2)$ and $\vec{v} = (1, 4)$ _____

b) $\vec{u} = (2, -5)$ and $\vec{v} = (3, 2)$ _____

16. Calculate, in each case, the angle θ formed by vectors $\overrightarrow{AB}$ and $\overrightarrow{CD}$.

a) A(–1, 2), B(2, 3), C(2, –3) and D(0, –4).

_____

b) A(2, 3), B(0, 5), C(–1, 2) and D(2, 6).

_____

17. Consider a triangle ABC whose vertices are A(2, 6), B(–1, 2) and C(4, 3). Calculate the measure of each angle of triangle ABC.

_____

_____

_____

18. Calculate, rounded to the nearest unit, the acute angle θ formed by lines $l_1: y = 2x + 1$ and $l_2: y = -2x + 3$.

_____

_____

_____

19. Consider lines l_1 and l_2 with respective equations $l_1: y = a_1x$ ($a_1 \neq 0$) and $l_2: y = a_2x$ ($a_2 \neq 0$). Show the equivalence: $l_1 \perp l_2 \Leftrightarrow a_1a_2 = -1$.

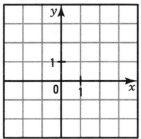

_____

_____

_____

20. A triangle ABC has vertices A(1, 3), B(–1, 1) and C(3, –1). Calculate the measure of angle ABC to the nearest tenth of a unit.

_____

_____

6.6 Orthogonal projections

a) Consider vectors $\vec{u}$ and $\vec{v}$ on the right.

Using a square, we projected vector $\vec{u}$ onto vector $\vec{v}$.

The vector we obtained, represented in blue, is the **orthogonal projection** of vector $\vec{u}$ onto vector $\vec{v}$. It is written $\vec{u}_{\vec{v}}$.

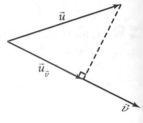

b) 1. In each of the following cases, represent the vector $\vec{u}_{\vec{v}}$, orthogonal projection of $\vec{u}$ onto $\vec{v}$. (Use a square)

1)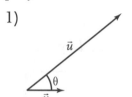

2)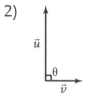

3)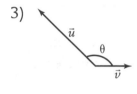

2. Let θ denote the angle between vectors $\vec{u}$ and $\vec{v}$. Answer true or false.

1) When θ is acute, vectors $\vec{u}_{\vec{v}}$ and $\vec{v}$ have the same direction. _____

2) When θ is obtuse, vectors $\vec{u}_{\vec{v}}$ and $\vec{v}$ have opposite directions. _____

3) When θ is right, vector $\vec{u}_{\vec{v}}$ is the zero vector. _____

ORTHOGONAL PROJECTION OF A VECTOR

- Given vectors $\vec{u}$ and $\vec{v}$ on the right, the vector represented in blue is the **orthogonal projection** of vector $\vec{u}$ onto vector $\vec{v}$.

  It is written: $\vec{u}_{\vec{v}}$.

- **Properties**
  - Vectors $\vec{u}_{\vec{v}}$ and $\vec{v}$ are **parallel**: $\vec{u}_{\vec{v}} \parallel \vec{v}$.
  - Vector $\left(\vec{u} - \vec{u}_{\vec{v}}\right)$ is **perpendicular** to $\vec{v}$: $\left(\vec{u} - \vec{u}_{\vec{v}}\right) \perp \vec{v}$.
- We distinguish the following 3 cases according to the angle θ between $\vec{u}$ and $\vec{v}$.

θ acute	θ obtuse	θ right
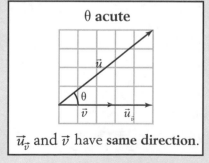	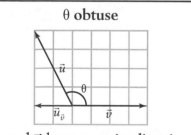	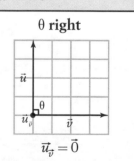
$\vec{u}_{\vec{v}}$ and $\vec{v}$ have **same direction**.	$\vec{u}_{\vec{v}}$ and $\vec{v}$ have **opposite directions**.	$\vec{u}_{\vec{v}} = \vec{0}$

ACTIVITY 2 Formula for the orthogonal projection of $\vec{u}$ onto $\vec{v}$

a) Consider vectors $\vec{u}, \vec{v}$ and vector $\vec{u}_{\vec{v}}$, orthogonal projection of $\vec{u}$ onto $\vec{v}$.

Justify the steps showing that $\vec{u}_{\vec{v}} = \dfrac{\vec{u} \cdot \vec{v}}{\|\vec{v}\|^2} \vec{v}$.

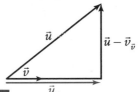

Steps	Justifications
1. $\vec{u}_{\vec{v}} \,/\!/\, \vec{v}$	
2. $\vec{u}_{\vec{v}} = k\vec{v}$	
3. $(\vec{u} - \vec{u}_{\vec{v}}) \perp \vec{v}$	
4. $(\vec{u} - k\vec{v}) \perp \vec{v}$	
5. $(\vec{u} - k\vec{v}) \cdot \vec{v} = 0$	
6. $\vec{u} \cdot \vec{v} - k\vec{v} \cdot \vec{v} = 0$	
7. $k = \dfrac{\vec{u} \cdot \vec{v}}{\vec{v} \cdot \vec{v}}$	
8. $k = \dfrac{\vec{u} \cdot \vec{v}}{\|\vec{v}\|^2}$	
9. $\vec{u}_{\vec{v}} = \dfrac{\vec{u} \cdot \vec{v}}{\|\vec{v}\|^2} \vec{v}$	

b) Consider vectors $\vec{u} = (2, 6)$ and $\vec{v} = (2, 1)$.

1. Show that $\vec{u}_{\vec{v}} = 2\vec{v}$.

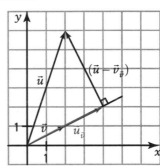

_____

2. Determine the components of $\vec{u}_{\vec{v}}$.

_____

3. Determine the components of vector $(\vec{u} - \vec{u}_{\vec{v}})$.

_____

4. Verify the property: $\vec{u}_{\vec{v}} \perp (\vec{u} - \vec{u}_{\vec{v}})$.

_____

_____

FORMULA FOR THE ORTHOGONAL PROJECTION OF $\vec{u}$ onto $\vec{v}$

$$\vec{u}_{\vec{v}} = \frac{\vec{u} \cdot \vec{v}}{\|\vec{v}\|^2} \vec{v}$$

Ex.: $\vec{u} = (5, 5); \vec{v} = (4, 2)$

$\vec{u} \cdot \vec{v} = 30; \|\vec{v}\|^2 = 20$

$\vec{u}_{\vec{v}} = \dfrac{3}{2} \vec{v}$

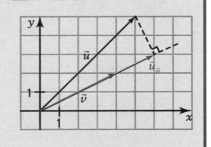

1. Consider vectors $\vec{u}$ and $\vec{v}$ on the right.

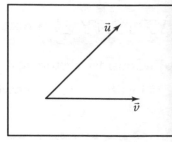

   a) Using a square, represent
   1. vector $\vec{u}_{\vec{v}}$, orthogonal projection of vector $\vec{u}$ onto $\vec{v}$.
   2. vector $\vec{v}_{\vec{u}}$, orthogonal projection of vector $\vec{v}$ onto $\vec{u}$.

   b) Show that $\vec{v}_{\vec{u}} = \dfrac{\vec{v} \cdot \vec{u}}{\|\vec{u}\|^2} \vec{u}$

---

2. Consider vectors $\vec{u} = (-3, 4)$ and $\vec{v} = (2, 3)$. Find the components of

   a) $\vec{u}_{\vec{v}}$ _____

   b) $\vec{v}_{\vec{u}}$ _____

3. An object, located in 0, is moving in the direction of vector $\vec{u} = (4, -2)$ under a force $\vec{F} = (4, 2)$.

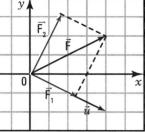

   We want to express $\vec{F}$ as a sum $\vec{F_1} + \vec{F_2}$ of two forces, one in the direction of the motion, the other perpendicular to this direction.

   a) Determine the components of $\vec{F_1}$.

   _____

   b) Determine the components of $\vec{F_2}$.

   _____

   c) Verify that forces $\vec{F_1}$ and $\vec{F_2}$ are perpendicular.

   _____

4. Consider triangle ABC with vertices A(6, 3), B(1, 2) and C(4, 8). Let $\overline{AH}$ be the height from vertex A relative to the base BC.

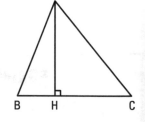

   a) What is the orthogonal projection of vector $\overrightarrow{BA}$ onto the direction of vector $\overrightarrow{BC}$?

   _____

   b) Determine the components of vector $\overrightarrow{BH}$.

   _____

   c) Deduce the coordinates of point H.

   _____

6.7 Vectors and geometric proofs

The vector supported by the median from a vertex of a triangle is equal to half the sum of the vectors supported by the sides from that same vertex.

Hypothesis: $\overrightarrow{AM}$ is the median from vertex A of triangle $\triangle ABC$.

Conclusion: $\overrightarrow{AM} = \frac{1}{2}(\overrightarrow{AB} + \overrightarrow{AC})$

Justify the steps of the proof leading to this conclusion.

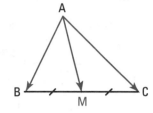

	Steps	Justifications
1.	$\overrightarrow{AM} = \overrightarrow{AB} + \overrightarrow{BM}$ ①	
2.	$\overrightarrow{AM} = \overrightarrow{AC} + \overrightarrow{CM}$ ②	
3.	$2\overrightarrow{AM} = \overrightarrow{AB} + \overrightarrow{BM} + \overrightarrow{AC} + \overrightarrow{CM}$	
4.	$2\overrightarrow{AM} = \overrightarrow{AB} + \overrightarrow{AC} + \overrightarrow{BM} + \overrightarrow{CM}$	
5.	$2\overrightarrow{AM} = \overrightarrow{AB} + \overrightarrow{AC}$	
6.	$\overrightarrow{AM} = \frac{1}{2}(\overrightarrow{AB} + \overrightarrow{AC})$	

ACTIVITY 2 Theorem on the midpoints of the sides of a triangle

The line segment joining the midpoints of the sides of a triangle is parallel to the 3rd side and measures half the length of the 3rd side.

Hypothesis: M is the midpoint of $\overline{AB}$ and N is the midpoint of $\overline{AC}$.

Conclusion: $\overrightarrow{MN} = \frac{1}{2}\overrightarrow{BC}$

Justify the steps of the proof leading to this conclusion.

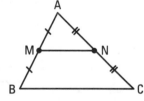

	Steps	Justifications
1.	$\overrightarrow{BA} = 2\overrightarrow{MA}$ ①	
2.	$\overrightarrow{AC} = 2\overrightarrow{AN}$ ②	
3.	$\overrightarrow{BA} + \overrightarrow{AC} = 2\overrightarrow{MA} + 2\overrightarrow{AN}$	
4.	$\overrightarrow{BC} = 2(\overrightarrow{MA} + \overrightarrow{AN})$	
5.	$\overrightarrow{BC} = 2\overrightarrow{MN}$	
6.	$\overrightarrow{MN} = \frac{1}{2}\overrightarrow{BC}$	

ACTIVITY 3 Parallelogram theorem

If a quadrilateral has two parallel congruent sides then this quadrilateral is a parallelogram.

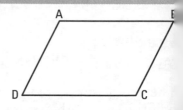

Hypothesis: $\overrightarrow{AB} = \overrightarrow{DC}$.

Conclusion: ABCD is a parallelogram.

a) Justify the steps of the proof leading to this conclusion.

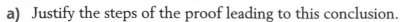

	Steps	Justifications
1.	$\overrightarrow{AB} = \overrightarrow{AD} + \overrightarrow{DB}$ ①	
2.	$\overrightarrow{DC} = \overrightarrow{DB} + \overrightarrow{BC}$ ②	
3.	$\overrightarrow{AD} + \overrightarrow{DB} = \overrightarrow{DB} + \overrightarrow{BC}$	
4.	$\overrightarrow{AD} = \overrightarrow{BC}$	
5.	$AD // BC$	
6.	ABCD is a parallelogram.	

b) Complete: $\overrightarrow{AB} = \overrightarrow{DC} \Leftrightarrow \overrightarrow{AD} = $ _____

ACTIVITY 4 Theorem on the midpoints of the sides of a quadrilateral

If we join the midpoints of adjacent sides of any quadrilateral, we obtain a parallelogram.

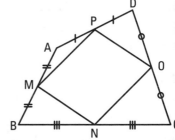

Hypotheses: M midpoint of $\overline{AB}$, N midpoint of $\overline{BC}$.

0 midpoint of $\overline{CD}$, P midpoint of $\overline{AD}$.

Conclusion: ABCD is a parallelogram.

Justify the steps of the proof leading to this conclusion.

	Steps	Justifications
1.	$\overrightarrow{MN} = \frac{1}{2}\overrightarrow{AC}$ ①	
2.	$\overrightarrow{PO} = \frac{1}{2}\overrightarrow{AC}$ ②	
3.	$\overrightarrow{MN} = \overrightarrow{PO}$	
4.	MNOP is a parallelogram.	

ACTIVITY 5 Parallelogram diagonals theorem

The diagonals of a parallelogram intersect at their midpoint.

Hypotheses: – ABCD is a parallelogram.

– 0 is the midpoint of $\overline{AC}$.

Conclusion: – 0 is the midpoint of $\overline{BD}$.

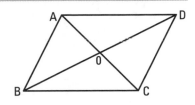

Justify the steps of the proof leading to this conclusion.

	Steps	Justifications
1.	$\overrightarrow{BC} = \overrightarrow{BO} + \overrightarrow{OC}$ ①	
2.	$\overrightarrow{AD} = \overrightarrow{AO} + \overrightarrow{OD}$ ②	
3.	$\overrightarrow{BO} + \overrightarrow{OC} = \overrightarrow{AO} + \overrightarrow{OD}$	
4.	$\overrightarrow{BO} + \overrightarrow{AO} = \overrightarrow{AO} + \overrightarrow{OD}$ ③	
5.	$\overrightarrow{BO} = \overrightarrow{OD}$	
6.	0 is the midpoint of $\overline{BD}$.	

ACTIVITY 6 Quadrilateral diagonals theorem

If the diagonals of a quadrilateral intersect at their midpoint, then this quadrilateral is a parallelogram.

Hypotheses: – 0 is the midpoint of $\overline{AC}$.

– 0 is the midpoint of $\overline{BD}$.

Conclusion: – ABCD is a parallelogram.

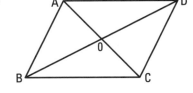

Justify the steps of the proof leading to this conclusion.

	Steps	Justifications
1.	$\overrightarrow{AD} = \overrightarrow{AO} + \overrightarrow{OD}$	
2.	$\overrightarrow{AD} = \overrightarrow{OC} + \overrightarrow{BO}$	
3.	$\overrightarrow{AD} = \overrightarrow{BO} + \overrightarrow{OC}$	
4.	$\overrightarrow{AD} = \overrightarrow{BC}$	
5.	ABCD is a parallelogram.	

ACTIVITY 7 Theorem on the angle inscribed in a half-circle

Any inscribed angle intercepting a half-circle is right.

Hypotheses: − $\mathscr{C}$ is a circle of radius r centred at 0.

         − $\angle BAC$ is an inscribed angle.

         − $\overline{BC}$ is a diameter.

Conclusion: $\angle BAC$ is right.

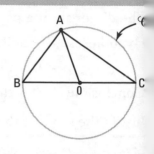

a) Justify the steps of the proof leading to this conclusion.

	Steps	Justifications
1.	$\overrightarrow{AB} \cdot \overrightarrow{AC} = \left(\overrightarrow{AO} + \overrightarrow{OB}\right) \cdot \left(\overrightarrow{AO} + \overrightarrow{OC}\right)$	
2.	$= \overrightarrow{AO} \cdot \overrightarrow{AO} + \overrightarrow{AO} \cdot \overrightarrow{OC} + \overrightarrow{OB} \cdot \overrightarrow{AO} + \overrightarrow{OB} \cdot \overrightarrow{OC}$	
3.	$= r^2 + \overrightarrow{AO} \cdot \left(\overrightarrow{OC} + \overrightarrow{OB}\right) - r^2$	
4.	$= r^2 + \overrightarrow{AO} \cdot \vec{0} - r^2$	
5.	$= 0$	
6.	$\angle BAC$ is right.	

b) Explain why

    1. $\overrightarrow{AO} \cdot \overrightarrow{AO} = r^2$ _____

    2. $\overrightarrow{OB} \cdot \overrightarrow{OC} = -r^2$ _____

ACTIVITY 8 Theorem on the centre of gravity of a triangle

If G is the centre of gravity of a triangle ABC, then $\overrightarrow{GA} + \overrightarrow{GB} + \overrightarrow{GC} = \vec{0}$.

Hypotheses: − $\overline{AA'}$ is a median of triangle ABC.

         − G is the centre of gravity.

Conclusion: $\overrightarrow{GA} + \overrightarrow{GB} + \overrightarrow{GC} = \vec{0}$

Justify the steps of the proof leading to this conclusion.

Hint: Use the following property of the centre of gravity:

    The centre of gravity G divides each median in a 2:1 ratio from each vertex, in other words
$\overrightarrow{AG} = 2\overrightarrow{GA'}$, $\overrightarrow{BG} = 2\overrightarrow{GB'}$ and $\overrightarrow{CG} = 2\overrightarrow{GC'}$.

	Steps	Justifications
1.	$\overrightarrow{GA} + \overrightarrow{GB} + \overrightarrow{GC} = \overrightarrow{GA} + \left(\overrightarrow{GB} + \overrightarrow{GC}\right)$	
2.	$= \overrightarrow{GA} + 2\overrightarrow{GA'}$	
3.	$= \overrightarrow{GA} + \overrightarrow{AG}$	
4.	$= \vec{0}$	

Evaluation 6

1. Complete:

   a) $\overrightarrow{AB} = \overrightarrow{CD} \Leftrightarrow \overrightarrow{AC} =$ _____

   b) $\overrightarrow{PQ} = \overrightarrow{RS} \Leftrightarrow PQSR$ is _____

   c) $\overrightarrow{AB} + \overrightarrow{AC} = \overrightarrow{AD} \Leftrightarrow ABDC$ is _____

   d) $\overrightarrow{AB} + \overrightarrow{BA} =$ _____

   e) $\vec{v} = k\vec{u}$ and $k \neq 0 \Rightarrow \vec{u}$ __ $\vec{v}$

2. True or false?

   a) $\vec{u}$ and $\vec{v}$ form a vector basis of the plane if and only if $\vec{u}$ and $\vec{v}$ are not parallel. _____

   b) Two perpendicular vectors in a plane always form a vector basis of this plane. _____

   c) $\{\vec{u}, \vec{v}\}$ is an orthonormal basis if and only if $\vec{u} \perp \vec{v}$ and $\|\vec{u}\| = \|\vec{v}\| = 1$. _____

   d) M is the midpoint of the line segment AB if and only if: $\overrightarrow{AM} + \overrightarrow{BM} = \vec{0}$. _____

   e) The scalar product of two vectors is negative if and only if the angle θ between the vectors is obtuse. _____

3. Determine the norm and orientation of the following vectors.

   a) $\vec{u} = \left(-2, 2\sqrt{3}\right)$ _____

   b) $\vec{u} = \left(\sqrt{2}, \sqrt{2}\right)$ _____

   c) $\vec{u} = (-3, -4)$ _____

   d) $\vec{u} = \left(\sqrt{3}, -1\right)$ _____

4. Simplify $3\overrightarrow{BC} - 2\overrightarrow{AC} + \overrightarrow{CB} + 3\overrightarrow{AD} - 2\overrightarrow{CD} + \overrightarrow{DA}$.

_____

_____

_____

_____

5. Consider vectors $\vec{u}$ and $\vec{v}$ on the right. Starting from point A, draw the vector $\overrightarrow{AB}$ representative of $2\vec{u} - 3\vec{v}$.

6. Consider A(–2, 1), B(1, 2) and C(2, –1). Calculate

  a) $3\overrightarrow{AB} - 2\overrightarrow{AC}$ _____

  b) $\|\overrightarrow{AB} + \overrightarrow{AC}\|$ _____

  c) $\overrightarrow{AB} \cdot \overrightarrow{AC}$ _____

  d) $(\overrightarrow{AB} + \overrightarrow{AC}) \cdot (\overrightarrow{AB} - \overrightarrow{AC})$ _____

  e) $\overrightarrow{AB}_{\overrightarrow{AC}}$ _____

7. Consider A(–1, 2) and B(2, 6).

  a) Find the two unit vectors $\overrightarrow{u_1}$ and $\overrightarrow{u_2}$ parallel to $\overrightarrow{AB}$.

  _____

  b) Find the two unit vectors $\overrightarrow{v_1}$ and $\overrightarrow{v_2}$ orthogonal to $\overrightarrow{AB}$.

  _____

  _____

8. Consider the rectangle on the right. Complete

  a) $\overrightarrow{AB} \cdot \overrightarrow{AD} =$ _____ **b)** $2\overrightarrow{A0} =$ _____

  c) $\overrightarrow{BA} + \overrightarrow{BC} =$ _____ **d)** $\overrightarrow{AD} - \overrightarrow{BA} =$ _____

  e) $\overrightarrow{AB} =$ _____ **f)** $\overrightarrow{AD} + \overrightarrow{CB} =$ _____

  g) $\overrightarrow{0A} + \overrightarrow{DC} =$ _____ **h)** $\overrightarrow{0A} + \overrightarrow{0B} + \overrightarrow{0C} + \overrightarrow{0D} =$ _____

9. Consider the orthonormal bases $\{\vec{i}, \vec{j}\}$ and $\{\vec{u}, \vec{v}\}$ as well as the vector $\vec{w}$.

  a) Express the following vectors as a linear combination of vectors $\vec{i}$ and $\vec{j}$.

   1. $\vec{u}$_____ 2. $\vec{v}$_____ 3. $\vec{w}$ _____

  b) Express vectors $\vec{w}$ as a linear combination of vectors $\vec{u}$ and $\vec{v}$.

  _____

  c) Verify the linear combination found in b) using the linear combinations found in a).

  _____

10. Consider points A(–1, 2), B(2, 1) and C(1, –3).

  a) 1. Find point D knowing that $\overrightarrow{AB} = \overrightarrow{CD}$.

  _____

   2. Find point E knowing that $\overrightarrow{AE} = 3\overrightarrow{AB} - 2\overrightarrow{AC}$.

  _____

b) What type of quadrilateral is quadrilateral ABDC? Justify your answer.

_____

_____

11. Calculate the acute angle θ formed by the lines $l_1 : y = \frac{3}{2}x + 1$ and $l_2 : y = -\frac{3}{2}x - 1$.

_____

_____

_____

12. Let $\vec{u}$ and $\vec{v}$ be two nonzero vectors. Indicate, for each statement, if it is true or false.

a) $(k\vec{u}) \cdot (k\vec{v}) = k(\vec{u} \cdot \vec{v})$ _____ **b)** $k(\vec{u} + \vec{v}) = k\vec{u} + k\vec{v}$ _____

c) $\vec{u} \cdot \vec{v} = \vec{v} \cdot \vec{u}$ _____ **d)** $\|\vec{u}\| = \sqrt{\vec{u} \cdot \vec{u}}$ _____

13. Consider the rectangular-based right prism on the right. Simplify.

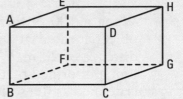

a) $\overrightarrow{AB} + \overrightarrow{ED}$ _____ **b)** $\overrightarrow{AH} - \overrightarrow{FE}$ _____

c) $\overrightarrow{AD} + \overrightarrow{CF} + \overrightarrow{GC}$ _____ **d)** $\overrightarrow{AG} - \overrightarrow{EF} - \overrightarrow{BG}$ _____

14. Consider the line l passing through points A(2, –3) and B(–4, 6).

a) Find the coordinates of point P dividing the line segment AB in a 2:1 ratio from A.

_____

b) Find the coordinates of point Q if $\overrightarrow{AQ} = \frac{-2}{3}\overrightarrow{AB}$.

_____

15. Two unit vectors $\vec{u}$ and $\vec{v}$ form a 60° angle. What is the norm, rounded to the nearest tenth of a unit, of vector $3\vec{u} + 4\vec{v}$?

_____

_____

_____

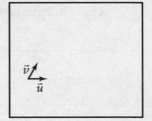

16. Consider vectors $\vec{u} = (1, 2)$ and $\vec{v} = (-2, 1)$.

a) 1. Show that $\vec{u}$ and $\vec{v}$ form a basis.

_____

2. Show that the basis $\{\vec{u}, \vec{v}\}$ is orthogonal. _____

b) Express vector $\vec{w} = (-1, 8)$ as a linear combination of vectors $\vec{u}$ and $\vec{v}$.

_____

17. Show the following property: the diagonals of a diamond are perpendicular.

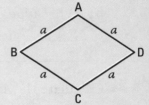

_____

_____

_____

18. Alan and Ben are pulling on an object located at point 0. They apply respectively forces of 80 N and 40 N, with orientations 40° and 120°. Find the resultant $\vec{r}$ (magnitude and orientation) of these two forces.

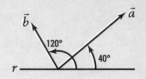

_____

_____

_____

19. When a 100 N force with orientation 30° is applied to an object located at 0, the object moves horizontally over a distance of 20 m. What is the work, rounded to the nearest unit, performed by this force? The work, expressed in joules, is defined as the scalar product of the force vector with the displacement vector.

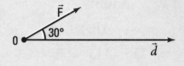

_____

20. A boat leaves port A and must go to port B. In the Cartesian plane on the right, measured in kilometres, points A(150, 100) and B(350, 250) represent the ports. During the crossing, a current represented by vector $\vec{c} = (15, -10)$ acts on the boat. The captain orients the boat so as to cancel the effect of the current. What is, to the nearest degree, the measure of the angle, with respect to the eastward direction, at which the captain must orient the boat to reach the port located in B?

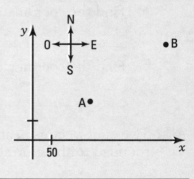

_____

_____

_____

_____

21. In a Cartesian plane, measured in km, town A is located at point (25, 50) and town B at point (150, 200). When there is no wind, the flight from town A to town B lasts one hour. If there is wind and the pilot does not take it into account, the plane will end up, after one hour of flight, at point C(160, 190). Find the speed of the wind as well as its orientation.

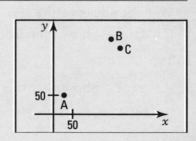

_____

_____

_____

Chapter 7

Conics

CHALLENGE 7

1. Name the set of points M in the plane

   a) located at the same distance from a fixed point. _____

   b) such that the sum of the distances to two fixed points is constant. _____

   c) such that the absolute value of the difference of the distances to two fixed points is constant. _____

   d) located at the same distance to a fixed point and a fixed line. _____

2. Determine the equation of the geometric locus defined by the set of points $M(x, y)$

   a) located 5 units from the origin $0(0, 0)$. _____

   b) such that the sum of the distances from point M to points $(-4, 0)$ and $(4, 0)$ is equal to 10.

   _____

   c) such that the absolute value of the difference between the distances from point M to points $(-10, 0)$ and $(10, 0)$ is equal to 12.

   _____

   d) located at the same distance from the point $(-2, 3)$ and the line with equation $x = 4$.

   _____

3. **a)** Draw, in the Cartesian plane, the curve whose equation is $x^2 - y^2 = -1$ and the curve whose equation is $y^2 = x + 1$.

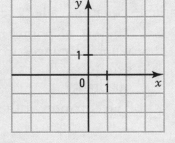

   b) Find algebraically the intersection points of these two curves.

   _____

4. Represent, in the Cartesian plane, the set of points $M(x, y)$ such that

$$\begin{cases} \dfrac{x^2}{9} + \dfrac{y^2}{4} \leq 1 \\ x^2 + y^2 \geq 4 \end{cases}$$

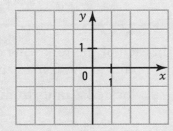

7.1 Geometric locus

ACTIVITY 1 Geometric locus

a) Given two distinct points A and B in a plane, what do we call the set of points whose distances from points A and B are equal?

• A   • B

_____

b) The set of points having a common metric property is called a **geometric locus**. Give examples of geometric loci.

_____

_____

c) In the Cartesian plane, a locus is defined by an equation called **locus equation**.

Given points A(–1, 2) and B(3, 4), find the locus equation of the points whose distances from points A and B are equal.

_____

_____

GEOMETRIC LOCUS

The set of points having a common characteristic is called a geometric locus.

In a Cartesian plane, the common property of the points (x, y) of a locus is translated by a two-variable equation called locus equation.

Ex.: The set of points in the 1st quadrant of the Cartesian plane whose distances from the x-axis and the y-axis are equal is a geometric locus corresponding to the bisector of the 1st quadrant.

The equation of the locus is: $y = x$ $(x \geqslant 0)$.

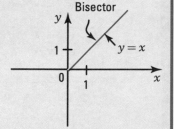

---

1. In each of the following cases, describe the geometric locus and give its equation if it is the set of points in the Cartesian plane

a) located 2 units from the x-axis and having a positive y-coordinate.

_____

b) located 3 units from the y-axis and having a negative x-coordinate.

_____

c) whose distances from the x-axis and the y-axis are equal.

_____

7.2 Circle

a) What is the definition of a circle of radius r centred at the origin?

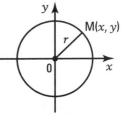

_____

b) Justify the steps allowing us to find the equation of a circle $\mathcal{C}$ of radius r centred at $O(0, 0)$.

	Steps	Justifications
1.	$M(x, y) \in \mathcal{C} \Leftrightarrow d(O, M) = r$	
2.	$\Leftrightarrow \sqrt{x^2 + y^2} = r$	
3.	$\Leftrightarrow x^2 + y^2 = r^2$	

CIRCLE CENTRED AT THE ORIGIN

- A circle centred at the origin is the set of points M in the plane located at constant distance from the origin.
  - The constant distance is the radius r of the circle.
  - The origin is the centre of the circle.

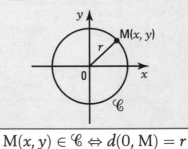

- The standard form of the equation of a circle of radius r centred at $O(0, 0)$ is:

$$\boxed{M(x, y) \in \mathcal{C} \Leftrightarrow d(O, M) = r}$$

$$\boxed{x^2 + y^2 = r^2}$$

1. Find the equation of the circle centred at the origin with radius

    a) $r = 2$ _____   **b)** $r = \sqrt{3}$ _____

2. Find the equation of the circle centred at the origin passing through $A(-2, 3)$. _____

3. Consider the circle with equation: $x^2 + y^2 = 5$. Indicate if the following points belong to the circle.

    a) $A(-2, 1)$ _____   **b)** $B(1, -2)$ _____   **c)** $C(-2, 2)$ _____

4. Consider the circle with equation: $x^2 + y^2 = 25$. Find the points $M(x, y)$ of the circle that have

    a) an x-coordinate equal to 4. _____

    b) a y-coordinate equal to -2. _____

ACTIVITY 2   Circle not centred at the origin

a) The equation of the circle $\mathscr{C}$ on the right, centred at $0(0, 0)$ with radius 2, is: $x^2 + y^2 = 4$. The image of circle $\mathscr{C}$ under the translation $t: (x, y) \Rightarrow (x + 4, y + 3)$ is circle $\mathscr{C}'$.

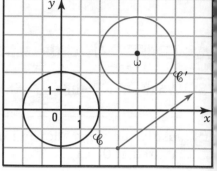

1. What are the coordinate of the centre ω of circle $\mathscr{C}'$?

   _____

2. What is the radius of circle $\mathscr{C}'$? _____

3. What is the equation of circle $\mathscr{C}'$? _____

b) A circle $\mathscr{C}$ of radius r centred at $\omega(h, k)$ is represented on the right.

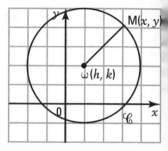

1. What is the property which characterizes every point M on this circle?

   _____

   _____

2. Justify the steps allowing us to find the equation of the circle in the standard form.

	Steps	Justifications
1.	$M(x, y) \in \mathscr{C} \Leftrightarrow \qquad d(\omega, M) = r$	
2.	$\Leftrightarrow \sqrt{(x - h)^2 + (y - k)^2} = r$	
3.	$\Leftrightarrow (x - h)^2 + (y - k)^2 = r^2$	

EQUATION OF A CIRCLE: STANDARD FORM

- The set of points M in the plane located at the same distance r from the centre ω, written $\mathscr{C}(\omega, r)$, is called circle $\mathscr{C}$ of radius r centred at ω.

$$M \in \mathscr{C}(\omega, r) \Leftrightarrow d(\omega, M) = r$$

- The standard form of the equation of a circle of radius r centred at $\omega(h, k)$ is:

$$(x - h)^2 + (y - k)^2 = r^2$$

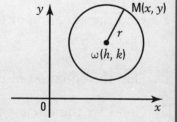

Ex.: The equation, in standard form, of the circle of radius $r = 5$ centred at $\omega(-3, 2)$ is:
$(x + 3)^2 + (y - 2)^2 = 25$.

---

5. Consider the circle $\mathscr{C}$ of radius 3 units centred at $0(0, 0)$ and the translation $t: (x, y) \rightarrow (x - 1, y + 2)$.

   a) Find the equation of circle $\mathscr{C}$. _____

   b) We draw circle $\mathscr{C}'$, image of circle $\mathscr{C}$, under translation t.

      1. Determine the coordinates of the centre of circle $\mathscr{C}'$ and its radius.

      _____

      2. Find the equation of circle $\mathscr{C}'$. _____

6. Determine the centre ω and the radius r of the following circles.

   a) $(x - 3)^2 + (y - 4)^2 = 16$ _____

   b) $(x + 2)^2 + (y - 1)^2 = 9$ _____

   c) $(x + 3)^2 + (y + 1)^2 = 17$ _____

   d) $\dfrac{(x+2)^2}{3} + \dfrac{(y-7)^2}{3} = 12$ _____

7. Find the equation of the circle, in the standard form, knowing the centre ω and a point M on the circle.

   a) $\omega(1, 3)$ and $M(1, 7)$ _____

   b) $\omega(-4, 5)$ and $M(2, -3)$ _____

8. The points $A(-1, 2)$ and $B(-3, -4)$ are the endpoints of a diameter AB of a circle. Find the equation, in the standard form, of this circle.

_____

9. The equation of a circle centred at the origin is $x^2 + y^2 = 16$.

Describe the translation which associates, with this circle, the circle of equation

   a) $(x - 1)^2 + (y + 4)^2 = 16$: _____

   b) $x^2 + (y - 3)^2 = 16$: _____

   c) $(x + 2)^2 + y^2 = 16$: _____

   d) $(x + 1)^2 + (y + 3)^2 = 16$: _____

ACTIVITY 3   Equation of a circle: general form

a) Consider the circle of radius $r = 4$ centred at $\omega(-1, 2)$.

   1. Find the equation of the circle in the standard form. _____

   2. Expand the standard equation in order to write the equation in the form
$x^2 + y^2 + ax + by + c = 0$, called **general form** of the equation of a circle.

_____

b) Each of the following expressions is a perfect square trinomial. Complete it and then factor it.

   1. $x^2 + 2x +$ _____ $=$ _____   2. $x^2 - 6x +$ _____ $=$ _____

   3. $y^2 + 4y +$ _____ $=$ _____   4. $y^2 - 8y +$ _____ $=$ _____

   5. $x^2 + 3x +$ _____ $=$ _____   6. $y^2 - 5y +$ _____ $=$ _____

c) The general form of the equation of a circle is: $x^2 + y^2 - 6x + 4y - 12 = 0$.

1. Justify the steps allowing us to write the equation in the standard form.

	Steps	Justifications
1.	$x^2 + y^2 - 6x + 4y - 12 = 0$	
2.	$x^2 - 6x + \ldots + y^2 + 4y + \ldots = 12$	
3.	$x^2 - 6x + 9 + y^2 + 4y + 4 = 12 + 9 + 4$	
4.	$(x - 3)^2 + (y + 2)^2 = 25$	

2. Identify the centre and the radius of the circle. _____

EQUATION OF A CIRCLE – GENERAL FORM

- Expanding the standard form of the equation of a circle $(x - h)^2 + (y - k)^2 = r^2$, we obtain the **general form**

$$x^2 + y^2 + ax + by + c = 0$$

Ex.: $(x + 3)^2 + (y - 2)^2 = 25$ (Standard form)
 $\Leftrightarrow x^2 + 6x + 9 + y^2 - 4y + 4 = 25$
 $\Leftrightarrow x^2 + y^2 + 6x - 4y - 12 = 0$ (General form)

- The curve with equation: $x^2 + y^2 + ax + by + c = 0$ is represented by a circle in the Cartesian plane if and only if $a^2 + b^2 > 4c$.

- From the general form of the equation of a circle, we can find the standard form of the circle equation (See activity 3c)).

---

10. In each of the following cases, find the equation of circle $\mathscr{C}$ in the standard form and then in the general form.

a) Centre $(-1, 3)$; radius 2.
 1. _____
 2. _____

b) Centre $(0, -3)$; radius 2.
 1. _____
 2. _____

c) Centre $(2, -1)$; M$(-1, 3) \in \mathscr{C}$.
 1. _____
 2. _____

d) $\overline{AB}$ is a diameter, A$(-2, 1)$ and B$(4, -3)$.
 1. _____
 2. _____

11. For each of the following circles,
 1. write the equation of the circle in the standard form.
 2. find the centre and the radius of the circle.

a) $x^2 + y^2 - 2x + 4y - 4 = 0$

_____

_____

b) $x^2 + y^2 + 8x + 4y + 19 = 0$

_____

_____

c) $x^2 + y^2 - 4x + 6y - 4 = 0$

d) $x^2 + y^2 - x + 3y - 1.5 = 0$

_____

_____

_____

_____

12. Explain why each of the following equations is not that of a circle.

a) $x^2 + y^2 - 4x + 6y + 14 = 0$ _____

b) $x^2 - y^2 - 2x - 4y - 19 = 0$ _____

13. Determine, if they exist, the intersection points of circle $\mathscr{C}$ with line l.

a) $\mathscr{C}: (x - 1)^2 + (y + 2)^2 = 9$
$l: y = -x + 2$

b) $\mathscr{C}: (x + 1)^2 + (y - 2)^2 = 2$
$l: x - y + 1 = 0$

c) $\mathscr{C}: (x + 2)^2 + (y + 1)^2 = 1$
$l: x - y - 1 = 0$

_____

_____

_____

d) $\mathscr{C}: x^2 + y^2 - 2x + 4y + 1 = 0$
$l: x - y - 1 = 0$

e) $\mathscr{C}: x^2 + y^2 = 9$
$l: x + y = 5$

f) $\mathscr{C}: x^2 + y^2 - 2x + 4y - 20 = 0$
$l: 3x + 4y - 20 = 0$

_____

_____

_____

14. Represent the solution set of the following inequalities in the Cartesian plane.

a) $x^2 + y^2 \leqslant 9$

b) $(x - 2)^2 + (y - 1)^2 \geqslant 4$

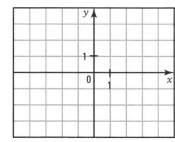

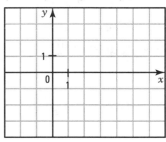

c) $x^2 + y^2 + 4x + 2y + 1 < 0$

d) $x^2 + y^2 + 2x - 3 > 0$

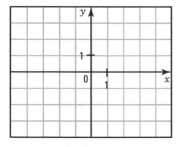

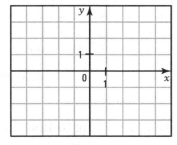

15. For each of the following regions, determine the inequality that defines it.

a)

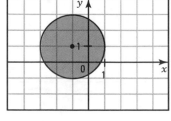

b)

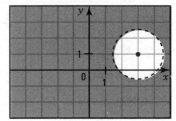

_____

_____

ACTIVITY 4 Line tangent to a circle

Consider on the right the circle $\mathscr{C}$ with equation: $(x-2)^2 + (y-1)^2 = 5$ and point $A(1, 3)$ on this circle.

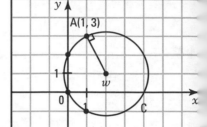

a) Find the coordinates of the centre ω of this circle. _____

b) Draw the line l passing through point A and perpendicular to the radius ωA.

This line l intersects circle $\mathscr{C}$ in only one point. Line l is called tangent to the circle at point A.

c) Find the equation of line l. _____

LINE TANGENT TO A CIRCLE

- A line is **tangent** to a circle if it intersects the circle in only one point called **point of tangency**.

  Ex.: Given the circle on the right,
  - line l is tangent to the circle at point A.
  - A is the point of tangency.

- **Properties of the tangent:**
  - The tangent is perpendicular to the radius at the point of tangency.

    $$\boxed{l \perp \overline{\omega A}}$$

  - The distance between the centre ω and the tangent l is equal to the radius r.

    $$\boxed{d(\omega, l) = r}$$

  - Given a point A on a circle, there exists **only one** line tangent to the circle at point A.

---

16. Consider the circle with equation: $(x+1)^2 + (y-2)^2 = 25$.

a) Verify that point $A(2, 6)$ is a point on this circle. _____

b) What are the coordinates of the centre ω of the circle? _____

c) Explain the procedure to find the equation of the line l tangent to the circle at point A.

_____

_____

_____

d) Find the equation of the tangent l at point A.

_____

17. Use the data from exercise 16. Justify the steps allowing us to find the equation of the tangent l at point A using the scalar product.

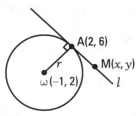

Steps	Justifications
1. $M(x, y) \in d \Leftrightarrow \overrightarrow{AM} \perp \overrightarrow{A\omega}$	
2. $\Leftrightarrow \overrightarrow{AM} \cdot \overrightarrow{A\omega} = 0$	
3. $\Leftrightarrow (x - 2, y - 6) \cdot (-3, -4) = 0$	
4. $\Leftrightarrow -3(x - 2) - 4(y - 6) = 0$	
5. $\Leftrightarrow -3x - 4y + 30 = 0$	
6. $\Leftrightarrow y = -\frac{3}{4}x + \frac{15}{2}$	

18. Find the equation of the tangent to the circle with equation: $x^2 + y^2 - 2x + 4y - 35 = 0$ at point $A(3, 4)$.

_____

19. Find the equation of the circle with centre $\omega(-2, 3)$ if the circle is tangent to

a) the x-axis. _____   b) the y-axis. _____

20. Consider the line $l: 2x + y - 4 = 0$ and a point $\omega(1, -3)$.

a) Find the equation of the circle $\mathscr{C}$ centred at ω and tangent to line l.

_____

b) Find the coordinates of the point of tangency A. _____

21. Consider the circle $\mathscr{C}$ with equation: $x^2 + y^2 = 18$.

a) Find the coordinates of points A_1 and A_2 on the circle which have an x-coordinate equal to 3. _____

b) Find the equation of the lines l_1 and l_2 tangent to circle $\mathscr{C}$ at points A_1 and A_2 respectively.

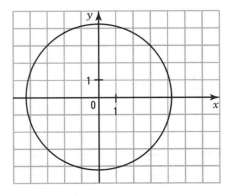

_____

c) Show that lines l_1 and l_2 meet at a point P located on the x-axis.

_____

d) Show that the quadrilateral $0A_1PA_2$ is a square.

_____

_____

e) Calculate the area of the region bounded by the line segment PA_1, the line segment PA_2 and the arc of circle A_1A_2. _____

_____

7.3 Ellipse

Consider two points $F_1(-4, 0)$ and $F_2(4, 0)$ located on the x-axis.

The set of points M in the plane such that the sum of the distances $d(M, F_1) + d(M, F_2) = 10$ is an **ellipse** with foci at points F_1 and F_2.

The four points $A_1(-5, 0)$, $A_2(5, 0)$, $B_1(0, -3)$ and $B_2(0, 3)$ represent the **vertices** of the ellipse.

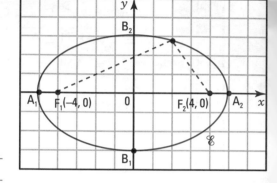

a) Verify that

1. $d(A_1, F_1) + d(A_2, F_2) = 10$ _____
2. $d(A_2, F_1) + d(A_2, F_2) = 10$ _____
3. $d(B_1, F_1) + d(B_1, F_2) = 10$ _____
4. $d(B_2, F_1) + d(B_2, F_2) = 10$ _____

b) Justify the steps allowing us to find the equation of this ellipse $\mathscr{E}$.

	Steps	Justifications
1.	$M(x, y) \in \mathscr{E} \Leftrightarrow d(M_1F_2) + d(M_1F_2) = 10$	
2.	$\Leftrightarrow \sqrt{(x+4)^2 + y^2} + \sqrt{(x-4)^2 + y^2} = 10$	
3.	$\Leftrightarrow \sqrt{(x+4)^2 + y^2} = 10 - \sqrt{(x-4)^2 + y^2}$	
4.	$\Leftrightarrow (x+4)^2 + y^2 = 100 + (x-4)^2 + y^2 - 20\sqrt{(x-4)^2 + y^2}$	
5.	$\Leftrightarrow x^2 + 8x + 16 + y^2 = 100 + x^2 - 8x + 16 + y^2 - 20\sqrt{(x-4)^2 + y^2}$	
6.	$\Leftrightarrow 16x - 100 = -20\sqrt{(x-4)^2 + y^2}$	
7.	$\Leftrightarrow (16x - 100)^2 = 400\left[(x-4)^2 + y^2\right]$	
8.	$\Leftrightarrow 256x^2 - 3200x + 10\ 000 = 400(x^2 - 8x + 16 + y^2)$	
9.	$\Leftrightarrow 256x^2 - 3200x + 10\ 000 = 400x^2 - 3200x + 6400 + 400y^2$	
10.	$\Leftrightarrow 144x^2 + 400y^2 = 3600$	
11.	$\Leftrightarrow \dfrac{x^2}{25} + \dfrac{y^2}{9} = 1$	

c) The equation of the ellipse in b) is in the form $\dfrac{x^2}{a^2} + \dfrac{y^2}{b^2} = 1$ $(a > 0, b > 0)$ called **standard form**.

1. Identify parameters a and b. _____
2. Verify that the major axis A_1A_2 containing the foci has a length of $2a$. _____
3. Verify that the minor axis B_1B_2 has a length of $2b$. _____
4. If $2c$ is the distance between the foci, identify c and verify that $b^2 + c^2 = a^2$.

_____

ELLIPSE CENTRED AT THE ORIGIN

- The **ellipse** with **foci** F_1 and F_2 is the set of all points M of the plane for which the sum of the distances to the foci is **constant**.
- We distinguish two cases according to the position of the **major axis** containing the foci.

Horizontal major axis	Vertical major axis
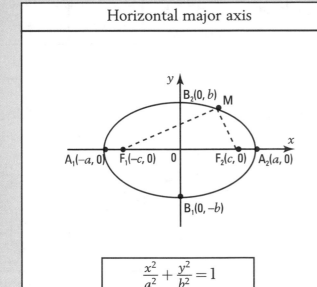	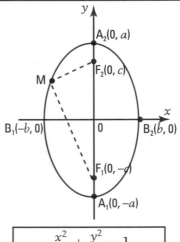
$\dfrac{x^2}{a^2} + \dfrac{y^2}{b^2} = 1$	$\dfrac{x^2}{b^2} + \dfrac{y^2}{a^2} = 1$

- For every point M on the ellipse we have: $\boxed{d(M, F_1) + d(M, F_2) = 2a}$

- The four **vertices** of the ellipse are: A_1, A_2, B_1 and B_2.
- The **major axis** is the line segment A_1A_2 with length $2a$. $(a > 0)$
  The foci F_1 and F_2 are located on the major axis.
- The **minor axis** is the line segment B_1B_2 with length $2b$. $(b > 0)$
- The **focal distance** is the length $2c$ between the foci F_1 and F_2. $(c > 0)$
- The axes of the ellipse are axes of symmetry.
- The centre 0 of the ellipse is a centre of symmetry.
- The parameters a, b and c of the ellipse verify Pythagoras' relation: $\boxed{a^2 = b^2 + c^2}$

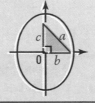

Ex.: $\dfrac{x^2}{25} + \dfrac{y^2}{9} = 1$ We have: $a = 5, b = 3, c = 4$ $A_1(-5, 0), A_2(0, 5)$ $B_1(0, -3), B_2(0, 3)$ $F_1(-4, 0), F_2(4, 0)$ 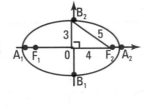	**Ex.:** $\dfrac{x^2}{9} + \dfrac{y^2}{25} = 1$ We have: $a = 5, b = 3, c = 4$ $A_1(0, -5), A_2(0, 5)$ $B_1(-3, 0), B_2(3, 0)$ $F_1(0, -4), F_2(0, 4)$ 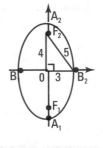

1. Consider the ellipse with equation: $\frac{x^2}{9}+\frac{y^2}{4}=1$.

   a) Draw the ellipse in the Cartesian plane on the right.

   b) Is the major axis horizontal or vertical? _____

   c) Find the coordinates of the vertices. _____

   d) Find the coordinates of the foci F_1 and F_2 and locate the foci in the Cartesian plane. _____

   e) If M is a point on the ellipse, determine $d(M, F_1) + d(M, F_2)$. ____

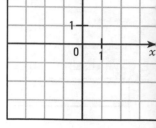

2. Consider the ellipse with equation: $\frac{x^2}{1}+\frac{y^2}{4}=1$.

   a) Draw the ellipse in the Cartesian plane on the right.

   b) Is the major axis horizontal or vertical? _____

   c) Find the coordinates of the vertices. _____

   d) Find the coordinates of the foci F_1 and F_2 and locate the foci in the Cartesian plane.

   _____

   e) If M is a point on the ellipse, determine $d(M, F_1) + d(M, F_2)$. ___

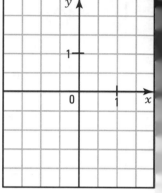

3. **a)** Explain the steps allowing us to write the standard form of the equation of an ellipse centred at the origin in the general form $ax^2 + by^2 + c = 0$.

   $\frac{x^2}{9}+\frac{y^2}{4}=1$ (standard form)

   1. $36\left(\frac{x^2}{9}+\frac{y^2}{4}\right)=36$ _____

   2. $4x^2 + 9y^2 = 36$ _____

   3. $4x^2 + 9y^2 - 36 = 0$ _____

   b) Write the equations of the following ellipses in the general form.

   1. $\frac{x^2}{4}+\frac{y^2}{5}=1$ 2. $x^2+\frac{y^2}{9}=1$ 3. $\frac{x^2}{\frac{4}{9}}+\frac{y^2}{16}=1$

   _____   _____   _____

4. Complete the following table.

Equation of the ellipse	Position of the major axis	Coordinates of the vertices	Coordinates of the foci	Length of the major axis	Length of the minor axis
$\frac{x^2}{169}+\frac{y^2}{25}=1$					
$\frac{x^2}{36}+\frac{y^2}{100}=1$					
$x^2 + 4y^2 - 4 = 0$					
$25x^2 + 4y^2 - 100 = 0$					

5. Determine the equation of each of the following ellipses.

a)
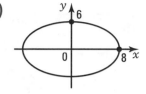

b)
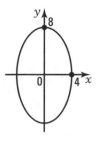

c)
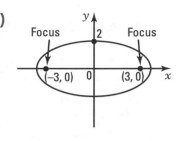

_____   _____   _____

d)
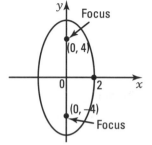

e)
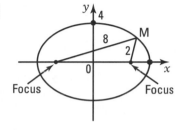

f)
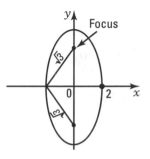

_____   _____   _____

6. Determine the coordinates of the foci of an ellipse centred at the origin whose vertices are the points

a) $(6, 0)$ and $(0, 4)$ _____   b) $(6, 0)$ and $(0, 7)$ _____

c) $(-10, 0)$ and $(0, -6)$ _____   d) $(-4, 0)$ and $(0, -6)$ _____

7. In each of the following cases, find the equation of the ellipse in the standard form.

a) The major axis of length 20 units is horizontal and the minor axis measures 12 units.

_____

b) The major axis of length 16 units is vertical and the minor axis measures 10 units.

_____

c) The major axis of length 10 units is horizontal and the focal distance measures 6 units.

_____

d) The major axis of length 20 units is vertical and the focal distance measures 16 units.

_____

8. Represent the following inequalities in the Cartesian plane.

a) $\dfrac{x^2}{9} + \dfrac{y^2}{4} \leqslant 1$ b) $9x^2 + 4y^2 - 16 \geqslant 0$ c) $x^2 + 4y^2 - 4 < 0$

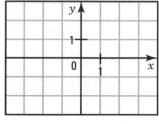
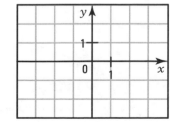
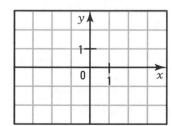

9. Describe each of the following regions using an inequality.

a)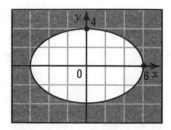

b)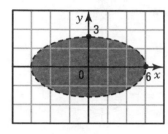

c)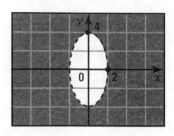

_____   _____   _____

10. Represent the following systems in the Cartesian plane.

a) $\begin{cases} 9x^2 + 25y^2 - 225 \leqslant 0 \\ 3x + 5y - 15 \geqslant 0 \end{cases}$

b) $\begin{cases} x^2 + y^2 - 9 \leqslant 0 \\ 9x^2 + 4y^2 - 36 \geqslant 0 \end{cases}$

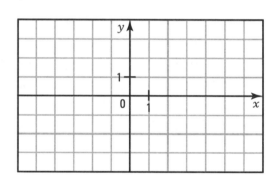

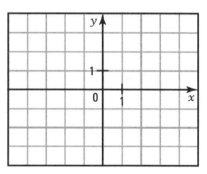

11. Describe each of the following shaded regions using a system of inequalities.

a)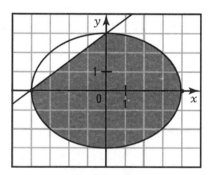

b)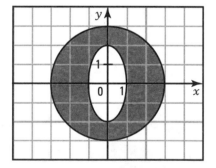

_____   _____

12. Determine the coordinates of the intersection points of the ellipse with equation $x^2 + 4y^2 - 25 = 0$ and the line with equation $x + 2y - 7 = 0$.

_____

13. An art exhibit is presented in a room whose ceiling has the shape of a half-ellipse as shown on the figure on the right.

Spotlights are installed on the ceiling at a horizontal distance of 5 m from the edges of the ceiling.

What is the height of the spotlights, as measured from the floor?

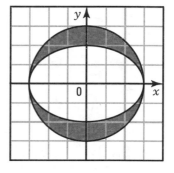

_____

14. The circle with equation: $x^2 + y^2 = 9$ and the ellipse with equation: $4x^2 + 9y^2 - 36 = 0$ are represented on the right. Calculate the area of the shaded region.

Note: The area of an ellipse with major axis measuring $2a$ and minor axis measuring $2b$ is equal to πab.

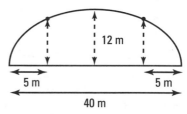

_____

15. A race track has an elliptical shape. The length of the major axis is 80 m and the focal distance is 64 m.

What is the length of the minor axis? _____

16. The measure of the chord perpendicular to the major axis and passing through one of the foci of an ellipse is called **latus rectum**.

Calculate the measure of the latus rectum of an ellipse defined by the equation $9x^2 + 25y^2 - 225 = 0$.

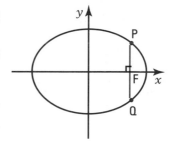

_____

_____

17. A rectangular garden has a perimeter of 72 m and an area of 320 m². A landscape architect wants to create a flowerbed shaped as an ellipse in this garden. Using a sketch, give the dimensions of the ellipse and locate the foci so that the flowerbed has maximum area.

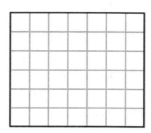

_____

7.4 Hyperbola

Consider two points $F_1(-5, 0)$ and $F_2(5, 0)$ located on the x-axis.
The set of points M of the plane such that the absolute value of the difference $|d(M, F_1) - d(M, F_2)| = 8$ is a **hyperbola** whose **foci** are the points F_1 and F_2.
The two points $A_1(-4, 0)$ and $A_2(4, 0)$ represent the **vertices** of the hyperbola.

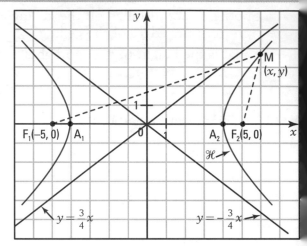

a) Verify that

1. $|d(A_1, F_1) - d(A_1, F_2)| = 8$

   _____

2. $|d(A_2, F_1) - d(A_2, F_2)| = 8$

   _____

b) Justify the steps allowing us to find the equation of the hyperbola $\mathcal{H}$.

	Étapes	Justifications
1.	$M(x, y) \in \mathcal{H} \Leftrightarrow |d(M, F_1) - d(M, F_2)| = 8$	
2.	$\Leftrightarrow \left| \sqrt{(x+5)^2 + y^2} - \sqrt{(x-5)^2 + y^2} \right| = 8$	
3.	$\Leftrightarrow \sqrt{(x+5)^2 + y^2} - \sqrt{(x-5)^2 + y^2} = \pm 8$	
4.	$\Leftrightarrow \sqrt{(x+5)^2 + y^2} = \sqrt{(x-5)^2 + y^2} \pm 8$	
5.	$\Leftrightarrow (x+5)^2 + y^2 = (x-5)^2 + y^2 + 64 \pm 16\sqrt{(x-5)^2 + y^2}$	
6.	$\Leftrightarrow x^2 + 10x + 25 + y^2 = x^2 - 10x + 25 + y^2 + 64 \pm 16\sqrt{(x-5)^2 + y^2}$	
7.	$\Leftrightarrow 20x - 64 = \pm 16\sqrt{(x-5)^2 + y^2}$	
8.	$\Leftrightarrow (20x - 64)^2 = 256\left[(x-5)^2 + y^2\right]$	
9.	$\Leftrightarrow 400x^2 - 2560x + 4096 = 256x^2 - 2560x + 6400 + 256y^2$	
10.	$\Leftrightarrow 144x^2 - 256y^2 = 2304$	
11.	$\Leftrightarrow \quad \dfrac{x^2}{16} - \dfrac{y^2}{9} = 1$	

The equation of the hyperbola obtained in b) is in the form $\dfrac{x^2}{a^2} - \dfrac{y^2}{b^2} = 1$ called **standard form**.

c) 1. Identify the parameters a and b. _____

   2. If the focal distance (distance between the foci) is $2c$, identify c and verify that $a^2 + b^2 = c^2$. _____

   3. Draw the rectangle having vertices: (a, b), $(-a, b)$, $(-a, -b)$, and $(a, -b)$ then verify that the diagonals of this rectangle are supported by the asymptotes of the hyperbola.

HYPERBOLA CENTRED AT THE ORIGIN

- The **hyperbola** with foci F_1 and F_2 is the set of all points M of the plane such that the absolute value of the difference of the distances to the foci is **constant**.
- We distinguish two cases according to the position of the **transverse axis** containing the foci.

Horizontal transverse axis	Vertical transverse axis
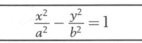	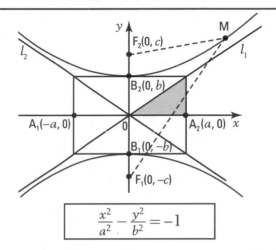
$$\frac{x^2}{a^2} - \frac{y^2}{b^2} = 1$$	$$\frac{x^2}{a^2} - \frac{y^2}{b^2} = -1$$
• The vertices are: $A_1(-a, 0)$ and $A_2(a, 0)$.	• The vertices are: $B_1(0, -b)$ and $B_2(0, b)$.
• The foci are: $F_1(-c, 0)$ and $F_2(c, 0)$.	• The foci are: $0\ F_1(0, -c)$ and $F_2(0, c)$.
• The transverse axis A_1A_2 has length $2a$. $(a > 0)$	• The transverse axis B_1B_2 has length $2b$. $(b > 0)$
• The conjugate axis B_1B_2 has length $2b$. $(b > 0)$	• The conjugate axis A_1A_2 has length $2a$. $(a > 0)$
• For every point on the hyperbola, we have:	• For every point on the hyperbola, we have:
$$\boxed{|d(M, F_1) - d(M, F_2)| = 2a}$$	$$\boxed{|d(M, F_1) - d(M, F_2)| = 2b}$$

- The **focal distance** is the distance $2c$ between the foci $(c > 0)$.
- The axes of the hyperbola are axes of symmetry and the origin 0 is a centre of symmetry.
- The hyperbola has two asymptotes passing through the origin: $l_1: y = \frac{b}{a}x$ and $l_2: y = \frac{-b}{a}x$.
- The parameters a, b and c of the hyperbola verify the relation:

$$\boxed{a^2 + b^2 = c^2}$$

Ex.: $\dfrac{x^2}{16} - \dfrac{y^2}{9} = 1$

We have:

$a = 4$, $b = 3$, $c = 5$

Vertices: $A_1(-4, 0)$; $A_2(4, 0)$

Foci: $F_1(-5, 0)$; $F_2(5, 0)$

For every point M on the hyperbola, we have:
$|d(M, F_1) - d(M, F_2)| = 2a = 8$

Asymptotes: $l_1: y = \frac{3}{4}x$; $l_2: y = -\frac{3}{4}x$.

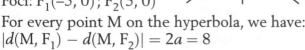

Ex.: $\dfrac{x^2}{16} - \dfrac{y^2}{9} = -1$

We have:

$a = 4$, $b = 3$, $c = 5$

Vertices: $B_1(0, -3)$, $B_2(0, 3)$

Foci: $F_1(0, -5)$, $F_2(0, 5)$

For every point M on the hyperbola, we have:
$|d(M, F_1) - d(M, F_2)| = 2b = 6$

Asymptotes: $l_1: y = \frac{3}{4}x$; $l_2: y = -\frac{3}{4}x$.

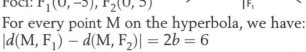

DRAWING THE HYPERBOLA

Let us use the following procedure to draw the hyperbola centred at the origin with equation: $\dfrac{x^2}{9} - \dfrac{y^2}{4} = 1$

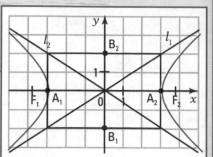

	Horizontal transverse axis
– We identify the position of the transverse axis according to the equation model. – We identify the parameters a and b.	$a = 3; b = 2$
– We deduce the parameter c knowing that $a^2 + b^2 = c^2$.	$c = \sqrt{13}$
– We locate the vertices A_1, A_2 and the foci F_1, F_2 on the transverse axis.	$A_1(-3, 0), A_2(3, 0)$ $F_1\left(-\sqrt{13}, 0\right), F_2\left(\sqrt{13}, 0\right)$
– We draw the asymptotes l_1 and l_2, supporting the diagonals of the rectangle centred at 0 with vertices $(a, b), (-a, b), (-a, -b),$ and $(a, -b)$. – We draw the hyperbola using a table of values.	$l_1 : y = \dfrac{2}{3}x$ $l_2 : y = \dfrac{-2}{3}x$

x	3	$\sqrt{13}$	4	5
y	0	$1.\overline{3}$	1.76	$2.\overline{6}$

– We draw one branch of the hyperbola approaching the asymptotes.
– We deduce the other branch by symmetry.

1. Consider the hyperbola $\dfrac{x^2}{9} - \dfrac{y^2}{4} = -1$.

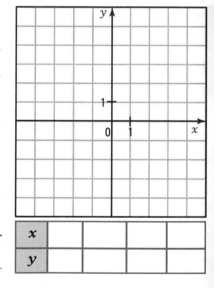

a) What is the position of the transverse axis? _Vertical_

b) Identify the parameters a, b and c. _$a=3$ $b=2$ $c=\sqrt{13}$_

c) Determine the coordinates of the vertices and the foci.

_____

d) Determine
  1. the length of the transverse axis. _____
  2. the length of the conjugate axis. _____
  3. the focal distance. _____

e) Draw the asymptotes of the hyperbola and determine their equation. _____

x				
y				

f) Draw the hyperbola.

g) If M is a point on the hyperbola, complete: $|d(M, F_1) - d(M, F_2)| = $ _____

h) Verify that the circle of radius c centred at 0 passes through the foci of the hyperbola and through the vertices $(a, b), (-a, b), (-a, -b)$ and $(a, -b)$ of the rectangle.

2. Consider the hyperbola $\frac{x^2}{9} - \frac{y^2}{16} = 1$.

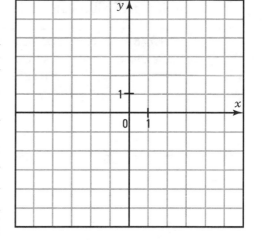

 a) What is the position of the transverse axis? _____

 b) Identify the parameters a, b and c. _____

 c) Determine the coordinates of the vertices and the foci.

 _____

 d) Determine

  1. the length of the transverse axis. _____

  2. the length of the conjugate axis. _____

  3. the focal distance. _____

 e) Draw the asymptotes of the hyperbola and determine

  their equation. _____

 f) Draw the hyperbola.

 g) If M is a point on the hyperbola, complete: $|d(M, F_1) - d(M, F_2)| =$ __

x	3	4	5
y			

 h) Verify that the circle of radius c centred at 0 passes through the foci of the hyperbola and through the vertices (a, b), $(-a, b)$, $(-a, -b)$ and $(a, -b)$ of the rectangle.

3. When the parameters a and b of the equation of the hyperbola $\frac{x^2}{a^2} - \frac{y^2}{b^2} = 1$ or $\frac{x^2}{a^2} - \frac{y^2}{b^2} = -1$ are equal, the hyperbola is called **equilateral**.

 a) 1. Determine the equations of the asymptotes of an
   equilateral hyperbola. _____

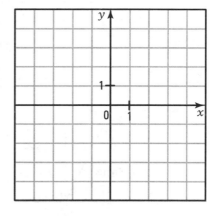

  2. Are the asymptotes of an equilateral hyperbola
   perpendicular? _____

 b) Draw, in the same Cartesian plane,

  1. the equilateral hyperbola with equation: $x^2 - y^2 = 4$.

  2. the equilateral hyperbola with equation: $x^2 - y^2 = -4$.

4. Write the equation of the following hyperbolas in the general form $ax^2 + by^2 + c = 0$.

 a) $\frac{x^2}{16} - \frac{y^2}{9} = 1$ **b)** $\frac{x^2}{36} - \frac{y^2}{64} = -1$ **c)** $\frac{x^2}{\frac{9}{16}} - \frac{y^2}{\frac{25}{16}} = 1$

 _____   _____   _____

5. Complete the following table.

Equation of the hyperbola	Position of the transverse axis	Coordinates of the vertices	Coordinates of the foci	Length of transverse axis	Length of conjugate axis	Equations of the asymptotes
$\dfrac{x^2}{9} - \dfrac{y^2}{16} = 1$						
$\dfrac{x^2}{9} - \dfrac{y^2}{16} = -1$						
$64x^2 - 36y^2 - 2304 = 0$						
$x^2 - 2y^2 + 2 = 0$						

6. For each of the following hyperbolas, determine its equation.

a)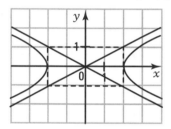

_____

b)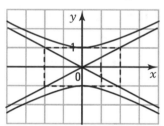

_____

c)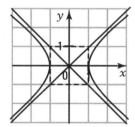

_____

d)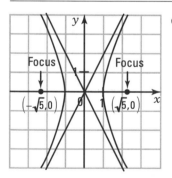

_____

e)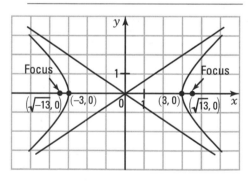

_____

f)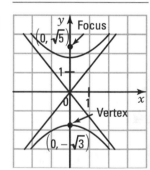

_____

7. Determine the coordinates of the foci of a hyperbola centred at the origin in each case.

a) The hyperbola has equation: $\dfrac{x^2}{3} - \dfrac{y^2}{2} = -1$. _____

b) The hyperbola has equation: $\dfrac{x^2}{4} - \dfrac{y^2}{5} = 1$. _____

c) The focal distance is equal to 12 and the transverse axis is vertical. _____

d) $(8, 0)$ is a vertex of the hyperbola and one of the asymptotes has equation: $y = \dfrac{3}{4}x$.

_____

8. Determine the coordinates of the vertices of a hyperbola centred at he origin in each of the following cases.

a) The hyperbola has equation: $\dfrac{x^2}{4} - \dfrac{y^2}{16} = -1$. _____

b) The hyperbola has equation: $\dfrac{x^2}{5} - \dfrac{y^2}{4} = 1$. _____

c) The transverse axis is horizontal and measures 6 units. _____

d) The conjugate axis is horizontal and has length 6 units and the focal distance is equal to 10 units.

_____

9. In each of the following cases, determine the equation of the hyperbola centred at the origin.

a) $F_1(-4, 0)$ and $F_2(4, 0)$ are the foci and $A_1(-3, 0)$ and $A_2(3, 0)$ are the vertices. _____

b) $F_1(0, -3)$ and $F_2(0, 3)$ are the foci and $B_1(0, -2)$ and $B_2(0, 2)$ are the vertices. _____

c) The transverse axis is vertical and measures 8 units and the focal distance is equal to 10 units.

_____

d) $(-2, 0)$ is a vertex of the hyperbola and one of the asymptotes has equation: $y = \dfrac{3}{2}x$.

_____

10. Represent the following inequalities in the Cartesian plane.

a) $x^2 - y^2 \leqslant 1$

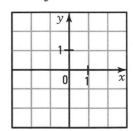

b) $\dfrac{x^2}{4} - y^2 \leqslant -1$

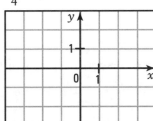

c) $x^2 - y^2 < -1$

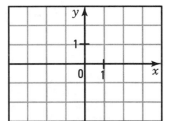

11. Describe each of the following regions using an inequality.

a)

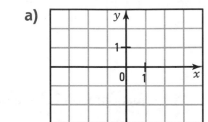

b)

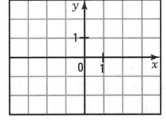

c)

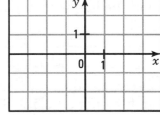

_____   _____   _____

12. Represent the following systems.

a) $\begin{cases} x^2 - y^2 \leqslant 1 \\ x^2 + y^2 \leqslant 4 \end{cases}$

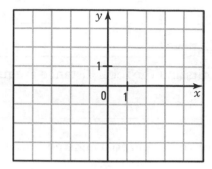

b) $\begin{cases} x^2 - y^2 \geqslant 1 \\ 4x^2 + 9y^2 - 36 \leqslant 0 \end{cases}$

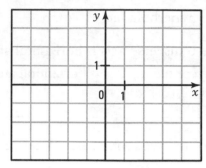

13. Describe each of the following shaded regions using a system of inequalities.

a)

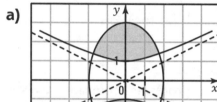

b)

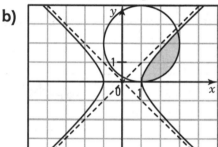

_____   _____

14. Determine the coordinates of the intersection points of the hyperbola with equation: $x^2 - y^2 = 1$ and the circle with equation: $x^2 + y^2 = 7$.

_____

15. Determine the coordinates of the intersection points of the hyperbola with equation: $x^2 - y^2 = -1$ and the line with equation: $y = 2x + 1$.

_____

16. Determine the coordinates of the intersection points of the ellipse with equation: $x^2 + 2y^2 - 2 = 0$ and the hyperbola with equation: $x^2 - 2y^2 + 2 = 0$.

_____

17. The logo of a company is represented on the right.

The curve shown is a hyperbola with equation: $16x^2 - 9y^2 = 3600$ where the measurement unit is the millimetre.

The line segment AB passes through the focus F of the hyperbola and is perpendicular to the transverse axis.

What is, rounded to the nearest hundredth of a unit, the length of line segment AB?

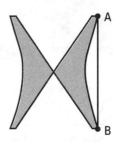

_____

_____

18. The outline of a chimney shaped like a hyperbola is represented on the right. The focal distance is equal to 10 m.

Determine, to the nearest hundredth of a unit, the height h of the chimney.

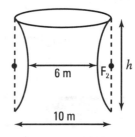

_____

_____

19. A mechanical part is composed of an ellipse and two arcs of hyperbola. The foci of the ellipse are the vertices of the hyperbola and the foci of the hyperbola correspond to two vertices of the ellipse.

The focal distance of the ellipse is equal to 16 cm while the focal distance of the hyperbola is equal to 20 cm. The width w of the mechanical part is equal to the measure of the minor axis of the ellipse. Determine the length L of the part, to the nearest tenth of a unit.

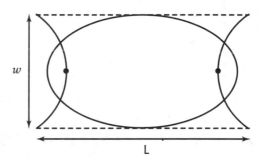

_____

_____

20. The two shores of a lake are shaped like the two branches of a hyperbola around the area where the distance between the shores is the shortest. We observed that the shortest distance is 30 m and that the focal distance is 50 m. What distance, rounded to the nearest unit, must we travel to cross this lake in the direction parallel to the transverse axis and at a distance of 15 m from this axis?

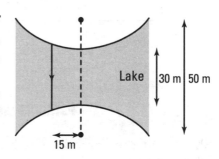

_____

_____

7.5 Parabola

Consider the line l with equation: $y = -c$ and the point $F(0, c)$, $(c > 0)$. The set of points M of the plane whose distances from line l and point F are equal is a **parabola** whose **focus** is point F and whose **directrix** is line l.

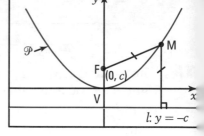

a) Verify that the vertex $V(0, 0)$ of the parabola is at the same distance from the focus F and the directrix l.

b) Justify the steps allowing us to find the equation of parabola $\mathcal{P}$.

	Steps	Justifications
1.	$M(x, y) \in \mathcal{P} \Leftrightarrow d(M, F) = d(M, l)$	
2.	$\Leftrightarrow \sqrt{x^2 + (y-c)^2} = y + c$	
3.	$\Leftrightarrow x^2 + (y-c)^2 = (y+c)^2$	
4.	$\Leftrightarrow x^2 + y^2 - 2cy + c^2 = y^2 + 2cy + c^2$	
5.	$\Leftrightarrow x^2 = 4cy$	

Activity 2 **Parabola with vertex V(0, 0) open downwards**

Show that the parabola $\mathcal{P}$ whose focus is the point $F(0, -c)$, $(c > 0)$ and whose directrix is the line $l: y = c$ has equation: $x^2 = -4cy$.

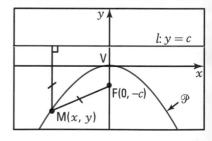

_____

_____

Activity 3 **Parabola with vertex V(0, 0) open to the right**

Show that the parabola $\mathcal{P}$ whose focus is the point $F(c, 0)$, $c > 0$ and whose directrix is the line $l: x = -c$ has equation: $y^2 = 4cx$.

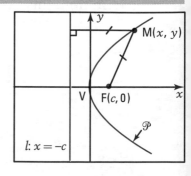

_____

_____

ACTIVITY 4 Parabola with vertex V(0, 0) open to the left

Show that the parabola $\mathcal{P}$ whose focus is the point $F(-c, 0)$, $(c > 0)$ and whose directrix is the line $l : x = c$ has equation: $y^2 = -4cx$.

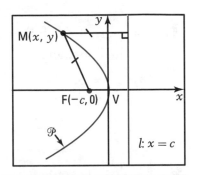

PARABOLA WITH VERTEX V(0, 0)

- The parabola with focus F and directrix l (line not passing through the focus) is the set of all points M of the plane whose distances from the focus and the directrix are equal.
- We distinguish four cases according to the concavity of the parabola with vertex $V(0, 0)$.

Concave upwards	Concave downwards
M F(0, c) V $l : y = -c$ $$x^2 = 4cy$$	$l : y = c$ V F(0, −c) M $$x^2 = -4cy$$

Concave to the right	Concave to the left
$l : x = -c$ M V F(c, 0) $$y^2 = 4cx$$	M $l : x = c$ F(−c, 0) V $$y^2 = -4cx$$

- The y-axis is an axis of symmetry when the parabola is concave upwards or downwards. The x-axis is an axis of symmetry when the parabola is concave to the right or to the left.

- In all cases, we have:
  - $d(V, F) = d(V, l) = c$ $(c > 0)$
  - The axis of symmetry passes through the vertex V, the focus F and is perpendicular to the directrix l.

Ex.: The parabola with equation $y^2 = 2x$ $\left(c = \frac{1}{2}\right)$, is open to the right.

We have: $V(0, 0)$; $F\left(\frac{1}{2}, 0\right)$; $l : x = -\frac{1}{2}$;

x	0	1	2	3	4
y	0	$\pm\sqrt{2}$	± 2	$\pm\sqrt{6}$	$\pm 2\sqrt{2}$

---

1. For each of the following parabolas with vertex V(0, 0), determine

    1. the concavity.   2. the coordinates of the focus.   3. the equation of the directrix.

   a) $x^2 = 6y$ **b)** $x^2 = -4y$ **c)** $y^2 = -12x$ **d)** $y^2 = 8x$

    1. _____   1. _____   1. _____   1. _____

    2. _____   2. _____   2. _____   2. _____

    3. _____   3. _____   3. _____   3. _____

2. A parabola with vertex V(0, 0), open to the left, passes through point A(–5, –5). What is its equation? _____

3. A parabola with vertex V(0, 0), passes through point A(4, 4). What is its equation if the parabola is

   a) open upwards? _____   **b)** open to the right? _____

4. Complete the following table knowing that each parabola has vertex V(0, 0).

Equation of the parabola	Focus	Equation of the directrix	Equation of the axis of symmetry	A point on the parabola
$x^2 = -6y$				A(6,)
$y^2 = 8x$	F(2, 0)			A(, –4)
$x^2 = 2y$		$y = -\frac{1}{2}$		A(–4,)
$y^2 = -x$			$y = 0$	A(, 1)

5. Consider the parabola $\mathcal{P}$ with equation: $y^2 = 4x$ and the line l with equation: $2x + y - 4 = 0$.

   a) Determine algebraically the intersection points of parabola $\mathcal{P}$ and line l.

   _____

   b) Represent the parabola and line l in the Cartesian plane and verify the answers found in a).

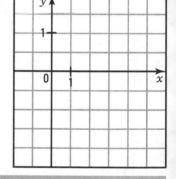

Activity 5 Parabola with vertex V(h, k)

Consider the parabola $\mathcal{P}$ with vertex 0(0, 0), equation $x^2 = 4y$, focus F(0, 1) and directrix $l: y = -1$.

   a) We apply to parabola $\mathcal{P}$, its focus F and its directrix l, the translation t defined by $t: (x, y) \rightarrow (x + 2, y + 3)$.

   Draw the parabola $\mathcal{P}'$, image of parabola $\mathcal{P}$, the image F' of the focus F and the image l' of the directrix l.

   b) What is, for parabola $\mathcal{P}'$

      1. its focus? _____   2. its directrix? _____

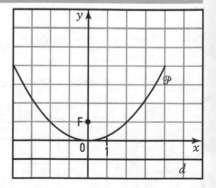

c) Determine
1. the coordinates of the vertex V of parabola $\mathcal{P}'$. _____
2. the coordinates of the focus F' of parabola $\mathcal{P}'$. _____
3. the equation of the directrix l' of parabola $\mathcal{P}'$. _____
4. the equation of the axis of symmetry of $\mathcal{P}'$. _____

d) Deduce the equation (in the standard form) of parabola $\mathcal{P}'$ from the equation of parabola $\mathcal{P}$.
_____

PARABOLA WITH VERTEX V(h, k)

We have the following four situations:

Concave upwards	Concave downwards
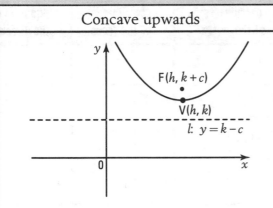	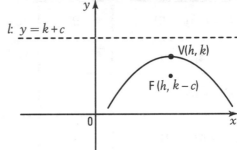
$(x - h)^2 = 4c(y - k)$	$(x - h)^2 = -4c(y - k)$

Concave to the right	Concave to the left
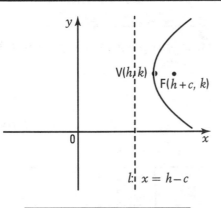	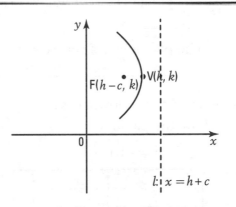
$(y - k)^2 = 4c(x - h)$	$(y - k)^2 = -4c(x - h)$

6. Complete the following table.

Equation of the parabola	Parameter c	Concavity	Coordinates of the vertex	Coordinates of the focus	Equation of the directrix
$(x + 3)^2 = 4(y - 1)$					
$(y - 2)^2 = 2(x + 1)$					
$(x + 1)^2 = -4(y + 3)$					
$(y + 2)^2 = -2(x - 1)$					

7. Complete the following table.

Equation of the parabola	Parameter c	Concavity	Coordinates of the vertex	Coordinates of the focus	Equation of the directrix
$(x - 1)^2 = -6(y + 2)$	$\dfrac{3}{2}$	Downwards	$V(1, -2)$		
$(x + 1)^2 = 4(y - 3)$	1	Upwards	$V(-1, 3)$		
$(y - 2)^2 = -2(x + 1)$			$V(-1, 2)$	$F\left(-\dfrac{3}{2}, 2\right)$	
$(y + 1)^2 = 6(x - 2)$				$F\left(\dfrac{7}{2}, -1\right)$	$x = \dfrac{1}{2}$

8. Determine the equation of the parabola in each of the following cases.

   a) The parabola has focus $F(1, 4)$ and directrix $l: y = 2$. _____

   b) The parabola has vertex $V(-1, 2)$, is open to the right and passes through point $A(3, 6)$.

   _____

   c) The parabola has vertex $V(1, 3)$, is open downwards and passes through point $A(3, 1)$.

   _____

9. In each of the following cases,
   1. draw the parabola.   2. locate the focus F.   3. draw the directrix l.

   a) $(x + 2)^2 = -4(y - 1)$

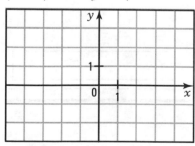

x					
y					

   b) $(y - 1)^2 = -2(x - 3)$

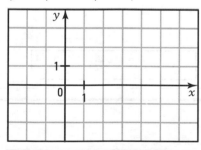

x					
y					

c) $(x + 1)^2 = 2(y + 2)$

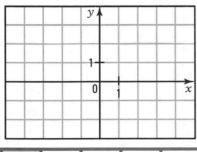

x					
y					

d) $(y - 1)^2 = 4(x + 1)$

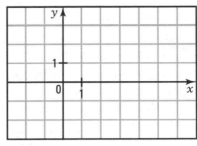

x			
y			

ACTIVITY 6 Equation of the parabola – General form

a) Consider the parabola with equation (standard form): $(x - 1)^2 = 2(y + 2)$. Expand this equation in order to write it in the form $y = ax^2 + bx + c$ called general form.

_____

b) A parabola has equation (general form): $y = 2x^2 - 4x + 1$.

1. Justify the steps allowing us to write the equation in the standard form.

	Steps	Justifications
	$y = 2x^2 - 4x + 1$	
1	$\Leftrightarrow y = 2(x^2 - 2x) + 1$	
2	$\Leftrightarrow y = 2(x^2 - 2x + 1) + 1 - 2$	
3	$\Leftrightarrow y = 2(x - 1)^2 - 1$	
4	$\Leftrightarrow (x - 1)^2 = \frac{1}{2}(y + 1)$	

2. Determine the coordinates of the vertex V, the coordinates of the focus F and the equation of the directrix l of this parabola.

_____

GENERAL EQUATION OF THE PARABOLA

- By expanding the equation $(x - h)^2 = 4c(y - k)$ of a parabola open upwards or the equation $(x - h)^2 = -4c(y - k)$ of a parabola open downwards, we obtain the **general form**:

$$\boxed{y = Ax^2 + Bx + C} \quad (A \neq 0).$$

- By expanding the equation $(y - k)^2 = 4c(x - h)$ of a parabola open to the right or the equation $(y - k)^2 = -4c(x - h)$ of a parabola open to the left, we obtain the **general form**:

$$\boxed{x = Ay^2 + By + C} \quad (A \neq 0).$$

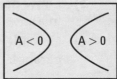

10. Write the equations of the following parabolas in the general form.

a) $(x-1)^2 = 2(y+1)$ _____

b) $(x+2)^2 = -4(y-1)$ _____

c) $(y+3)^2 = \frac{3}{2}(x-4)$ _____

d) $(y-2)^2 = \frac{-1}{2}(x+2)$ _____

11. Write the equations of the following parabolas in the standard form.

a) $y = x^2 + 2x + 3$ _____

b) $x = y^2 - 6y + 10$ _____

c) $y = -x^2 + 4x + 6$ _____

d) $x = -y^2 - 2y + 1$ _____

12. Determine the coordinates of the focus F and the equation of the directrix l of the following parabolas.

a) $y = x^2 - 2x - 1$; _____

b) $x = \frac{1}{4}y^2 - y - 1$; _____

13. Represent the solution set of the following inequalities in the Cartesian plane.

a) $(x-2)^2 \leqslant -4(y-1)$

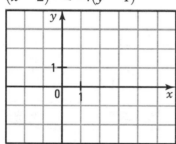

b) $(y-1)^2 \geqslant 2(x+1)$

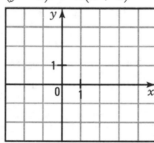

c) $(y-1)^2 < -4(x-3)$

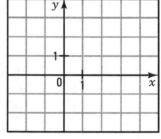

14. For each of the following regions, determine the inequality that defines it.

a)

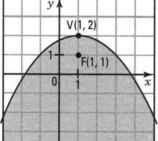

_____

b)

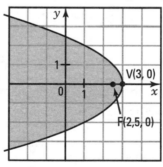

_____

c)

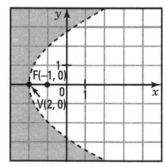

_____

15. Consider the parabola $\mathcal{P}$ with vertex V(−2, 1) and focus $F\left(\frac{-3}{2}, 1\right)$ and the line l passing through points A(2, 1) and B(4, 3).

a) Find the intersection points C and D of parabola $\mathcal{P}$ and line l. _____

_____

b) Draw parabola $\mathcal{P}$ and line l and verify the results found in a).

c) Consider the closed region $\mathcal{R}$ whose boundary is parabola $\mathcal{P}$ and line l.

Describe region $\mathcal{R}$ using a system of inequalities. _____

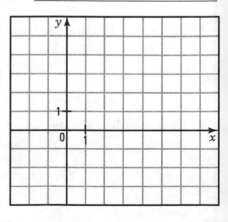

16. Consider the hyperbola $\mathcal{H}$ with equation: $x^2 - y^2 = 1$ and the parabola $\mathcal{P}$ with equation: $x + 1 = y^2$.

a) Find the intersection points of the hyperbola and the parabola.

_____

_____

_____

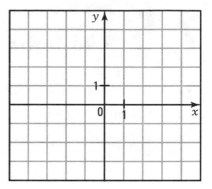

b) Represent, in the Cartesian plane, the region defined by the system $\begin{cases} x^2 - y^2 \leqslant 1 \\ x + 1 \geqslant y^2 \end{cases}$.

17. In each of the following cases, represent the region defined by the system.

a) $\begin{cases} x^2 + y^2 \leqslant 3 \\ y^2 \leqslant 2x \end{cases}$

b) $\begin{cases} y^2 \geqslant -2(x-2) \\ 4x^2 + 9y^2 - 36 \leqslant 0 \end{cases}$

c) $\begin{cases} x - 1 \leqslant \dfrac{-1}{2}y^2 \\ x^2 - y^2 \leqslant 1 \end{cases}$

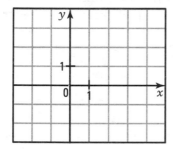 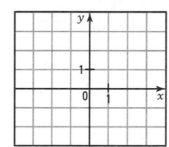 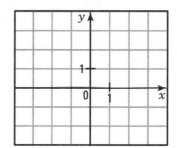

18. Consider the circle $\mathcal{C}$ and the parabola $\mathcal{P}$ on the right. The vertex of the parabola is the centre $\omega(1, 2)$ of the circle. The points A(4, 6) and B(4, –6) are the intersection points of the circle and the parabola.

Describe, using a system, the shaded region.

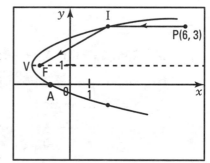

_____

19. The parabola on the right, open to the right with vertex V(–2, 1) crosses the x-axis at point A(–1, 0).

Calculate the distance traveled by a light ray going from point P(6, 3) in a direction parallel to the x-axis, hitting the parabola at point I and reflected at the focus F.

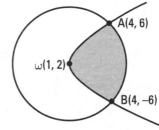

_____

_____

7.6 Problems on conics

1. Find the equation in the standard form of each of the following conics.

a) Ellipse with foci $F_1(-8, 0)$ and $F_2(8, 0)$ whose major axis measures 20 units. _____

b) Hyperbola with foci $F_1(-10, 0)$ and $F_2(10, 0)$ whose transverse axis has a length of 12 units.

_____

c) Circle centred at $O(0, 0)$ passing through $A(-2, 3)$. _____

d) Parabola with vertex $V(0, 0)$ and focus $F(0, -3)$. _____

2. For each of the conics defined by the following equations, describe the conic by giving:
- for a circle, the centre and the radius,
- for an ellipse, the coordinates of its foci and its vertices,
- for a hyperbola, the coordinates of its foci, its vertices and the equations of the asymptotes,
- for a parabola, the coordinates of its vertex, its focus and the equation of the directrix.

a) $x^2 + y^2 - 5 = 0.$ _____

b) $x^2 + 4y^2 - 16 = 0.$

_____

_____

c) $4x^2 - 9y^2 - 36 = 0.$

_____

_____

d) $y^2 + 2x - 2y + 7 = 0.$

_____

_____

3. In each of the following cases, name the geometric locus and give its equation.

a) Set of points $M(x, y)$ located at a distance of 3 units from the origin. _____

b) Set of points $M(x, y)$ whose distances from the point $(-1, 2)$ and the line with equation $x = 3$ are equal. _____

c) Set of points $M(x, y)$ such that the absolute value of the difference of the distances from point M to points $(-5, 0)$ and $(5, 0)$ is equal to 8 units.

_____

d) Set of points $M(x, y)$ such that the sum of the distances from point M to points $(0, -4)$ and $(0, 4)$ is equal to 10 units.

_____

4. The ellipse centred at the origin on the right has a major axis measuring 10 units and a minor axis measuring 8 units.

The vertex of the parabola on the right coincides with one of the vertices of the ellipse and its directrix passes through one of the foci of the ellipse.

Calculate the area of rectangle ABCD if line segment BC corresponds to the horizontal minor axis of the ellipse.

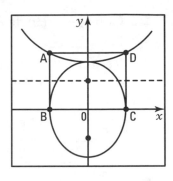

_____

_____

_____

5. Consider the circle centred at 0 passing through point A(–4, 3) and the rectangle ABCD whose sides are parallel to the axes. Consider the hyperbola $\mathcal{H}$ whose transverse axis is on the x-axis, whose vertices are points E and G and whose foci are points S and Q and the hyperbola $\mathcal{H}'$ whose transverse axis is on the y-axis, whose vertices are points F and H and whose foci are points P and R.

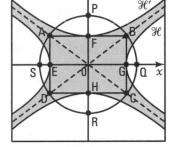

a) Determine the system of inequalities representing the shaded region.

_____

_____

b) What can be said about the supports of the diagonals of rectangle ABCD. Justify your answer.

_____

_____

6. A circle $\mathcal{C}$ centred at $\omega(-1, 2)$ passes through point A(2, 6). Find the equation of the line l tangent to the circle at point P(3, –1).

_____

7. Circle $\mathcal{C}$ centred at $\omega(4, 3)$ on the right is tangent to line l with equation: $4x + 3y + 25 = 0$.

a) Find the equation of circle $\mathcal{C}$.

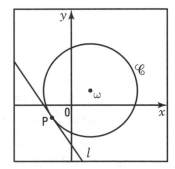

_____

_____

b) Find the coordinates of the point of tangency P.

_____

7.6 Problems on conics   **353**

8. Consider triangle ABC having vertices A(–5, 10), B(–7, –4) and C(9, 8).
Find the equation of the circumscribed circle of triangle ABC.
Recall that: The circumscribed circle's centre is the intersection point of the perpendicular bisectors of the sides of the triangle.

_____

_____

_____

9. What is the intersection point of the directrices of parabolas
$\mathcal{P}_1 : (y - 1)^2 = -8(x + 1)$ and $\mathcal{P}_2 : (x + 3)^2 = 4(y + 2)$?

_____

10. The difference between the radii of two concentric circles is 3 cm.
If the equation of the larger circle is: $x^2 + y^2 + 6x - 4y - 36 = 0$, determine the equation of the smaller circle.

_____

11. The major and the minor axes of the ellipse centred at the origin shown on the right measure 10 and 6 units respectively.

A circle of radius 2 units centred at one of the foci of the ellipse was drawn.

Determine the length of the chord CD knowing that $\overline{CD} \perp \overline{A_1A_2}$.

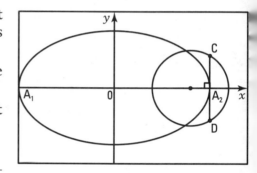

_____

_____

12. The asymptotes of the hyperbola centred at the origin shown on the right are the lines with equations: $y = x$ and $y = -x$. Its transverse axis measures 12 units. The circle on the right, of radius 8 units and centred at the origin, intersects the hyperbola at four points P, Q, R and S.

Calculate the area of rectangle PQRS.

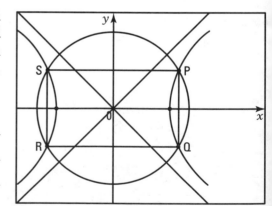

_____

_____

_____

_____

13. The major and the minor axes of the ellipse on the right measure 10 units and 6 units respectively. Calculate the area of the right triangle PQR inscribed inside the ellipse knowing that the side PQ passes through one of the foci of the ellipse.

_____

_____

_____

14. On the figure on the right, the circle centred at the origin passes through the vertex V of the parabola and the ellipse passes through its focus F. The minor axis B_1B_2 of the ellipse is a diameter for the circle.

If the equation of the parabola is $x^2 = 4(y - 3)$, describe the shaded region using a system of inequalities.

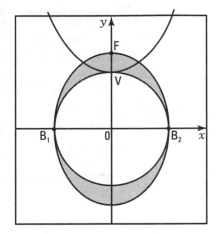

_____

_____

15. In an elliptical shaped pool, two points P and Q on the side of this pool are joined by a cable. This cable passes through a focus of the ellipse and is perpendicular to its major axis.

Knowing that the major axis and the minor axis measure 200 m and 160 m respectively, calculate the length of the cable when it is stretched.

_____

_____

16. The interior region of a hyperbola centred at the origin has been shaded.

Knowing that one of the asymptotes of the hyperbola passes through point (4, 3) and that the distance between the vertices of the hyperbola is equal to 6 units, describe the shaded region using an inequality.

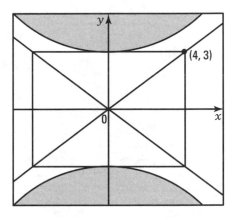

_____

17. Consider an ellipse centred at the origin with equation: $\frac{x^2}{25} + \frac{y^2}{16} = 1$.

Determine the equation of each of the parabolas whose vertex and focus are respectively the foci of the ellipse.

_____

_____

Evaluation 7

1. In each of the following cases, name the geometric locus and give its equation.

a) The set of points $M(x, y)$ located at a distance of 3 units from the origin.

_____

b) The set of points $M(x, y)$ whose distances from the point $(-2, 1)$ and the line with equation $x = 2$ are equal. _____

c) The set of points $M(x, y)$ such that the sum of the distances from point $M(x, y)$ to the points $(0, -3)$ and $(0, 3)$ is equal to 10.

_____

d) The set of points $M(x, y)$ such that the absolute value of the difference of the distances to the points $(0, -10)$ and $(0, 10)$ is equal to 12.

_____

e) The set of points $M(x, y)$ whose distances from the point $(3, -4)$ and the line $y = 2$ are equal. _____

2. For each of the conics defined by the following equations, describe the conic by giving
 – for a circle, the centre and the radius,
 – for an ellipse, the coordinates of its foci and its vertices,
 – for a hyperbola, the coordinates of its foci, its vertices and the equations of the asymptotes,
 – for a parabola, the coordinates of its vertex, its focus and the equation of its directrix.

a) $(y - 3)^2 = 8(x - 1)$. _____

_____

b) $\frac{x^2}{3} + \frac{y^2}{3} = 1$ _____

c) $x^2 - 4y^2 = 4$. _____

_____

d) $9x^2 - 25y^2 - 225 = 0$. _____

_____

3. Give the equation of each of the following conics.

a) Ellipse with foci $F_1(0, -12)$ and $F_2(0, 12)$ and minor axis equal to 10 units. _____

b) Hyperbola with foci $F_1(0, -13)$ and $F_2(0, 13)$ and transverse axis equal to 10 units.

_____

c) Circle centred at the origin and passing through point $A(-2, 4)$. _____

d) Parabola with vertex $V(-3, 2)$ whose directrix is the line with equation $x = -6$.

_____

4. A circle $\mathscr{C}$ centred at the origin is tangent to the line l: $3x - 2y - 13 = 0$.

   a) Find the equation of the circle. _____

   b) Find the coordinates of the point of tangency A. _____

5. Consider the hyperbola $\mathscr{H}$ with equation: $x^2 - y^2 = -1$ and the circle $\mathscr{C}$ with equation: $x^2 + y^2 = 5$.

   a) Find the intersection points of hyperbola $\mathscr{H}$ and circle $\mathscr{C}$.

   _____

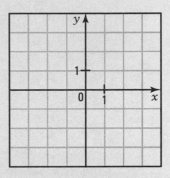

   b) Represent hyperbola $\mathscr{H}$ and circle $\mathscr{C}$ in the Cartesian plane.

   c) Colour, in the Cartesian plane, the region defined by the system: $\begin{cases} x^2 - y^2 \geqslant -1 \\ x^2 + y^2 \leqslant 5 \end{cases}$.

6. Represent the following regions in the Cartesian plane.

   a) $x^2 + y^2 - 9 \leqslant 0$ **b)** $x^2 - 4y^2 + 4 \geqslant 0$ **c)** $4x^2 + y^2 - 4 \geqslant 0$

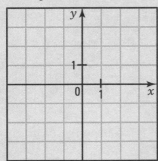 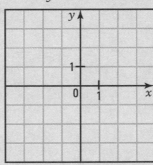 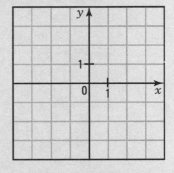

   d) $(y - 1)^2 \leqslant -(x - 2)$ **e)** $\begin{cases} x^2 + 4y^2 - 4 \geqslant 0 \\ x^2 + y^2 - 4 \leqslant 0 \end{cases}$ **f)** $\begin{cases} y - 2 \leqslant -\dfrac{1}{2}x^2 \\ x^2 - y^2 \geqslant 1 \end{cases}$

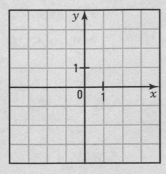 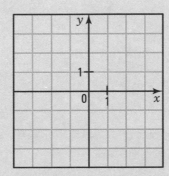 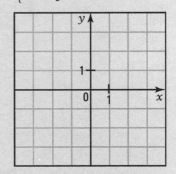

7. The roof of a tunnel is shaped like a half-ellipse. If traffic is not allowed at a distance of 3 m from the edges of the tunnel, determine, to the nearest unit, the maximum height allowed for a vehicle entering this tunnel.

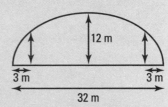

_____

SYMBOLS

$\mathbb{N}$	set of natural numbers
$\mathbb{N}^*$	set of nonnegative natural numbers
$\mathbb{Z}$	set of integers
$\mathbb{Z}_+$	set of nonnegative integers
$\mathbb{Z}_-$	set of nonpositive integers
$\mathbb{Q}$	set of rational numbers
$\mathbb{Q}'$	set of irrational numbers
$\mathbb{R}$	set of real numbers
$\in$	belongs to
$\subset$	is a subset of
$\notin$	does not belong to
$\not\subset$	is not a subset of
$=$	is equal to
$\approx$	is approximately equal to
$\neq$	is not equal to
$<$	is less than
$>$	is greater than
$\leq$	is less than or equal to
$\geq$	is greater than or equal to
$\forall x$	for all x
$\Rightarrow$	logically implies
$\Leftrightarrow$	is logically equivalent
$[a, b]$	closed interval
$[a, b[$	left-closed and right-open interval
$]a, b]$	left-open and right-closed interval
$]a, b[$	open interval
$]-\infty, a]$	left-unbounded and right-closed interval
$]-\infty, a[$	left-unbounded and right-open interval
$[a, +\infty[$	left-closed and right-unbounded interval
$]a, +\infty[$	left-open and right-unbounded interval
$\varnothing$	empty set
$\sqrt[n]{a}$	n^{th} root of real number a
Δ	discriminant
S	Set of solutions
AB	line AB
$\overline{AB}$	line segment AB
$m\overline{AB}$	measure of line segment AB
$\cong$	is congruent to
$\angle AOB$	angle AOB
$m \angle AOB$	measure of angle AOB
$\perp$	is perpendicular to

//	is parallel to
$\triangle ABC$	triangle ABC
$M(x, y)$	coordonates of point M
~	is similar to
R^{-1}	inverse of relation R
$f(x)$	image of x by function f
dom f	domain of a function f
ran f	range of function a f
max f	maximum of a function f
min f	minimum of a function f
$g \circ f$	composition of f by g
$|a|$	absolute value of a
$[a]$	greatest integer of a
$\log_c$	logarithm in base c
$\log$	logarithm in base 10
In	logarithm in base e
sin A	sine of angle A
cos A	cosine of angle A
tan A	tangent of angle A
sec A	secant of angle A
csc A	cosecant of angle A
cot A	cotangent of angle A
°	degree
gr	gradian
rd	radian
$P(t)$	trigonometric point
p	period
F	frequency
arcsin	arcsine
arccos	arccosine
arctan	arctangent
Sin	principal sine
Cos	principal cosine
Tan	principal tangent
$\overrightarrow{AB}$	vector $\overrightarrow{AB}$
$\|\overrightarrow{AB}\|$	norm of vector $\overrightarrow{AB}$
$\vec{0}$	zero vector
$\theta_{\overrightarrow{AB}}$	orientation of vector $\overrightarrow{AB}$
$\vec{u} \cdot \vec{v}$	scalar product of two vectors $\vec{u}$ and $\vec{v}$
$\vec{u}_{\vec{v}}$	orthogonal projection of vector $\vec{u}$ onto vector $\vec{v}$

INDEX

INDEX OF THEOREMS

NOTES

NOTES

NOTES

NOTES

NOTES

PRINTED IN THE YEAR
TWO THOUSAND
NINE
BY
GUÉRIN, ÉDITEUR
MONTRÉAL, QUEBEC.